"The Ethical Investor (1995) changed my views on what could done to harness investment to social responsibility in the UK context. This book now moves the agenda to the world stage and is essential reading for all those who can see the need to harness capitalism to SRI objectives in the post Sept. 11th world, and that after the Enron and Worldcom scandals, SRI can deliver the better world we need"

Tony Colman MP, House of Commons International Development Select Committee

"The growth of SRI has been one of the most important - but often misunderstood − investment trends of the past decade. Russell Sparkes provides an invaluable analysis of the main SRI developments and issues for both professional and private investor alike, writing with true authority and insight"

Stuart Bell, Research Director, PIRC Ltd

"Russell Sparks has filled a huge need. In this magisterial volume, he has brought together the history, language and lore of shareholder activism and responsibility into coherence. For everyone searching for ways for owners to make corporations part of the solution for global problems, this book is a must read"

Robert A.G. Monks, Chairman, Lens Investment Management and Publisher of http://www.ragm.com concerned with corporate governance and shareholder responsibility

"... a useful tool for investors and managers. Not the untested ideals of someone wishing to jump on the ethical band wagon but the considered and tested observations of a successful institutional investor of conviction"

"... having compared *Socially Responsible Investment* to an iceberg, Russell Sparkes explains many of those aspects of the subject not obvious on the surface."

J.E. Rogers, Chief Executive, UKSIP The Society of Investment Professionals

Socially Responsible Investment

Series Editors: John Goodchild and Clive Callow

Socially Responsible Investment
A Global Revolution

Russell Sparkes

JOHN WILEY & SONS, LTD

0471499536

Copyright © 2002   John Wiley & Sons Ltd, The Atrium, Southern Gate, Chichester, West Sussex PO19 8SQ, England

Telephone   (+44) 1243 779777

E-mail (for orders and customer service enquiries): cs-books@wiley.co.uk
Visit our Home Page on www.wileyeurope.com or www.wiley.com

Other Wiley Editorial Offices

John Wiley & Sons, Inc., 111 River Street, Hoboken, NJ 07030, USA

Jossey-Bass, 989 Market Street, San Francisco, CA 94103-1741, USA

Wiley-VCH Verlag GmbH, Boschstr. 12, D-69469 Weinheim, Germany

John Wiley & Sons Australia Ltd, 33 Park Road, Milton, Queensland 4064, Australia

John Wiley & Sons (Asia) Pte Ltd, 2 Clementi Loop #02-01, Jin Xing Distripark, Singapore 129809

John Wiley & Sons Canada Ltd, 22 Worcester Road, Etobicoke, Ontario, Canada M9W 1L1

Library of Congress Cataloging-in-Publication Data

Sparkes, Russell.
    Socially responsible investment : a global revolution / Russell Sparkes.
       p. cm.—(UKSIP series)
    Includes bibliographical references and index.
    ISBN 0-471-49953-6 (alk. paper)
    1. Investments—Moral and ethical aspects. I. Title. II. Series.

    HG4515.13 .S63 2002
    332.67'8—dc21   2002027205

British Library Cataloguing in Publication Data

A catalogue record for this book is available from the British Library

ISBN 0-471-49953-6

Typeset in 11/13pt RotisSerif by TechBooks, New Delhi, India
Printed and bound in Great Britain by TJ International, Padstow, Cornwall, UK
This book is printed on acid-free paper responsibly manufactured from sustainable forestry in which at least two trees are planted for each one used for paper production.

To Rosemary, without whose constant help and support this book could never have been written

Contents

Contents

Contents

Foreword by Tim Smith

(Tim Smith is Senior Vice President at Walden Asset Management, a Boston based money management firm involved in socially responsible investing for over 25 years. Walden is involved in screening, community development investing, public policy and shareholder advocacy. Before joining Walden, in October 2001, Tim worked at the Interfaith Center on Corporate Responsibility for 30 years. In 2002 he was elected as President of the Social Investment Forum, the U.S. trade association for social investors.)

I am pleased to provide this foreword to a book that is both timely and extremely relevant. I am also pleased that Russell felt comfortable in asking someone from the United States to add some thoughts leading into this important book. In a sense, this symbolizes the fact that ethical investing or socially responsible investing is increasingly a global reality, as relevant in London or Paris as in New York or Sydney. It's not just a global reality that we watch from afar as independent observers, but it is an evolving process where investors are working together to insure that their investments mirror their value and that corporations are being held accountable for their social and environmental impact.

Russell Sparkes is not only a commentator on this reality, he has been involved in its creation for many years as a leader in the faith community in the U.K. He also represents the bridge, personally and institutionally, between the money management world and that of a values based organization. In that sense we have walked a similar path. I moved to Walden after 3 decades at ICCR, a remarkable Interfaith organization that co-ordinated the work of 275 Protestant, Roman Catholic and Jewish institutions. I served as the Executive Director but I was but one of scores of remarkable religious leaders who worked passionately for economic justice and for greater corporate accountability and business responsibility.

No ordinary activists here, no labels of anti-corporate criteria could stand. Instead, they worked as people of faith, committed to making changes in the world, reflective and spiritual yet tireless advocates for economic and social justice. What were the faith foundations that led to this work and sustained people in this journey? A passion for justice – whether expressed in the Old Testament or the New Testament (Amos or Matthew), we were led not just to be of service but to challenge and change unjust systems. The contradiction of patience blended with a great sense of urgency – the issues need to be addressed now and solved yesterday. Blended with this was a conviction that we needed to persevere even when our work did not result in immediate success. A global vision – a commitment to have our work on corporate responsibility focus on global issues.

Inevitably as we looked at the systems impacting our lives, we looked at the power and influence of the business community. But not from a distant, prophetic vantage point sitting on a mountain top as a comfortable prophet. The leaders representing the faith community looked at their institutions and their institutions and their investment decisions and observed that we were connected. They were participating in the policies and decisions of the global corporate community, not removed from it. These religious organizations from ICCR owned a piece of the rock – their investment portfolios were worth $100 billion plus. Thus they could not sit as moral outsiders. It forced them as participants in the economic system to get their hands dirty and get involved in interacting with companies and the marketplace. It led us all to some very strange places to corporate board rooms, stockholder meetings, to dialogues with CEOs. The religious community played an essential role planting seeds in the 1960's and 1970's – seeds regarding ethical investing and corporate social responsibility. Without these prophets involved in profits the marketplace might be much different.

What is the landscape of this debate about ethical investing and corporate social responsibility in 2002? Let me wear my new hats, as President of the Social Investment Forum (SIF), a trade association of socially concerned investors and Senior Vice President of Walden

Asset Management who manages money for individuals and institutions in a socially responsible manner. While not using the words of the faith community, Walden and other social investors, mirror the same values and passion for change. We work to make a difference with our invested assets. What does this SRI landscape in the U.S. look like now?

A recent SIF Trends report discloses that individuals and institutions with over $2 trillion, are now involved in some way shape or form in social investing e.g. tobacco screening e.g. shareholder resolutions e.g. community investing. Players in the U.S. now include the City of New York and State of Connecticut and California pension funds – foundations, unions, mutual funds, money managers and individuals. Moral voices merged with words like 'fiduciary responsibility' urge companies to be good corporate citizens. The acoustics change when the City of New York, with $100 billion, gets involved.

And on the corporate side is the message being heard? Look at the websites of Shell, BP, Sun Oil or Ford Motor Company and you see declarations and progress not seen a decade ago. New energy on the environment, diversity, human rights, sustainability workplace safety and enhancement. But we also see hundreds of companies that don't think it and don't get it! Whose focus is solely on the bottom line whatever the price paid. Thus the urgent need for moral voices to be raised by individuals and institutions, by investors and consumers, citizens and advocates. The corporate community is more powerful, more global than ever before. The acts of leadership in business – in small companies and large corporations are vital. Whether our voices are mandated by faith or values like decency and fairness, they need to heard. But they need not simply be voices of moral urgency. To be effective in this marketplace, they need to be instruments of economic clout and power as well.

Russell Sparkes has created a powerful tool in this new book. It describes well the new reality in the U.K. as investors assess new realities as they make investment decisions. In fact, the U.K. community of socially concerned investors may well have grown larger than its U.S. counterpart. This book is one more step in the mainstreaming of SRI that we have seen over the last decade. It is an issue discussed in corporate boardrooms, investment houses and mutual funds, in pensions funds and around family dinner tables. It is significant that a prominent business publisher like Wiley understands the importance and is publishing this book.

Russell and I were both caught in the aftermath of September 11, both of us marooned at a conference on SRI in Tucson, Arizona, unable to travel because of the closing of airports. There and upon our returns to London and Boston, we reflected on the meaning of September 11 for the work we did. Both of us felt our work in encouraging corporate responsibility globally was more important than ever. It is my hope that this book will help illuminate the minds and breech the myths surrounding social investing while warming our hearts to be even more active leaders in this important social movement.

Series Preface

When *The Ethical Investor* was published in 1995 it marked an important step towards a wider recognition of socially responsible investment within the fund management industry. Russell Sparkes' new book outlines the changes that have occurred since the mid 1990s and examines their significance for the professional and the lay person. As in the earlier work, his ideas are presented with style and clarity.

This is the fourth title in the John Wiley/UKSIP series. Future subjects that are being considered include the effect of general (and presidential) elections on stock markets and the 'structure' of football finance in Britain. The aim of the series is to provide a challenging perspective on current investment themes. *Socially Responsible Investment* meets that criterion.

John Goodchild and Clive Callow
May 2002

Preface

Eight years ago I wrote the first UK book on socially responsible investment (SRI) to be produced by a mainstream publisher. When John Wiley first suggested I should write another book on the subject, my first thought was to update the earlier work. I quickly realised, however, that this would be impossible and that I would have to write a totally new book.

There were two reasons for this. First, socially responsible investment has changed beyond all recognition since the previous book was written. Then it was a small fringe activity carried out by a small number of unit trusts and mutual funds in the US and the UK. Now it has become a core part of mainstream investment management. As the book's subtitle indicates, there has been a global revolution and SRI has spread out around the world. Even the name has changed. When I wrote my first book 'ethical investment' was the standard term, but this has now been replaced by 'socially responsible investment'.

The second reason for writing a completely new book is a personal one. My thoughts on the subject have changed significantly from what they were in 1993–94. I hope they are deeper and more wide-ranging, and I hope this change is reflected in the scope of my new book. If my thoughts on socially responsible investment have deepened, this is largely due to what I have learned over the last eight years from Bill Seddon and other colleagues at the Central Finance Board of the Methodist Church (CFB).

This book is written in a personal capacity and should not be interpreted as a reflection of the views of the CFB. For this reason the CFB is described in the third person in Chapter 10. It has been written for anybody who feels that they need to understand the concept of socially responsible investment for professional or personal reasons. They may include trustees of pension funds and charitable trusts, financial advisers, pension consultants, company executives, policy makers and investment managers. I often describe SRI as resembling an iceberg whose visible surface is only 20% of the total. The visible portion of SRI consists of unit trusts and mutual funds. However, these form only a small fraction of the global SRI universe.

The book is divided into three parts. Part I describes the visible portion of the iceberg, looking at screening in practice, and profiling the typical investor in SRI retail funds. Part II examines the issues that are increasingly dominating SRI discussion: the environment, human rights and corporate social responsibility. Part III concentrates on the institutional side of socially responsible investment, something which has received relatively little coverage until now. Anyone who is sceptical about the importance of SRI to pension funds, charitable trusts and insurance companies is encouraged to read Chapter 1, which sets out the 'paradigm shift' travelled by SRI as it has moved from the fringe to the mainstream.

Russell Sparkes
London, March 2002

PART I

Exploring Socially Responsible Investment

Part I describes the essence of socially responsible investment (SRI). It analyses SRI into its structural components and explores its historical development. One chapter profiles the typical investor in socially responsible funds, while another looks at screening, the best-known SRI technique. However, it starts with the British SRI pension fund legislation that came into force in July 2001, the moment when SRI came of age.

1

Socially Responsible Investment Comes of Age

My aim in writing this book has been to document the major changes that have taken place in the field of socially responsible investment (SRI) over the last few years. Until recently SRI was essentially a fairly fringe activity carried out by a limited number of unit trusts or mutual funds. The relatively small amounts of money invested in these funds meant that they had little impact on business and society. I suspect that most people still think of SRI like that.

That view is now quite outdated. Socially responsible investment has become something that pension advisers, charity trustees, and indeed corporate executives need to know about. There are two reasons why this is so. SRI has entered the vocabulary and consciousness of mainstream finance, while it has moved from on its origins in the UK and US to become a global movement. Up to now books on SRI have been written for retail investors; I produced one myself in 1995 called *The Ethical Investor*. However such books are of little use to pension fund trustees or their advisers struggling to combine social responsibility concerns with the legal duty of fiduciary duty. They are also not much good to corporate executives wondering why they are becoming bombarded with requests for information on their company's social and environmental performance, or indeed, why major shareholders are increasingly filing shareholder resolutions on these issues.

The aim of this book is to fill that gap. Rather than looking at individual funds, it considers particular topics in a structured way based upon evidence from the UK and the US. The first part examines the history and development of SRI before moving on to profile the typical investor in socially responsible retail funds. It then describes some leading SRI unit trusts and mutual funds. The main section of the book examines the main issues of concern to institutional investors considering socially responsible investment: the environment, human rights, corporate governance, *and* financial performance. The final part of the book looks at American and British evidence of 'the mainstreaming of socially responsible investment', followed by an examination of its increasingly global reach.

A HISTORIC DATE

The normal trend in financial markets is for US-based innovations — hedge funds, risk arbitrage, private equity, etc. — to be copied in the rest of the world. However, by issuing the 1999 socially responsible pension fund regulations, the UK took a lead that was followed elsewhere. This chapter therefore concentrates on Britain, whereas the rest of the book examines SRI issues from a structural perspective looking at each issue from the combined viewpoint of US and UK experience. It examines the new SRI pension fund regulations and explains the process of consultation and discussion that led to their declaration.

Since I was an eyewitness to these developments, and indeed actively involved in the discussions leading up them, I thought it important to put them down on record. In fact, it is my belief that history will consider the day the UK's SRI pension fund regulations came into effect, 3 July 2000, as a momentous day in the evolution of investment management. It was a date of global rather than of local importance. For the first time ever pension funds, the building blocks of the world's capital markets, were legally obliged to consider non-financial issues in setting their investment policy.

The SRI pension regulations were important in their own right, but it is essential to try to uncover the various forces that encouraged the UK government to issue the new measures. Many people working in financial markets have historically taken a fairly jaundiced view of socially responsible investment, regarding it as a fringe product for a niche 'green' customer base. This opinion can no longer be justified. The new UK pension fund regulations were not some trivial, superficial measure drafted for party political reasons; rather they reflected political awareness of growing pressure from a variety of sources for such policies to be implemented. Since similar forces for change were also obviously present in other countries, it was only a matter of time before authorities elsewhere copied them. In fact, within a year of the UK measures coming into force, similar regulations had been passed in Germany, Sweden, and Australia and were actively under consideration by the European Parliament.

For the sake of argument it will be assumed (here) that the two terms 'ethical investment' and 'socially responsible investment' are synonymous. Chapter 2 considers whether there is any meaningful difference between them. SRI has always been the normal description in the US, and it is increasingly replacing 'ethical investment' as the standard term in the UK. In any case the basic meaning is an investment philosophy that combines social and environmental objectives with financial objectives.

Social scientists sometimes talk of 'a paradigm shift' in public awareness, when a belief that is generally accepted becomes obviously outmoded and rejected. A good example would be the relative importance of the Earth and the Sun; before Galileo it was universally accepted that the Sun rotated round the Earth, after him everybody knew that the reverse was true. I believe that we are now in a similar situation regarding institutional investment, and that ultimate beneficiaries such as pension schemes and charitable foundations are now starting to question the conventional wisdom that the sole purpose of investment is the maximisation of short-term financial returns. A comparable paradigm shift in investment would be that resulting from Markowitz's assertion in the 1950s that investors should analyse the overall risk of a portfolio, rather than seeking gains from individual stocks.[1]

THE UK SRI PENSIONS REGULATIONS

The new measures oblige all UK private sector pension funds to consider socially responsible investment and voting rights as part of their overall investment policy. (Equivalent regulations were drafted by the Department of Environment, Transport and the Regions (DETR), which at that time was the regulatory body for local authority pension schemes.) This came about under a regulation issued by the Department of Social Security (DSS) under section 35 of the 1995 Pensions Act, which provides a statutory obligation for all private sector pension schemes to have a Statement of Investment Principles (SIP). These statements must cover the types of investment, the balance between investments, risk, return and realisations. The new regulation required all trustees to add the following two considerations to their fund's SIP:

(i) The extent (if at all) to which social, environmental or ethical considerations are taken into account by trustees in the selection, retention, and realisation of investments; and

(ii) the policy (if any) directing the exercise of the rights (including voting rights) attaching to investments.

At first sight these clauses do not look particularly dramatic. It is important to stress that they do not force pension funds to invest along SRI lines; the new rules simply oblige them to take social and environmental considerations into account and disclose their policy about this. It is worth repeating that the regulations are about consideration and disclosure, not about compulsion. Nevertheless, their issuance was a major watershed in the evolution of investment management, even from a global perspective. To the best of my knowledge, the new SRI requirements represented the first time anywhere in the world that a government had obliged pension funds to consider environmental and social factors in their investment policy. As is shown in Chapter 13, the new regulations gave a powerful stimulus to the growing number of UK pension funds that considered socially responsible investment to be a normal part of their investment strategy.

Similar shifts occurred in the attitude of most pension funds to investment in emerging markets around 1990, or to venture capital in the early 1980s. In each case something that had previously been regarded as a 'fringe' part of the potential investment universe became suddenly accepted as 'core' or 'mainstream'. It would be unthinkable now for any significant investment management company not to have expertise in emerging markets or venture capital, and I suspect that the same thing has now become true of SRI. The reader might well ask why this should happen. The answer, I think, is that the new measures provide a mechanism that enables pension scheme members to translate their increasing awareness and interest in social investment into investment policy. It also facilitates other interested parties to persuade trustees of the appropriateness of such a strategy.

Before the new measures became law, pension fund trustees and their professional advisers were able to resist growing pressure for their funds to invest along socially responsible lines on the grounds that this contravened the requirements of fiduciary duty. This was the 'old paradigm' generally accepted up to that date by fund managers and pension consultants. It was conventional wisdom that SRI was bound to produce lower financial returns, and that pension funds were therefore prohibited from adopting SRI principles as they would thereby breach their 'fiduciary duty' to get the best returns on the funds entrusted to them. However, the Government's imposition of the new pensions regulations gave an explicit suggestion that this could not be true, otherwise the UK Government would have been forcing pension funds to consider potentially unlawful acts. In other words, 3 July 2000 saw socially responsible investment come of age as it moved from fringe to mainstream in the investment community. The new paradigm had begun.

THE ROAD TO REGULATION

It may seem appropriate that it was a New Labour government who created a 'new paradigm' in investment management. However pension fund scheme regulation is a fairly obscure subject that is top of few politicians' action lists. When Labour came to power in May 1997 the new Government's plans for social security reform meant a lot of challenges for the Department of Social Security (DSS), the parent department of the pensions ministry. Nevertheless, plans for pension funds to be able to consider ethical investment were high up the political agenda. According to one civil servant who worked on the measure:

We started work on the project in October 1997, and after discussions with lawyers and pensions consultants, we reported back that it was impossible. Financial returns on ethical unit trusts were described as sub-optimal – which ruled them out under the Scargill case. However the Minister was not satisfied with this answer, and instructed us to look further.[2]

The legal reference was to two classic judgements in UK trust law that placed severe restrictions on the extent to which pension trusts could adopt non-financial objectives in their financial policy: *Cowan v. Scargill* in 1984, and the *Bishop of Oxford et al. v. the Church Commissioners* in 1990. However, these cases were quite old. Many leading law firms had since gone on record to express their view that the 'climate of legal opinion' regarding the ability of pension funds to consider social and environmental factors had 'moved on' since the Scargill case. According to Charles Scanlan of Simmons & Simmons:

> Pension scheme trustees need not feel constrained by trust law to ignore ethical investment. On the contrary, provided that they take into account only the legally relevant considerations, trustees can fairly regard an ethical investment policy as a modern expression of the traditional principles of trust law'.[3]

Despite this 'shift in the climate of legal opinion' in the 1990s, pension schemes were still being advised by their advisers on the basis of the old paradigm that fiduciary duty ruled out what was then called 'ethical investment'. In fact, as early as 1993 the Goode Committee Report on pension funds, which led to the 1995 Pensions Act, had made a clear statement of the rights of pension funds to consider socially responsible investment:

> As trustees they are perfectly entitled to have a policy on ethical investment and to pursue that policy, as long as they treat the interests of the beneficiaries as paramount and the investment policy is consistent with the standards of care and prudence required by law. This means that they are free to avoid certain kinds of prudent investment which they consider the scheme members would consider objectionable, so long as they make equally advantageous investments elsewhere.[4]

The government first broached its intention to add SRI to pension scheme regulations in a speech by the then Pensions Minister, John Denham, to the UK Social Investment Forum (UKSIF) annual general meeting on 9 July 1998. UKSIF was of course a partisan audience, but I well remember the collective intake of breath, followed by applause, when the minister announced his intentions:

> I am minded to take action which will ensure that trustees set out the extent to which their investment strategy takes account of ethical and social considerations in the circumstances I have just described, so that scheme members are made aware of the existence and nature of that policy.[5]

One of the problems facing any government is the limited amount of parliamentary time that is available to create major legislation. The new government elected in 1997 had an ambitious legislative programme, and it is doubtful whether they would have proceeded with the SRI pension fund measures if this required the tabling of a substantial bill. However, in his speech Denham announced that he had found a way to proceed without the need for primary legislation, by using the powers already existing in the 1995 Pensions Act, and in particular Section 35 requiring trustees to compile a statement of investment principles governing decisions about scheme investments.

The UKSIF speech was followed by an extensive consultation process, resulting in the issuance of a Green Paper in December 1998. In the meantime John Denham had moved on, being replaced by Stephen Timms as Minister of State with responsibility for pensions. Timms made his first major statement on the issue in April 1999. He noted that Denham's proposal had led to extensive feedback to the pensions ministry (emphasis added):

> When my officials were briefing me on the issues I would face on taking office as Minister of State, one of them was the Government's proposal to require pension fund trustees to state their policy, on what I prefer to call socially responsible investment.... I want to turn back now again to our proposal for requiring pension fund trustees to state the policy that they take on this issue. *We received more responses about this proposal than any other measure in the consultation paper which we*

issued just after the Green Paper...I was very impressed by the
level of informed comment on it. In the main this focussed on
the wording.[6]

Timms made his speech at a Pensions and Investment Research
Consultants (PIRC) conference on corporate social responsibility. I
was in the audience at the PIRC conference as I had been at the
UKSIF AGM eight months earlier, but this time there was no audi-
ble intake of breath at the minister's stated plans. Expectations had
moved on. Timms firmed up the outline proposals described in the
consultation paper. What the minister said was this:

I want to turn to our proposal for requiring pension fund
trustees to state the policy that they take on this issue....The
wording shall be changed to make our policy intention clear.
This means, I think, including the inclusion of direct references
to socially responsible, environmentally responsible and ethical investments, as well as the exercise of rights, including voting rights.[7]

Right from the beginning of their enquiry into the possibility of linking pension funds and socially responsible investment, civil servants
from the Pensions Ministry had received cautious, fairly negative advice about the feasibility of SRI for pensions schemes. Indeed, had it
not been for ministerial insistence, they would probably have aban-
doned the proposed measures. Timms' speech mentioned the high
level of response the DSS received on this proposal, most of it believed to be negative. Nevertheless, the DSS persevered in its policy,
and Timms announced that the appropriate regulations would be laid
before Parliament in July 1999. This statement seemed to crystallise
opposition to the new measures. The public face of this opposition
was probably the National Association of Pension Funds (NAPF). In
June 1999, shortly before the new regulation was due to be put before Parliament, NAPF chief Alan Pickering warned that what he
described as 'artificial restrictions' on pension scheme investment
could damage the UK corporate sector.[8] NAPF heightened the political tension by writing to the DSS suggesting the proposals could
lead to compulsion. The *Financial Times* reported warnings by NAPF
(emphasis added):

The NAPF, whose members control almost a third of the stock market, *launched its most aggressive assault yet on the government's plans*, which it has warned would lead to higher administrative costs for companies and pension funds.[9]

The political climate got hotter, with lobbying and campaigning for and against the proposed measures. *The Guardian* went on to accuse the NAPF 'of a late effort to block it' (the proposed regulation) and of 'an attempt by pension fund managers to derail government legislation on ethical investment'.[10] For a time it looked as if the Government's intentions to proceed might falter. However, it was strengthened in the place where it mattered most, the House of Commons. On 14 July 1998 Putney MP Tony Colman inaugurated the All-Party Group on Socially Responsible Investment, becoming its first Chair. (An all-party group is simply a group of backbench MPs or peers (ministers are excluded) with a common interest in a topic.) The All-Party Group on Socially Responsible Investment started with the stated purpose 'to promote debate and understanding about socially responsible investment, and to ensure that socially responsible investment issues are considered wherever relevant during the framing of legislation'. Tony Colman argued:

> The NAPF is wrong to suggest that artificial restrictions are going to be placed on the investment decisions of pension funds. The regulation is a step forward and company managers should not be afraid of it.[11]

On 11 June 1999 the All-Party Group encouraged the Government by tabling an Early Day Motion in the Commons, backed by over 30 MPs, supporting the proposed regulations:

> That this House welcomes the Government's proposed regulation which will require trustees of pension funds to make a statement on the ethical and environmental principles to which investments are made; welcomes the democratic principle behind the regulation which will make trustees more accountable to their members; urges advisers to provide trustees with

acceptable ways to include socially responsible considerations in their investment.[12]

The regulation was passed on 1 July 1999, although it was announced that it would not come into effect for just over a year, until 3 July 2000, in order to give trustees and their advisers time to consider the issues fully. The NAPF was reassured by the DSS that the new regulation was about disclosure and consideration, not compulsion, and on that basis it withdrew the earlier warning about potential damage to the UK stock market and the British economy'.[13]

Denham used the older model of a 'tiebreaker', i.e. that trustees could take social considerations into account when there was a choice between two investments that appeared equally attractive on financial grounds. Timms moved on to put the emphasis on 'engagement', i.e. the belief that institutional investors should use their power as shareholders to press for change from the corporate sector — this could be by quiet dialogue, or more aggressively though shareholder activism or direct use of shareholder voting power. The pensions ministry carried out a considerable amount of consultation before the regulation was passed, and they seem to have climbed up a steep learning curve while developing the SRI disclosure policy. The term 'ethical investment' was dropped. As one adviser said to me, 'We came to the conclusion that the phrase "ethical investment" came with too much negative baggage, and switched to "socially responsible investment" instead'.[14]

One of the problems facing ministers and their officials was the fact that most of the information available on SRI derived from retail unit trusts, that in Denham's words were 'relying heavily on relatively simplistic negative techniques'. It was hard for the civil servants working in the pensions ministry to advocate SRI for pension funds until they could find viable models of this being achieved in practice. They were particularly keen to find examples of a more sophisticated approach better suited to pension funds. I remember their repeated visits to the Central Finance Board of the Methodist Church (CFB), and how pleased they were to discover that the CFB had a track record of successful institutional fund management while using SRI constraints (further information on the CFB's investment performance is given in Chapter 10).

THE PRESSURES FOR CHANGE

It is worth looking in more detail at the forces for change that led to this significant development. They show that the UK Government was acting in relation to pressures and concerns of global importance, rather than responding to purely domestic considerations. The first of these was geopolitical, and should not be ignored in any account of governmental thinking. The 1980s and 1990s saw privatisation and deregulation roll back the boundaries of state regulation of the economy in most developed countries, and power on people's lives was increasingly devolved to market forces. The 'anti-globalisation' riots seen in Seattle and Prague demonstrated, albeit in extreme form, the worries felt by many people about this. Politicians became aware that socially responsible investment was an available mechanism that could put the genie of unregulated free-market forces back into the bottle of some kind of social restraint.

As long as SRI was confined to relatively small sums invested in 'ethical' unit trusts, it could have little effect on corporate behaviour, but things would look very different if pension funds, the goliaths of the investment world, were to adopt socially responsible investment criteria. In most developed countries, pension funds are the most important group of shareholders in quoted companies – in the UK they own about 35% of all UK publicly quoted companies. They therefore have the influence, and if necessary the power, to compel company managements to focus on other matters than maximising profits. Given rising public concern about corporate behaviour in areas like environmental damage, human rights, and executive pay, it was hardly surprising politicians empowered pensions funds, and perhaps even encouraged them, to address these issues. John Denham put it this way in his 1998 speech:

> The investment of such huge sums [£830 billion in pension funds] is bound to have an effect on the wider world. As such the nature of the investments made on their behalf shapes the world in which fund members live, work, and retire. In many ways, whether or not investors are aware of it, investment decision-making has an ethical dimension. . . . I would like to mention one example. The Department of International Development have

13

provided funding for the Ethical Trading Initiative which seeks to encourage voluntary company action on codes of conduct within supply chains.[15]

Reviewing this regulatory process, I have been struck by how keenly the government pursued this aim despite a crowded legislative agenda and in the teeth of some highly negative publicity. And reshuffles at the DSS meant that three ministers (John Denham, Stephen Timms, Jeff Rooker) were in charge of pensions over the last two years, yet the SRI policy was consistently supported. It suggests to me that this policy objective had the blessing, and probably the active support, of the highest level of government. Socially responsible investment dovetails naturally with Prime Minister Tony Blair's statement that:

> It is surely time [that] we shift the emphasis in corporate ethos from a company being a mere vehicle to be traded, bought and sold as a commodity, towards a vision of the company as a community or partnership in which each employee has a stake, and where a company's responsibilities are more clearly delineated.[16]

If the geopolitical feature of stakeholding was one major influence spurring the government's new policy, the second was much closer to home – the needs of local government, and in particular their environmental commitments under Local Agenda 21. By 1996 over 50% of all the local authorities in the UK had made a commitment to Local Agenda 21, including the creation of detailed action strategies. Local authorities discovered, however, the frustrating fact that no matter how great the political will of the council to assert sustainable development, the law seemed to insist that local authority pension schemes should focus solely on maximising financial rewards irrespective of the environmental cost. Over time local authorities increasingly realised that they faced a potential charge of hypocrisy, in that they were using ratepayers' money to encourage local communities to act in a sustainable way, while ignoring such issues in the investment strategy of their own pension funds. As Roger Latham, county treasurer of Nottinghamshire County Council described it:

Many of the issues around SRI are part of the natural agenda for local government. National government has laid specific environmental obligations on local government by asking each authority to have a policy in place.... As a public body, we have to take account of public attitudes. In the past SRI has been a fringe issue, but it is becoming increasingly central. The public is becoming more aware. Green consumerism is on the increase. People are looking for an integrated relationship between an organisation, its pension fund, and the wider community.[17]

John Denham specifically referred to Local Agenda 21 in his 1998 speech introducing the planned measures:

The Department of the Environment, Transport and the Regions is demonstrating the Government's overall commitment to sustainability by encouraging all local authorities to adopt the principles of Local Agenda 21, i.e. sustainable development that protects and enhances the environment, meets social needs, protects human health, and promotes economic success.[18]

I would identify concerns over corporate governance as the third impulse prompting government action. There seemed growing political frustration about the apparent failure of institutional investors to use the votes and influence resulting from their ownership of shares to assert some control over executive behaviour. The criticisms of the 1992 report of the Cadbury Committee on Corporate Governance sent shock waves through UK boardrooms. The majority of shares in UK quoted companies are owned by institutional investors, yet there has been growing public and governmental concern that they are acting as 'absentee owners', i.e. ignoring the responsibilities of share ownership. Despite the best efforts of Cadbury and subsequent corporate governance reports such as Hempel, repeated surveys showed that the majority of fund managers were failing to vote their shares.

The 1990s saw increasing public criticism of what were perceived as corporate excesses, with senior executives awarding themselves huge pay rises, extended notice periods, and lucrative bonuses and share options. Criticism turned to bitterness when some companies combined large executive pay rises with restructuring and job losses.

British Gas even had a pig named after its chief executive kept out-side in its 1995 AGM during a row over executive pay. In the US executive remuneration at Disney was a similar *cause célèbre*. The apparent disinterest of institutional investors in corporate gover-nance during the 1990s coincided with an escalation of executive pay on both sides of the Atlantic. A significant corporate governance industry grew up in response to such concerns, yet British govern-ments (of both political parties) became increasingly frustrated that institutional investors, the one group with the power to compel (or dismiss) executives, seemed to be doing nothing to stop such exec-utive abuse. Shortly after taking office as head of the Department of Trade and Industry (DTI) in 1997, Margaret Beckett publicly ex-pressed such concern:

> I look forward to more institutions actively using their voting assets, and to pension fund trustees, and other clients, routinely asking managers how they have voted. Better still, institutions should explain their voting policies and volunteer the informa-tion on how they have voted.[19]

For someone such as the author, who has followed the evolution of socially responsible investment for many years, perhaps the most revolutionary thing about the 1999 pensions regulations was the clause about 'the policy (if any) directing the exercise of the rights (including voting rights) attaching to investments'. It would be fair to say that the general public does not associate corporate governance with SRI, and it seems legitimate to wonder why the DSS did so. The answer was provided in a November 1999 speech by Jeff Rooker, who had recently been appointed as Pensions Minister. The Minister explained that while the Department of Social Security drafted the new SRI pensions regulations,

> The inclusion of a requirement to state policy on the exercise of (voting) rights is there because the DTI [Department of Trade and Industry] wanted to move that issue forward but didn't have a legislative vehicle of its own available — an example of 'joined-up Government'.[20]

POLITICAL RECOGNITION OF PUBLIC INTEREST IN SRI

The new pension regulations also met the Government's desire to increase transparency and disclosure, particularly in financial services. Another driver behind them was the Government's awareness of growing public awareness and interest in socially responsible investment. John Denham specifically referred to this in his 1998 speech to the UKSIF AGM:

> As a politician I am interested in what people think about ethical and green issues. There have been a number of surveys over the years. In 1996 analysis of regular Mori polls identified that 41% of British adults qualified as 'green consumers'. In the same year Ogilvy and Mather reported that 67% of adults consider a company's ethical stance when buying a product. The EIRIS survey last year showed that over 70% of those interviewed wanted their pension scheme assets invested ethically.[21]

Denham was referring to an opinion poll carried out by NOP for the ethical investment research service EIRIS in September 1997. Forty-four percent of the 700 adults questioned stated that their pension scheme should operate an ethical policy if that could be done without any reduction in financial return. Interestingly, a further 29% of the sample argued for their pension scheme to adopt ethical policies even if this led to reduced returns, making 73% wanting ethical pensions. (Nineteen percent of the survey thought that pension schemes should ignore ethics and concentrate on financial return, while 8% didn't know.) When the poll was repeated in 1999, NOP found the proportion wanting their pension fund to have an ethical investment policy had risen further from 10% to 83%. Stephen Timms followed a similar line of argument when he laid the new SRI regulations before the House of Commons:

> There is undoubtedly a significant groundswell of public interest in socially responsible investment. Ordinary people want to know what is being done with the money invested on their behalf.[22]

Table 1.1   *UK SRI retail funds 1990–1999*

Year	1990	1993	1996	1999
Total (£m)	321	728	1480	3197
Total Funds	30	41	45	60

Note: The criteria used to distinguish retail from institutional products are that the 'retail' total include any collective investment scheme or 'pooled fund' that is open to all qualifying members. Hence personal pensions are defined as retail products, but segregated defined benefit pension schemes are classified as institutional.

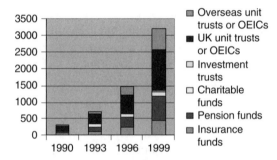

Figure 1.1   *Growth of UK SRI retail funds (£m) 1990–99*

The most visible sign of public interest in SRI was probably the continuing strong growth in the number and size of socially responsible funds available to the public. This included unit trusts, open-ended investment companies (OEICs) and related pension and insurance funds. In 1994 my article 'The Rewards of Virtue'[23] demonstrated the rapid growth of ethical unit trusts in their first ten years of life, following the launch of Friends Provident Stewardship in June 1984. This showed that over the period 1987–93 the total assets invested in UK SRI unit trusts were doubling in size every three years. When I updated the research for the six years to 1999, I was surprised to see that the SRI industry was still demonstrating the same extraordinary growth rate (Figure 1.1 and Table 1.1).

The growth in retail SRI products was hardly surprising. The last twenty years have seen a steady erosion of public support for political parties and the established churches, combined with continued growth in support for environmental and social campaigning groups such as Greenpeace, Friends of the Earth, and Amnesty International. Socially responsible unit trusts offer a vehicle for supporters of such groups to ensure their investments mirror the values that they feel are crucial.

Probably the last significant driver for change was political recognition of increasing activism from pension scheme members themselves for their fund to adopt SRI policies. The campaign Ethics for USS is a good example of the pressure brought to bear on a large pension fund, the Universities Superannuation Scheme (USS). This is one of the largest pension schemes in the UK, with £22 billion in assets. Ethics for USS was set up in 1998 to persuade USS to adopt a comprehensive ethical and environmental investment policy. The campaign was supported by 3500 individual members as well as the Association of University Teachers, and reached a successful conclusion. In September 2000 USS recognised this challenge by recruiting two SRI advisers whose role was to help the fund formulate socially responsible investment policies and to engage with company investments of USS on these issues.

For most ordinary people their pension entitlements are by far their largest single financial asset, a fact recently recognised in divorce law. Prior to the 1995 Pensions Act, contributors and beneficiaries of pension schemes had minimal rights over how their funds operated. The new act, with its requirements for the election of representative trustees, enabled scheme members to have a greater say in fund operation. One consequence of this democratic development has been an increasing trend among some scheme members to campaign for their own fund to adopt SRI principles. However, they found that their wishes were frustrated by a legal logjam, as investment managers and pension consultants adopted the traditional narrow interpretation of the law, which seemed to rule out SRI for pension schemes. The new pensions regulations can therefore be seen as the Government giving its blessing to such an expression of pension fund democracy.

I end this chapter with a quotation from a civil servant who worked on the new SRI regulations right from their beginning, and who had little doubt about the eventual outcome (original emphasis):

You cannot take away knowledge. This measure will enable scheme members to push for their pension funds, those great capital engines of the financial markets, to actually get involved in social and environmental issues. I suspect that within three to five years it will be *unthinkable* for pension funds *not* to invest their funds in socially responsible ways.[24]

REFERENCES

1. H.M Markowitz, 'Portfolio Selection', *Journal of Finance*, 1952.
2. Pensions adviser in conversation with the author, March 1999.
3. Charles Scanlan, quoted in *The Ethical Investor*, EIRIS, May 1999.
4. The Goode Committee on Pension Fund Trust Law, HMSO 1993.
5. John Denham MP, speech to the UKSIF annual general meeting, 9 July 1998, 'Building a Better World: The Future of Socially Responsible Pensions'.
6. Stephen Timms MP, speech to PIRC Corporate Responsibility Conference, 21 April 1999.
7. *Ibid.*
8. Quoted in the *Financial Times*, 'Ethics Disclosure Plan Prompts Share Price Warning', 9 June 1999.
9. *Ibid.*
10. *The Guardian*, 'MPs Criticise Pension Fund Stalling on Ethics Rule', 12 June 1999.
11. *Ibid.*
12. House of Commons, Early Day Motion 710: Pensions Disclosure Regulation.
13. *Financial Times*, 2 July 1999, 'Pension Funds End Opposition to Rules on Ethical Stance'.
14. Pensions adviser in conversation with the author, March 1999.
15. Denham, *op. cit.*
16. Tony Blair, speech on stakeholding, Singapore, March 1996.
17. Speech by Roger Latham, county treasurer of Nottinghamshire County Council, to Local Authority Pension Forum, 1998.
18. Denham, *op. cit.*
19. Margaret Beckett, speech October 1997.
20. Jeff Rooker, 'Ethics Policies for Company Pension Funds', speech to PWC/FIS Conference, 23 November 1999.
21. Denham, *op. cit.*
22. Timms, *op. cit.*
23. This article has just been reprinted in *Double Takes*, published by John Wiley & Sons.
24. Pensions adviser in conversation with the author, April 2000.

2

What Is Socially Responsible Investment?

Chapter 1 described the road to regulation, and described how all UK pension schemes have been obliged to disclose 'the extent (if at all) to which social, environmental or ethical considerations are taken into account by trustees'. One thing that struck me about this clause was that nowhere does it actually define what the terms 'socially responsible investment' or 'ethical investment' might mean. Contacts with the civil servants who advised ministers on the issue suggest that such silence was deliberate. It probably made sense to politicians and their official advisers to skate over this issue.

Yet surely at some point along the line somebody needs to define what is meant by 'socially responsible investment' as people need to know what it is, and what it isn't. SRI has grown up as a practical movement built by practical people, with relatively little thought being given to a deeper analysis of the basic ideas and concepts. While it is true that business ethics has become a booming academic speciality over the last twenty years, business ethicists have produced curiously little analysis of SRI. The aim of this chapter is to fill that gap, by attempting to categorise the different types of activity that make up socially responsible investment. It is very much a pioneering development in this respect. I would not be surprised if some people violently disagree with its conclusions, or if I modify them in a future work. However, in my opinion the attempt should be made. Confusion between closely related activities such as shareholder activism and single-issue advocacy can lead to a distorted view of SRI, and can also lead to disappointment if things are asked of social investing that it cannot be expected to deliver.

A DEFINITION OF SOCIALLY RESPONSIBLE INVESTMENT

> It is probably time to clarify what is normally meant by 'ethical investment'. It does not mean a moral campaign to clean up the Stock Exchange, or raise the standards of those who work in the financial field.... Ethical investment is straightforward, and simply means an investment philosophy that combines ethical or environmental goals with financial ones.[1]

The above was my attempt at a definition of ethical investment back in 1994. Many writers had described the phenomenon of SRI before that, but this was one of the first attempts to provide a precise definition. In my opinion the best summary definition of SRI was produced in the same year by Chris Cowton, Professor of Accounting at Huddersfield University Business School and one of the very few academics to address this question. Taking the terms SRI and ethical investment to be 'equivalent', he stated:

> Ethical investment may be defined as the exercise of ethical and social criteria in the selection and management of investment portfolios, generally consisting of company shares (stocks). This contrasts with standard depictions of investment decisions, which concentrate solely on financial return.... Ethical investors care not only about the size of their prospective financial return and the risk attached to it, but also its source – the nature of the company's goods or services, the location of its business or the manner in which it conducts its affairs.[2]

I am impressed with the precision of Cowton's definition, and wish I had seen it before making my own attempt. He is surely right to concentrate on the use of ethical and social criteria in the selection and management of investment portfolios, a much more precise category than the vague term 'investments'. Cowton also makes the valuable suggestion that financial return is important, a fact overlooked by many commentators. I have argued elsewhere that concern for financial returns is one of the key factors distinguishing SRI from charitable giving.[3] Many writers have described socially responsible investment as based on the avoidance of certain activities, but Cowton's use of the term 'source', defined as activity, location, or manner of business, indicates correctly that things are more complicated.

Although my earlier book used the phrase 'ethical investment', I now prefer 'socially responsible investment'. While both terms specify the same thing, there is a definite trend for 'ethical investment' to be replaced by 'socially responsible investment' as the standard descriptive term. That switch has already happened in the US. I would guess that the reason for the change is the 'mainstreaming of SRI', i.e. the move to SRI being dominated by institutional investors rather than retail SRI funds. In the Anglo-Saxon tradition 'ethics' is generally seen as something individual, about personal values. It made sense to call SRI 'ethical investment' when it described people investing along with their personal values in unit trusts or mutual funds. It makes less sense to describe pension fund investment as 'ethical', whereas 'socially responsible' seems to fit them much better.

It is also true that many people simply feel uncomfortable about using the word 'ethical' to describe investment. Stephen Timms described his dislike of the term 'ethical investment' in his 1999 speech announcing the new pensions regulations:

> [It] has traditionally been referred to as ethical investment, but what I prefer to call socially responsible investment. I believe that when a name becomes so loaded a term that the very mention of it stifles intelligent debate rather than encourages it, then it's time for a change.[4]

Stephen Timms is not the only one to be wary of the phrase 'ethical investment'. Chris Cowton points out the apparent contradiction of using the word 'ethical' to describe a profit-maximising activity of the financial services industry:

> At one level, ethical investment can be seen as just another product innovation that helps widen choice.... The irony is that its occurrence can be explained in pure, profit-seeking capitalistic terms, as financial institutions seek to influence and exploit their environment in the interests of profitability. Thus individual investors, potentially at least, have their values met or satisfied by institutions/people who do not share these values at all, whose sole motive might be to make more money.[5]

However, Cowton's criticisms were mild compared to the onslaught levelled by the Social Affairs Unit (SAU) in 1996:

> The criteria [used] reflect the criteria demanded by investors... the investment companies have indeed satisfied a customer demand. But that does not mean what they are doing has a right to be labelled 'ethical' with the least occasional implication that other investments are unethical.... This Report suggests that their own investments might variously be accurately labelled 'investments reflecting investors' opinions', 'investments reflecting fashionable causes', 'scrupulous investments', 'ethically simplistic investments'... the overall objection to ethical investment codes is their aggressive simplicity... a simplicity which ill fits them for their ethical work.[6]

People sometimes ask whether there is a difference between SRI and 'green investing'. Tessa Tennant, founder of the NPI research unit, has long been one of the UK's leading thinkers on the subject of the relationship of financial markets to environmental issues. She has consistently argued that there is no real difference between the two:

> The two are part and parcel of the same thing — investors avoiding tobacco companies on ethical grounds will almost certainly choose to avoid them on environmental grounds if they are appraised of the fact that for every 300 cigarettes made from third world tobacco, one tree is burnt.... Socially responsible investment should take into account both ethical and environmental issues.[7]

Of course there is an obvious difference between investment in environmental activities carried out to maximise profits, and that carried out to encourage sustainable development, with only the latter deserving the term 'green'. However, like most writers on SRI, I normally include funds investing in environmental technologies within the SRI universe on the grounds that many of the underlying investors do so for environmental reasons, rather than to make a quick profit. In such a case the 'ethics' derive from the underlying investors, rather than being explicitly stated in the fund's objectives. Over time asset management companies have discovered that the socially responsible investing public regards the environment as a core issue alongside the older negative exclusions of tobacco, defence, etc. In practice, therefore, virtually all SRI funds now use environmental criteria, regardless of whether they started out by doing so. Cowton again describes this accurately:

> It remains the case that some investors are interested in environmentalism for value-based reasons, and a number of ethical investment products recognise that. Therefore, when I refer to ethical investment I take it to encompass green investment too, when that investment is being undertaken for other than purely commercial motives.[8]

Another issue which needs clarification is the relationship of 'community development' to SRI. *The 2001 Trends Report on SRI in the United States* characterises SRI as consisting of three 'dynamic strategies': screening, shareholder advocacy, and community investing.[9] I beg to differ. There is no doubt that screening and shareholder advocacy are the two basic pillars of SRI, but I do not think that community development should be included. Both are certainly aspects of 'social investment', i.e. where investors integrate social factors into financial decisions. However, community development is based on a banking model rather than on equity finance, and indeed is sometimes described as 'ethical banking'.

The banking model works rather well in such targeted development, as savers in effect give the use of their capital (which can be guaranteed in banking), while waiving most or all of the interest due upon it. In other words, investors voluntarily accept lower returns than they could otherwise achieve on these loans to promote social objectives. The best-known example is probably the community development carried out by the South Shore Bank in Chicago. In the US, state or federal governments sometimes play a role by providing loan guarantees, which means that such loans automatically become investment grade. In the UK, Shared Interest and Triodos have pioneered low- or zero-interest savings accounts, with the money used to finance 'fairtrade' projects in developing countries. There is also the extremely valuable work carried out by micro-credit banks following the trail pioneered by the Grameen Bank in Bangladesh.

I would argue that such activity should be clearly distinguished from SRI for two reasons. Firstly, one of the key attributes of socially responsible investment is to affect corporate behaviour by using the power and influence of shareholders. This means that it must be centred upon holding stocks and shares in companies, i.e. equities. In the US the use of shareholder resolutions to pressurise corporations has been an integral part of SRI since the movement's inception. Community development in contrast is essentially a debt-based activity. The second difference relates to financial returns. The essence of ethical banking is that savers deliberately accept below-market returns in order to help others, which is not the intention in SRI. In community development, savers give up the use of their capital for a certain period, and waive their right to receive market rates of interest from it, but they expect to have their capital repaid in full in due course. In SRI, on the other hand, there is a general expectation of achieving a return on capital, although that capital is subject to the vagaries of the stock market. Both of these are subclasses of what may be called social investing, i.e. investment with some kind of social component.

I have revised my earlier definition of socially responsible investment in the light of the preceding discussion. One major change made to the earlier definition lies in the additional weight given to financial objectives. The reason for so doing so lies in the fact that many commentators on SRI have tended to overemphasise social and environmental considerations at the expense of neglecting financial factors. This is fair enough for retail SRI investors, as we shall see in later chapters, but the growing importance of institutional investors within socially responsible investment has changed that; see the ICCR definition of its members' aims (page 33). In fact, I would argue that these two aspects of SRI could be formally modelled in distinct ways: retail investors want the maximum avoidance of social and environmental concerns, with financial performance a secondary consideration, whereas institutional investors want to maximise financial returns within SRI constraints. Readers interested in pursuing such arguments further are referred to the author's article on the subject in the business ethics literature.[10] Anyway, here is my new definition of SRI:

> The key distinguishing feature of socially responsible investment lies in the construction of equity portfolios whose

investment objectives combine social, environmental and financial goals. When practised by institutional investors this means attempting to obtain a return on invested capital approaching that of the overall stock market.

IS THERE MORE TO SRI THAN SCREENING?

The oldest significant 'ethical investors' were the UK church investors (notably the Church of England, the Methodist Church, and the Society of Friends or Quakers). The first of these was running investment portfolios subject to certain ethical constraints as early as 1948. These pioneers used what would now be called a simple avoidance approach, with investment portfolios excluding certain sectors of the stock market traditionally judged inimical in the Protestant, and particularly Nonconformist, tradition: alcohol, tobacco, defence, and gambling. Later some secular commentators jocularly called this methodology 'sin stock' avoidance.

The Society of Friends and the Methodist Church were the main sponsors behind the foundation of the UK ethical research service EIRIS in 1983. Similar groups and individuals were likewise behind the launch of the first UK commercial 'ethical' unit trust, Friends Provident Stewardship, in 1984; see Chapter 3 for further details. While the churches had tended to talk in general terms of 'ethical constraints being applied to investment', or the 'ethics of investment', such subtleties were lost when the media described the new commercial activity, which became generally known as 'ethical investment'. Likewise, the first modern American SRI mutual fund was the Pax World Balanced Fund, launched by two United Methodist ministers in August 1971.[11] Like many Americans at that time, they were particularly keen to exclude any investment holding that could be profiting from the Vietnam War.

This is the basic model of socially responsible investment that has been used by SRI unit trusts and mutual funds ever since − a form of investment based on what some would call arbitrary exclusion criteria. These funds set out certain activities of concern to them, traditionally alcohol, tobacco, defence, and gambling, with more recent additions such as the environment, human rights or pornography.

Filter screens are then established to rule out unacceptable invest-ments; typically a maximum percentage of a company's turnover, perhaps 5% or 10%. Screening in practice is covered in Chapter 5, which examines the practice of two UK SRI funds and two US SRI funds. Over time some retail funds have made changes to the basic model. A small number now try and take into account positive fac-tors when analysing companies, such as charitable donations, em-ployment of ethnic minorities, etc. The problem with this approach is that there is relatively little agreement on what such positive issues should be, and not much data on which to assess them.

One of the difficulties with the classic SRI avoidance approach is that it reduces diversification and reduces potential growth opportu-nities. While investors in retail funds such as unit trusts and mutual funds are willing to accept this, these factors are hard for pension funds to swallow. Most asset managers have therefore tried to refor-mulate the original model to make it more acceptable to potential pension fund clients. Until recently US pension funds and charitable foundations have been wary of making any SRI exclusions at all for fear of falling foul of the 'prudent man' rule of fiduciary duty. Their approach eliminates exclusion, making shareholder activism the basis of their SRI policy. The activity of ICCR and other leaders in the field of US shareholder activism is covered later in this chapter. A variant that is increasingly popular in the UK is to emphasise dia-logue with companies over sensitive issues, generally known as the 'engagement' approach.

Another variant of SRI that is growing in popularity with institu-tional investors is to accept investment in all sectors of the market, but to try and identify the 'best in class'. The advantage of this style of SRI is that it need not negatively affect financial returns. Innovest data on environmental performance suggests that it can actually im-prove them (see Chapter 10 for more details). Another SRI investment style that has been tried, particularly by SRI funds with a strong en-vironmental bias is a positive approach with a title such as 'indus-tries of the future'. This has a strong appeal to green investors as it offers them the dual benefits of a commitment to sustainability plus the hoped-for financial benefits of investing in industries with significant long-term growth prospects. In general, however, avoid-ance remains the dominant model for unit trusts, with best in class

Table 2.1 *Varying investment methods within SRI*

Method	Risk	Class of investors
Avoidance of certain activities	Lack of diversification and potentially lower returns	Retail funds, unit trusts, mutual funds
Targeting positive activities	Limited data	None at present
Shareholder activism	Must own 'problem' shares	Institutions-not liked by retail investors
Best in class	Data to do this limited, but could produce good returns	Few at present
Industries of the future	Highly concentrated portfolios so high portfolio risk	Few at present
SRI risk optimisation	Low portfolio risk	Some institutions

and engagement more common for the growing institutional interest in SRI.

A final investment style which seems well suited to pension funds is SRI risk optimisation, i.e. using internal market correlations to minimise the risk of SRI exclusions. This enables institutional port-folios to be created that avoid certain sections of the stock market, but are designed to produce a risk/reward performance similar to that of a benchmark index such as the FTSE All-Share in the UK, or the S&P 500 in the US. This is the approach of the Central Finance Board of the Methodist Church in the UK, and the Domini Social Index in the US. These varying approaches are shown in Table 2.1.

THE ROLE OF SHAREHOLDER ACTIVISM

Technically 'shareholder activism' simply means the use of voting rights attached to ordinary shares to assert political, financial or other objectives. It occurs when a group of shareholders get together to raise public awareness of something that a company is doing, and it represents an attempt to use shareholders' unique power as the owners of companies to facilitate change. Shareholder activism can be classified into three types of action: publicity, dialogue, and the filing of shareholder resolutions. It is also practised by some active funds for purely financial reasons, as such investors hope to profit from the stock market's recognition of a greater focus on shareholder value by targeted companies. SRI resolutions are often described in the US as social proxy resolutions, or just social proxies, to distinguish them from shareholder resolutions motivated by financial considerations.

Shareholder activism has always been an integral feature of socially responsible investment in the US. Landmark events include Ralph Nader's action to force General Motors to discuss workers' rights and consumer issues at its 1970 annual meeting, and the US Episcopal Church resolution on South Africa at General Motors' AGM the following year. People often seem to think that the essence of SRI lies in negative screening. This is misguided. The following two quotations may help to dispel this impression: (a) describes the aims and objectives of the founders of the Pax World Fund in 1971; (b) is from the 2001 ICCR annual report:

(a) Their second goal was to create a vehicle to challenge corporations to establish and live up to specific standards of social and environmental responsibility. They thought they could best influence corporations from the inside, as shareholders.[12]

(b) Rather than simply selling stock when a company acts irresponsibly, ICCR members use these investments to open doors at corporations and raise social and environmental concerns at the highest levels.[13]

It is no accident that shareholder activism has flourished in the United States. American shareholders benefit from the closely defined legal rights to file shareholder resolutions issued by the Securities and Exchange Commission (SEC). Primary sponsors of a resolution must own a minimum of $2000 worth of stock in the corporation (a threshold increased from $1000 in 1992) and they must have held this for at least a year. To be resubmitted, a resolution must receive at least 3% of the votes in year 1, 6% in year 2, and 10% subsequently. When US institutions started filing social proxies in the early 1970s, the atmosphere was often highly charged and adversarial. By the 1990s things had changed through what Tim Smith, the long-time head of ICCR, called 'a process of maturation'. In other words, each side of the process recognised that the other had something of value to offer, that the objective of the exercise was to benefit the corporation by improving its behaviour; it was not aimed at damaging it. In Smith's words:

> Today a generation of parties to these negotiations has become accustomed to the idea that the interests involved are not mutually exclusive but are often complementary. In fact, this is what the corporate social responsibility movement has contended from the beginning. A 'maturation' process is taking place on both sides. Increasingly investors are recognising and affirming the constructive role of social investors such as the churches to raise and work though issues that must be of concern to the corporation.[14]

Shareholder rights are not unlimited, however, as the SEC only allows 'resolutions going beyond ordinary business which are therefore suitable subjects for shareholder review through the proxy process'. Probably the most high-profile SEC decision in this regard was over Cracker Barrel in 1992. Cracker Barrel was a US store chain that was alleged to have a policy of not employing homosexuals. In 1992 the New York City Employee Retirement System attempted to file a shareholder resolution requesting the company 'to implement non-discriminatory policies relating to sexual orientation and to add explicit prohibitions against such discrimination to their corporate employment policy statement'. The SEC ruled that this was a 'personnel' matter, and as such was part of the 'ordinary business' of the company, meaning that the resolution could not be filed. Another factor encouraging shareholder activism in the US is the legal duty of American pension funds to make use of the voting rights of the shares they own. US pension plans are supervised by the Department of Labor under the Employee Retirement Income Security Act of 1974 (ERISA). Under the Reagan administration, Department of

Labor officials insisted that fiduciary duty under ERISA extended to the use of shareholder votes. As one senior official stated in 1988:

> A fiduciary who manages a portfolio has a duty to evaluate issues that can have an impact on the economic value of the stock in the portfolio and to vote on those issues. Shares should be voted based upon a careful analysis of the impact of the vote on the ultimate value of the plan's investments.[15]

Over time US shareholder activism has developed a recognised code of procedure. Informal dialogue with corporate executives informs them of SRI concerns held by institutional investors. If this dialogue does not result in change, a resolution is then filed. Often the mere existence of such a resolution is enough to concentrate executives' minds over the issue, and the matter is then settled, with the resolution being amicably withdrawn by the proposers before the company's annual general meeting. By the 1990s many social resolutions were receiving the support of 10–25% of the vote, putting huge pressure on corporate executives to respond positively to them. Tim Smith wrote in 1992:

> The movement has evolved from the stage when shareholder resolutions were considered an annoying irritation by gadflies to one where only corporate executives with their head in the sand would ignore the power – if not the sensibilities – of these investor petitions. As one analyst stated, 'the acoustics change at a stock-holders meeting when the resolution is jointly sponsored by investors with one to three million shares'.[16]

It is extremely rare for a social proxy resolution to actually win 50% of the vote. Any social proxy that receives 10% or more is normally considered to be a great success that sends a strong message to the company's directors on the issue. The *2001 Trends Report* produced by the Social Investment Forum collated some interesting statistics on US social shareholder resolutions (Table 2.2).

Of the 261 shareholder resolutions filed in 2001, a total of 135 were filed by one organisation and its constituent members, the Interfaith Center on Corporate Responsibility (ICCR). ICCR has been the leader in US shareholder activism since it was founded in 1973.

Table 2.2   *US shareholder resolutions*
2000–2001

	2000	2001
Resolutions introduced	251	261
Resolutions voted on	150	156
Average share of vote (%)	7.5	8.5

Source: 2001 Report on Socially Responsible Invest-
ing Trends in the United States, Social Investment
Forum, 28 November 2001.

ICCR's 2001 annual report described some of the key issues it had campaigned on in the previous year, as well as its basic ethos:

> Best known for advocacy, ICCR Members are serious, long-term investors for whom the financial performance of their socially screened portfolios is crucial to their investment strategy. Distinguishing us from traditional investors, ICCR Members also examine companies in our portfolios for their social and environmental performance.... This year saw a 'higher than usual number' of social responsibility resolutions 'with the support of at least 10% of the shares voted'. Backed by billions of dollars of shares, these votes send out powerful messages to corporations and contribute to significant progress towards a better world.[17]

Here are some manifestations of ICCR's shareholder activism during 2000–2001:[18]

- *Environment*: pressed multinational companies to reduce emissions of greenhouse gases, and change practices and products that contribute to global warming and climate change.
- *General Electric*: publicised GE responsibility for dumping 1.3 million pounds of PCBs in the Hudson River prior to this practice being outlawed in 1977.
- *Genetically Modified Foods*: campaigned to raise awareness among senior US corporate executives, institutional investors, and the American public of the widespread prevalence of GM material in foodstuffs.

- *Predatory Lending*: initiated major reforms in lending practices of leading financial institutions accused of predatory lending.
- *Maquiladoras*: documented huge gap between wages paid in *maquiladoras* (US-owned plants located just inside the Mexican border) and local basic living costs.
- *Smoking*: persuaded Wendy's burger chain to make its restaurants no-smoking.
- *Pharmaceuticals*: pressed leading US pharmaceutical companies to make affordable prescription drugs available in developing countries.

Shareholder activism on social issues has been less successful outside the US. In Canada it was illegal until late 2001 (Chapter 12), while practical difficulties in continental Europe and Asia make it almost impossible. The UK is the only other country apart from the US where shareholder activism has been tried on a significant scale. Filing shareholder resolutions in the UK requires crossing a higher hurdle than in the US. They can only be tabled if they receive the support of 100 separate investors who each own shares with a nominal value of £100 (i.e. based on the par value of the shares, not current market price), or own over 5% of the total voting capital of the company. These provisions of UK company law date back to the 1948 Companies Act. As early as 1982 the World Development Movement filed a resolution to force the Brooke Bond tea company to give better pay and conditions to the workers on its tea plantations. However, the resolution received little support and was generally forgotten.

The real beginnings of UK shareholder activism on SRI issues can be precisely dated to 14 May 1997. This was the date of the 1997 annual general meeting of the Shell Transport and Trading Company. Shell had already received negative publicity in 1995–96 over its planned disposal of the Brent Spar oil platform, and concern over human rights abuses in Nigeria culminating in the execution of Ken Saro-Wiwa. In 1997 an NGO-led coalition was able to assemble enough support from local authority pension funds (coordinated by PIRC) and church investors led by ECCR to file a shareholder resolution. This requested the management to behave in a more socially and environmentally responsible way, asking the company to draw up a detailed policy on the environment and human rights, with a specific board member responsible for its implementation, and that it should be independently audited. While the resolution was rejected, the proposal received the support of over 11% of the votes cast, an astonishingly high total for such a huge company. Within a year Shell management responded positively towards the measures suggested in the resolution.

Other large UK multinationals subject to SRI resolutions in recent years have included BP, Rio Tinto, and Balfour Beatty. The 2000 BP AGM saw a proposal calling on the company to cease development of its Northstar development off the coast of Alaska, and reinvest the proceeds into renewable energy. This resolution received 13.5% of the vote. Rio Tinto, the world's largest mining company, faced a resolution at its 2000 AGM asking the company to adopt the International Labour Organisation (ILO) standards on labour rights at work which gained the support of 17.3% of the votes cast. It has been generally accepted in UK legal circles that once the conditions set out above have been met, SRI shareholder resolutions should be presented to the AGM. However, in February 2001 the board of BP declined to accept four social resolutions as ordinary business for its AGM, although it had accepted one the previous year. BP justified its decision by stating that the four resolutions should only be moved in the form of an arcane procedure called a special resolution, thus raising a legal precedent.

ADVOCACY CONTRASTED WITH ACTIVISM

Shareholder activism is also of interest to NGOs in pursuit of their advocacy campaigns. Such groups are normally driven by a single-issue agenda that is perceived to be of overwhelming importance to their activist members. One of the main themes of this book is that the essence of SRI is the attempt to combine social concerns with a reasonable financial return. If this definition is correct, it is important to distinguish SRI from such single-issue campaigns, as there is quite a lot of general confusion about this. Advocacy campaigns use shareholder rights to force attendance at a company's annual general meeting where critical questions can be asked of the senior executives. The main aim of such groups is to be able to complain in a public forum about a company's activities in a particular field, such as the environment, animal rights, or indigenous peoples. Here is an example (emphasis added):

> Each year Partizans, a tiny but dogged London-based campaigning group, has launched a campaign on RTZ, the world's largest mining company. Partizans wants RTZ to act in a more environmentally responsible way, and to treat indigenous people with more respect. Partizans does not table resolutions, instead it asks difficult questions and seeks to attract press publicity for the causes it represents. *Occasionally it has stormed the podium in an effort to make the company and the press listen.*[19]

For such campaigning activists, maintaining the value of the shares they have bought, normally for only a small sum, is not an object of concern. It seems quite legitimate for them to want to cause financial harm to a company, perhaps by encouraging consumer boycotts, if that is seen as the most effective way to achieve their aims. On the other hand, it is hard to conceive of any circumstance in which SRI fund managers would actually want to see a decline in the value of the shares they hold. Socially responsible investors want a financial return from their investments, something immaterial for advocacy campaigns. If SRI shareholder activism seeks to improve corporate behaviour, NGO advocacy campaigns may even seek to close down a particular company on the basis that they believe its whole basis of operation to be immoral, e.g. nuclear power (British Energy), mining (Rio Tinto), or tobacco (Philip Morris). It also seems fair to describe confrontation and publicity as standard tools of campaigning groups, whereas quiet discussion with corporate executives is more characteristic of SRI. Perhaps Table 2.3 will make this distinction clearer.

In practice there is a significant overlap between single-issue advocacy campaigns and the social objectives of SRI investors. The two groups may share the same concerns, and they may often work together to pressurise a certain company on a particular issue. The two types of activities may share the same means, i.e. the utilisation of the voting rights attached to ordinary shares to assert non-financial objectives, although the aims and objectives are different. As part

Table 2.3 *Advocacy compared to SRI*

Advocacy campaigns	Socially responsible investment
Single-issue focus	Multi-issue concerns
No financial concerns	Strong financial interest
Seeks confrontation	Seeks engagement
Seeks publicity	Avoids publicity

of these campaigns it is normal practice for ICCR staff members to work with advocacy groups. I find it interesting that ICCR has set out a series of obligatory 'ground rules' for any NGO who wants to work with it, to ensure that the aims, objectives and methods of each party are made clear before they start to work together. For instance, companies in private discussions with ICCR regarding proposed shareholder resolutions may disclose confidential information to support their case. The ground rules prohibit any such confidential information being placed in the public domain without the prior approval of the company.[20]

Recent years have also seen a sea change in the attitude of many NGOs regarding contact with companies, particularly the larger NGOs. The older 'confrontational' approach described above has been replaced by a more pragmatic stance that fits in well with SRI. Such pragmatic approaches are described in depth in *The Campaigners' Guide to Financial Markets*, a 200-page book on the subject that was published in 2002.[21] This examines cases like BP and its proposed drilling in Alaska, Del Monte and non-recognition of union rights in Costa Rica, and American investment banks and the Three Gorges Dam in China. The campaign led by Friends of the Earth against the UK company Balfour Beatty is described in the book, and seems a good example of the pragmatic approach.

In 1997 the civil engineering company Balfour Beatty became a member of a consortium planning to build a 1200 megawatt dam at llisu in south-eastern Turkey. The $2.2 billion project received the backing of the US Export-Import Bank, and an initial favourable reception from the UK government for $200 million in export credits. The llisu dam is highly controversial on a number of environmental, human rights and historical grounds. It is believed that the dam's construction will result in the flooding of over 200 square miles, as well as seriously affecting the water supply to the river Tigris. The planned dam site is in the Kurdish region of Turkey, an area of political unrest and under a state of emergency by the Turkish government. The dam's construction is forecast to flood 15 towns and 50 villages, displacing up to 78 000 people, most of them Kurds. Lastly the area contains a number of important archaeological sites, particularly the historic town of Hasankeyf. An international campaign grew up to try to persuade the export credit agencies of the major countries involved in the project of the importance of these issues, and convince them to withdraw.

In the UK the llisu Dam Campaign decided to organise a campaign against Balfour Beatty's involvement in the project, which included sending petitions to the company, and holding demonstrations at its offices. In 2001 the Ilisu Dam Campaign decided to work together with Friends of the Earth in a focused shareholder activism campaign, based on the following shareholder resolution:[22]

- that the company recognises the importance of the principles, criteria, and guidelines of the World Commission on Dams Report; that the company hereby adopts as formal company policy that it shall endeavour to ensure that all future hydropower contracts in which it is involved comply with the set of Guidelines for Good Practice;
- that the company considers the potential to use those Guidelines in other areas of its operations; and
- that the Business Practices Committee reports to shareholders on the company's implementation of the Guidelines.

The two NGOs carried out a sophisticated lobbying campaign of institutional investors who owned shares in Balfour Beatty. Detailed dossiers were produced to back up the case for the resolution, and interviews were held with many of the largest shareholders in the company. The group argued for Balfour Beatty's compliance with the World Commission on Dams Report not on ethical grounds, but on the risk to its reputation by involvement in the Ilisu project. It claimed that the company had insufficient structures and policies in place to manage those risks:

This emphasis on reputational, and therefore financial risk, rather than moral arguments, was crucial for communicating our message to investors for two reasons. First, it put the issues to fund managers and analysts in language which made sense to them. Second, the argument that the current operating policy was financially risky enabled us to show investors that, unless it changed, Balfour Beatty could be jeopardising its future profits.

We also specifically targeted local authority pension funds. ... We used a two-pronged approach: we wrote directly to every local authority pension fund in the country (almost 100), enclosing a briefing and the resolution, and to our own supporters, asking them to send letters to their local authority, asking the latter to support our resolution. We also produced a spoof annual report – *Balfour Beatty counter-report 2000, Balfour Beatty's annus horribilis* [which] highlighted key controversial projects – including the Ilisu dam – in which the company was involved and argued that Balfour Beatty lacked a coherent strategy to manage reputational risks. We used the report to brief the media, institutional investors and shareholders.[23]

Although the Ilisu dam resolution received the support of only 1% of the votes cast, 40% of institutional shareholders decided to abstain on the issue. Pensions and Investment Research Consultants (PIRC) described the Balfour Beatty abstentions as follows: 'Abstentions should usually be read as (institutional) shareholders who sympathise with the resolution but don't want to go the whole hog'.[24] In November 2001 Balfour Beatty publicly announced that it would be pulling out of the Ilisu dam project. The company denied this decision had been made in response to the campaign against it. It did, however, state that the decision followed 'thorough and extensive evaluation of the commercial, environmental, and social issues' involved in the project. Balfour Beatty's withdrawal from the Ilisu dam consortium was quickly followed by that of the Swedish construction firm Skanska. In February 2002 UBS, one of the main bankers to the planned dam, also pulled out. It stated:

The decisive factor behind this termination is the general progress of the project has been unsatisfactory in recent years, and that there has been no definitive decision on what accompanying measures are to be taken to minimise the social and environmental impact of the project.[25]

A THEORETICAL JUSTIFICATION FOR SRI

It seems undeniable that retail SRI unit trusts and mutual funds are providing a product that their clients want. It is also hard to argue against churches and charities ensuring that their values are enshrined in their investment strategies. For example, if the UK charity the Cat's Protection League declines to invest in companies that test cosmetics on cats, it is surely being both morally consistent with its objectives, and commercially sensible as not doing something that might offend its donors and other supporters. (This commercial possibility is the legal basis that allows UK charities to have restricted 'ethical investment' policies even at some financial cost.) It is much harder to see why more broadly based investment institutions, such as insurance companies and pension funds, should adopt SRI principles. Pension schemes are financial trusts whose sole function is to produce a financial return sufficient to adequately fund an individual's retirement. In this section I would like to develop some ideas I briefly touched upon in 1998 that may provide an answer to this question.[26]

The first point is that such SRI responsibilities are only a reasonable reflection of the legal privileges given to pension funds. The legal privilege of incorporation is something that is often overlooked; individuals can pool their individual pension contributions into a joint fund that is a legal entity on its own account, and whose actions have no immediate legal or tax consequences for the potential pensioners. There are also financial privileges that include tax relief on contributions; employers' contributions not treated as taxable income, and immunity from capital gains tax. There seems a strong case that pension funds should repay such a privileged status by acting in socially responsible ways.

In this book I have repeatedly stressed the importance of not forgetting the 'investment' in socially responsible investment. Now in this context 'investment' normally refers to investment in equities, shares in limited companies quoted on a stock market. It seems to me that it is this word 'limited' which is crucial in terms of a general justification of SRI for most investment funds. The point is that it describes limited liability. In effect, such a company is a legal entity of its own; while shareholders control it, they are not liable for damages for the company's actions. Here is surely what economists call an agency problem, in that the asymmetric nature of the risk to shareholders in such companies may encourage antisocial behaviour. This can perhaps be most clearly seen in the case of the environment, where a profit-maximising company has every incentive to externalise as many costs as possible onto society if this adds to its own profitability. This agency problem was of course identified in 1776 by Adam Smith in his landmark book *The Wealth of Nations*.[27]

Those looking for a greater theoretical justification of SRI may find it in the concept of stakeholding. Applied to investment, stakeholding theory states that investors have responsibilities as owners of a company's shares, as well as the rights to the benefits of its success. In 1997 Steve Lydenberg, one of the leading US thinkers on SRI, together with the academic Karen Paul attempted to integrate stakeholder theory with socially responsible investment.[28] They used a classic model: 'it is based on the premise that firms have both explicit and implicit contracts with those constituents which make the corporations responsible for honouring the resulting contracts, explicit and implicit'. Lydenberg and Paul went on to use the example of financial theory, which states that the return shareholders receive from a quoted equity should be proportional to the risk involved. They argued that employees, suppliers and local communities also share risks in the success or failure of a business, so they too should be compensated for the risk. The authors then use this idea to generate a new definition of a well-managed company:

> If all stakeholders are being similarly treated, with employees getting lower compensation, investors getting lower returns, communities getting lower contributions etc., then we might say that this is fair. When one stakeholder benefits disproportionately, receiving disproportionately more rewards, and others receive disproportionately fewer rewards over time, we say we observe a lack of corporate social responsibility, poor social performance, and poor management.... Socially responsible

investors aim to create and support a business environment where managers are mindful of the risks their operations impose on society, to avoid incalculable risks, and in the case of calculable risks to be as equitable as possible in minimising societal costs, along with compensating fairly for their imposition.[29]

In my opinion the Lydenberg and Paul stakeholding thesis offers an original and interesting idea that justifies the theoretical application of SRI to all financial institutions. There is certainly an argument that corporate limited liability has had a negative impact on corporate social responsibility, and it seems only logical to put the genie back into the bottle by requiring investors to consider and assert the values of corporate responsibility. In fact, I would also argue that corporate social responsibility (CSR) and socially responsible investing are in essence mirror images of each other. Each concept basically asserts that business should generate wealth for society but within certain social and environmental frameworks. CSR looks at this from the view point of companies, SRI from the viewpoint of investors in those companies.

In essence SRI has three main mechanisms to assert corporate social responsibility: avoidance (exclusion), engagement (dialogue), and shareholder activism (coercion). These have already been discussed in some depth, but there is one more that should be briefly mentioned − public disinvestment. Church and charity investors can use their unique moral authority to publicly announce the sale of a holding in a company on ethical grounds. For example, in 1995 the UK Methodist Church generated worldwide publicity when it announced the CKB was selling shares in BSkyB because BSkyB had links with the Playboy Channel.

REFERENCES

1. Russell Sparkes, *The Ethical Investor*, Harper Collins 1995.
2. Professor Chris Cowton, 'The Development of Ethical Investment Products', published in *ACT Guide to Ethical Conflicts in Finance*, Blackwell 1994.
3. Russell Sparkes, 'Through a Glass Darkly: Some Thoughts on the Ethics of Investment', the Beckley Lecture 1998; published in the *Epworth Review*, Vol. 25, No. 3, July 1998.
4. Stephen Timms MP, speech to PIRC Conference, 21 April 1999.
5. Cowton, *op. cit.*

6. Digby Anderson, editor, *What Has 'Ethical Investment' to Do With Ethics?* Social Affairs Unit, London 1996.
7. Tessa Tennant, 'The Ethical Issue', *Planned Savings*, February 1991.
8. Cowton, *op. cit.*
9. *2001 Report on Socially Responsible Investing Trends in the United States*, Social Investment Forum, 28 November 2001.
10. Russell Sparkes, 'Ethical Investment: Whose Ethics, Which Investment', *Business Ethics: A European Review*, July 2001.
11. Anita Green, quoted in 'Socially Responsible Mutual Fund Assets Rose 5 Times Faster Than All Other Funds in Last 30 Years', press release issued on behalf of Pax World Management, 8 August 2001.
12. *Ibid.*
13. ICCR Annual Report 2000–2001, *The Corporate Examiner*, 9 October 2001.
14. Tim Smith and Edgar Crane, 'The Impact on Corporations of Shareholder Actions', Chapter 17 of *The Social Investment Almanac*, Henry Holt, 1992.
15. David M. Walker, Assistant Secretary of Labor, address to the Pension Research Council, 12 May 1988.
16. Tim Smith, 'Shareholder Activism', Chapter 7 of *The Social Investment Almanac*, Henry Holt, 1992.
17. ICCR Annual Report 2000–2001, *The Corporate Examiner*, 9 October 2001.
18. *Ibid.*
19. Craig Mackenzie, 'Shareholder Action', published in *The Christian Democrat*, No. 39, 1997.
20. Author's notes from discussions with ICCR staff.
21. Nicholas Hildyard and Mark Mansley, *The Campaigners' Guide to Financial Markets*, Corner House, 2002.
22. Author's notes from speech by Simon McRae of Friends of the Earth, 'Shareholder Resolutions: An NGO Perspective', London, February 2002.
23. Kate Geary, Ilisu Dam Campaign, and Hannah Griffiths, Friends of the Earth, quoted in Nicholas Hildyard and Mark Mansley, *The Campaigners' Guide to Financial Markets*, Corner House, 2002.
24. *Ibid.*
25. 'UBS Becomes Latest Company to Pull Out of Turkish Dam', Bloomberg Newswire, 27 February 2002.
26. Russell Sparkes, 'Through a Glass Darkly: Some Thoughts on the Ethics of Investment', the Beckley Lecture 1998; published in the *Epworth Review*, Vol. 25, No. 3, July 1998.
27. Adam Smith, *The Wealth of Nations*, Book V, *The Expenses of the Sovereign*, original edition 1776, Everyman edition 1977.
28. S. Lydenberg and K. Paul, 'Stakeholder Theory and Socially Responsible Investing: Toward a Convergence of Theory and Practice'; unpublished manuscript, 1997; available from Kinder Lydenberg Domini Inc., 129 Mt Auburn Ave, Cambridge, Mass 02136 USA.
29. *Ibid.*

3

From the Beginning

Chapter 1 described the broad range of factors that persuaded the UK government to issue socially responsible pension fund regulations, observing that these political pressures were global in extent. Chapter 2 provided a detailed analysis of the different types of activity that make up socially responsible investment. This chapter examines the main historical events that lie behind the growth of SRI, as a chronological account can sometimes illuminate the key elements of a complex process better than the kind of structural analysis given in Chapter 2. The historical record also sheds some interesting light on the growth of socially responsible investing. While conventional wisdom has it that SRI began in the early 1970s over the issue of South Africa, in practice things were more complicated than that.

Many accounts of SRI give the impression that it just 'growed like Topsy', but it didn't. One important factor behind this rising trend was ethical consumerism, a growing trend for people to want their values reflected in their purchases and their investment holdings. However, an examination of the history of SRI shows that the major drivers behind its growth over the last thirty years were in fact geopolitical issues: the Vietnam War, South Africa, environmental concern, human rights and outsourcing issues, and worries over globalisation. Each of these issues led to a significant increase in the number and amount of investment funds taking social, environmental and ethical issues into account.

A PRECURSOR

Socially responsible investing is essentially a modern phenomenon. Many of the original pioneers are still alive and still active. However, men and women have struggled with issues of ethics and economics long before the age of ethical investment in its modern form. I will therefore briefly describe one of these, a precursor who anticipated much of what was to come later.

John Wesley (1703–91) was not only a great preacher who brought Christianity back to the working people of England. He was also a social reformer who campaigned against the squalid life of the poor at that time, and was one of the first public figures of his day to speak out against the slave trade. In 1760 his sermon 'The Use of Money' was published, based on the parable of the unjust steward (Luke 16: 1–13). In it Wesley stressed the importance of the right use of money, and poured scorn on those who want to have nothing to do with it. The point is 'to employ it to the greatest advantage', and the role of the Christian is to act 'not as a proprietor, but as a steward'. He went on to say that we should gain all we can but

> not at the expense of life nor at the expense of our health, nor without hurting our mind. Therefore we may not engage or continue in any sinful trade; any that is contrary to the law of God, or of our country... without hurting our neighbour in his substance, nor by hurting our neighbour in his body... nor by hurting our neighbour in his soul.[1]

Wesley's point was that making money in ways which injure our neighbour cannot be right. Hence he ruled out obtaining his property through gambling or pawnbroking or excessive interest rates, while he also condemned profits made through the supply of products which damage health, such as strong liquor. Finally, he vetoed profit made through encouraging moral corruption, such as drunkenness or sexual licence. Avoidance of investment in alcohol is a standard feature of most socially responsible unit trusts, but few of them explain why alcohol should be forbidden. Wesley set out his reasons:

We may not gain by hurting our neighbour in his body. Therefore we may not sell anything which tends to impair health. Such is, eminently, all that liquid fire, commonly called drams, or spirituous liquors.... We may not gain by hurting our neighbour in his soul, by ministering, either directly or indirectly, to his chastity or intemperance... it concerns all those who have anything to do with taverns.[2]

Wesley castigated profiting from spirits, but he was not a 'killjoy' and did not prohibit wine. He cautioned against profits made from 'taverns', which from the context seem to be defined as places whose main function is to encourage drunkenness, arguing that heavy drinking leads to the loss of self-control and to further ills like violence. Wesley was also strongly aware of social justice issues, i.e. that the tavernkeepers were exploiting the weakness of the poor to make themselves richer, and putting the poor further into penury. Elsewhere in the same sermon Wesley condemned those, such as pawnbrokers, who exploited others to gain their money. Wesley's thinking seems highly sophisticated for its time. A secular generation may take from it the underlying idea that human life is short, and that each generation is only the steward for the generations to come.

It was striking that in his 1999 speech setting out the proposed new SRI regulations, the Pensions Minister Stephen Timms used this Wesley sermon as the basis of his speech, and particularly its emphasis on stewardship:

In Wesley's words, penned some 250 years ago, we are told we are 'placed here (on earth) not as proprietors, but as stewards... we are entrusted for a season with goods of various kinds; but the sole property of them does not rest with us'. Central to his message is the idea of stewardship: that everything we gain or are given is only conditionally ours. We are not the absolute owners of our wealth; rather we are custodians or stewards. This is a way of thinking that has become more familiar to us in recent years: we recognise that our children and grandchildren will have to deal with the environmental problems we leave them, and we have already begun to address the damage we have done. So perhaps Wesley's words have a resonance for us that they did not have for the people of his own time.[3]

AMERICAN BEGINNINGS

In 1919 America carried out a great experiment in social engineering. This was the Volstead Act, the 28th Amendment to the US Constitution, generally known as Prohibition. This prohibited the production or sale of alcohol throughout the US for the next fifteen years. Led by President Woodrow Wilson, the old Puritan ideals of the original American colonists were very strong in the US at that time. Not just over alcohol. For example, gambling was also banned throughout most of the US. In 1928 temperance groups led to the introduction of the world's first socially responsible mutual fund, the Pioneer Fund, which banned investment in alcohol or tobacco. However, this fund made relatively little impression and remained fairly small.

In the UK, SRI has normally been identified with ethical unit trusts based on an avoidance approach, in essence an example of ethical consumerism. In the US, on the other hand, shareholder activism by pension funds and charitable foundations has always been a major factor. There is a simple explanation for this, as religious and charitable endowments are much bigger in the US than in the UK. This is particularly true for university endowments, where as British universities are essentially funded by central government, whereas Harvard University's endowment fund alone is currently worth around $65 billion.

Modern socially responsible investment arose in the US in the late 1960s driven principally by shareholder activism on several fronts: the civil rights campaign of the time; opposition to college endowment funds profiting from the controversial Vietnam War; and Ralph Nader's consumer rights activism. A few years later the desire to put pressure on the apartheid regime in South Africa became a powerful force. One of the very first examples of shareholder advocacy took place in 1967, when the campaigning group FIGHT bought some shares in Eastman Kodak in order to attend and ask awkward questions at that company's AGM. FIGHT had been in negotiation with Eastman Kodak since 1965 following race riots in Rochester, New York. The city of Rochester was where the company's head office was based, and FIGHT argued that the company should provide better living conditions and job opportunities for black employees. Following FIGHT's attendance at Eastman Kodak's 1967 AGM, the company agreed to work with the advocacy group to address its grievances.

The Vietnam War (1965–74) probably polarised US society more than any issue since the Civil War. The period saw violent demonstrations on many US campuses about the war, and the refusal of many students to obey the draft obliging them to fight in it. It was only a natural development for American universities and religious bodies to question whether they should (a) own shares in companies supplying war materials, and (b) whether they should use their power as shareholders to force change. These questions culminated in a major conference at Yale in 1970 where the first sustained debate about SRI took place.

In the meantime the first socially responsible shareholder resolution was submitted to Dow Chemical's AGM in 1969, questioning the morality of the production by the company of the war materials napalm and Agent Orange. Agent Orange was an extremely powerful defoliant, so named because it was stored in orange drums. University foundations discussed whether they should sell their shareholdings in Dow on ethical grounds. An estimated 50 million litres of the chemical were sprayed on the forests of Vietnam and Cambodia from 1963 to 1971 with the aim of destroying the jungle cover of Vietcong guerrillas. From 1969 onwards it was suspected of causing birth defects in laboratory animals, with its US production suspended in 1971. Agent Orange has subsequently been alleged to be linked to a number of diseases in the children of US veterans of the conflict, such as spina bifida and the normally rare acute myeloid leukaemia. In 1979 US veterans brought a class action against the manufacturers of Agent Orange such as Dow Chemical and other manufacturers and the case was settled out of court for $180 million in 1987. In 1991 the US Congress passed the Agent Orange Act, requiring two-year health checks for Vietnam veterans and their children. (In 2000 President Clinton visited Vietnam and was shown terribly deformed children whose disabilities were attributed to the effects of Agent Orange.)

Concerns about the Vietnam War also led to the establishment of the first 'modern' SRI mutual fund on 8 August 1971, the Pax World Fund. It started with $101 000 in total assets. It was created by two New Hampshire Methodist ministers, Luther Tyson and Jack Corbett, with the assistance of two local businessmen. Thirty years later Pax celebrated its thirtieth birthday with assets under management having grown to over $1 billion. Anita Green, the company's director of research commented:

> Tyson and Corbett had two goals. First, they wanted to make it possible for people to invest in keeping with their values. Their second goal was to create a vehicle to challenge corporations to establish and live up to specific standards of social and environmental responsibility. They thought they could best influence corporations from the inside, as shareholders. That line of thought led directly to what we know today as socially responsible mutual funds.[4]

The idea of setting up Pax came to Tyson and Corbett when they discovered there was no existing mutual fund available to them that would avoid investment in companies believed to be profiting from the Vietnam War. The new fund excluded traditional Nonconformist 'sin stocks' such as tobacco and gambling. However, as its name suggests (*pax* is Latin for peace), the key idea behind Pax was the promotion of peace and the avoidance of profiteering from war. This is explicitly spelled out in the fund's investment objectives:

> To make a contribution to world peace through investment in companies producing life-supportive goods and services. It does not invest in arms, but seeks out nonwar-related industries, firms with fair employment practices, companies exercising pollution control, and some international development.[5]

Another powerful motive force behind the growth of SRI was consumer activism, a reflection of growing public suspicion that big business was ignoring consumers' interests in order to maximise profits. This burst into public awareness in 1966 with the publication of Ralph Nader's book *Unsafe at any Speed*, which highlighted the poor safety record of US automobiles. It is hardly surprising that another of the first social proxy resolutions was filed at General Motors' 1970 annual general meeting. Campaign GM, a Nader organisation, drafted nine resolutions dealing with the needs of minorities, workers and consumers, although the Securities and Exchange Commission (SEC) only allowed two of them to be submitted to shareholders.

General Motors was deliberately targeted as at that time it was the largest US company in terms of market capitalisation.

The late 1960s and early 1970s also saw the foundation of a number of organisations dedicated to social research and the assertion of corporate social responsibility. The Council for Economic Priorities (CEP) was founded in 1969 to carry out in-depth analysis of corporate America from a social viewpoint, the first organisation ever set up to analyse companies on social and environmental issues. In 1971 the US churches formed a number of shareholder activism groups, these eventually merging to form the Interfaith Center on Corporate Responsibility (ICCR) in 1973. The Investor Responsibility Research Center (IRRC) was also founded in 1971. The creation of the Pax fund was followed in 1972 by the launch of the Third Century Fund by the Dreyfus Group, one of the largest mutual fund managers in America. The fund focused on two areas: environmental protection and improvement, and social factors like health and safety at work, and equal opportunities in employment. It employed a complex company evaluation system ranking these factors. The retail market for SRI mutual funds in the US grew slowly during the 1970s. Less visible but more important in terms of size was the management of private client and charity endowment funds by specialist teams within large investment banks. Individuals prominent in this area included Robert Schwartz and Joan Bavaria. Joan Bavaria went on to found Boston-based Franklin Research, the first asset management company specialising in social investing.

In the early 1970s plans were devised to launch an SRI retail fund in the UK, although ethical investment had been carried out by the UK church investment bodies since at least 1948. There were three significant church investors: the Church Commissioners and CCLA Investment Management for the Church of England, and the Central Finance Board of the Methodist Church (CFB). In 1973 Charles Jacob, the CFB investment manager, attempted to establish a UK ethical unit trust on similar lines to Pax in the US. He prepared

> proposals for the formation of a trust to create an increased awareness of the responsibility of ownership....To provide a suitable avenue through which those members of the public

already conscious of their social responsibility are enabled to invest in equity without disturbing conscience.[6]

Despite support from a large number of churches and charities, it was rejected by the Department of Trade in November 1973:

> To our utter surprise and dismay it was turned down! It appeared that we were ahead of our time – the Inspectors were apparently concerned with a conflict of capital and conscience, and were not prepared to sanction the new concept.... There was no mention of an ethical unit trust in this country for the next five years.[7]

In 1984 Charles Jacob finally received regulatory approval for the establishment of an 'ethical unit trust'. This was carried out by the insurance company Friends Provident, using Jacob's name of Stewardship. There was considerable scepticism about the new venture, but in fact it proved highly popular with investors, and the next few years saw the launch of some similar funds such as the Credit Suisse Fellowship trust and Abbey Ethical. However, the next major spur to SRI was another geopolitical phenomenon: South Africa.

SOUTH AFRICA: A DEFINING ISSUE

If Vietnam unlocked the door to socially responsible investment, South Africa kicked it open. After 1970 many US civil rights activists felt they had achieved the bulk of their domestic US objectives. It was natural for them to turn their attention to South Africa, the country where civil rights seemed to be most grievously breached. As the decade progressed, South Africa was progressively isolated in sporting terms; eventually it felt obliged to withdraw from the United Nations before it was forcibly ejected. It also became one of the major issues driving US shareholder activism over the period. In 1977 the Reverend Leon Sullivan, a veteran civil rights activist and close associate of Martin Luther King, issued minimum standards for US companies operating in South Africa:

1. Non-segregation of all races in eating, comfort, locker room and work

2. Equal and fair employment practices for all employees
3. Equal pay for equal work
4. Training programmes for blacks and coloureds to prepare them for supervisory jobs
5. Steadily increase number of blacks in supervisory positions
6. Help employees outside work in such areas as housing, transportation, schooling, recreation, and health

In 1982 Connecticut became the first US legislature to establish social performance criteria for state investments. This required all companies in which it invested to follow the Sullivan Principles. Trust funds run by the University of Wisconsin went further; following a period of consistent campus unrest and a legal opinion from the Wisconsin State Attorney-General, university funds sold all their holdings of US companies which did not pass the Sullivan test. Repression proceeded to deepen in South Africa, particularly following the state of emergency in 1985. This led to an intensification of efforts by US anti-apartheid groups who campaigned for local government and labour pension funds to exclude all direct investment in the country, and to sell the shares of all US companies that operated there.

In 1983 the state of Massachusetts passed a measure prohibiting the investment of state funds in companies or banks doing business in South Africa. In 1984 the two biggest pension funds in America, those of New York City and the State of California, issued social investment guidelines concerning South Africa. The New York pension funds had over $15 billion in total assets, while the combined value of California's state pension funds was over $50 billion. Given the massive size of their investment assets, this action compelled the mainstream US financial system to take note of socially responsible investment. While the New York State legislature did not order its pension funds to sell their South African shareholdings, which would have been of dubious legality under the 'prudent man' rule, it could and did require its trustees to be aware of such issues:

Critical elements include our right to vote proxies in ways that will help shape the broad social environment, our sponsorship and support of shareholder proposals and, ultimately, our decision to selectively divest both equities and fixed income securities supporting the regime in South Africa....US corporations doing business abroad are virtual extensions of the US itself and should embody its laws and ethical standards. It is quite proper to ask them this: if they abide by anti-discrimination and equal opportunity laws in the US, should they not then be required to resist the immorality of apartheid in South Africa?[8]

In 1986 the Californian state legislature passed a legislative amendment requiring the state's pension funds to divest over $6 billion from companies which had activities in South Africa. The importance of South Africa as the next big issue driving forward the growth of socially responsible investment in the US can be seen from Figure 3.1. The total amount of US funds using SRI screens, mostly based in South Africa, surged following the declaration of a state of emergency in South Africa on 20 June 1985. In fact, they grew tenfold over the period, with screened assets rising from $40 billion to over $400 billion.

Historically, South African banking was dominated by British and American banks. Financial boycotts pressurised each group to leave. In 1984 Citicorp was threatened with the loss of the $20 billion in deposits the bank held on behalf of the New York City pension fund if it did not cease making new loans to South Africa. Not surprisingly, in February 1985 Citicorp agreed to do so. In summer 1987 Citicorp also sold its stake in its South African subsidiary to First National Bank of South Africa. This represented a concession to the continuous pressure from US investors for the bank to withdraw completely, but it also reflected the fact that its customers were disappearing. In July 1985, following the state of emergency, the second largest US lender, Chase Manhattan, followed Citicorp's example and stated

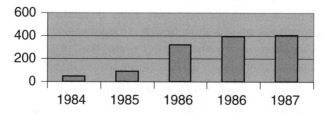

Figure 3.1 *US SRI assets ($bn) 1984–87*

that not only would it not make new loans, but it would not renew old ones when they expired.

Similar pressure was put on the UK banks that were at the heart of the South African financial system, Barclays in particular. A 'shadow board' was set up that helped to coordinate one of the biggest consumer boycotts ever held in Britain. Trades unions, charities and a number of educational establishments, including several Oxford colleges, as well as a significant number of individuals, all withdrew their money from Barclays. Possibly the most significant in terms of size was the actions of local authorities; for example, Rochdale Council took all its £200 million deposit business away from Barclays in 1985. In August 1985 Barclays submitted to pressure when it announced that it would not be taking up its rights in a share issue by Barclays National in South Africa. This changed the status of Barclays South Africa from a subsidiary to an associated company in which Barclays merely owned 40%.

UK shareholder activism regarding South Africa was centred on the UK churches, and led to the famous Bishop of Oxford court case in 1990. The Central Finance Board of the Methodist Church had informal discussions on ethics of investment for many years, but acrimonious debate within the Methodist Church over the issue of South Africa led to a decision to formally establish an Ethics of Investment Committee in 1983 'to advise the Central Finance Board of ethical considerations relating to finance'. This was one of the first ethical advisory committees ever created, and it began with a mandate to produce an annual 'ethics report' on its activities. The giant Anglo-Dutch oil company Royal Dutch/Shell was believed to be a significant supplier of oil to South Africa, and was therefore the subject of a share action campaign like the one against Barclays. This campaign obtained the official support of the Methodist Conference and involved substantial shareholder support for motions opposing oil being supplied to South Africa at both the Shell and Royal Dutch AGMs for many years. Eventually the CFB sold its shareholdings in Shell and Barclays.

Demands within the churches for more information on corporate involvement in South Africa also led to establishment of the Ethical Investment Research Service (EIRIS) in 1983. The main initial supporters were the Society of Friends (Quakers), Quaker charitable trusts, and the Methodist Church. The aim was to produce the information required to apply ethical criteria to investment, to identify alternative investments for ethical investors, and to promote a wider debate on issues of corporate responsibility. Its director, Peter Webster, later wrote:

> When EIRIS was launched in 1983 I think we were clearer about the research that people needed than we were about who might buy it. We hoped that there would be enough demand to replace our grant funding, and the hope was fully justified.[9]

South Africa became effectively cut off from the global debt markets. Big US investors such as the state of Californian pension fund cautioned the world's largest investment banks who dominate this market – Goldman Sachs, Morgan Stanley, Merrill Lynch, etc. – not to deal with South Africa, or risk losing all their highly profitable US business. It was obviously in their interest to comply. In August 1985 South Africa simply ran out of money, and was forced to declare a default on its loans. This was surprising as South Africa's debt service ratio was only 9% in 1985, a level which would have been easily sustainable in normal circumstances. This showed the effectiveness of the financial boycotts.

The value of the currency collapsed despite the introduction of a system of stringent foreign exchange controls, with the value of the

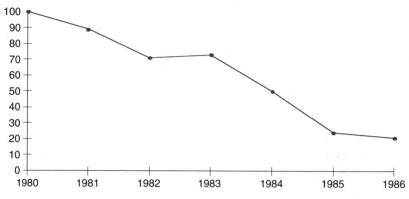

Figure 3.2 *Value of the financial rand (US cents) 1980–86*

financial rand falling from $1.00 in 1980 to $0.21 by the end of 1986 (Figure 3.2). The financial squeeze reached breaking point in the summer of 1990, when the bulk ($13 billion) of South Africa's foreign debt was due to be repaid. By the beginning of 1990 the foreign exchange reserves of South African Reserve Bank were virtually exhausted.

The death throes of apartheid began in February 1990, when Nelson Mandela was released from 28 years of captivity and the state of emergency was lifted. Clearly a number of factors combined to bring about the end of apartheid in South Africa, but financial boycotts coordinated by socially responsible investors played a significant part in this. According to the ANC, 'Financial sanctions have been a critical pressure point which has pushed the process of political transformation to where it is today'. Or in the words of the Commonwealth Heads of Government summit in Harare, October 1991: 'Financial sanctions were the most demonstrably effective of all sanctions'. According to Robert Schwartz, one of the original pioneers of SRI in the US:

> What SRI did in regard to South Africa should be considered a major victory.... Corporate executives have a strong interest in the price of their company's stock options and were influenced in leaving South Africa because of the pressures by public employee and university funds. I know. They told me so.[10]

In October 1993 the Division of Social Responsibility together with the Overseas Division of the Methodist Church issued a joint statement on South Africa together with its ethics committee. The statement was called 'Responsible Investment – the Fruit of Anti-Apartheid Action' and declared:

> The creation of the Transitional Executive Council (TEC) structures and the setting of 27th April 1994 as the date for elections, are clear marks of the long awaited victory for the democratic process. These political advances have been won by a courageous and tenacious struggle of those within and without South Africa who have kept faith in the vision of a fully participatory, non-racial state. No other issue in our time has involved such a broad global consensus of people and organisations, and the

effect of their combined concerted action against apartheid has been immense.... The ethical responsibility of investors and investment policies is now an accepted principle in the commercial world, largely pioneered by anti-apartheid action.[11]

GROWING ENVIRONMENTAL CONCERNS

Opposition to the apartheid regime in South Africa united people around the world in asserting that their savings should reflect their social values. While concern over South Africa faded from 1993, another geopolitical issue took its place that had the same galvanising effect in persuading public opinion to back socially responsible investment. This was, of course, global concern over the environment. The environment is such a major issue for SRI in the modern period that I have devoted two chapters of this book to it. In this section I just want to provide some historical background describing its development.

It is hard to date the exact beginnings of the modern environmental movement. Many people would attribute it to the 1961 publication (1962 in the UK) of Rachel Carson's book *Silent Spring*, a thorough-going analysis of the dangers of modern industrial chemicals to the natural world, particularly pesticides such as DDT. Another milestone was probably the Club of Rome's 1972 book *The Limits to Growth*, which argued that the rapid economic growth experienced during the 1950s and 1960s could not continue at the same pace. The report argued forcibly that such growth was based on the exploitation of natural resources at a rate that would quickly lead to their exhaustion and that it ignored the soaring costs of pollution.

Environmental concerns grew throughout the 1970s following a series of major environmental accidents such as the Seveso dioxin leak in Italy, and public disquiet over the Love Canal situation in the US. In the 1930s and 1940s Love Canal in upstate New York, near Niagara Falls, was used as a disposal site for chemical waste stored in steel drums. The site was later covered over, and housing and a school built on top. In the 1970s the chemicals started to leak. Analysis showed the presence of over 80 toxic chemicals, including 10 carcinogens, and a high incidence of birth defects, liver failure, and various cancers. In 1978 President Carter declared the area a federal emergency, and the population was evacuated. Love Canal was believed to be just one example among many of a community poisoned by America's industrial legacy. The political response was to pass the Federal Comprehensive Environmental Response, Compensation and Liability Act, generally known as Superfund, in 1980. The name derived from the creation of the Hazardous Substance Response Trust Fund, or Superfund, to pay for the clean-up. The Environmental Protection Agency (EPA) was charged to create a National Priorities List (NPL) of the most hazardous sites; potentially responsible parties (PRPs) either had to pay for clean-ups themselves or reimburse the Superfund for having done so.

In 1979 there was a potentially serious accident at the Three Mile Island nuclear power facility that effectively ended the construction of new commercial nuclear power plants in the US. Twenty-two years later the George W. Bush administration stated it was considering restarting the nuclear building programme in America. Public environmental concerns grew during the 1980s as a result of a number of major environmental disasters. These included the deaths of 3500 people in 1984 following a toxic gas leak at Bhopal in India which also injured 50 000 people. The plant that exploded at Bhopal was a subsidiary of a major US chemical company. Rising public unease over toxic chemicals within the US itself led to Congress passing the Emergency Planning and Right to Know Act, which mandated the establishment of a national database on toxic chemical production. In 1988 American wildlife groups launched a campaign that aimed to persuade the US tuna industry to adopt wider nets and other fishing techniques to stop dolphins being caught along with tuna. As part of this campaign the leading US tuna brand 'Starkist' was targeted for a consumer boycott. Starkist's parent company, Heinz Foods, received shareholder resolutions urging the adoption of dolphin-friendly fishing techniques, and in 1990 it agreed to do so.

Public opinion in Europe was also increasingly worried about the environment in the 1970s, particularly about *Waldsterben* or forest death. These concerns escalated in 1986 following two major disasters. The first was severe pollution of the Rhine near Basel in Switzerland when a chemical plant leaked pesticides and mercury into the river, killing all the fish in the vicinity. The same year saw the explosion of the Chernobyl nuclear power plant in the Soviet Union, spreading radioactive material across Europe. There was of course a global political response to such growing public concern, which led to the United Nations establishing of a World Commission on Environment and Development in 1983. The committee, led by Gro Harlem Brundtland, went further than examining specific environmental disasters; it adopted a holistic approach looking at the Earth as one ecological unit. The committee's report, *Our Common Future* (the Brundtland Report), was notable for its definition of sustainable development:

> Humanity has the ability to make development sustainable — to ensure that it meets the needs of the present without compromising the ability of future generations to meet their own needs.[12]

The most high-profile environmental disaster in America was probably the *Exxon Valdez*. On 23 March 1989 the oil supertanker *Exxon Valdez* ran aground on Bligh Reef off Alaska's Prince William Sound. Eleven million gallons of North Slope crude oil were spilled in the worst environmental disaster in American history. Thirteen hundred miles of pristine coastline were fouled, and long-term damage was inflicted on 23 species of local wildlife, only two of which have since recovered. Most of the oil was converted by wind into an emulsion called mousse that will not burn and is very difficult to remove from the sea surface or the shoreline. In 1990 Exxon made a $900 million civil settlement with the local government to compensate local fishermen. In June 1994 a US federal court in Anchorage, Alaska, found the company guilty of recklessness over the oil spill caused by the *Exxon Valdez* tanker disaster. The recklessness verdict opened the way for the jury to assess punitive damages of $5 billion, in addition to the $3.5 billion damages Exxon had already paid, $1.1 billion in federal and state charges, and more than $2 billion to clean up the contaminated coastline. The day the verdict was announced, the price of Exxon shares fell sharply on Wall Street, knocking $5 billion off the company's stock market value.

In late 1988 the Social Investment Forum, the umbrella body for US socially responsible investment, met with various environmental groups to form the Coalition for Environmentally Responsible

Economies (CERES). CERES then launched a set of ten principles to guide industrial companies to better environmental performance (see page 149). There seems little doubt that public alarm at the *Exxon Valdez* incident led to the CERES principles receiving faster recognition than might otherwise have been the case. The head of New York City pension fund, the second largest pension fund in the US, acted quickly:

> We felt that when corporations treat the environment badly, they treat their investors badly by exposing their investments to enormous liability and negative publicity. We are such large investors that we cannot quickly sell holdings in problem companies, therefore it makes sense to exercise the power of ownership when faced with environmental negligence, and press for changes. Our primary job is to protect the assets of our beneficiaries, that's our fiduciary responsibility. But that responsibility includes protecting our portfolio investments from being damaged by corporate environmental carelessness.
>
> We owned six million shares in Exxon, and after the Exxon Valdez disaster I organised a meeting with ourselves and other big pension funds and the Exxon management to express our concerns. We then went further in recommending that companies should adopt the CERES Principles, and when Exxon declined to publish an environmental report, we filed a proxy resolution instructing them to adopt the CERES principles. Note that we only file such resolutions as a last resort, and subject to four criteria:
>
> 1. the company must be associated with a severe environmental accident like the Valdez spill.
> 2. the company must be the subject of legal action for environmental injury, and therefore liable to pay fines.
> 3. the environmental damage must involve a specific community.
> 4. an assessment of whether the company's financial performance is poor.

To sum up, as long-term investors pension funds should practice responsible investment — avoiding environmental risk is part of their fiduciary duty. As shareholders they are responsible for examining their investment portfolios, and responsible investment is informed and intelligent investment.[13]

Public awareness of the environment as a critical issue received a major boost on both sides of the Atlantic following the 1992 Earth Summit in Rio. In 1990 the Green Party won 15% of the vote in the UK European elections, causing the Conservative government of Margaret Thatcher to adopt a much higher environmental profile. In 1993 Greenpeace Business worked with SRI fund managers to prevent the London flotation of Barito Pacific, an Indonesian timber company alleged to be responsible for significant deforestation. Rising public interest in the environment can perhaps be best illustrated by a table of membership of some UK environmental organisations in the 1970s and 1980s. This was a period when church attendance fell steadily, when membership of political parties dropped away and even community groups like the Scouts saw declines in membership. However, membership of environmental organisations grew steadily (Table 3.1).

The conjunction of factors such as the Brundtland Report, Chernobyl, the *Exxon Valdez* disaster, and the Earth Summit led to rapid growth in the number of specialist environmental funds in the US and the UK at a rate never seen before or since. Table 3.2 illustrates this using UK data.

Table 3.1 *Growth in environmentalism:*
membership numbers (000s) 1971−93

	1971	1981	1993
National Trust	278	1046	2189
RSPB	98	441	850
Greenpeace	0	30	410
Friends of the Earth	1	20	150
Worldwide Fund for Nature	12	60	207

Source: Social Trends 1995.

Table 3.2 *UK environmental fund launches 1988–92*

Year	Fund
1988	Merlin Jupiter Ecology Trust, first 'green fund'
1989	Merlin International Green, first SRI investment trust
1989	Henderson Green PEP
1989	Homeowners Green Chip Trust
1989	Eagle Star Environmental Trust
1989	TSB Environmental Investor Trust
1990	CIS Environ Trust
1990	Clerical Medical Evergreen Trust
1991	NPI Global Care Trust, strongly green
1992	Commercial Union Environmental Investment Trust

Source: Russell Sparkes, *The Ethical Investor*, Harper Collins, 1995.

ETHICAL CONSUMERISM

The most recent major theme to emerge that has helped drive the sales growth of SRI unit trusts and mutual funds is ethical consumerism. The 1980s saw a boom in the sales of products perceived to help the environment, such as recycled paper or enzyme-free detergents. This was followed in the 1990s by rapid growth in the sale of foodstuffs which appeal to the customer's sense of justice as much as their tastebuds, i.e. ethical consumerism. In October 1993 a poll by NOP found that 68% of the thousand adults polled would be willing to pay more for products that guaranteed a fair return to farmers and workers in the Third World; in fact, the average consumer was prepared to pay a 25% price premium to achieve this. A similar RSPCA poll found that 30% of the population were sufficiently concerned about animal rights that they were prepared to pay up to 50% more for meat from animals which had been well treated.

The most visible sign of this trend has been the growth of fairly traded products. The Fairtrade Foundation was launched in the UK in March 1994 by a group of mostly development charities; it awards a consumer label to fairly traded goods. Cafedirect has been the most successful Fairtrade brand, achieving the significant market share level of 5.8% of UK ground coffee sales. Cafedirect buys coffee beans from countries including Costa Rica, Mexico and Peru, paying the farmer a price that is significantly above the market rate. Despite this, its retail price is little more than standard ground coffee, and is stocked by the majority of retail chains in the UK. The number of farmers directly supplying Fairtrade products rose from 13 000 in 1992 to 120 000 in 2000. However, the majority of Fairtrade coffee is produced by over 300 producer cooperatives that represent over 500 000 local coffee growers. The cooperatives are able to use their profits to improve schools, clinics and hospitals, in the local area, while they are also able to help the individual growers to fund their cash needs and keep them out of the hands of extortionate money lenders. The essence of the Fairtrade approach lies in its conditions and terms of trading:[14]

- Fairtrade production conditions
  - Based on the local democracy of small-scale farmers
  - Trade unions are encouraged rather than prohibited
  - There is no forced child or adult labour
  - Health and safety standards are supported, as is good environmental practice
- Fairtrade terms of trading
  - A price that covers the cost of production
  - A 'social' premium to invest in social and business development programmes
  - Advance payments to prevent workers falling into debt
  - Longer-term relationships to allow sustainable production

The success of the Fairtrade movement is illustrated by the rapid growth in sales of such products in the UK, which grew by 51% in 2000 and 40% in 2001 (Table 3.3).

The close identity between Fairtrade products and the growing focus on outsourcing within SRI can be seen if Fairtrade's terms of trade and production conditions are compared with the criteria of many SRI funds on this subject (Chapter 8). There is also a close similarity between the average social investor and the standard purchaser of Fairtrade products. The latest survey of such consumers was carried out by MORI for Fairtrade in May 2001. This found that Fairtrade

Table 3.3   *UK retail sales (£m) of Fairtrade products*

	1994	1998	1999	2000	2001
Coffee	undisclosed	13.7	15.0	15.5	18.5
Tea	undisclosed	2.0	4.5	5.1	5.6
Chocolate	undisclosed	1.0	2.3	3.6	4.5
Other	undisclosed	n/a	n/a	7.8	17.3
Total	2.8	16.7	21.8	32.0	45.9

Source: The Fairtrade Foundation.

supporters were mainly over 55 and drawn from social classes A
or B. They were in full-time work and were significantly better educated than average with a first degree or higher. This customer profile
shows a very close correlation with the typical average SRI investor
as described in the next chapter.

FEARS OVER GLOBALISATION

This chapter gave a brief overview of the growth in socially responsible investment and the forces behind it during its first thirty years. I
thought it important to show that there was more to this than South
Africa as is sometimes claimed, particularly in the US.[15] The high
visibility of SRI unit trusts in the UK has led to the impression in
the British media that SRI is little more than an example of ethical
consumerism. Ethical consumerism has certainly been an extremely
important factor in the 1990s, but history indicates that ethical consumerism is just one geopolitical development among many that
have driven the growth of SRI. Table 3.4 summarises how the growth
of SRI has been correlated with geopolitical issues:

I end this chapter with some thoughts over what may become the
driving issue behind the growth of SRI in the new millennium, *corporate social responsibility*. The equation SRI = CSR simply means socially responsible investment and corporate social responsibility are
inextricably connected. CSR and SRI are two sides of the same coin.
Of course there is a risk that both can degenerate into an exercise

Table 3.4 *Geopolitical factors and SRI*

Event	Consequence	Date
Vietnam War	Birth of SRI, Dow Chemical	1969
Consumer activism	GM proxy resolution, safety	1970
South Africa	Surge in US pension fund activism	1980s
Chernobyl/*Exxon Valdez*	Growth in green funds and awareness	1980–
Fairtrade/ethical consumer	Rapid growth in retail SRI funds	1990–
Globalisation concerns	Pension funds: SRI = CSR	2000–

in public relations a green fig leaf often given the derisory title of 'greenwash'. However, neither need do so.

The 1980s and 1990s saw privatisation and deregulation roll back the boundaries of state regulation of the economy in most developed countries, and power on people's lives increasingly devolved to market forces. While few people would deny that the 'anti-globalisation' riots seen in Seattle, Prague and Gothenburg were the work of a 'lunatic fringe', other events demonstrate that there are widespread worries about the growing power of companies. Nobody thought that the protests in autumn 2000 about high fuel prices would spread from France to the rest of Europe including, to everybody's surprise, the UK. Monsieur Bove, a French farmer wrecked a McDonald's restaurant and became a national hero. Lord Melchett, the head of Greenpeace UK, admitted wrecking a field of GM-planted corn in the UK, but was acquitted by the jury who agreed with him.

Growing public concern about corporate behaviour is likely to force politicians in many countries of the world to look for ways to harness such disquiet in peaceful and democratic ways. Political encouragement of pension funds to assert the values of corporate social responsibility by using their rights of share ownership seems an obvious way to do so. For example, the Lisbon EU Head of State Summit in March 2000 stressed the importance of corporate social responsibility as a mechanism to meet the challenges of globalisation. The EU Summit on Corporate Social Responsibility held in Brussels in

November 2000 had a specific section on the role of SRI in promoting CSR. From a political viewpoint, the expected rapid growth of funded pension schemes, coupled with growing public unease about global capitalism, provides a powerful force to assert corporate social responsibility. Such developments are also likely offer significant and rewarding opportunities to those financial institutions that are able to offer attractive SRI products to pension scheme clients.

REFERENCES

1. Revd John Wesley, 'The Use of Money', *47 Sermons*, original edition 1760, Epworth Press edition 1974.
2. *Ibid.*
3. Speech by Stephen Timms MP to the PIRC Corporate Social Responsibility Conference, 21 April 1999.
4. Anita Green, quoted in 'Socially Responsible Mutual Fund Assets Rose 5 Times Faster Than All Other Funds in Last 30 Years', press release on behalf of Pax World Management, 8 August 2001.
5. Pax World Fund, quoted in *Ethical Investing*, Domini/Kinder, Addison-Wesley, 1984.
6. Charles Jacob, 'Proposals Relating to the Formulation of the Stewardship Unit Trust', September 1973.
7. Charles Jacob, 'History of Ethical Investment in the UK', speech at Friends Provident Conference, November 1993.
8. Nicers, quoted in Anne Simpson, *The Greening of Global Investment*, Economist Books, 1991.
9. Peter Webster, quoted in *The Ethical Investor*, August 1993.
10. Robert Schwartz, letter to *The Nation*, 21 June 1993.
11. 'Responsible Investment: the Fruit of Anti-Apartheid Action', joint statement of the Division of Social Responsibility together with the Overseas Division of the Methodist Church, October 1993.
12. *Our Common Future*, World Commission on Environment and Development, Oxford University Press 1987.
13. Author's notes from a speech by Elizabeth Holtzman, treasurer of New York City pension funds, to CEIG conference, Windsor, May 1994.
14. The Fairtrade Foundation.
15. See, for example, Geoffrey Heal, professor of public policy at the University of Columbia, 'The Bottom Line to a Social Conscience', *Financial Times*, 2 July 2001.

4

Profiling the Investors

For many people, negative screening is the 'heart' of SRI, and this is certainly true for the retail funds (unit trusts in the UK, mutual funds in the US) that are the public face of socially responsible investing. It is often taken as read that companies with significant operations in areas such as alcohol, tobacco, defence or gambling should be excluded from any socially responsible portfolio. Few people seem to take the trouble to ask why. Of course, these exclusion criteria reflect the mainly Methodist origins of SRI in both the UK and the US. However, commercial socially responsible unit trusts and mutual funds have now been around for over thirty years. They have come a long way from these modest beginnings.

This chapter therefore examines the issues that most retail funds use as part of their exclusion screens, but from the viewpoint of the underlying investor. Successful SRI funds will aim to meet the 'ethical' requirements of their clients as accurately as possible. In other words, retail SRI fund providers (asset managers) have the task of creating funds that as far as possible match the public's ethical concerns, while not forgetting the need to generate acceptable investment returns. A lot has been written about SRI over recent years, but there is relatively little information available on the following important points:

- What are the key issues for the average SRI investor?
- What type of person are they?
- What performance costs are they prepared to accept?

These questions seem to me to be absolutely key in any evaluation of socially responsible investment. The general silence on the subject reflects the scarcity of information on these topics. I hope that the information presented here will give the reader a representative picture of the 'average investor' in SRI funds, and of the issues that he or she believes to be most important.

IDENTIFYING THE ISSUES

One of the first attempts to analyse the public's social responsibility concerns systematically was carried out in 1992, by Chris Cowton, now a Professor at the Huddersfield Business School. Cowton analysed 125 questionnaires completed in 1989 by clients of the ethical investment research service EIRIS. They were invited to specify the grounds on which they wished to avoid investing by filling in an acceptable list questionnaire (ALQ). In my opinion there were certain conceptual problems with this survey, e.g. that the questionnaire presented respondents with a fixed list of 14 different headings, each beginning with the question 'Do you want to exclude...'. Nevertheless, while accepting these limitations, Cowton considered that they were outweighed by the benefits:

> The ALQs were later retrieved from the EIRIS filing cabinets and summarised by one of the authors (i.e. Cowton). The questionnaires therefore represent primary data and there is every reason to believe that the clients took the privilege of completing them seriously, since they were paid a fee for the privilege of doing so. However, there were concomitant disadvantages in that the questionnaire design was given and it was not possible to collect further information on the clients.[1]

The raw data produced by the survey was later published in Table 4.1. One of the most interesting aspects of Cowton's research was the use of sophisticated statistical techniques to see if there was any underlying pattern to the scores. This 'multi-variance factor analysis' showed that about half of the responses fell into two distinct clusters, which Cowton called 'political' and 'religious'. These two groups each accounted for about 25% of the total survey, so the other half of the survey did not reveal any clear tendency of issues to group together. This clustering effect can be seen most

Table 4.1   *EIRIS clients: main SRI exclusions*

Issue	Frequency	Rank
Advertising (upheld complaints)	50	9
Alcohol (production or sale)	49	10
Animals (meat, fur or leather, animal testing)	57	7=
Armaments	111	2
Gambling	59	6
Newspaper production	6	14
Nuclear power	82	4
Overseas interests (operating in over 10 countries)	24	11=
Overseas operations (over 33% of sales overseas)	24	11
Political donations	54	7=
Size (in top 100 UK companies)	16	13
South Africa (any operations in South Africa)	120	1
Tobacco (production or sale)	87	3
Financial institutions	70	5

Source: The Ethical Investor (EIRIS newsletter), May 1992.

easily if the scores are turned into percentages, and then shown in descending order of importance. Table 4.2 shows the result of this cluster analysis. Cowton's evaluation of the results was as follows:

> The issue that concerns us is the more general attributes of which these choices are particular manifestations. Because the data were elicited under conditions which were both strongly incentive compatible (encouraged revelation of true preferences), and because there was little reason to suppose that any other sources of noise had influenced the data, a principal components analysis was used.[2]

It is easy to see from Table 4.2 that the 'political' and 'religious' groups each had a consistent set of issues that formed a coherent cluster. The traditional 'sin stocks' of alcohol, gambling, and tobacco were highly important to the 'religious' grouping, while these were of little interest to the 'political' group. The reverse

Table 4.2   *Cluster analysis of SRI concerns: all figures are percentages*

	Religious	Political	Total
South Africa	100	85	96
Armaments	84	76	89
Tobacco	94	9	70
Nuclear power	28	58	66
Financial institutions	16	46	56
Gambling	56	12	47
Animals	3	39	46
Political contributions	16	30	46
Advertising	31	0	40
Alcohol	63	3	39
Overseas interests	0	9	26
Size of company	6	9	13
Newspapers	0	3	5

Source: Reprinted from the *Journal of Economic Psychology*, Volume 14, 1993, P. Anand and C. Cowton, 'The Ethical Investor: Exploring Dimensions of Investment Behaviour'. Copyright 1993 with permission from Elsevier Science.

was true of issues like the environment (avoiding nuclear power) and animal testing. However, each of these two groups had strong and overlapping concerns about the issues of South Africa and armaments, which therefore dominated the rankings in the overall survey.

The NM Conscience Fund (later taken over by Friends Provident) was one of the first SRI unit trusts to try to find out the issues of major concern to its underlying investors, which it did at the end of 1993. Questionnaires were sent out to owners of units in its fund asking them to rank positive and negative criteria on a scale of 1 to 5, where 1 meant unimportant and 5 meant very important. The response confirmed the traditional negative bias of ethical investors, as there were six negative factors placed highly compared to only four positive ones (Table 4.3). Brian Wilkinson, NM's head of marketing noted that the range of issues was broadening out beyond

Table 4.3 *Survey of actual SRI investors 1993*

Negative criterion	Score	Positive criterion	Score
Oppressive regimes	4.72	Environmental awareness	4.67
Armaments	4.55	Employee welfare	4.24
Animal exploitation	4.36	Community involvement	3.54
Tobacco	4.05	Charitable donations	2.62
Gambling	3.17		
Alcohol production	2.66		

Source: 'Ethical Views', *Charities Management,* Spring 1994.

traditional 'sin stocks' or 'green issues':

> These results show that ethical investment goes further than just 'green issues'. Environmental awareness is important, but so too is the avoidance of companies which profit from totalitarian governments, the arms trade, or animal exploitation.[3]

NM's research was followed quickly by two surveys carried out in 1994 and 1995 by NOP, one of the UK's leading market research firms, for the Friends Provident Stewardship Trust. The basic methodology used was that of the NOP Omnibus survey, a regular representative sample of all adults in telephone-owning households in the UK. The research was conducted among a sample of 1000 adults structured to be representative of the UK population. Hence it was a survey of general public opinion, rather than a focus group of existing SRI investors or subscribers to an ethical investment research service. This is an important point that deserves to be highlighted. It seems quite likely that there could well be significant differences between the general public's opinion of social and environmental issues of concern, and the concerns of people actively committed to socially responsible investment. That said, the results coming out of the 1995 survey (Table 4.4) were consistent with earlier research, the main change being the public's growing environmental concerns and awareness that became so evident in the 1990s.

Subsequent research has tended to confirm the general conclusions of the above findings. The latest UK study was carried out in

Table 4.4   *1995 survey of key issues*

Negative criterion	Important (%)	Positive criterion	Important (%)
Environmental damage	90	Pollution control	93
		Energy conservation	91
Animal exploitation	89	Employee welfare	90
Oppressive regimes	80	Good stakeholder relations	90
Pornography	75	Products of community	89
Nuclear power	74	benefit	
Armaments	71	Openness about activities	87
Offensive advertising	70	Equal opportunities	85
Alcohol or tobacco	49	Community Involvement	80

Source: NOP Ethical Investment Research Summary 1995.

2000 by Dr Therese Woodward, then a senior lecturer at the University of Bournemouth (now Principal Lecturer in Accounting, Kingston Business School, Kingston University). She stated:

Ethical investors are interested in making a positive impact on society and the environment. They want to make a financial return on their investments and ease their conscience but they are not prepared to sacrifice their ethics for the sake of a profit....This report goes some way to redress the paucity of information about ethical investors by providing a description of these individuals concentrating on the non-financial criteria they apply to their investments.[4]

Dr Woodward contacted 650 people drawn from a database of 2421 potential SRI investors known to be interested in SRI and who had requested a copy of a guide to socially responsible investment produced by one of the leading independent financial advisers (IFAs) specialising in this area. Her sample also included 388 known investors in SRI funds. A total of 560 people replied – quite a high response rate for such a survey – of whom 485 had in fact invested using SRI principles. Her study found that investment screening could be analysed by three vectors: product/service; process, and philosophy. It could also be categorised by its effect on three objects:

Table 4.5 *Important issues for SRI investors 2000*

Process/philosophy	Important (%)	Product	Important (%)
Third World people	97.7	Armaments	96.5
Fair employment	97.7	Protecting environment	94.0
Openness	96.7	Improving environment	91.1
Efficient material use	94.8	Pornography	87.2
Environment pollution	93.2	Tobacco	86.4
Community relations	92.3	Gambling	81.6
Repressive regimes	91.8	Nuclear power	81.5
Sustainable materials	91.4	Basic requirements	71.5
Animal test cosmetics	89.3	Health	50.9
Director remuneration	79.0	Alcohol	46.9
Political donations	66.8	Animals, clothing	46.2
Charitable donation	59.4	Animals, food	43.7
Animal test, medical	55.2		

Source: Based on notes from a presentation by Dr Therese Woodward, 24 October 2000.

Table 4.6 *SRI cluster analysis 2000*

Religious	Political
Sin stocks (alcohol, tobacco, gambling)	Fair play (treatment of employees and suppliers)
Quality of life	Abuse of nature
Animal exploitation	Eco-worries
War machinery	Abuse of power (oppressive regimes)

Source: Based on notes from a presentation by Dr Therese Woodward, 24 October 2000.

people, the environment and animals. The Woodward analysis produced the results in Table 4.5.

Factor analysis of the Woodward data identified the underlying concerns as falling into two groups, similar although not identical to the 'religious' and 'political' groupings identified by Cowton eight years earlier (Table 4.6).

PROFILING THE INVESTORS

One of the first attempts to identify the typical SRI investor was a study published in 1998 by Professor Alan Lewis, a researcher in the Department of Psychology in the University of Bath. This analysed the survey results of over 1100 individual SRI investors. The study discovered a strong correlation between SRI fund purchases and general lifestyle, with self-image being a strong motivating factor behind decisions to purchase such funds. The majority of these investors were middle-aged, highly educated and often working in a caring profession such as teaching, social work or medicine.[5]

The Woodward study also tried to discover whether SRI investment formed part of an individual investor's overall lifestyle. It found that most SRI investors surveyed carried out individual activities such as product recycling, boycotting goods judged to be unfairly produced, and buying environmentally friendly products. However, most SRI investors had limited links with campaigning groups such as Greenpeace or Amnesty International. Most of them were members of one or two such groups, while the third largest proportion of the survey were not members of any campaigning groups.[6]

The average SRI investor in Woodward's research was well educated, as 83% of them had a first degree. They were middle-aged and working in managerial or professional occupations. It is hardly surprising that they were better educated and with higher incomes and professional status than the public as a whole. This is true of all unit trust investors as a whole, presumably reflecting the fact that they have more spare income to invest. However, Woodward's results confirmed other findings that SRI investors tend to have a significantly higher average income or professional status than the average unit trust investor, which makes this a highly desirable sector of the market for investment management firms considering new product launches. It would be natural to assume that SRI would be particularly attractive to younger investors, but research shows this to be false. For example, only 13% of the investors in the sample were aged 35 or less, 30% were aged 36–45, and 29% were aged 46–55.

Woodward's research found no significant gender difference among SRI investors. However, there was a suggestion that the raw data masked a definite bias towards women. This seemed to arise because among older age groups women with an interest in SRI tended to get their husbands to invest for them, so the motivating factor behind the investment was female but the actual investment was carried out by a male. Other UK studies have found that more women than men favour SRI. In September 1997 NOP carried out a survey on behalf of EIRIS enquiring about pension funds and ethical investment. This discovered that more women (32%) than men (26%) wanted their pension scheme to operate an ethical policy even if this resulted in lower financial returns. Twenty-three percent of men thought that pension schemes should concentrate on financial return to the exclusion of other factors, while only 13% of women agreed with this statement.[7]

Indeed, female financial empowerment among younger women may prove to be a driving force behind the growth of SRI. In March 1998 the Standard Life insurance company examined the responses received from mailshots of marketing literature announcing the launch of the Standard Life Ethical Fund. It was surprised to discover an unexpectedly high response rate from younger women. Commenting on this fact, EIRIS noted:

> When Standard Life started advertising its new ethical unit trust, it discovered something that might make ethical funds even more attractive to the rest of the financial services industry. It is well known that women are one of the social groups which financial advertising struggles to attract. When Standard Life looked at the response from its ethical advertising, it found there was a surprisingly high response rate from women aged 30–35.[8]

NOP carried out a follow-up poll called Pensions and Ethical Policies in June 1999; it surveyed 493 adults and found similar gender differences to the earlier survey. Only 22% of women thought their pension scheme should concentrate solely on financial objectives, compared to 37% of men. Women were also stronger supporters of the government's proposed plans to compel pension funds to disclose whether they took SRI decisions into account in their investment strategies (75% of women compared to 67% of men). This survey also showed gender differences emerging in ethical exclusion criteria, particularly the issues in Table 4.7.

Table 4.7   *SRI: revealed gender preference differences*

	Women %	Men %
Weapons	61	40
Oppressive regimes	66	50
GM food	53	40

Source: EIRIS news release, June 1999.

Table 4.8   *Age profile of NPI SRI client base*

Age	Percent by age	Percent of UK adult population by age
0–24	6.4	13.2
25–34	19.5	19.7
35–44	25.2	18.0
45–54	23.8	15.0
55–64	13.1	13.3
65+	12.1	20.8

Source: Based on notes from a presentation by Mark Campanale, Henderson Investors, March 2000.

In 2000 Henderson Global Investors (which acquired NPI in 1999) disclosed some interesting results derived from a survey of the NPI client base. This research found there was little gender difference between the clients but it found a great age disparity (Table 4.8). The data for Henderson/NPI's client base confirmed the age profile of earlier studies, as they were overwhelmingly middle-aged and middle class. In fact, almost half of the SRI clients surveyed were aged between 35 and 54, while they were predominantly professionals with high incomes (Table 4.9).

UK studies have all shown that the average socially responsible investor shows a strong occupational bias towards the caring professions such as teaching, social work and medicine. The same is true in the US; this can be seen in Table 4.10, based on US data compiled by the Calvert Group in 1996.

Table 4.9   *Age and profession of SRI investors*

Occupation	Percent	Income band (£)	Percent
Professional	56.6	0–10000	5.8
Retired	17.4	10001–15000	13.2
Managerial	10.0	15001–25000	27.9
Director	6.4	25001–35000	20.9
Technical	3.6	35001–50000	19.0
Unemployed*	2.1	£50000+	13.2

*Includes unpaid carers looking after children or the ill.
Source: Based on notes from a presentation by Mark Campanale, Henderson Investors, March 2000.

Table 4.10   *Occupational profile of US SRI investors*

Occupation	Percentage of all working shareholders
Schoolteacher	10%
College professor	6%
Lawyer	5%
Social worker	3%
Nurse	3%
Doctor	3%
Engineer	3%
Computer programmer	3%
Psychotherapist	2%
Clergyman	2%

Source: The Calvert Group 1996, quoted in a presentation by Mark Campanale, Henderson Investors, March 2000.

The evidence presented in this section provides a fairly consistent and detailed picture of the typical investor in socially responsible investment funds. However, a complete profile should also offer some explanation of why he or she behaves in this way. It would also be useful to understand the factors driving the rapid growth of SRI over the last ten years. What little work has been produced in this area comes from the US. For many years the Princeton scholar Ronald Inglehart has carried out intensive analysis of opinion poll data to try to identify shifts in America's underlying basic values. Inglehart's work suggests that the 1990s saw a major move in popular values, in both North America and Europe, away from the materialism which had dominated the 1980s to a cluster of preferences placing greater emphasis on quality of life, what he described as 'postmaterialism'. Thus people have increasingly rejected the crude moneymaking ethos of the yuppie period in search of personal values. They have left highly paid jobs to downshift, and they have moved beyond selfish individualism to concern over human rights and the environment. They have also rediscovered a quest for meaning beyond materialism, searching for values in philosophy and a variety of spiritual paths.[9]

The Californian social analyst Paul Ray produced a detailed analysis of these postmaterialists in his recent book *The Cultural Creatives: How 50 Million People Are Changing the World*.[10] Preferring to describe them as 'cultural creatives', Ray argues that there are 50 million people of this type in the US alone at present, and that they are the fastest-growing affinity group in America. While Ray notes that affinity groups can be found in all age groups in America, he contrasts cultural creatives with 'traditionalists' and 'moderns'. The traditionalists are concentrated in the oldest age groups, whilst there is less of a difference in age profile between the moderns and the cultural creatives. His conclusion is that the growth in number and influence of cultural creatives results from the arrival to political and economic power of the age group who grew up in the 1960s, reflecting that period's social movements and search for alternative spiritual and philosophical paths. The gap between the two main groups can be seen from Table 4.11.

Ray makes the perceptive and intriguing point that the values of cultural creatives are very different from those of conventional investors, values that are not being recognised by the majority of asset managers who sell socially responsible mutual funds. He argues that the culture of the asset management company is important to SRI investors, who look beyond the fund itself. This feature would explain why SRI in both the UK and the US has remained dominated by a few specialist firms seen as committed to the field, and why

Table 4.11   *Moderns and cultural creatives*

	Moderns (%)	Cultural creatives (%)
Interested in other cultures	92	100
Believe in sustainable development	63	99
Emphasise simple life over money	60	98
Value relationships	58	98
Emphasise altruism	35	67
Financially materialistic	50	15
Value spiritual development	30	50

Source: Based on notes from a presentation by Paul Ray at SRI in the Rockies, September 2001.

attempts by ordinary asset management firms to 'get a slice of the SRI action' have failed to make significant inroads. Ray suggests that SRI investors want a gentler, softer, more people-oriented approach from their investment management fund providers – they do not want brief bullet points. He makes the following suggestions for the future of socially responsible investment:[11]

1. What would an SRI industry 'good practice' award look like?
2. What does 'socially responsible' mean now, and in the future?
3. What are the world's best practices?
4. Can SRI funds justify claims of using positive and negative screens?
5. Isn't there a need for all potential SRI investors to have access to funds' SRI approach, overall investment philosophy, and holdings?

HOW IMPORTANT IS FINANCIAL RETURN?

The third and final question posed at the start of this chapter was the sensitive topic of financial returns. In particular, the extent to which investment returns were an important consideration for potential SRI investors. The first fund to investigate this subject was the NM Conscience Fund at the end of 1993. It discovered that 87% of unit holders in its fund had bought their units in view of the stated ethical investment policy, and that only 7% had done so on the grounds of investment performance.[12]

Further research was carried out from 1994 to 1997 on this subject as part of the ESRC Morals and Money Project, headed by Professor Alan Lewis at the University of Bath, with Dr Craig Mackenzie as research officer. The project involved surveying the 1146 people who had replied to a questionnaire sent out to 3672 people known to hold units in the two largest UK SRI unit trusts. The results confirmed the occupational profile of SRI investors described earlier: 31% of the investors in the survey worked in education, while a further 14% worked in healthcare. The survey found that 'conscience' or easing guilt over owning investments was a major factor behind the purchase of SRI funds, but only to a limited extent:

> Many investors invested ethically in order to assuage their guilty consciences, others did so in order to make a statement. However, for all the investors in the survey, their ethical investments constituted only a minority of their total portfolio, in some cases a tiny minority. Therefore, it seems that, in order to be assuaged, these particular consciences only require a gesture in the right direction, rather than total commitment.[13]

Respondents were asked their opinions of the likely risks and returns from SRI unit trusts (Table 4.12). They were then asked how achieved

Table 4.12 *Expected risk and return from SRI unit trusts*

	Percent		Percent
Much riskier	0.3	Much lower returns	1.7
Slightly riskier	18.3	Slightly lower returns	40.7
Average risk	57.9	Average returns	40.8
Less risky	18.8	Slightly higher Returns	12.9
Much less risky	2.3	Much higher returns	0.8
Don't know or n/a	2.4	Don't know or n/a	3.2
Total	100.0		100.0

Source: Reprinted by permission of Sage Publications Ltd from Lewis, Alan, and Mackenzie, Craig, 'Morals and Money: Ethical Investing and Economic Psychology' in *Human Relations* Vol. 53 February 2000 Copyright © the Tavistock Institute 2000.

Table 4.13 *Effect of SRI relative returns on behaviour: all figures are percentages*

	Comparative return	Reduce ethical	Do nothing	Increase ethical
Ethical returns	8	5.2	80.8	12.9
Standard funds	10			
Ethical returns	5	35.8	56.5	3.6
Standard funds	10			
Ethical returns	12	0.6	34.3	61.1
Standard funds	10			

Source: Reprinted by permission of Sage Publications Ltd from Lewis, Alan and Mackenzie, Craig, 'Morals and Money: Ethical Investing and Economic Psychology' in *Human Relations* Vol. 53 February 2000 Copyright © the Tavistock Institute 2000.

returns above or below those of comparable 'standard' unit trusts would affect their subsequent behaviour (Table 4.13). In other words, how would the perceived financial performance affect the decisions to buy SRI unit trusts?

The data showed that for most investors the likely financial return from socially responsible investing was an important consideration, although not the only one. The prospect of a slightly lower return than from equivalent conventional funds seemed to have little impact on investor behaviour. Presumably they accepted that SRI might involve a small performance cost. However the prospect of a significant relative loss, or a modest financial gain, did have a significant impact on potential purchase behaviour. The investors were also asked to describe the motives underlying their purchase of ethical unit trusts. The objective most frequently stated was to avoid investing in companies that were doing harm (94.0%), followed by 89.7% wishing to help companies making a positive contribution to society. Active engagement came a long way behind, with only 62.4% of those surveyed wanting campaigns to change company behaviour.[14]

The Morals and Money Project interviewed a number of EIRIS subscribers about the motives underlying their purchase of socially responsible unit trusts. This found that the more sophisticated investors, about 40%, were well aware of the idea that investment portfolios should contain a spread of assets, such as UK and international funds, equities and bonds, liquid building society deposits and illiquid long-term investments. They were also fully aware that SRI investments did not offer exposure to all these investment types. Hence these investors invested in funds which they considered to be unethical because they wanted diversified financial portfolios, and they accepted that following such an investment policy ruled out investing purely in SRI funds. The survey's conclusions were that investors adopted a 'portfolio approach' to ethical investments. (Woodward's research found a similar pattern of a 'portfolio approach to ethics', as she found that the average investor in her survey had less than £25000 invested in SRI funds.) The Morals and Money Project concluded:

> The problem ethical investors faced is that while they had ethical concerns they were not prepared to sacrifice their essential financial requirements to meet these concerns. So they had to find a compromise, which included categorising a small part of their money as supplementary to their essential financial requirements and devoting this to meeting their ethical objectives, and deciding that their ethical objectives could be met satisfactorily if they only invested a small part of their portfolio ethically. These steps allow investors to take a compromise 'portfolio approach' to ethics, not dissimilar to their portfolio approach to investment.[15]

The 1999 NOP survey Pensions and Ethical Policies was mentioned earlier. All of the 493 adults interviewed had a personal or occupational pension, or were thinking of starting such a pension. This fact makes the data of the greatest importance in assessing the public's overall views on financial return within SRI. The evidence described above suggests that investment in SRI unit trusts or mutual funds is often carried out on a 'portfolio approach', i.e. it normally represents only a small proportion of an individual's wealth. This means that the investors can be relatively indifferent to financial performance. However, pension fund investments are the single largest financial asset for most people. For both personal and defined contribution pension schemes, financial performance is crucial if the fund

Table **4.14**   *The 1999 NOP/EIRIS pension fund survey: support (%) for pension funds having an SRI policy*

	Strongly agree	Mildly agree	Total agree	Disagree
If reduces returns	4	35	39	61
No effect on returns	26	51	77	23
Ignoring ethics	9	23	32	68

Source: EIRIS/NOP Pensions and Ethical Policies, summary of findings, June 1999.

is to assure the future pensioner a financially secure retirement. One consequence of this important consideration was that the NOP pension fund survey showed a significantly lower proportions of people were willing to advocate SRI screening than was the case for SRI mutual fund investors in similar surveys.

The NOP survey also showed significant support for the idea that pension funds should actively pressurise companies to change corporate behaviour. Fifty-four percent of respondents thought that pension funds should limit excessive pay deals for directors, and 47% of those surveyed advocated lobbying companies to produce better working conditions in developing countries. Forty-six percent of the respondents supported better relations with employees, local suppliers and the local community, while 42% wanted pension funds to push for better environmental disclosure and reduced environmental impact from their companies. The NOP data showed strong support for pension funds adopting SRI policies, but it was fairly sensitive to the effect this might have on financial performance (Table 4.14).

Before moving on from the topic of SRI criteria, we should note that they can and do vary significantly between countries, reflecting cultural factors. For example, US SRI investors are very concerned about racial and gender diversity, i.e. that women and ethnic minorities are well represented in the senior management of a company. This is less of an issue in the UK or Europe. On the other hand SRI in Europe often stresses 'inclusivity', i.e. that workers are included in management decisions, or that the salaries of senior managers should not exceed certain multiples of the average worker, issues rarely covered in the US.

The treatment of animals has always been a major issue for socially responsible investors in the UK. Historically this is a subject which has had a relatively low ranking among US SRI criteria, but it seems to be growing in importance to American socially responsible investors. (In January 2000 the first explicitly 'animal-friendly' SRI fund was launched in Washington DC by the Humane Society of the US together with Salomon Brothers Asset Management.) The same also seems to be true of genetically modified food. I remember visiting a number of US SRI fund managers in October 1999 and finding little interest in GM foods. In contrast, GM foods were highly controversial, and indeed front-page news in the UK and Europe at that time. GM foods are now certainly on the map as far as SRI in America is concerned.

To sum up, we can say that retail investors in SRI unit trusts or mutual funds seem to fall into two distinct groups who share overlapping concerns about issues such as human rights. The religious investors naturally feel comfortable with the issues that SRI funds inherited from the churches, i.e. sin stocks such as alcohol, tobacco, defence and gambling. The politically aware investors are much more troubled by issues surrounding outsourcing, animal rights, etc. The two groups have overlapping concerns about the environment and human rights, and these are the issues which therefore tend to dominate the polls in terms of high levels of overall concern.

We can also draw some conclusions about the average SRI investor. They are well educated and probably work in one of the caring professions. While there seems to be little obvious gender differentiation, female financial empowerment may be a powerful factor behind the growth of socially responsible investment. The average SRI investor is of professional status and possesses an income well above average. It is not surprising this is an attractive area for financial services companies.

REFERENCES

1. 'The Ethical Investor: Exploring Dimensions of Investment Behaviour', P. Anand and C. Cowton, *Journal of Analytical Psychology*, Vol. 14, 1993.
2. Anand and Cowton, *op. cit.*
3. 'Ethical Views', *Charities Management*, spring 1994.

4. Dr Therese Woodward, *The Profile of Individual Ethical Investors and Their Choice of Investment Criteria.*
5. 'Ethical Investing Linked to Lifestyle and Image', *Financial Times*, 12 September 1998.
6. Author's notes from presentation by Dr Therese Woodward, 24 October 2000.
7. *The Ethical Investor* (EIRIS newsletter), March/April 1999.
8. *The Ethical Investor* (EIRIS newsletter), March/April 1999.
9. Ronald Inglehart, *Culture Shift in Advanced Industrial Societies*, Princeton, 1995.
10. Paul Ray and Ruth Anderson, *The Cultural Creatives: How 50 Million People Are Changing the World*, Three Rivers Press 2001.
11. Author's notes from a presentation by Paul Ray, SRI in the Rockies, September 2001.
12. 'Ethical Views', *Charities Management,* spring 1994.
13. 'Morals and Markets: Ethical Investing and Economic Psychology' Alan Lewis and Craig Mackenzie, *Human Relations*, Vol. 53 February 2000.
14. The Morals and Money Project, summary of findings, October 1997.
15. Lewis and Mackenzie, op cit.

5

Screening in Practice

SCREENING IN PRACTICE

SRI unit trusts and mutual funds are the the best-known part of so-cially responsible investing i.e. the retail market. These funds are nor-mally characterised by the use of social and environmental exclusion criteria alongside standard financial goals. The retail market for SRI funds has grown rapidly on both sides of the Atlantic over the past decade, and this, coupled with its high visibility, has led many people to see negative screening as the heart of SRI. In the previous chapter I examined survey evidence describing the social responsibility issues that are of greatest concern to the investing public. The next step is to move on and look at the varying ways that SRI unit trusts and mutual retail funds have put these concerns into practice.

Chapter 3 described the way investment management firms adopted ethical exclusion criteria traditionally used by the Protestant churches when they first launched SRI funds for sale to the public. These standard avoidance criteria prohibited investment in compa-nies producing weapons, alcohol, tobacco, or providing gambling services. Yet a lot has changed since the Pax Fund started in the US in 1971, or the Friends Provident Stewardship Trust was launched in the UK in 1984. It is obvious from even a brief study of contem-porary SRI funds that a number of issues have been added to the original list inherited from the churches, particularly subjects like the environment, human rights, animal testing and pornography.

I decided that the best way to tackle the changing nature of SRI screening would be to describe the exclusion criteria of two older funds in some depth, and contrast these with two newer ones. The analysis is based on two US SRI mutual funds and two UK SRI unit trusts. The two old-established funds I have chosen are the Calvert Social Investment Fund and the Friends Provident Stewardship Trust, the market leaders in SRI retail funds in the US and UK respectively. This is followed by briefer consideration of the screening criteria used by Citizens Funds and Standard Life's UK Ethical Fund, two more recent entrants into the SRI field. An individual fund's SRI criteria, tend to reflect the culture of the asset manager providing them, so I have given some background information on each investment management group in order to put the screens into a broader context.

CALVERT SOCIAL INVESTMENT FUND

Based in Bethesda, Maryland, the Calvert Group was founded in 1976 as a mutual fund company specialising in bonds and money market funds. The group moved into socially responsible investing in October 1982 with the launch of the Calvert Social Investment Fund (CSIF). Calvert's president, Wayne Silby, stated the group's aim as follows:

> To provide an economic return to its investors and an economic and social return to society that will contribute to the quality of life for all.[1]

Calvert marketed the CSIF and did the screening, while the investment adviser was US Trust Company. Thus Calvert used a classic twin-track SRI model, whereby SRI research and fund management were kept strictly separate. In this case Calvert devised assessment screens and marketed the funds to the public, but an external asset manager carried out the actual investment of the funds. Growth of CSIF was initially fairly slow, but speeded up with the launch of a pure equity fund in 1987. In March 1998 a larger company fund was added to the Calvert SRI range with the introduction of the CSIF Enhanced Equity Portfolio, based on the Russell 1000 large-cap index. Barbara Krumsiek, Calvert's chief executive officer (CEO), explained:

> That's about as close as we can get to a large to mid cap index with social screening. We'll be the first socially screened

fund that sets itself up against a conventional index. We believe that businesses that meet the socially responsible criteria are generally well managed which should be reflected in good long-term financial performance. We think that by looking at these characteristics, you're looking at a proxy for good management. These aren't areas that are going to have an impact on the stock price today, but they could have an impact down the road.[2]

In 1982 the Calvert Social Investment Fund became the first US mutual fund to use South African exclusion screens and to campaign against the apartheid regime. However, following the democratic revolution in that country in 1994 the Calvert South African mutual fund was launched to invest there, although interest from Main Street USA was not high. In June 2000 the Calvert Social Index Fund was opened, a passively managed fund based on the US benchmark index, the S&P 500. The aim of the new fund was to create a broad-based, rigorously constructed benchmark for measuring the social responsibility performance of large-cap US companies. This had assets under management of around $20 million going into 2001.

CSIF's total assets broke through the $1 billion barrier for the first time in 1992, a large chunk of the total group's then assets under management of $3.4 billion. The financial performance of the Calvert Social Investment Fund was disappointing relative to the S&P 500 index during the mid 1990s, but picked up in the late 1990s, as shown in Table 5.1.

By the end of 2000 the Calvert Group had the largest family of socially screened mutual funds in the US, and hence the world. Total

Table **5.1** *Calvert social equity performance: annualised returns (%) for n years to December 2000*

	1 year	3 years	10 years
CSIF (Equity) NAV	11.6	15.1	12.2
Lipper Multi-Cap Fund Average	−2.9	10.8	16.3
S&P 500	−9.0	12.1	17.5

Source: Calvert Group and author's analysis.

assets under management at that date were $6.7 billion, with a total of $2.4 billion invested in the Calvert SRI portfolios. The group as a whole had 220 000 individual shareholders investing in 27 screened and non-screened portfolios, calling itself

> the leading provider of the broadest array of SRI mutual funds across equity, bond and money market portfolios.[3]

The Calvert Group seems a fairly dynamic group that is forward-looking in its thinking. It was notable that in 1997 the group hired Barbara Krumsiek from Alliance Capital as CEO, making Calvert one of the few companies within the $3700 billion US mutual fund industry to have a female CEO. Krumsiek's arrival seems to have sparked a more innovative period for the company, with a variety of new SRI funds being launched. For example, in November 2000 it issued the first ever SRI technology fund. Krumsiek explained the logic thus:

> There is no socially screened technology fund available in the market place, so we thought that it would be an important new product for Calvert and also the mutual fund industry.... Interestingly though, technology generally has a very high [SRI] pass rate, about 85%. These are relatively new companies, and they are started with what we believe is a good perspective with respect to the environment and workplace issues.... We are committed to expanding the choices for investors that are interested in being able to tap into a full array of investment strategies within a socially screened discipline.[4]

The philosophy underlying Calvert's SRI work is that long-term rewards accrue to investors from organisations whose products, services and methods add to human well-being. These basic principles have been crystallised into the positive and negative assessment criteria in Box 5.1. There is an important difference between the four negative screens. The first three are low tolerance, i.e. companies are avoided that are judged to be 'significantly engaged' in the prohibited areas. The screening criteria for alcohol, tobacco and gambling are applied in a less stringent way, only prohibiting investment in a company 'primarily engaged' in the products. (The criteria have been abridged and slightly simplified by the author to save space.)

Box 5.1 Calvert SRI Criteria

Positive: companies are sought that are

1. *Environmentally friendly.* Produce safe goods and services in ways which sustain the environment, such as producers of renewable energy, while heavy polluters are avoided.
2. *Inclusive management style.* Staff participation encouraged in decision making, and employee stock ownership or profit-sharing plans are offered.
3. *Diversity.* Treat workers fairly, with no discrimination on the basis of race, gender, religion, age, disability, ethnic origin or sexual orientation. Provide opportunities for women, disadvantaged minorities and others for whom equal opportunities have often been denied.
4. *Creativity and community awareness.* A commitment to human goals, such as creativity, productivity, self-respect and responsibility, and provision of a working environment in which these goals can be realised. Also companies with an above average commitment to community affairs and charitable giving.

Negative: investment is avoided in companies which

1. *Nuclear energy.* Either produce nuclear energy directly, or manufacture equipment used to produce nuclear energy.
2. *Oppressive regimes.* Have business operations in oppressive regimes.
3. *Armaments.* Manufacture weapon systems.
4. *Alcohol, tobacco, gambling.* Manufacture alcoholic beverages or tobacco products, or operate gambling services, e.g. casinos.

The Calvert Social Investment Fund uses a variety of social research procedures. The most wide-ranging is a search process using news items from over 1200 publications to produce data on corporate social responsibility issues. It also uses a number of well-known external research providers on social responsibility and corporate governance issues, such as the Investor Responsibility Research Center, KLD and the Council on Economic Priorities. CSIF also works with the Interfaith Center on Corporate Responsibility on shareholder activism issues. The in-house research department also trawls through data published by US government agencies such as the Environmental Protection Agency, the Department of Defense and the National Labor Relations Board. Calvert's analysts also produce detailed reports on each company investment using traditional financial information sources such as the report and accounts and other regulatory filings, while regular contact with corporate executives is also maintained. CSIF notes the useful role played by community groups or other non-governmental organisations (NGOs) in providing specific information on an issue from a viewpoint that may not be flattering to the company concerned:[5]

> We have found each potential investment to be more or less unique. For this reason, we must rely on a wide range of organisations with specific industry or geographic knowledge to ensure a comprehensive analysis. Here are some examples:
>
> - In researching Bank of America's commitment to community reinvestment, we tracked the company's lending record at a national level, through San Francisco based CANICCOR, and at a local level, through groups like Communities for Accountable Reinvestment in South-Central L.A.
> - When considering Intel Corporation, we were pleased with the company's pollution prevention programs and energy efficiency improvements, but had concerns with other policies and their operations in New Mexico. We contacted the Southwest Organising Project near Albuquerque to gain a more local perspective.

Calvert's basic philosophy seems to be that its social screening can identify good company management who are proactive in meeting the social and environmental challenges increasingly faced by business, rather than poor management who choose, ostrich-like, to ignore such challenges. In stock market terms, if you can identify good management, you have a formula that should produce good financial returns for investors. In CSIF's own words:

CSIF believes that social and technological change will continue to transform America and the world for the balance of this century. Those enterprises which exhibit a social awareness measured in terms of the above attributes and considerations should be better prepared to meet future societal needs for goods and services. By responding to social concerns, these enterprises should maintain flexibility and further social goals. In so doing they should not only avoid the liability that may be incurred when a product or service is determined to have a negative social impact or has outlived its usefulness, but also be better positioned to develop opportunities to make a profitable contribution to society. These enterprises should be ready to respond to external demands and ensure that over the longer term they will be viable to provide a positive return to both investors and society as a whole.[6]

FRIENDS PROVIDENT STEWARDSHIP

During the 1970s and early 1980s a great debate took place within the Society of Friends on ethics and investment. This in turn led to intensive discussion within Friends Provident, a mutual insurance company (i.e. unquoted), established on Quaker principles in 1832, as to what extent these principles could still be followed in the 1980s. It was decided that the bulk of the company's funds should be invested on normal commercial lines, but that a specialist ethical fund, the Friends Provident Stewardship Trust, should be established for the small minority believed to want such a product. (In view of the subsequent growth of the Stewardship funds, it is ironic that conventional wisdom at that time thought the new fund would be lucky to reach £5 million of investment assets.)

Right from its beginning, the Stewardship funds had a clear philosophy that combined negative exclusion criteria with positive aspirational values:

This Trust aims to invest, as far as practicable, in companies whose products or services make a positive and healthy contribution to society.... We seek out companies with healthy track records in labour relations, pollution control and environmental

95

protection.... We make every effort to avoid investing in the tobacco industry, in alcohol, and in oppressive regimes... nor in
companies involved in the arms trade, gambling, or exploitation
of animals. Our experience shows that this policy can achieve
excellent long-term results. We believe that there is a good
reason for this: concerned companies are usually operated by
diligent, concerned managements, and this shows up in their
financial performance. It's also true that 'socially conscious'
companies tend to avoid adverse publicity, strikes and boycotts
of their products.[7]

One of the most distinctive features of the Friends Provident Stewardship approach has always been the immense amount of time and
trouble spent on developing and improving its SRI procedures. Right
at the beginning of Stewardship's life, this resulted in the establishment of a Committee of Reference to determine general principles
and assess their application via detailed investment criteria. I have
always felt that the establishment of the Stewardship Committee of
Reference was one of the most important aspects of Stewardship's
creation, and something that sadly has not been followed by the
many other SRI unit trusts which have copied its approach in other
ways. This is an aspect of SRI that has received relatively little academic scrutiny or coverage in the media. I discussed its role with
Charles Jacob MBE, a founder member of the committee. Known as
the 'father of ethical investment' for his trail-blazing work in exploring the legal possibility of setting up an ethical unit trust as early
as 1973, it was Jacob's pioneering efforts which led to the establishment of the first 'ethical' unit trust by Friends Provident in 1984:

When the concept of Stewardship, the first UK ethical trust
was being developed, the requirements of both capital and
conscience were matters of individual concern. The final selection of investments was required to be in the hands of
professional investment managers. Equally essentially, an independent qualified body appeared necessary not only to ensure
that the advertised policy of the trust was adhered to, but also
to consider the ethical merits of shares available for investment.
Thus the idea of a Committee of Reference was born. The analysis of individual companies, however, goes far beyond products

and services, and encompasses such issues as employment practices, attitudes towards local communities, natural resources, pollution control, and the political and social environment of countries in which companies operate.

The investment selection criteria, with its positive and negative aspects, covers over ten pages. It is not unusual for an agenda of 200 foolscap sheets to be presented every six weeks for consideration by the Committee. As a result, the analysis of over 800 companies has resulted in less than half being acceptable for further consideration for investment. I doubt whether any other ethical fund is able to go into the depths of research that is required by Stewardship, if only because the sheer size of the funds enables us to afford it. Much of the research is done by EIRIS, although internal sources also contribute to the analysis. I cannot stress too much that considerable discussion and consideration of company merits is necessary. Few situations can be defined as black and white, and the weighing up of positives against negatives is necessary when considering shares in several sectors.[8]

Stewardship was the UK pioneer of the twin-track model subsequently followed by the majority of UK SRI unit trusts. The essence of this approach lies in the existence of a totally separate SRI research department whose responsibility is to produce an 'SRI approved list' of potential investments. The fund managers, who are not involved in the ethical discussions, then use the company names on the approved list to create investment portfolios they hope will generate good financial returns. Stewardship fund manager Richard Singleton put it this way:

> It was felt important to separate the investment management side, which considers companies purely in terms of financial considerations, from the ethical view provided by the Committee of Reference.[9]

In its earlier days, Stewardship's 'ethical' advice was based on external research produced by the SRI research service EIRIS, whose role also included monitoring the activities of current and potential investments against the established investment criteria. EIRIS produced extensive SRI research dossiers on industries, issues and particular companies, using annual reports and other published information supplemented by questionnaire surveys probing specific ethical issues among individual companies. Representatives from EIRIS attended every Committee of Reference meeting to provide expert guidance on the issues being discussed. EIRIS still plays an important role in Stewardship's SRI effort, although this is now complemented by research produced by the internal research unit. Stewardship is scrupulous in weeding out any company that it believes falls foul of its ethical criteria, and this has caused it to exclude from investment the majority of the shares in the UK's main benchmark index, the FTSE All-Share. It has also resulted in the Stewardship unit trust having a strong bias to smaller companies, as they are purer plays and therefore much less likely than a large conglomerate to have a subsidiary involved in questionable activities.

The original Stewardship equity fund was followed by Stewardship Income in 1987, a high-yielding equity fund of a type that is popular in the UK, although so far it is the only UK income fund with SRI screens. The same year also saw the arrival of Stewardship North America, a screened fund for UK investors to invest in North American equities. (This was rebranded as a global SRI fund in 1998.) The group also issued an SRI investment trust in 1993 (closed-end mutual fund), the Friends Provident Ethical Trust.

Box 5.2 is my abridged version of the Stewardship ethical screens.[10]

Box 5.2 Stewardship SRI Criteria

Companies involved in the following activities: investment is generally excluded

1. *Environmental damage and pollution.* Companies producing unacceptable levels of water pollution, destruction of natural woodlands or forests, high use of fossil fuels, and the manufacture or use of pesticides or ozone-depleting chemicals.
2. *Unnecessary animal exploitation.* This includes the fur trade, intensive or factory farming, and the production or processing of meat or meat products where this is a company's main

business. It also prohibits investment in companies that manufacture cosmetics, soaps or toiletries unless their products are animal test free. However, investment is not excluded in companies that use animal testing in the production of medicines, food additives, veterinary products or household and industrial chemicals; instead it is referred to the overall judgement of the advisory committee.

3. *Oppressive regimes.* Investment in companies with significant operations in countries with oppressive regimes (as defined by Freedom House). However, account is taken of their operations (e.g. medical support) and the terms and conditions of employment.

4. *Exploitation of the Third World.* This excludes, for example, companies violating the International Code of Marketing Breast-Milk Substitutes, or marketing tobacco products in the Third World.

5. *Manufacture and sale of weapons.* This encompasses contracts of a military nature, including the manufacture or sale of weapons or products with military uses.

6. *Nuclear power.* Any significant involvement in the nuclear power industry, such as construction of nuclear power stations or associated plant or equipment, supply or transport of nuclear fuel or uranium ore, and disposal or transport of radioactive waste.

7. *Tobacco or alcohol production.* The sale of tobacco or alcohol products where the proportion of turnover attributable to such activity exceeds 10% of the total, though in the case of alcohol consideration is also given to the nature of the business.

8. *Gambling.* Supplies of gambling machines, and operators of betting shops, horse and greyhound tracks and licensed bingo halls. Any company involved in running the National Lottery, and any company whose sale of lottery tickets account for more than 10% of turnover.

9. *Pornography.* Companies which produce, print, publish or distribute material of a clearly offensive nature.

10. *Offensive or misleading advertising.* Advertising which is clearly deceitful or offensive, as indicated by complaints

upheld by the Advertising Standards Authority during the previous two years.

Companies making a positive contribution to society: investment is positively sought

1. *Supplying basic necessities.* Supplying food, water, fuel, clothing, etc.
2. *Products and services of benefit to the community.* This includes
   the production and supply of life-saving or life-enhancing
   products such as medicines or safety equipment, as well as
   community services such as public transport.
3. *Conservation of energy or natural resources.* A company policy of not using or supplying tropical hardwood or tropical hardwood products or using only independently certified
   wood and wood products. The avoidance of ozone-depleting
   chemicals.
4. *Good employment practices.* This covers a company's approach
   to the management of its staff, including the terms and conditions of employment.
5. *Community involvement.* Charitable donations amounting to at
   least 1% of UK pre-tax profits in the most recent financial year,
   and the provision of products and services on reasonable terms
   to disadvantaged groups within the community.
6. *Equal opportunities.* The presence of women and ethnic minorities on the board and in managerial positions, and the provision
   of carers' benefits.
7. *Environmental improvement.* The provision of specialist pollution control equipment, the sponsoring of major conservation
   projects, and the publishing of an environmental policy statement or an independent environmental audit report in the past
   three years.
8. *Stakeholding.* Good relations with customers and suppliers and
   with the general public.
9. *Training and education.* The provision of training or educational resources to schools, colleges, universities, employees or
   individuals.

The Stewardship funds did well in the second half of the 1980s and early 1990s. They deserve credit for 'creating the market' for retail SRI products in the UK in the face of significant scepticism from the independent financial advisers, the main sales channel for unit trusts and insurance products in the UK. The financial return from the Stewardship funds was also strong on the back of the good investment performance of smaller companies then seen. In 1993 Friends Provident's investment manager Peter Sylvester expressed the group's high level of confidence at that time in its approach to socially responsible investment:

> While growth in ethical funds is impressive, we believe it is just the tip of the iceberg. Some people are holding back because they do not understand what an ethical investment is and how it can compete with a traditional fund. Once the arguments have been explained, they are hard to refute.... We're looking for companies that have good products, good practices and good markets. If you're doing that, you'll find you're in the right pool for healthy companies — we haven't found it any handicap at all when it comes to performance.... The evidence is that most of our ethical funds have actually outperformed the rest of our funds, particularly on the pensions side.[11]

However, while the market for SRI funds did grow rapidly during the mid 1990s and beyond, some market observers felt that the Stewardship approach rather lost its way in this period. Stewardship's small-cap bias had been a positive factor as regards investment performance in the early 1990s, but as the decade progressed it became a negative. For example, performance data for Stewardship and Stewardship Income showed that the total return from Stewardship for the five years to October 2000 was only 84.7% compared to 97.1% produced by the FTSE All-Share index, while Stewardship Income lagged behind with a return of only 46.7%.[12]

Aggressive new entrants such as Jupiter and Henderson/NPI developed new techniques that moved away from the rather rigid screening methods practised by Stewardship. These groups promoted positive approaches such as 'best of class' and 'industries of the future', while they also encouraged 'engagement' with companies rather than prohibiting investment. For example, in April 1998

Table 5.2   *Friends Provident range of retail SRI funds: asset value (£m)*

	Launch	1990	1993	1996	1999
FP Steward Insurance	1984	56	90	178	300
NM Conscience	1987	1	2	3	3
FP Steward Pension	1984	25	92	215	568
Unit trusts					
FP Stewardship	1984	90	154	312	605
FP Steward Income	1987	14	44	66	79
FP Steward North America	1987	3	5	13	37
Investment trusts					
FP Ethical	1993	–	30	32	46
Total		188	418	818	1638
Total market		321	728	1479	3197
FP market share		59%	57%	55%	51%

Source: Data compiled by the author.

Henderson/NPI launched the UK's first socially responsible index, tracking the performance of companies with strong social and environmental records. Stewardship's UK market share in SRI declined (Table 5.2). More importantly, this enabled Henderson/NPI in particular to gain a large market share of the SRI pension fund and charity market that opened up in the late 1990s. (There is more on this subject in Chapter 13.)

Rapid changes were made in the shape of the Friends Provident Group following the appointment of a new chief executive, Keith Satchell, in 1997. In February 1998 the long-established Scottish investment trust manager Ivory & Sime was taken over. This added some £3 billion of assets under management to the Friends Provident existing total of £19 billion. It also gave the group greater depth of fund management expertise, so that a new company, Friends Ivory & Sime (FIS), became the group's asset management centre. This was followed in February 1999 by the acquisition of London & Manchester, an Exeter-based life insurance company, which added London & Manchester's strength in corporate pensions business to

Friends Provident's existing leading position in traditional life and personal pensions products. The acquisition also brought £5.1 billion of London & Manchester's investment assets. As a result of these deals, combined with organic growth, FIS assets under management nearly doubled from £19 billion at the end of 1997 to £37 billion at the end of 2000.

There were also significant developments in Friends' SRI approach. The original Stewardship model of the SRI policy being set by the advisory committee primarily on the basis of external research supplied by EIRIS was already looking rather dated by the mid 1990s. In 1998 the group hired Dr Craig Mackenzie, the research officer of the Morals and Money project described in Chapter 4, to set up and then head a new six-person internal ethics unit for the Stewardship funds. Mackenzie was also given a mandate to examine Stewardship's negative screening bias. On 8 May 2000 Friends Provident unveiled plans to use its total £15 billion equity portfolio to press companies on issues such as human rights, child labour and environmental pollution. This engagement approach, given the proprietary name of Responsible Engagement Overlay (REO) was the responsibility of the ethics unit of FIS, previously responsible only for the firm's £1.5 billion Stewardship ethical funds. The ethics unit was expanded from 6 to 11 people, and FIS announced that it would be increasing the number of specialist fund managers from 8 to 12. Keith Satchell described the group's belief that REO would positively influence corporate behaviour while resulting in good returns for shareholders:

> Good corporate practice on human rights, child labour and environmental pollution is good for society but it's also good for shareholders. It is right that we use our influence to encourage responsible business practices while serving the financial interests of our customers.[13]

In December 2000 Friends Provident announced what may have seemed a revolutionary step to people who had observed the growth of Stewardship from the beginning, a comprehensive review of Stewardship's policies:

> The Ethics Unit – now renamed the Socially Responsible Investment Team – has grown over recent years to a staff of 11.

The team is now able to undertake much more extensive in-house policy research than in the past, allowing us to deepen and broaden our knowledge of the issues, and therefore to better inform our investment decisions. Changes will be modest and aim to reflect areas where perceptions have evolved over the 16 years since Stewardship was launched. For example, we will aim to reflect the fact that the standards which companies are expected to reach in terms of social and environmental performance and reporting have increased in recent years. Further, we will give much more extensive and sophisticated consideration to some issues, such as human rights, which have grown in scope and complexity in recent years. Business is increasingly expected to play a much more proactive role in upholding and protecting human rights wherever they operate, and to manage human rights related issues affecting their suppliers.[14]

It is always difficult for a market leader to accept that its way of doing business may need updating. I think that Friends Provident deserves credit for the way it responded to the growing challenges facing Stewardship in the late 1990s. It made a significant investment in building up its internal SRI research capacity, and was one of the pioneers of a broadly based 'engagement' approach in the UK.

CITIZENS FUNDS

If Calvert and Friends Provident are long-established players, Citizens Funds is a relatively new entrant into SRI equity funds. Based at Portsmouth, New Hampshire, the group was founded in 1982 under the name of Working Assets Capital Management. However, funds under management remained relatively modest until the entrepreneur Sophia Collier took control in 1992, moving away from purely cash funds into the equity investment arena. Citizens Funds grew rapidly in the late 1990s on the back of strong investment performance, so that by the beginning of 2001 Citizens had some $2 billion in assets. It describes its objectives thus:

To generate the best possible returns for our clients by investing in companies that are fundamentally strong and socially responsible. A growth orientation is at the heart of Citizens Funds' investment process. We believe that a company's financial strength is ultimately affected by how well it treats its employees, customers, community and environment. It is our belief that sound investing requires responsible investment managers to evaluate a broad array of factors about how companies do business — to look carefully at the numbers in combination with all the variables that affect performance over time.[15]

Citizens has what to me seems an interesting approach, in that while it is a specialist in socially responsible investment — all the equity funds operate within SRI constraints — there is also a strong commitment to generating equity growth, and to managing the risk of SRI exclusions. I have chosen to illustrate Citizens' social screens by using the Citizens Core Growth Fund, formerly known as the Citizens Index Fund, launched in 1995. This is a domestic large-cap growth fund with 300 holdings and with about $450 million invested in the spring of 2001. Its social screening is described as in Box 5.3.[16] Note that the exclusionary process is straightforward and absolute:

Box 5.3 Citizens exclusion screens

Exclusion

- Tobacco
- Alcoholic beverages
- Nuclear power
- Weapons
- Gambling as a main line of business
- Lack diversity (women or ethnic minorities on board)
- Test cosmetics on animals

Qualitative screening (assessment)

Negative screens: companies are avoided which produce or have

1. *Products*: products with poor safety records, products marketed inappropriately to children, and products that promote negative social stereotypes.

2. *Environment*: products or services particularly harmful to the environment, or with poor environmental track records for their industries.
3. *Human rights*: utilise child labour, forced labour, or sweatshops, or do not have codes of conducts or vendor standards.
4. *Diversity/equal opportunities*: a pattern of discrimination relating to age, religion, race, disability or sexual orientation.
5. *Employee relations*: violate basic labour laws, or lack policies to promote employees' health and safety.
6. *Community relations*: manufacturers who are unresponsive to community concerns about emissions or other local impacts of manufacturing.
7. *Animal issues*: companies that test on animals in excess of legal requirements.

Positive screening: companies are sought which

1. *Environment*: whose operations have a minimal impact on the environment, with rigorous environmental policies.
2. *Human rights*: companies with codes of conduct, vendor standards for overseas operations and suppliers.
3. *Diversity/equal opportunities*: companies that actively promote equal opportunities and seek to hire ethnic minorities.
4. *Employee relations*: companies with family-friendly benefits, good relations with trade unions, and provide benefits to same-sex partners.
5. *Community relations*: companies that support their local communities by charitable contributions or encouraging staff to undertake voluntary activity.
6. *Animal issues*: companies that use alternative methods to animal testing or produce artificial alternatives to fur, and have public disclosure of testing methods.

In the author's opinion, the future of SRI mutual funds lies in moving beyond just screening. In addition to devising social responsibility exclusion criteria, successful mutual funds and SRI unit trusts will need to be able to generate good investment returns, manage the risk of their exclusions, and also possess a good level of transparency and disclosure. This fourfold combination is what I think SRI fund management is all about, although it must be admitted that not all SRI funds seem to share this viewpoint. I would rate Citizens Funds highly for its progress using the author's four metrics. It was notable that when *Business Ethics* magazine held the first Annual Social Investing Leadership Awards in 1999, the US small-medium cap award was won by the Citizens Emerging Growth Fund. The judges reported:

> Through third quarter 1998, Citizens Emerging Growth Fund enjoyed an annualised three year return of 14.9% – more than double the comparable Russell 2000 index at 6.9%. And it achieved this while employing Citizens Funds social screens, which are among the most stringent in the industry. For example, the fund avoids companies that have a below-average environmental record, test personal care products on animals, and have material involvement in the manufacture of weapons. In sweatshop concerns, Citizens Funds has been a special leader, and was an early participant in the White House's Apparel Industry Partnership.[17]

'We screen out companies with the poorest social profiles,' said Diane South, manager of social research. 'For example, we don't own ExxonMobile or Wal-Mart, two companies that some other socially responsible investment managers have held in their portfolios.'

Like Calvert and Stewardship, Citizens Funds has a distinct philosophy that lies behind its social responsible work. Like them it believes there is more to socially responsible investment than just 'conscience investing', i.e. creating investment vehicles that enable members of the public to avoid investing in company activities of concern to them. I would describe it as the belief, shared with the author, that over the long-term the detailed evaluation of social and environmental factors, and their inclusion into the financial decision-making process, adds to, and does not subtract from, financial returns. This approach adds value in two ways. First, it identifies potential risks such as asbestos liability or reputational damage that might be missed by analysts examining only financial data. Secondly, it helps fund managers identify corporate managements who are proactively grappling with potential problems, rather than ignoring them in the hope they will go away. Spotting good management is one of the best indicators of future stock market success. Citizens' president, John Shields, explained the logic behind its approach:

> Citizen Funds' investment process is driven by the belief that evaluating a company's record of corporate responsibility contributes to investment success in two ways: it helps eliminate companies whose behaviour increases risk, and it helps identify more forward-thinking and potentially more promising companies. Coupled with fundamental analysis as performed by our portfolio managers – no investment is ever made for social reasons alone – social screening provides a unique and more comprehensive view of the companies we consider for investment. Screening is the responsibility of our in-house research department. Through a disciplined process these dedicated professionals produce a detailed evaluation of corporate policies and practices culled from over 300 data sources and direct dialogue with the company under review.[18]
>
> Quantitative financial screening is a defining component of our investment approach. But there's a very specific reason why we also engage in what the financial industry calls 'social screening'. We know that share prices can be trampled when companies are called to the carpet for violations of environmental sanctions, child labour laws or the like. Frankly, we'd rather our portfolios steered clear of those kinds of companies. It just makes good investment sense to do so. I point you to the long-term track record of our funds as evidence of that.[19]

Citizens does relatively little shareholder advocacy, and it files few shareholder resolutions. There are two reasons for this. First, its main aim is to avoid investment in problem companies, rather than working to improve them. Secondly, the Citizens Emerging Growth Fund has a fairly high turnover, 245% in 1998, so that often it does not own shares long enough to be eligible to file resolutions.[20] However, it does engage in dialogue with the growth companies that form the basis of the fund's long-term holdings on issues it considers important. One issue that it does pursue is diversity. It has discussed this with companies as varied as retailing giant Home Depot and semiconductor company Micron Technology. 'Our resolution asking American Power Conversion to nominate qualified women and minorities to its board was the most successful board diversity resolution in the United States in 2001, receiving a 28% yes vote, compared with an average 19% yes vote for board diversity proposals,' South said. 'We believe that a diverse board is better equipped to operate in the global marketplace.'

STANDARD LIFE ETHICAL FUNDS

Standard Life is one of the giants of the UK life insurance industry with over £78 billion in assets under management and 4 million customers in the UK. Edinburgh-based Standard Life is one of the few large UK life insurance companies to remain a mutual, i.e. it is owned by policyholders rather than by shareholders. Its financial strength has been recognised by the awarded of a triple A from financial rating agencies. In November 1998 Standard Life announced that its fund management division would be set up as a stand-alone investment management company called Standard Life Investments. It described aggressive plans to achieve a substantial and dynamic increase in its funds under management from an initial level of £60 billion to a target of funds under management of £100 billion within five years. Increasing the company's existing strong market share in the corporate pooled pensions market was a particular objective.

The Standard Life UK Ethical Fund, an OIEC, was launched in February 1998, reaching investment assets of £14 million on behalf of 2500 individual investors by the end of the first year. This was one of three SRI funds run by the company, the others being the Pension Ethical Fund and the Life Ethical Fund. Whereas the older generation of investment management firms such as Calvert and Friends Provident launched SRI funds at least in part to assert their own commitment to social responsibility, Standard Life launched its 'ethical' fund in response to customer feedback; in other words, to fill a gap in its product range in an area that it saw was growing rapidly. Intensive research was carried out with both IFAs and customers before the launch of the new fund to identify the issues potential customers wanted. Standard Life's ethical policy and screening criteria reflect its customer-driven origin. EIRIS was actively involved in developing the criteria, while an ethical advisory committee was also established. According to Standard Life's Gail Gibson:

> We had a tremendous amount of feedback from independent financial advisers (IFAs) asking us if we had this kind of fund. This is being targeted at a specific gap in the market. Our view is that the market seems to be doubling every two years and we do not want to see key business going to our competitors as a result of not offering what the customer wants.[21]

In 1998 Standard Life Investments showed its awareness of the growing pension fund interest in environmental and social issues when it started the Standard Life Ethical Pension Fund, a retail pension fund product that was opened to corporate pension funds in 1999. The investment strategy of the new fund was to invest mainly in UK equities for growth, with 15% of the fund invested in corporate bonds to provide stability and income. Stephen Acheson, investment director at Standard Life Investments, explained the launch of the new fund thus:

> With corporate pooled pension funds under management now approaching £2 billion, of which £300 million has been attracted over the last six months, we are now taking the opportunity to widen our corporate fund range by adding a Corporate Ethical Fund. Feedback from our corporate investors has highlighted their requirements to invest in a fund that reflects their concerns on environmental and social issues.[22]

Standard Life's positive and negative socially responsible screens are shown in Box 5.4.[23] Note that the basis of the fund's SRI policy is derived from issues that the company's market research among investors and financial advisers identified as being of general interest or concern, and is validated and updated each year by investor surveys. Standard Life's corporate ethos has no impact on the social responsibility policy.

Box 5.4 Standard Life's SRI Criteria

Negative criteria

In trying to identify companies which have a harmful effect on the environment and its inhabitants, Standard Life's Ethical Funds look at the background of companies in the following areas:

Environmental damage and pollution

The Funds will avoid investment in the following areas:

- *Water pollution*: companies which have repeatedly discharged effluent into rivers, estuaries, coastal waters or underground, in the last year.
- *Ozone-depleting chemicals*: companies which manufacture or supply ozone-depleting chemicals.
- *Pesticide production*: companies which manufacture pesticide products.
- *Environmental pollution*: companies which have been convicted following a prosecution by the Environment Agency or the Scottish Environmental Protection Agency.

Test products on animals

The Funds will avoid investment in companies whose products or ingredients are tested on animals by themselves or their suppliers.

Genetic engineering

The Funds will avoid investment in companies that carry out genetic engineering of crops, genetic engineering of animals or gene patenting.

Intensive farming

The Funds will avoid investment in companies that use intensive farming methods and own or operate fish farms.

Operate in countries which violate the political and civil rights of their people

Companies that operate in two or more countries which are rated poorly by Freedom House, an organisation based in the United States which monitors human rights worldwide, and the Observer Human Rights Index will be avoided.

Pornography

Companies that publish, print or wholesale magazines which portray men, women or children, in a sexually explicit and degrading manner, including sexual violence, are avoided. The Funds' Ethical Policy also excludes companies that distribute pornographic films or videos through cinemas and shops.

Produce or sell weapons

Companies that produce or sell weapons, including nuclear weapons, will be avoided.

Process nuclear power

Under this criterion companies that own or operate nuclear power stations will be avoided.

Produce alcohol

The Funds will avoid investment in companies which produce alcohol.

Produce tobacco

The Funds will avoid investment in companies that manufacture tobacco products.

Are involved in gambling

Companies which derive any turnover from gambling will be avoided by the funds.

Positive criteria

In identifying companies which are regarded as having a positive effect on society and the environment, Standard Life's Ethical Funds look at the background of companies which:

Make a positive contribution to the environment

For example, companies which:

- Publish an environmental policy or statements or produce an environmental report.
- Produce environmental technologies, for example, technologies associated with pollution control and conservation of natural resources.
- Develop or use renewable energy, for example, solar, wind and wave energy.
- Do not use or supply products which are commonly made from tropical hardwood, unless from sustainable sources.

Promote sound employment practices

We encourage companies which maintain good employee welfare standards and conditions of employment, including:

- Good equal opportunities practice, including equal treatment of women and ethnic minorities.
- Training and education, including providing appropriate training of employees and having been awarded the Investors in People award.
- Good conditions of employment, including job-sharing, career breaks and providing good maternity and paternity conditions.
- Health and safety: have demonstrated a good health and safety record.

Promote products and services which benefit the environment or human life including

Companies that provide environmental products and services which are of benefit to the community or life-saving and life-enhancing products such as medicines and safety equipment.

113

Donate to charities or are strongly involved in the community

Companies which have made it clear that they have an employee secondment scheme in the UK or made gifts in kind to the UK community.

Do not hide the amount paid to their directors

Companies that are open about their activities and how much they pay directors.

In February 2001 the Trades Union Congress (TUC) announced that it would be offering a Standard Life SRI pension option as one of five low cost 'stakeholder' pension products it was offering to its members.[24] The emphasis of Standard Life Investments on corporate governance, and in particular on executive pay, was rewarded in May 2001 when it won the contract to run the TUC's £28 million superannuation scheme. A TUC spokesman explained their decision thus:

> We are already involved with the Standard Life Group who are key players in our group stakeholder scheme and whom we admire as a strong mutual organisation. We are also very impressed with Standard Life Investments' strength and positioning on issues of corporate governance, a subject close to the heart of the TUC and its members.[25]

REFERENCES

1. '14 Firms Launch Alternative Mutual Funds', *Labor and Investments*, December 1982.
2. Barbara Krumsiek quoted on Bloomberg News, 15 December 1997.
3. Calvert Group website, May 2001.
4. Barbara Krumsiek quoted on Bloomberg News, 6 November 2000.
5. 'Funds Seek to Do the Right Thing', *Wall Street Journal*, 21 August 2000.
6. Calvert website, May 2001.
7. Friends Provident Stewardship marketing material 1987.
8. Charles Jacob in conversation with the author 1994.
9. Quoted in *The Ethical Investor*, May/June 1999.
10. Friends Provident Stewardship marketing material 1987.
11. Quoted in 'How Ethical Funds Have Performed', *Daily Telegraph*, 14 November 1993.

12. Friends Provident, *Stewardship Newsletter*, winter 2000.
13. Quoted in 'Friends Plans to Give Ethics a Boost', *Financial Times*, 8 May 2000.
14. Friends Provident, *Stewardship Newsletter*, winter 2000.
15. Citizens website, May 2001.
16. *Ibid.*
17. *Business Ethics*, January/February 1999.
18. Citizens Funds website, May 2001.
19. Citizens Funds, president's letter, 2 January 2001.
20. *Business Ethics*, January/February 1999.
21. Quoted in *The Ethical Investor*, January/February 1998.
22. Standard Life website, June 2001.
23. Copyright Standard Life Investments. Reproduced with permission.
24. 'Friendly Societies Go Back to the Future', *The Independent*, 10 February 2001.
25. Standard Life website, June 2001.

PART II

Issues for Institutional Investors

Part I discussed SRI from the viewpoint of the retail investor, i.e. someone who buys socially responsible unit trusts or mutual funds. That is without doubt the best-known aspect of SRI. However, socially responsible investment is like an iceberg – what you see is only a small fraction of the whole. The hidden part of socially responsible investment is the social responsibility work quietly carried out by major investment institutions such as pension funds, religious groups and charitable foundations.

Institutional investors are increasingly finding SRI to be a part of their standard approach to fund investment. However, the issues they consider are more focused than those used by retail funds. There is, in fact, an emerging consensus that centres 'mainstream SRI' on four key subjects: the environment, human rights, corporate governance and financial performance. These core issues are described and evaluated in Part II. We start with the environment.

6

From Environmental
Risks...

WHY THE ENVIRONMENT IS FUNDAMENTAL

Of all the varying concerns that make up the social responsibility component of SRI, the environment is the most fundamental. Philosophically speaking, if the Earth's ability to support life is essentially impaired, there seems little point in worrying about the other issues. As a result of this fundamental importance, the environment is an issue that has been adopted by practically all socially responsible investors. Even the older church-inspired funds whose list of SRI criteria was originally limited to areas like alcohol, defence and tobacco have generally added the environment to their list of key concerns.

However, the sheer range and ubiquity of environmental issues in the social investing universe can also make it difficult to identify what is really important. While there is growing demand for environmental factors to be incorporated into investment decision-making, a lack of definitional clarity can make it difficult to move on to specifics. For example, investors may be confused by varying claims for environmental management, and wonder how this relates to eco-efficiency and sustainability.

I decided that it would make the subject of the environment more manageable if I split it into two chapters. The first describes the environmental concerns most frequently expressed by the investing public, and hence reflected in SRI fund criteria; the second takes a more positive line, examining investment opportunities within the framework of sustainable development. Ascertaining the environmental issues that most worry the public is important in its own right. Such a process is crucial for SRI unit trusts and mutual funds whose sales rely on meeting such concerns. However, there is more to it than this. The more the public is worried by an environmental issue, the greater the risk it will turn into a corporate banana skin. Although Wall Street and the City of London have tended to ignore environmental risks, these can be deadly when they emerge.

In December 2001 an adverse court judgement on asbestos liability knocked almost 50% off the market capitalisation of the US oil services company Halliburton, on fears that its subsidiary Dresser Industries faced asbestos liabilities totalling over $150 million.[1] At the same time it was estimated that growing worries over asbestos liabilities had reduced the market value of the Swedish/Swiss engineering giant ABB by $20 billion.[2] These are not isolated examples. The devastating impact of thirty-year old asbestos liability on some of the most famous names in the US construction and chemical sectors is described later in the chapter. Another example was the huge cost of cleaning PCBs out of the Hudson River imposed in August 2001 by the EPA on General Electric. This chapter therefore ends with a discussion of some environmental risk factors that all investors need to be aware of, if only to avoid potential financial loss.

THE INVESTING PUBLIC AND THE ENVIRONMENT

The public's environmental concerns are reflected in the screening criteria used by SRI unit trusts and mutual funds. Surveys of socially responsible retail funds therefore provide a reasonably accurate picture of the public's main environmental concerns. A good example was produced by the ethical research service EIRIS in 1991, based on a survey of the majority of UK SRI unit trusts (Table 6.1). Further information on EIRIS is given in Chapter 11.

Reviewing this list ten years after the original survey, I was surprised to see how little it had changed. The latest EIRIS survey, carried out in December 2000, showed the environmental issues that topped

Table 6.1 *A 1991 survey of main environmental concerns*

Single issue	Vote (%)	Weighted voting	Vote (%)
1. Nuclear power	32	1. CFCs	59
2. CFCs	25	2. Polluting water	50
3. Polluting water	21	3. Greenhouse gases	48
4. Greenhouse gases	20	4. Hazardous chemicals	47
5. Hazardous chemicals	20	5. Nuclear power	46
6. Tropical hardwoods	18	6. Tropical Hardwoods	45
7. Pesticides	10	7. Pesticides	22

Source: '"Green Investment" – What Does It Mean to the Ethical Investor?', EIRIS 1991.

the poll in 1991 still did so in 2000. There were, however, three important additions to the earlier list: environmental management and policy, biodiversity, and genetic engineering. Of course, any single list has its limitations. Reliance on database sources runs the risk that the criteria may be driven by what data is publicly available rather than based on key indicators where hard data is more difficult to obtain. For example, in the environmental field this might mean monitoring breaches of pollution permits rather than key sustainability data such as reductions in carbon dioxide emission. It seems appropriate to discuss the main environmental issues of Table 6.1 in some detail, although global warming and environmental management will be covered in the next chapter. Two important topics omitted from Table 6.1 are also discussed in this chapter: smog/acid rain and biodiversity.

NUCLEAR POWER

It is hardly surprising that the production of nuclear materials comes high up the public's social responsibility concerns. Some writers have argued that, right from its beginning, 'peaceful' nuclear power generation was tied up with the production of plutonium for military purposes; see, for example, Walter Patterson's *The Plutonium*

Business.[3] Recent declassified military documents have confirmed this suspicion. The *Financial Times* recently described British Nuclear Fuels Ltd (BNFL) as

> a company with a history of insularity and covering up that dates back to its origins in the late 1940s as a weapons-grade plutonium manufacturing plant.[4]

For many SRI investors this would rule it out as a possible investment on ethical grounds alone, thus providing yet another example of how frequently 'ethical' and 'ecological' concerns are interlinked. There is also widespread suspicion that the cumulative exposure to low levels of radiation may be far more dangerous than governments have admitted, as the clusters of childhood leukaemia sufferers which have been found around UK nuclear power stations would suggest. The Canadian expert Rosalie Bertell estimated in 1985 that nuclear power worldwide had caused some 16 million casualties.[5]

Public confidence in nuclear power snapped in the US in 1979, following an accident at the Three Mile Island nuclear reactor, and the US building programme of commercial nuclear reactors came to a sudden halt as a result of this. However, in 2001–2 the George W. Bush administration did announce plans to reconsider nuclear power plant construction as part of its National Energy Strategy plan. In 1986 the catastrophic explosion at the Chernobyl nuclear power station in the former USSR spewed radioactive material across Europe, and was probably the key factor leading to the effective end of the nuclear power building programme then taking place across Europe. In 2000 the German government announced plans to close down all of their nuclear generating capacity, following a lead taken earlier by Sweden. This will be a massive undertaking for Germany, as the country's 19 nuclear power plants currently produce 35% of its annual electrical power needs. Nevertheless, the German government is adamant that by 2025 they will all be shut.

In July 2001 there was intensive lobbying in favour of nuclear power at the Bonn summit discussions over the implementation of the Kyoto Protocol on climate change. However, despite diplomatic pressure from the US, Canada, Japan, Australia and Russia, other delegates led by the EU refused to include nuclear power in the Clean Development Mechanism. This provides credits to industrialised countries who invest in emission reduction programmes in developing countries. Nuclear power was also excluded from the Joint Implementation Programme, which grants credits to industrialised countries financing emission reduction projects in other developed countries or in Eastern Europe.

Advocates of nuclear power contend that it offers the only realistic alternative to fossil fuels given concerns over global warming. However, opponents argue that the whole industry is irretrievably dangerous to human health. They point out the health risks resulting from nuclear power generation, the dangers of reprocessing and transporting radioactive waste, and ultimately the difficulty of storing material that will be dangerous for thousands of years. Electricity generated by nuclear power plants may seem cost-effective, as its operating costs are normally below that of other competing fuels. However, critics contend that the apparently low cost of nuclear-generated electricity massively understates the costs of decommissioning, and ignores the need for centuries of safe storage of radioactive waste material.

Friends of the Earth (FoE) have pointed out that no definitively safe method of storing nuclear waste has yet been devised. They also note that weapons-grade plutonium can be extracted from nuclear waste, so that even commercial nuclear power plants produce waste material that could be used to make nuclear weapons.[6] Such fears may have seemed exaggerated before 11 September 2001. However, in the light of evidence that the Al-Qaeda terrorist network was planning to make nuclear bombs, their seriousness is unquestionable. The evidence on the safe storage of spent nuclear fuel is not reassuring. A UK report in 1995 by the Nuclear Installations Inspectorate reported that it was 'increasingly concerned' about the condition of over 50% of the 70 000 cubic metres of intermediate nuclear waste stored at 22 locations around the UK.[7] Given the innate caution of bureaucratic language, this might be translated as 'gravely worried'. It warned of potential risks including fires, explosions, and leaks of radioactive materials including plutonium.

OZONE-DEPLETING CHEMICALS

The stratosphere contains a significant layer of ozone (a form of oxygen) that plays a vital part in absorbing the majority of the ultraviolet radiation the Earth receives from the Sun. In the early 1980s scientists were stunned to discover that an ozone hole had appeared over the Antarctic pole, while a similar hole was subsequently discovered over the Arctic. It was realised that certain chlorine-based chemicals called chlorofluorcarbons (CFCs), reacted with sunlight in the upper atmosphere to form bromine and chlorine, highly destructive to ozone. At that time CFCs were in general use as refrigeration agents, cleaners and as the propellant in aerosols. Such ozone holes are highly dangerous, as increased ultraviolet radiation can lead to blindness, skin cancer, and damage to crops and the phytoplankton that forms the base of many marine food chains. In October 1989 an ozone hole lingered over Punta Arenas, a city at the tip of Patagonia, the first time in history that an inhabited area was subjected to unscreened ultraviolet light. An American research team from Johns Hopkins University noted several cases of animal eye diseases and severe human sunburn, unusual in such a cold climate.[8] Plants kept outside withered, whereas those in greenhouses thrived.

The Montreal Protocol in 1987 led to a ban in the developed world on the production of CFCs, although their production was allowed to continue in developing countries. Large-scale production of CFCs still occurs in China, Russia and India, possibly for Western corporate clients, although these countries have agreed to terminate their production by 2010. The problem is that the CFCs circulating in the upper atmosphere are long-lived chemicals, so even if CFC production is stopped completely, the ozone layer is not expected to recover for many years. The latest detailed scientific study published in 1998 estimated that the global ozone shield would be at its thinnest by 2000–2002, and would not recover fully until 2050. The Montreal Protocol recommended that CFCs should be replaced by the similar chemicals HFCs and PFCs. It is now believed that these are a contributory factor in global warming, and a search is on for a new replacement for CFCs. Other substitutes for CFCs include halon gases, used mostly in fire extinguishers, but these also have similar negative factors to HFCs.

WATER POLLUTION

Water pollution has both environmental and economic impacts, for example from discharges of untreated human sewage, or from toxic chemical waste that may kill marine life. Over the past twenty years water pollution has become highly monitored in the EU and the US. Detailed information is provided by government agencies such as DETR in the UK (now separated into two departments) and the Environmental Protection Agency (EPA) in the US on companies fined or suffering other penalties for polluting water. In the UK, DETR has produced a Red List of chemicals it believes to be particularly dangerous if released into water supplies. This list includes cadmium and other heavy metals, DDT, trichlorobenzene and mercury.

Not all dangerous water pollutants are covered by this Red List; for example, it does not monitor agricultural discharge consents. Excessive use of artificial fertilisers, which then run off into surrounding groundwater, is one of the major water pollution issues in developed countries. These chemicals are normally nitrate or phosphate based, and high concentrations in rivers and lakes encourage algal growths that starve the water of oxygen in a process called eutrophication. The result is to kill fish and other aquatic creatures, leaving the rivers dead, sterile. In 1999 FoE published a league table of major water polluters based on Environment Agency data.[9] This identified ICI's Wilton plant on Teesside as releasing far more alkylphenols, chemicals used in industrial-grade detergents, into the UK's water system than any other company. FoE claimed that ICI Wilton released over 8 tonnes of alkylphenols into water in 1998, about 40% of all major alkylphenols discharged in that year. Alkylphenols are known to disrupt hormone development, causing male fish to develop female characteristics and hence become sexually sterile. Canadian research implicates them in the collapse of the Atlantic Coast salmon stocks.

HAZARDOUS CHEMICALS

While many industrial chemicals are potential health hazards, two types of chemical are the subject of major environmental concerns: pesticides, and PVC and phthalates. There is increasing public concern that pesticides can linger in water and the food chain, creating health hazards for animals and humans. They may also produce health risks for farm workers and others exposed to them. In fact, there is a growing body of scientific evidence on the significant health risk posed by pesticides.

In 2000 US scientists at Emory University, Atlanta, found evidence that long-term exposure to low doses of a common pesticide called rotenone produced all the characteristics of Parkinson's disease.[10] Perhaps the most rigorous study was published in the prestigious medical journal *The Lancet* in October 1999.[11] This study examined patients with pancreatic cancer and used genetic trackers to identify the link with chemical pollutants. It found that people with high blood concentrations of organochlorines such as the pesticide DDT, or polychlorinated biphenyls (PCBs) were five times more likely to have a genetic mutation believed to cause pancreatic cancer. DDT has been banned in the EU since the 1970s, while production of PCBs, mostly used for insulating and cooling electrical equipment, was outlawed in the US in 1977.

A US study carried out in 2001 by the University of West Michigan found that while high PCB exposure immediately killed tadpoles, lower dosages led to genetic damage that resulted in later death, even though the lower-dosage tadpoles initially appeared healthy.[12] This study was carried out in Michigan because of concerns about heavy historic dumping by US paper companies of PCBs in the Kalamazoo River, which flows through Michigan. State officials decided to ban the eating of fish caught in the Kalamazoo, on the basis that it was unsafe. The EPA expressed similar concerns about PCBs that had been dumped in the Hudson River, New York (page 140).

Synthetic chemicals such as phthalates and dioxins are used to manufacture PVC, and are produced when PVC is incinerated. It is believed they can accumulate in body tissue, and it is also believed they have strong negative impact on hormone levels, leading to reduced fertility, immune deficiency illnesses, and possibly cancer. An EPA report suggested that the risk of cancer from dioxin exposure could be as high as one in a hundred for people who eat extremely high-fat diets.[13] About 1 million tonnes of phthalates are produced in the EU annually, with five main types: DEHP, DBP, DINO, DIDP and BBP. The main industrial function of phthalates is as a plastic softener, with uses ranging from medical tubing to children's toys. A Swedish medical study in July 2001 found that DEHP poses negative health risks, particularly to the reproductive and developmental health of children.[14] Growing political pressure to reduce their use led the EU in December 1999 to impose a temporary ban on the use of phthalates in toys for children under 3. This ban has been constantly renewed ever since. The EU has also planned restrictions on PVC use, in order to reduce the volume of PVC waste produced. In 1998 *The Lancet* published a study identifying the high health risks of living near landfill sites. It found that pregnant women living near such sites had a significantly higher risk of producing children with birth defects such as spina bifida, holes in the heart and malformation of blood vessels.[15]

TROPICAL HARDWOODS

Tropical forests are home to half of all species on Earth, so the felling of forests has negative consequences for biodiversity. Forests are also home to native peoples, and play a major role in absorbing carbon dioxide, so limiting global warming. Some small-scale deforestation is carried out by local farmers, but most forests are damaged or destroyed as a result of commercial logging activities, or by commercial companies seeking to clear land for agriculture or construction. The normal method in the latter case is to set timber on fire. Burning forests releases large amounts of carbon dioxide into the atmosphere, and can lead to massive palls of smoke of the type that hung over Malaysia and Indonesia during the summer of 1998. Deforestation can also leave surrounding land vulnerable; for example, in Central America hillsides that were previously hurricane resistant collapsed into mudslides, killing thousands of people in low-lying villages. Commercial logging is normally carried out as an export industry targeted at the developed world, with the logs used in the construction industry (including DIY) or as raw pulp in paper manufacture.

One of the most depressing aspects of the 'green consumerism' of the early 1990s was the way genuine environmentally friendly products were swamped by the introduction of a rush of 'me too' products whose green credentials seemed to be concentrated in the colour of their packaging. This has led to widespread scepticism among the public about products claiming environmental or social benefits. For example, a study produced in October 2001 by the Nader organisation Public Citizen found that 95% of the price premium paid by Californian power users for 'green electricity' went on marketing and other costs, with only 5% supporting renewable energy.[16]

The only way to overcome such scepticism is for a trusted non-governmental organisation (NGO) to produce some kind of a quality mark, logo or eco-label guaranteeing that the product really has been produced in accordance with the claims made by it. In the UK the Soil Association has worked with British farmers to ensure that produce carrying the Soil Association mark meets its stringent rules governing the use of the description 'organic food'. In the US the Energy Star is a voluntary programme inaugurated by the EPA to identify products produced in an energy-efficient way. The most successful project in this regard seems to be the Forest Stewardship Council (FSC), an independent body founded in 1994, and funded by organisations as diverse as the European Union, Greenpeace, the World Wide Fund for Nature (WWF), and the Swedish furniture store Ikea. It has been followed by the Marine Stewardship Council, run on similar lines, which guarantees that fish carrying this eco-label have been caught using sustainable methods. The FSC's certification system confirms that timber bearing its label has been produced by methods that ensure sustainable forest management. FSC inspectors supervise logging in the areas it gives accreditation to. The FSC started by monitoring 800 000 hectares in 1995, but within five years this had grown to 18 000 000 hectares, an area larger than England and Wales. Here are the FSC core principles:[17]

- Logging practices do not threaten the health of the forest.
- Endangered animals and plants must be protected.
- Logging practices must not pollute rivers or use significant herbicides.
- Hillsides must not be left bare, leaving them vulnerable to erosion.
- Rights of workers and indigenous peoples must be respected.

The FSC's greatest triumph probably came in August 1999, when US group Home Depot, the world's largest DIY retailer, announced that it would stop selling the most endangered species of wood, and give preference to FSC certified products in its 1100 stores. Home Depot was the target of an unusual campaign by activist group Rainforest Action. The idea of a traditional consumer boycott was rejected on the grounds that so few US retailers stocked certified wood products that consumers would not be able to find alternatives. Instead Rainforest Action carried out a high-profile campaign using press advertising and sending activists into Home Depot stores to lecture customers, as well as 'ethical shoplifting', which involved publicly attempting to remove old forest timber from the stores without paying.[18] This campaign was supported by shareholder resolutions urging the company to stock sustainable wood. In August 2000 Lowe's, the second largest home improvement retailer in the US, announced that it too would be working with suppliers to avoid using 'old-growth' timber. By 2000 FSC certified wood accounted for about 40% of all wood sold in the UK home improvement market. The FSC explained that the campaign for sustainable timber was aimed to work with, rather than against, British DIY retailers such as Homebase and B&Q:

> Initially it was aimed at companies that had the greatest exposure to consumers. In this case it was do-it-yourself retailers like Homebase in the UK. They were able to answer consumers' questions about the use of tropical hardwoods by pointing to the certification their products carried, confirming that they were made from sustainable timber sources. In turn, the producers were able to see a market for these products.[19]

In fact, obtaining FSC certification is increasingly being seen as a way to preserve old woodland that can also produce a more profitable product for the landowner. It will perhaps achieve its greatest success if it can persuade timber-exporting countries such as Thailand and Malaysia, whose tropical rainforest is under threat, that it is in their own interest to seek FSC certification, as shown by quotation (a). Quotation (b) shows that Japanese producers have also woken up to this possibility:

> (a) Malaysian timber exporters are, for now, left with no alternatives but to subscribe to the Mexico-based Forest Stewardship Council (FSC) timber certification to achieve

greater success in the developed nation markets. Industry sources said the environment-conscious consumers of these countries trust the timber certification of FSC, a non-governmental organisation (NGO). He noted that the local timber exporters without FSC certification will continue to lose out, it indicates that Malaysia's timber come from a sustainable and well-managed forest and certification allows better pricing and value for money.[20]

(b) Trees from Japanese forests have been undermined by imported lumber. They have been poorly managed after deforestation, and although reforestation has been carried out, maintenance efforts have tended to be inadequate. What we must do is appeal more to the consumers [to use certified timber products] to protect the forests for the future.[21]

SMOG AND ACID RAIN

From the Industrial Revolution of the 1780s to the 1960s the UK relied on coal burning for power generation. In winter this resulted in what the Victorians described as pea-souper fogs, but what later generations would call smog, an oily emulsion of soot and caustic gases in a yellowish-green mist. Pea-souper fogs probably killed hundreds of people each winter, but the death scale rose to 4000 in December 1952. For five days a giant smog extended some twenty miles over London. Coal normally contains around 3–4% of sulphur, which is released as sulphur dioxide into the atmosphere. Once there, the interaction of sunlight and water vapour turns it into sulphuric acid, which falls as acid rain. It was believed that it was the combination of small soot particles, coated with sulphuric acid droplets, that proved fatal to people with breathing difficulties.

The government commissioned a committee of inquiry, which led to the passage of the Clean Air Act in 1956, giving local councils powers to establish smokeless zones, and provided grants to consumers to convert to smokeless fuel. Aided by the arrival of cheap natural gas from the North Sea in the 1960s, domestic coal burning became a thing of the past. By 1980 average smoke levels in London were only 10% of their 1950s levels, while sulphur dioxide levels had fallen 80%. (Coal-fired power generation is also a major contributor to global warming, as the combustion of coal produces about 250% of the carbon dioxide that results from the burning of natural gas per energy equivalent.) The 1956 Clean Air Act has been largely forgotten, but it was in fact the world's first major piece of environmental legislation. As such it is something the UK should be proud of. It also shows how major changes can be made to lifestyles for environmental reasons, if the political will is present. Smog may have gone away in the UK, but its prevalence is rising around the world, particularly in developing countries. In developed countries it is generally caused by the internal combustion engine.

BIODIVERSITY

Biological diversity is a sign of how efficiently the natural world uses the incoming energy from the Sun, from the abundant life forms seen in tropical forests to the sparse lichens of the frozen Arctic tundra. Generally speaking, the more diverse an ecosystem, the more robust it is, and the more able to withstand outside shocks. A single disease organism can wipe out an artificial plantation, but it will normally only target a small percentage of the trees that make up a natural forest. Reasons for being concerned about biodiversity range from the ethical to the instrumental. The former inquires what right humanity has to push other life forms to extinction. The latter notes that the manifold plant and animal life forms that exist in the tropics almost certainly contain chemicals and biological information that could be of great use in human medicine. Human action is the major cause of loss of biodiversity, which can result from deforestation, intensive agriculture, pollution and growing urbanisation, particularly in developing countries. Wetlands are other environmentally rich areas also at serious risk.

I was struck by the book *The Miner's Canary* by Niles Elridge, one of the world's leading palaeontologists, which discusses the repeated mass extinctions in the Earth's history, all of them probably resulting from abrupt changes in the planet's temperature. In it Eldridge notes that a mass extinction is occurring now:

> In the days before sophisticated sensing technology, miners often took canaries with them as they ventured down in to the bowels of the earth. The canaries were their early warning system for poisonous gas.... We destroy habitats for our own short-term economic good. We change the proportion of gases in the atmosphere, decreasing ozone and raising global temperatures.... All we have to do is to check the skies every spring to see the drastic decline of the songbird. Migrating songbirds fill the same role on a global scale that those caged canaries used to perform for miners. By now it is abundantly clear to all who will look that the global miner's canary is not at all well.[22]

As Eldridge says, those who will listen can hear numerous examples of biological alarm bells. Global amphibian populations have fallen markedly in recent years. Since amphibians breathe through their skin, and live on both water and land, they are particularly sensitive to environmental change. It is suggested that there are three factors decimating the frog and toad populations: infectious diseases, chemical pollution, and increased ultraviolet radiation resulting from the declining ozone layer. US research has found that salamander spawn shielded from ultraviolet light developed normally, while those exposed to sunlight either failed to hatch or they developed abnormally. There is also a substantial body of evidence that pesticides distort the development of young frogs and toads, so that they grow up with hideous deformities and soon die.[23]

Coral reefs are one of the most sensitive of the world's ecosystems to climate change. In the late 1990s thousands of miles of coral reef died in the Indian Ocean, the Pacific, and the Caribbean. They left bleached white stalks that could be seen from satellites. Coral reefs have been estimated to provide developing countries with revenues from fish and tourism worth $500 billion a year. They are also a specialised habitat for 93 000 fish species, 25% of the global total. Dr Thomas Goreau, an expert in coral reefs told the 1998 Buenos Aires summit on climate change:

This is an unprecedented natural disaster. The coral reefs are the canary in the mine for global warming. They will go first.... Unless this conference takes effective action, coral reefs and the benefits they provide will be condemned to death. Other ecosystems will follow.[24]

Biodiversity is also important in financial terms, i.e. a huge potential asset is being destroyed. In 1997 a paper in the journal *Nature* estimated that the world's ' ecosystem and natural capital' was worth $33 000 billion, a larger sum than the planet's entire domestic product. This figure included the value of wild species in providing a precious gene pool for agricultural and medicinal purposes, as about 25% of all prescription medicines contain ingredients derived from plants. Research produced in 1999 estimated that the combined annual global market for genetic resources in pharmaceuticals, crops, horticulture, cosmetics, etc., was between $500 billion and $800 billion.[25] However, there have been growing fears over biopiracy, i.e. that major Western corporations will patent naturally occurring genes found in developing countries, and make fortunes in the process. In his book *The Biotech Century* writer Jeremy Rifkin compared this process to the seizure of traditional common land in Tudor England. Land that had been used for community benefit in medieval England for centuries was suddenly enclosed, leading to riches for local landowners and impoverishment for the ordinary villagers.[26] According to Dr Pennapa Subcharoen of the Thailand Ministry of Public Health:

When drug companies come here and collect samples, they say it is the collective heritage of mankind. Then they study it, copy it, claim intellectual property rights on it, and come back to Thailand and make us pay for it.[27]

The 1992 Convention on Biological Diversity, signed by 158 countries, aims to rule out biopiracy by making genetic resources part of the patrimony of the state where they are found, rather than being owned in common by mankind, as was the case previously. The objective of the convention is to trade access to genetic resources in exchange for a fair and equitable sharing of benefits. Suffice it to say that this is a highly controversial subject where there is much scepticism over the benefits of the convention to either local communities or the living world. In 1995 one hundred different NGOs campaigned against the European Parliament's proposed directive on patenting living organisms, The Legal Protection of Biological Inventions. They claimed:

> Granting exclusive monopoly rights over plants, animals and human genetic material to corporations could prevent farmers from freely reproducing patented livestock, and place restrictions on the re-use of patented seed, as well as allow companies to claim ownership over entire species of food crops, medicinal plants, and livestock. This threatens the food security and self-reliance of countries in the Third World.[28]

GENETICALLY MODIFIED FOODS

Genetic modification (GM), known as genetic engineering by its opponents, is the biggest single new environmental issue to have arisen in recent years. Simply put, it describes the newly found ability of the biotechnology industry to take a gene found within one species and transplant it into another, e.g. a cold-resistant gene from a bacteria into a tomato, enabling the tomato to be grown in more northerly climes. Advocates of this technology claim it will enable the 'production' of naturally pest-resistant grains of rice and wheat that will vastly increase the Earth's ability to feed humanity. A good example is Golden Rice, rice that has been genetically modified to hold significant quantities of beta-carotene, something absent from normal rice. This can be metabolised in the human body to form vitamin A; in developing countries, vitamin A deficiency leads to millions of people becoming blind each year. There are several current and potential applications of GM technology, but these four seem the most important:

- *Agriculture.* At the moment, the biggest market for GM products is in food, particularly soya beans or maize, that has been genetically modified to increase crop yields and increase resistance to pests and diseases.

- *Medicine.* This includes the transplantation of human genes into animals to increase their productivity of medicinal ingredients, or to make them more accurate predictors of diseases and drug response in humans. GM bacteria are also used to manufacture products such as insulin.
- *Industrial.* GM bacteria are increasingly being used to produce food ingredients.
- *Human testing.* Genetic technology can be used to make accurate predictions of human health risks, e.g. propensity to heart attacks or breast cancer.

When I visited the US in late 1999 I was surprised by the apparent complacency of the US public over GM technology at a time when there were widespread demonstrations against GM food in Europe. In the UK in 1998–99 a wave of consumer protests and adverse media reports led large UK supermarket groups such as Tesco, Sainsbury and Marks & Spencer to impose tight GM labelling, and work to eliminate GM ingredients from their food products. Similar action was taken by France's largest retailer Carrefour, Delhaize of Belgium, and Migros of Switzerland. This action had global implications as Brazil, a large supplier of soya to the EU, scrapped plans to grow GM soya. There was a general suspicion in Europe that far too little was known about the effects of transposed genes for them to safely enter the human food chain. Critics noted the lack of detailed testing over GM products, which seemed to be in stark contrast to the exhaustive testing demanded of new pharmaceutical products. MORI polls showed that 77% of the UK population did not want GM crops grown in the UK, and 61% of the public did not want to consume genetically modified organisms (GMOs).[29]

US agribusiness and the US chemical industry have made massive investments in GM, which may explain why GM products have greater acceptance in America. For example, a US Department of Agriculture survey found that 68% of all the soya beans planted in the US in 2001 contained a Monsanto gene giving the plants immunity to Monsanto's widely used herbicide Roundup. This figure was an increase on the 54% of the American soya crop using GM the previous year.[30] About 25% of the US maize (corn) crop had also been sown with GM seed making it resistant to the corn borer, a common pest in the southern US. However, US consumer opposition has grown in recent years. For example, in September 2000 Kraft Foods ordered an instant recall of all taco shells it sold in the US, after learning they contained GM maize, called Starlink, that was supposed to be used for industrial purposes such as ethanol manufacture.[31]

Growth of GM agribusiness has been held back by unwillingness of other countries to take GM products. GM maize is effectively outlawed in the EU, which has not approved it for human consumption, while the EU has also imposed strict labelling requirements on food containing GM soya. Since there is low enthusiasm among EU consumers for GM products, such tight labelling requirements have resulted in very limited EU demand. There has been political pressure from the US for the EU to modify its tough anti-GM approach, as soya for example is one of the largest agricultural crops by value in the US, used in a variety of products such as cooking oil, baby food, and most vegetarian dishes. Indeed, Lord Clinton-Davis, UK trade minister in the first Blair government, warned that US pressure could lead to a trade war between the two blocs.[32]

One of the most controversial aspects of GM was the development by the Monsanto company of a terminator gene, a gene added to its products so that its GM seed would only grow for one year. Farmers would therefore not be able to save grain for next year's planting, standard practice in developing countries. There was such a public outcry against this that Monsanto dropped the idea. There is also a known risk that GM organisms may interbreed with natural ones to produce hybrids with potentially devastating consequences, e.g. insects with resistance to insecticides. (The above sentence was originally written by the author in a speculative vein in May 2001. Within six months of my writing it, it came true.) In August 2001 US scientists discovered that the US cotton moth was starting to develop resistance to the natural pesticide *Bacillus thuringiensis*. This was genetic material which had recently been inserted into US cotton plants.[33] Once GM material is released into the general environment, it is impossible to get it back. In 2000 the Church of England Ethical Investment Advisory Group produced a twelve-page report on genetically modified products. This led to a decision to ban

GM trials from being carried out on land owned by the Church. It stated:

> The genetic modification of crops is not beyond the range of acceptable human activities, but has called for a clear ethical framework for practical application of the science.... [It] considers the potential benefits of genetic modification for humankind to be too great to ignore, but does not feel it is yet appropriate to grant tenancies for crop trials on Church land given the uncertainties caused by the lack of an ethical framework.[34]

The Prince of Wales made a very public attack on GM foods:

> GM crops are presented as an essentially straightforward development that will increase yields through techniques that are merely an extension of traditional methods of plant breeding. I am afraid I cannot accept this. The fundamental difference between traditional and genetically modified plant breeding is that in the latter, genetic material from one species of plant, bacteria, virus, animal, or fish is artificially inserted into another species, with which they would never naturally breed.... Most of the GM plants marketed so far contain genes from bacteria which make them resistant to a broad spectrum weedkiller available from the same manufacturer. When the crop is sprayed with this weedkiller, every other plant in the filed is killed. The result is an essentially sterile field, providing neither food nor habitat for wildlife.[35]

ENVIRONMENTAL LIABILITY

Financial markets may ignore environmental concerns, but they have the unpleasant habit of turning into significant financial problems. Trustees of pension funds and charitable foundations may feel that the fiduciary duty to maximise financial returns prevents them from taking environmental considerations into account. In the author's opinion this approach is misguided, as fiduciary duty also obliges institutional investors to avoid possible calamitous losses, as indicated by environmental risks. While pension schemes may not have the expertise to do this themselves, it seems only reasonable to expect such skills from their investment managers.

Here is a practical example. Asbestos was widely used in the US construction and automotive industries from 1940 to 1970 as a cheap insulating and braking material. It was then realised that handling asbestos releases microscopic fibres that can lead to severe lung diseases. These run from the breathing difficulties of asbestosis to mesothelioma, a highly malignant cancer of the lining of the lung. These diseases typically have a long latency period, so the illness may not arise for twenty or thirty years after the critical exposure. While asbestos is no longer used in the developed world, it is still in general use as a cheap building material in developing countries. It is estimated that this could lead to over 1 million further deaths over the next thirty years. As the 1980s developed it was realised that this latency factor meant that companies who had produced or used asbestos before 1970 would face massive health liability suits in the US. By 1995 it was estimated that total personal injury damages could cost the US asbestos industry $80 billion. Yet despite this, investors continued to buy shares in companies whose potentially disastrous asbestos liabilities were well known.

Disaster finally struck in 2000–2001 when many leading US chemical and construction companies were forced into Chapter Eleven bankruptcy as a result of being financially overwhelmed by the asbestos litigation hitting them. In the winter 2000 of these included such industrial giants as Owens Corning (insulation materials), and Armstrong World Industries (building materials), even though Armstrong had last processed asbestos back in 1969.[36] In April 2001 they were followed into Chapter Eleven by the speciality chemical company W.R. Grace.[37] This was forced upon USG, the largest US manufacturer of plasterboard (gypsum drywall) in June 2001 when the company announced that it too would be seeking US federal bankruptcy court protection in the wake of spiralling asbestos costs.[38] Although the industry had paid billions of dollars in damages in the 1980s and 1990s, it was estimated that outstanding claims could still be over $30 billion.[39] As we saw at the beginning of this chapter, asbestos liability continued to destroy shareholder value in 2001–2, as shareholders in Halliburton and ABB discovered. Equity investors in Owens Corning, USG and W.R. Grace lost over 80–90% of the value of their investment in 2000. These asbestos cases indicate why environmental risks should be investigated by investment professionals on purely financial, due-diligence grounds.

At least US investors have the advantage that the SEC requires contingent environmental liabilities to be revealed in annual financial filings (10k filings). There is no such requirement in the EU. Chapter 3 noted how the US Superfund legislation came into being in the wake of the environmental emergencies such as Love Canal in the 1970s. The Superfund legislation was the first major legal vehicle to place environmental risk at the heart of the financial system – the banks and insurance companies. The essence of Superfund was the 'polluter pays' principle, written in very stringent legal language: *no-fault, joint and several, and retroactive.* 'No-fault', and 'retroactive' meant that the liability for cleaning up a site existed even if the disposal was legal at the time and irrespective of the degree of care applied. 'Joint and several' implied that anyone connected with the site was liable, even if totally different from the original polluter. In other words, if the original polluters were unable to pay or to be traced, banks and insurance companies with a contractual relationship to the site 'inherited' the liability. Not surprisingly this clause resulted in a spate of lawsuits targeted at financially strong companies viewed as having deep pockets even if they had only a slight connection with the original polluted site. The American insurance rating agency A.M. Best estimated in the spring of 1994 that the US insurance industry would need to set aside $260 billion to meet future environmental and pollution claims. Best described potential environmental liabilities as constituting the single largest threat to the financial well-being of the US non-life insurance sector.

It seems fair to state that while relatively little attention appears to have been paid to potential environmental liabilities by equity market analysts, banking and insurance companies have taken environmental risks much more seriously. All the major banks set up environmental risk assessment units in the 1990s. In the UK the National Westminster Bank created an environmental management unit (EMU) to integrate environmental risk into its loan-pricing structure. The process was to look at the industries a company operated in, and allocate a risk category accordingly. This stated:

> We have already started to formulate an informal policy to-
> wards the environment as a result of the deals that we have
> chosen to reject and those we have adopted.... By financing
> projects where environmental risks are deemed to be within en-
> vironmental tolerances, we are effectively shaping environmen-
> tal practice on a case by case basis. Environmental risk is just
> another aspect of risk management. All the usual risks are there:
> market, financial, capital cost, liabilities actual and contingent,
> reputational and strategic.[40]

Such large potential liabilities created a market for detailed environmental risk assessment. The Washington-based Investor Responsibility Research Center (IRRC) used EPA data to build a massive
environmental database on US companies. Corporate environmental risk ratings were constructed using quantitative data based on
three variables: emissions efficiency, a spill index and a compliance
index. The IRRC argued that investors in corporate bonds automatically checked a company's credit rating, and that increasingly they
would combine this with environmental risk ratings. According to
IRRC:

> Investors who fail to...assess environmental risk in a system-
> atic way...may be setting themselves up for lower returns.
> Once the financial community realises companies are having
> to spend hundreds of millions on this issue, the market reacts
> immediately.[41]

Environmental liability received a lot of media attention in the
1980s, but press coverage tailed away in the 1990s. However, the new
millennium seems likely to see greater media interest after the shock
announcement in August 2001 that the US company General Electric
(GE) would be required by the EPA to clean up the Hudson River at an
estimated cost of $460 million. GE was required to dredge 40 miles
of the Hudson downstream from Albany and remove 2.65 million
cubic yards of soil contaminated with PCBs. The EPA stated its belief that PCBs were possible carcinogens, in line with the medical
data on page 126. GE had manufactured electrical capacitors using
PCBs at two sites on the Hudson from 1947 until 1977, when the federal government outlawed their production. The EPA estimated that

1.3 million pounds of PCBs may have been deposited in the river. As a result, New York State law banned the eating of fish caught in a 43 mile stretch south of Albany, and urged pregnant women and children under 15 not to eat any fish caught in the lower Hudson. The day the EPA ruling was announced, GE stock fell $0.75, reducing its market capitalisation by $7.5 billion. Although $460 million was not a critical sum to a huge company like GE, investors may have been worried that this was just the first of a series of clean-up costs facing the company, which was believed to be linked to 80 more Superfund sites.[42]

Environmental risks extend beyond the level of the individual company. Historically, major development banks such as the World Bank have negotiated with national governments about development loans. Many international resource companies seek World Bank involvement in projects in developing countries as a kind of political risk insurance. However, in the 1990s the World Bank received severe criticism from a number of environmental agencies for ignoring the environment, biodiversity and native peoples in its deliberations over projects that could cause massive construction works and disruption. In 1996 the World Bank announced that henceforth it would carry out detailed environmental audits of any projects in which it was involved. These require it to:[43]

- Carry out detailed local consultations
- Assess any costs due to loss of crops
- Ensure all possible measures are taken to prevent oil spillages
- Assess disruption caused to native peoples, and compensation due
- Assess revenue management, and how much of the revenues go to the local communities

The need for extensive environmental audit and consultation has also moved to Asia, a region where historically people have tended to unquestioningly accept the wisdom of governments. Not any more. A good example is the controversy that blew up in the late 1990s over the construction of the Samut Prakarn wastewater plant, planned outside Bangkok in Thailand. The Asia Development Bank (ADB) was the main backer of this plan through a $750 million long-term loan. The ADB thought the project would go ahead smoothly once it had received the approval of the Thai government. However, the plant would also send effluent over mussel farms in the Gulf of Thailand, destroying the livelihood of traditional mussel farmers. They raised such an outcry over the Samut Prakarn proposals that in 2001 the ADB was forced to commission an independent health and environmental audit of the project, the first time the ADB had ever felt obliged to carry out such a step.[44]

REFERENCES

1. 'Asbestos Claims Played Down', *Financial Times*, 11 December 2001.
2. 'ABB Takes Asbestos Claim Charge', *Financial Times*, 31 January 2002.
3. Walter Patterson, *The Plutonium Business*, Penguin, 1982.
4. 'Tough Love for the Nuclear Industry', *Financial Times*, 9 February 2001.
5. Rosalie Bertell, *No Immediate Danger*, The Women's Press, 1985.
6. Rachel Weston, nuclear research officer for Friends of the Earth, quoted in *ENI Bulletin*, 6 August 1997.
7. 'Nuclear Waste "Is a Disaster in Waiting"', *Daily Telegraph*, 17 December 1995.
8. 'Sheep and Trees Are Acting Strangely at "End of World"', *Wall Street Journal*, 15 January 1990.
9. Friends of the Earth press release, March 1999.
10. 'Pesticide May Be the Cause of Disease', *Financial Times*, 6 November 2000.
11. 'Pesticide Pollution Is Linked to Cancer', *The Times*, 29 October 1999.
12. 'Studying Toxins' Link to Genes', *Wall Street Journal*, 1 August 2001.
13. 'EPA Draft Report Finds High Risk in Dioxin', *Wall Street Journal*, 18 May 2000.
14. 'Swedish Study Finds Phthalates Pose Health Risks', *Wall Street Journal*, 4 July 2001.
15. 'Baby Defects "Linked" to Toxic Dumps', *Daily Telegraph*, 7 August 1998.
16. 'Green Products: Consumers Count Cost over Ideology', *Financial Times*, 5 November 2001.
17. FSC website.
18. 'Greyer and Wiser, Environmental Activists Tinker with Tactics', *Wall Street Journal*, 7 September 2000.
19. FSC press release, June 2001.
20. *Business Times* (Malaysia), 19 June 2001.
21. 'Forest Certification Takes Root Across Nation', *Yomiuri Shimbun*, 8 September 2000.
22. Niles Eldridge, *The Miner's Canary: Unravelling the Mysteries of Extinction*, Virgin Books, 1992.
23. 'Are Frogs Dying to Tell Us Something?', *Financial Times*, 15 August 1998.
24. 'World Coral Reefs Destroyed by Global Warming', *Daily Telegraph*, 13 November 1998.
25. Kate and Laird, *The Commercial Use of Biodiversity*, Earthscan 1998.
26. Jeremy Rifkin, *The Biotech Century*, Gollancz, 1998.
27. Quoted in 'Genetic Pirates Walk the Plank', *Financial Times*, 9 January 1999.
28. Quoted in 'MEPs Urged to Vote Against "Patents on Life"', *Financial Times*, 9 January 1995.
29. MORI, source the Soil Association, *Genetic Engineering: the Key Issues*, 1999.

30. 'US Farmers Expand Use of Genetically Modified Seeds', *Wall Street Journal*, 2 July 2001.
31. 'Kraft Urges Tougher Oversight of Crop Biotechnology', *Wall Street Journal*, 25 September 2000.
32. 'Ex-minister Warns of Clash with US on Modified Food', *Financial Times*, 29 September 1998.
33. 'Mutations Could Make Organic Pesticides Useless', *The Independent*, 6 August 2001.
34. The Church of England Ethical Investment Advisory Group, *Genetically Modified Organisms*, April 2000.
35. HRH The Prince of Wales, 'Seeds of Disaster', *Daily Telegraph*, 7 June 1998.
36. 'Asbestos Litigation Hits US Stocks', *Wall Street Journal*, 28 December 2000.
37. 'W.R. Grace in Bankruptcy to Cope with Asbestos Suits', Bloomberg, 2 April 2001.
38. 'Payouts Cause USG to Seek Protection in Bankruptcy Court', *Wall Street Journal*, 26 June 2001.
39. 'Asbestos Sparks New Jitters in the US', *Financial Times*, 31 January 2001.
40. 'Finance with Strings', *Investors' Chronicle*, 20 September 1991.
41. 'Balance Sheet Poison: Environmental Liability Comes to Europe', *Institutional Investor*, August 1993.
42. 'GE Told by EPA to Spend $460m Dredging Hudson', Bloomberg newswire, 1 August 2001.
43. The World Bank website.
44. 'The Toxic Politics of Waste Water', *Financial Times*, 25 January 2002.

7

...To Sustainable Development

AN INTEGRATED APPROACH TO THE ENVIRONMENT

There has been a significant change in general environmental thinking over the last twenty years. In the 1970s and early 1980s the majority of environmental problems were relatively small and localised. They could be solved by specific remediation (clean-up) measures, or by national pollution regulations designed to reduce smog, acid rain and water pollution. In other words, they were 'end of pipe solutions'. However, the threat of global warming has brought a totally different dimension to environmental thinking; the problems are obviously on a global scale, with the consequences stretching out far into the future. Indeed, one of the major problems inhibiting action to reduce global warming has been the political difficulty of persuading a generation requiring instant gratification to curb current consumption in order to improve the life chances of future generations. Global warming also requires an international political consensus, and a fundamental rethink of the way energy is used.

Traditionally people working within financial markets have tended to be sceptical about the need to move towards sustainability. However, such people, even if they are personally dubious about the threat from global warming, should note that the combination of consumer pressure and government action implies major consequences for the operation of financial markets. There may be significant downside risks in some areas, but there are also likely to be great opportunities for financial practitioners who are able to exploit emerging new financial markets. Examples of potentially attractive new businesses include renewable energy, emissions trading, corporate environmental evaluation, and pollution liability risk assessment. Hence there are pragmatic, as well as value-based reasons to incorporate both sustainability and financial factors in the evaluation of a company's prospects. (True also for the bond market; global warming is likely to have particularly adverse impacts on some countries.)

It is easy to see how the investment in new growth industries can make sense from a financial viewpoint. However, doing so solely to make investment profits, without the deeper knowledge and commitment that derives naturally from socially responsible investing, is in fact likely to prove disappointing as a financial strategy. For example, the late 1980s saw the rise of 'green consumerism', and capital flowed into allegedly green stocks seeking a high financial return. Investors were attracted by the apparent growth prospects of retailers supplying green consumers such as Body Shop in the UK, or Ben & Jerry's ice cream in the US. There also seemed ample scope for profits from reducing or treating pollution (end-of-pipe solutions). In fact, as demonstrated in Chapter 10, these proved to be disappointing investments from a financial viewpoint. This episode demonstrates perhaps one recurring theme of this book, that the deeper environmental and social knowledge of specialist SRI asset managers gives them a competitive edge compared to conventional investors who just see the environment as a source of profit.

THE CASE FOR SUSTAINABILITY

Public disquiet that industrial pollution was resulting in anthropogenic (human-made) climate change led to the creation in 1972 of the United Nations Environment Programme (UNEP), mandated to analyse the evidence of environmental change. In 1983 UNEP founded the World Commission on Environment and Development, led by the former Norwegian prime minister Gro Harlem Brundtland. The Brundtland Report was published in May 1987, creating a framework for environmental thinking that has been used ever since. The Report's description of 'sustainable development' is generally regarded as definitive:

Development that meets the needs of the present without compromising the ability of future generations to meet their own needs. At a minimum, sustainable development must not endanger the natural systems that support life on Earth: the atmosphere, the waters, the soils, and the living beings. It contains within it two key concepts:

(a) the concept of 'needs', in particular the essential needs of the world's poor, to which overriding priority should be given; and
(b) the idea of limitations imposed by the state of technology and social organisation on the environment's ability to meet present and future needs.[1]

Critics of environmentalism sometimes accuse it of ignoring the needs of millions of people who live in dire poverty. However, the Brundtland Report explicitly condemned what it called such a 'naive approach'. It stressed that it is normally impossible to separate economic development from environmental issues, adding that over the longer term, environmental degradation undermines economic growth. It did not condemn economic growth as such, for it argued that such growth was essential for poverty eradication. The Brundtland Report did point out however that much economic growth only benefits people living in developed countries, as it leaves growing numbers of people in developing countries in absolute poverty, as well as degrading the physical environment. The report avoided detailed policy recommendations, but it did highlight certain areas of concern:

- *Native peoples.* The traditional rights of tribal peoples should be recognised.
- *Eco-diversity.* Diversity of species should be preserved, particularly when development involves destruction of tropical forests.
- *Energy use.* The world should develop 'low-energy paths' based on renewable sources, which would form the foundation of the global energy structure during the twenty-first century.
- *Economic added value.* The pattern of world trade in minerals should be modified to allow exporters a higher share in the value added from mineral use.[2]

From the viewpoint of socially responsible investment, the key point to note is that protection of the environment is irretrievably linked to the other core SRI issues. This linkage was aptly described by Amory Lovins, head of the Rocky Mountain Institute in Colorado, and author of *Natural Capitalism*:

> Industrial capitalism is inadvertently liquidating its two most important sources of capital – the natural world and properly functioning societies. There are four forms of capital – goods, money, people, and nature, providing ecosystems without which there is no life and no economic activity....It is essential to use nature more productively, wringing four or ten or a hundred times more work from each unit of topsoil, energy, water, or anything we borrow from the planet. We need to redesign production on biological principles, with closed loops, no waste, no toxicity. We need to adopt a business model from an economy that occasionally makes things and sells them, to a continuous flow of value and service, so that both the provider and the customer are rewarded for following the first two steps. Then, any profit is reinvested in natural capital because that's what we are shortest of.[3]

The concept of sustainability is therefore quite clear; the problem for socially responsible investors is how to assess the success of companies in integrating it into their operations. In the author's opinion the CERES principles, launched by the US Social Investment Forum in 1989, are the best general statement of environmental good practice for the corporate sector. CERES stands for Coalition for Environmentally Responsible Economies, and by the end of 2001 CERES had over 70 members working in the socially responsible or environmental field, including some of the leading names in US SRI who hold over $300 billion in investment assets. These include Calvert Group, Friends Ivory & Sime, the Interfaith Center on Corporate Responsibility (ICCR), KLD, the New York City Comptroller's Office, and Trillium Asset Management. It also has 58 corporate members who have committed themselves to its principles. The list includes some of the largest companies in America: American Airlines, Bank of America, Baxter International, Bethlehem Steel, Coca-Cola USA,

Bethlehem Steel, Ford Motor Company, General Motors, ITT Industries, Nike, Northeast Utilities, Polaroid, and Sunoco. Here are the CERES principles:[4]

1. *Protection of the biosphere.* We will reduce and make continual progress towards eliminating the release of any substance that may cause environmental damage to the air, water, or the Earth or its inhabitants. We will conserve non-renewable natural resources through efficient use and careful planning.
2. *Sustainable use of natural resources.* We will make sustainable use of renewable natural resources, such as water, soils, and forests. We will conserve non-renewable natural resources through efficient use and careful planning.
3. *Reduction and disposal of wastes.* We will reduce and where possible eliminate waste through source reduction and recycling. All waste will be handled and disposed of through safe and responsible methods.
4. *Energy conservation.* We will conserve energy and improve the energy efficiency of our internal operations and of the goods and services we sell. We will make every effort to use environmentally safe and sustainable energy sources.
5. *Risk reduction.* We will strive to minimise the environmental, health, and safety risks to our employees and the communities in which we operate through safe technologies, facilities, and operating procedures, and by being prepared for emergencies.
6. *Safe products and services.* We will reduce and where possible eliminate the use, manufacture, or sale of products and services that cause environmental damage or health or safety hazards. We will inform our customers of the environmental impacts of our products or services and try to correct unsafe use.
7. *Environmental restoration.* We will promptly and responsibly correct conditions we have caused that endanger health, safety or the environment. To the extent feasible, we will redress injuries we have caused to persons or damage we have caused to the environment, and will restore the environment.
8. *Informing the public.* We will inform in a timely manner everyone who may be affected by conditions that might endanger health, safety or the environment. We will regularly seek advice

and counsel through dialogue with persons in communities near our facilities. We will not take any action against employees for reporting dangerous incidents or conditions to management or to appropriate authorities.

9. *Management commitment.* We will implement these principles and sustain a process that ensures that the Board of Directors and Chief Executive Officer are fully informed about pertinent environmental issues and are fully responsible for environmental policy. In selecting our Board of Directors we will consider demonstrated environmental commitment as a factor.

10. *Audits and reports.* We will conduct an annual self-evaluation of our progress in implementing these Principles. We will support the timely creation of generally accepted environmental audit procedures. We will annually complete the CERES Report which will be made available to the public.

EVALUATING THE THREAT OF CLIMATE CHANGE

According to mainstream scientific opinion, the substantial increase in global energy consumption over the last fifty years has had a material and accelerating affect in causing global warming. This has occurred as a result of the accumulation of greenhouse gases in the atmosphere, principally carbon dioxide, methane and nitrous oxide. The process of rapid climate change is believed to result in much more severe weather patterns, with a growing frequency of major storms, droughts and flood disasters. The forecast melting of the vast amount of water currently locked in the Greenland and Antarctic ice sheets will also resulting in the drowning of much low-lying land. The thesis of global warming squares with the evidence of our own eyes. In the UK, for example, summers are becoming hotter and dryer, winter and spring rainfall more intensive, leading to widespread flooding exactly as predicted by models of global warming.[5] The Climate Change Unit at the University of East Anglia has found that the average UK temperature was essentially stable from 1700, when accurate measurements began, to 1940. By 1997 the average UK temperature was almost 1°C higher than the previous baseline.[6] Republican US Senator Ted Stevens of Alaska is no natural ally of the green movement, but he admitted his concerns over the impact on climate change on his state in February 2002:

> Pack ice, which insulates our coastal villages from winter storms, has shrunk. Our forests are moving north where it is warming, and airports near coastal villages are inundated with sea water.[7]

Of course some loud voices argue forcefully that climate change is not taking place. Their arguments against global warming tend to be of two types: (a) that there is considerable uncertainty about the world's meteorology, and (b) that there is a natural long-term variation in the Earth's mean temperature. There is much truth in both points, if not in the conclusions drawn from them. The most authoritative data on global warming is produced by the Intergovernmental Panel on Climate Change (IPCC), set up by the United Nations in 1988 to advise governments on the whole question of global warming. It consists of data and models produced by around 300 of the most eminent scientists in the world working in the field of meteorology and climate modelling. The IPCC's first assessment report was published in 1990 and warned that 60–80% reductions in carbon dioxide emissions were necessary in order to stabilise atmospheric carbon dioxide levels. In July 2001 the Universities Superannuation Scheme hosted a seminar on global warming, based around 'Climate change: a risk management challenge for institutional investors', a detailed paper by Mark Mansley of Claros Consulting and Andrew Dlugolecki. The authors addressed this issue:

> For those who are not climate experts, and particularly when making a risk assessment of climate change, the IPCC provides outsiders with an unparalleled summary of a very complex area of science. In particular, we note that as a summary, encompassing a wide range of models and different perspectives, the IPCC reports are far more credible than any single paper or observation.[8]

The second IPCC assessment report, published in 1995, simply stated that 'the balance of evidence suggests a discernible human influence on global climate'. The culprit behind global warming is the rising proportion of greenhouse gases that keep the Sun's radiation penned in the Earth's atmosphere. There are three main greenhouse gases: carbon dioxide (CO_2); nitrous oxide (NO_2) and methane. Their concentrations in the atmosphere can be independently measured, and they show a clear correlation with global warming. There is also increasing evidence that three fluorine-based gases also play a significant part in climate change: HFCs, PFCs and sulphur hexafluroride. The latest IPCC report on global warming, published in January 2001, made for depressing reading. It warned that surface temperatures could rise by 1.4–5.8°C over the next hundred years, far higher than the previous estimate of 1 to 3.5°C. It added that this would be catastrophic for low countries such as Bangladesh that would see much of their landmass disappear under the sea. It concluded:

> New and stronger evidence [indicates] that most of the observed warming of the last 50 years is attributable to human activities.[9]

Recently the work of the IPCC was independently assessed by two distinguished groups of scientists: (a) the National Academies of Science of seventeen different countries, and (b) the US National Academy of Sciences. Here are their conclusions:

(a) The IPCC is the world's most reliable source of information on climate change and its sources.... It is evident that human activities are already contributing adversely to global climate change. Business as usual is no longer a viable option.[10]

(b) The IPCC's conclusion that most of the observed warming of the last 50 years is likely to have been due to the increase in greenhouse gas concentrations accurately reflects the current thinking of the scientific community on the subject.... The full IPCC Working Group report is an admirable summary of the research activities in climate science, and the full report is adequately summarised in the Technical Summary.[11]

Over the years I have noticed that many of the critics of global warming do so for reasons that are not based on climate science. Many of them seem to be economists with no specialist training in the complex subject of meteorology. The arguments are often of the form that if there were a problem, the market would price it in; the market is not pricing it in, therefore there is no problem. The George W. Bush administration was advised against signing the Kyoto Protocol by various economists who wrote papers with titles like 'Requiem for Kyoto'. Richard Schmalensee, an MIT economist, predicted that the protocol would require the US to close all of its coal-fired power plants to get 50% of the way to its Kyoto targets, while another economist stated that implementing the protocol could amount to a $400 tax on every American.[12] I suspect that there would be a loud outcry if meteorologists denounced conventional economic thinking as nonsense, and yet economists feel free to do the same in reverse! There are also groups who attack the consensus on global warming for what seems purely ideological grounds, a phenomenon observed by Jonathan Porritt in 1994:

> One reason might be the emergence of the so-called contrarians; predominantly right wing groups who devote their lives to rubbishing the consensus about global warming. There are dozens of such organisations in the US, many of them funded by the businesses which stand to lose most as the world moves to do something about global warming....As eminent meteorologist Sir John Houghton commented 'the quality of their work is simply pathetic'.[13]

As Porritt mentioned, some of the attacks on global warming come from organisations linked to oil producers and oil companies with a vested interest in persuading the public that climate change is nothing to worry about. President George W. Bush comes from Texas, and has strong links with the oil industry, which was one of the leading donors to the Bush campaign during the 2000 election. It was hardly a great surprise in April 2001 when he publicly stated that he opposed the Kyoto Protocol on the grounds that it would 'cause serious harm to the US economy', and that he had no intention of imposing emission limits on US power stations. The *Wall Street Journal* reported Bush's plans to boost the oil industry and open up the hitherto sacrosanct Alaskan National Wildlife Reserve to oil drilling, under the headline 'Bush's Big Backers Now Seek a Return on Their Investment'.[14]

I will end this section will the assessment of the IPCC's work by quoting again from the detailed study of climate change for investors produced by Mansley and Dlugolecki:[15]

Understanding climate change is a major challenge for scientists and stretches the scientific community's ability to understand and model complex phenomena to the limit. As such, investors need to come to an informed judgement of the credibility of the science and the implications of any uncertainties.... The work of the IPCC is essentially to draw together the vast body of scientific knowledge in an understandable way that can be used by policy-makers and others. It has much to recommend it:

- It is an inclusive process, with sceptical scientists and others able to take part.
- It is based on a review of the best available science.
- Its own work is subject to external review by experts and by governments.
- The summaries are subject to line by line approval by governments: nothing which cannot be justified is accepted.
- The way IPCC has evolved through three major iterations has enhanced its credibility: weaknesses have been addressed and many conclusions have been strengthened or refined. There has been no major reversal of earlier conclusions.
- Potential alternative explanations for climate change, such as 'aerosol' cooling, variations in solar radiation, historic climate data, potential 'carbon fertilisation' of plants, and difficulties in cloud modelling, have either been used to refine the models or are included in the consideration of uncertainty.

RIO, KYOTO, AND BEYOND

The first IPCC assessment report led to the calling of the Earth Summit, held in Rio de Janeiro in June 1992, where ten thousand delegates discussed the threat posed by global warming. The concerns of the IPPC were then ratified into the Framework Convention on

Table 7.1 *Climate change: diplomatic timetable*

1988	Intergovernmental Panel on Climate Change (IPCC) set up
1990	First assessment report of IPPC published
	First meeting of the Advisory Group on Greenhouse Gases (AGGG)
	First meeting of the Intergovernmental Panel on Climate Change (IPCC)
1991	First meeting of the Intergovernmental Negotiating Committee (INC)
1992	Fifth meeting of INC/II prior to Rio Earth Summit
	UN Conference on Environment and Development, or Earth Summit, Rio de Janeiro Framework Convention on Climate Change (FCCC) ratified
1995	First Conference of the Parties (COP-1) in Berlin
1996	Second Conference of the Parties (COP-2) in Geneva; Geneva Declaration adopted
1997	Third Conference of the Parties (COP-3) in Kyoto; Kyoto Protocol adopted
1998	Fourth Conference of the Parties (COP-4) in Buenos Aires
1999	Fifth Conference of the Parties (COP-5) in Bonn
2000	Sixth Conference of the Parties (COP-6) in the Hague
2001	Seventh Conference of the Parties (COP-7) in Bonn

Climate Change (FCCC) in May 1992. The FCCC then led continuing negotiations on implementing its recommendations, to the point in December 1997 when the Kyoto Protocol came into existence (Table 7.1). Technically the Kyoto agreement was a protocol to the FCCC, while the Conference of the Parties (COP) is the executive body charged with implementing them.

The 1997 Kyoto Climate Conference set detailed procedures to reduce greenhouse gas emissions. It came close to collapse when the US negotiators refused to set any binding targets to cut carbon dioxide emissions. However, after long and intense negotiations, the Clinton administration finally agreed the targets set by the Kyoto Protocol. (Jeremy Leggett's book *The Carbon War*[16] is an invaluable source of reference on this momentous decision.) The Kyoto Protocol decreed that total greenhouse gas emissions by the main industrial countries should fall by 5.2% from their 1990 benchmark level by 2008–12. The US agreed to a 7% reduction, the EU 8% and Japan 7%. It was a

155

Table 7.2 *Forecast global CO_2 emissions (millions of tonnes) 1990–2010*

	OECD	Transition economies	Developing countries	World
1990	10640	4066	6171	20878
1997	11467	2566	8528	22561
2010	13289	3091	13195	29575
2020	14298	3814	17990	36102

Source: Copyright © OECD/IEA 2001. Reproduced by permission.

legal requirement of the Kyoto Protocol that it would not come into force unless it was ratified by 55 countries that accounted for 55% of the developed world's greenhouse gas emissions.

It has to be said that progress on meeting the Kyoto guidelines has been slow. In fact the EU seems the only major economic bloc that has actively sought to implement Kyoto measures by raising energy taxes and implementing tougher emissions regulations. As a result, in 1999 EU greenhouse gas emissions were 4% below 1990s levels. The US was a long way off, with emissions 16% above Kyoto levels, while Japanese emissions were 7% above 1990 levels despite Japanese economic stagnation. In 1999 the UN forecast that by 2010 the emissions from Organisation for Economic Cooperation and Development (OECD) countries would be about 18% above the 1990 baseline, rather than the 5% agreed reduction.[17] Indeed, it also forecast that rapid growth in emissions from developing countries would raise their total carbon dioxide emissions by 73% from their 1990 levels by 2010 (Table 7.2).

The Conference of the Parties held in Bonn in July 2001 was a tense and fractious affair. The blunt refusal of the George W. Bush administration to be involved meant the Kyoto Protocol came close to collapse. Since the US accounted for about 34% of Annex I emissions, there was little room for manoeuvre on the condition that it had to be agreed by countries accounting for 55% of OECD (Annex I) 1990 greenhouse gas emissions. The chairman of the Bonn summit, Dutch environment minister Jan Pronk, took the summit to the wire before a deal was finally agreed by the representatives of the 178 countries present. This resulted in the Kyoto Protocol coming into force without the US. George W. Bush rejected Kyoto on the grounds that it would cost too much for the US economy, but a study by the European Commission found that compliance with Kyoto could cost the EU €3.7 billion in the period 2008–12, or 0.06% of EU gross domestic product.[18] The failure of America to participate in the Kyoto Protocol means that US companies will not be able to participate in the planned emissions trading system.

The US opt-out from the Kyoto Protocol has generated fears that it could lead to increased trade difficulties between the EU and the US, as European manufacturers are forced to bear additional costs not borne by American competitors. It has also generated fears within the US that European countries that ratify the treaty will get a head start in developing innovative technologies in renewable energy and in emission trading. The US chemical giant Du Pont voiced concern about both issues:

> It is realistic to expect some pressure from Europeans and others if they are going forward under Kyoto, to want to insulate their industry from the potentially competitive implications of taking on that burden unilaterally.... The global warming issue will create fundamental changes in energy generation and usage. If the US is not subject to significant pressure and incentives to improve, it may not make significant technological advances. From a competitive standpoint the economies that get ahead on that curve will be in a better position to compete in that environment.[19]

THE RISING COST OF NATURAL DISASTERS

The most immediate impact of global warming, both on people and financial markets, is likely to be felt in increasing numbers of weather-related catastrophes such as severe storms and flooding. The reinsurance company Munich Re has collected data on natural disasters for many years. Its annual reports offer powerful confirmation that a significant deterioration of the world's weather has taken place. Table 7.3 illustrates the rising number of natural disasters over the last four decades expressed in number of incidents

Table **7.3** *Major natural disasters 1960–2001: all dollar amounts are indexed to 2001 values*

	1960–69	1970–79	1980–89	1990–1999	1992–2001
Number	27	47	63	89	78
Economic loss ($bn)	75.7	136.1	211.3	652.3	579.9
Insurance loss ($bn)	7.2	12.4	26.4	123.2	103.7

Source: Climate Change and Natural Disasters: Effects on the Insurance Industry. Copyright the GeoRisks Research Department, the Munich Reinsurance Company. Reproduced by permission.

and in their real cost. The report for 2000 expressed the company's belief that climate change was instrumental in increasing the number of catastrophic climatic events. The year 2000 saw a significant increase in the number of natural catastrophes. By good fortune none of them hit a major population centre, so the money cost to the insurance industry actually fell. The company's geoscience research unit stated:

> The year 2000 saw a record 850 natural catastrophes, 100 more than 1999, and around 200 more than the average for the 1990s.... If the trends of the last ten years continue, the climate in a few decades will exceed anything man has experienced. A great number of people will be at risk.... Global warming is already causing extreme weather events, but there will be more heatwaves, floods, and windstorms as it accelerates turbulence in the atmosphere's 'heat engine'.[20]

Table 7.3 shows how the insurance costs of natural disasters have soared over the last decade. The credit rating agency Standard & Poor's noted the progressive ratcheting up of natural catastrophe insurance claims during the 1990s; 1999 was the worst year on record (2000 was less bad as described above), with eight mega-disasters occurring that cost over $1 billion each. Standard & Poor's interest was the effect of this on the global reinsurance industry; the agency warned that it might be obliged to downgrade the credit rating of most reinsurers as a result.[21]

It seems worth adding that the UK government has done serious contingency planning for the severe consequences of global warming. In February 2001 the UK's Ministry of Defence (MOD) warned that future wars were likely as a result of global warming, while a severe shortage of fresh water supplies by 2025 could also trigger conflict.[22] The MOD was also concerned that growing natural catastrophes in the UK would put additional demands on the UK's armed forces. The UN has also warned that growing water shortages would lead to future wars.[23] The chief medical officer for the UK's National Health Service (NHS) warned that climate change was predicted to add to the burden on the NHS through rising levels of skin cancer. He also expressed anxiety about the arrival of tropical diseases such as malaria in the UK as a result of mosquitoes becoming resident in the salt marshes of southern England.[24] The Department of the Environment and the Regions (DETR) stated its concern that the cost of maintaining the UK's flood defences could quadruple to £600 million a year due to global warming, while water supplies in England and Wales could fall 20% by 2020.

The impact of climate change on the UK is expected to be relatively mild compared to its effect on many other parts of the world. Asia is likely to be one of the worst-affected regions, as the effects of global warming will be felt on top of those resulting from the region's own environmental degradation. Asia's problems stem from rapid urbanisation, including the worst air pollution levels in the world. The region has already seen the destruction of 90% of its native wildlife habitats to construction and agriculture; in part this has caused the march of deserts and growing pressure on water supplies. The Asian Development Bank (ADB) warned in 2001 that the region was on 'the brink of environmental catastrophe'. It reported that Asia would replace the OECD as the world's major source of greenhouse gases by 2015. Measured by levels of particulates in the air, 12 of the world's city's with the worst air pollution were in Asia, causing an estimated 100 000 premature deaths a year, and the loss of 1 billion work days. ADB environmental specialist Tahir Qadri warned:

Environmental degradation in the region is pervasive, accelerating, and unabated. Rapid population growth has contributed to pressure on land being the most severe in the world....Environmental mismanagment affects the poor first. Air pollution affects people living on the street, not in cars.

You can't separate poverty reduction from environmental management.[25]

NEW MARKETS FOR RENEWABLES

Having discussed the adverse consequences of climate change, I shall now examine its beneficial aspects. Ratification of the Kyoto Protocol, albeit without the participation of the US, will encourage the growth of a number of new businesses geared to sustainability. Today's 'industries of the future' include wind power, solar energy and fuel cells, all designed to replace older, polluting technologies. The world's major financial centres, New York, Tokyo and London, are all well aware that emissions trading could become a major business opportunity.

One of the key drivers behind the increased use of renewable energy is global deregulation of electricity distribution, which in turn enables consumers to choose 'green electricity'. In California and certain parts of Europe consumers can do so for a premium price, while in Germany houses generating their own solar energy are able to sell surplus electricity to the national grid at a profit. The US does not have the same kind of national grid, but 36 states have agreed to offer some kind of net metering. This means that homes generating solar and wind power can offer it to the local power company, and draw down the credits when they need to. This was not possible in the UK until liberalisation of the power supply market occurred in 1999 under compulsion from a European directive. From that date over ten suppliers have offered green energy for a small premium of 3–10%. The way the system works in the UK is that a supplier anywhere in the country can provide electricity to a customer in a distinct geographical region. Under the 'green tariff' system, the supplier agrees to supply the National Grid with electricity guaranteed to be produced from renewable sources equal to the units of electricity their customer has used.

In November 1999 Scottish and Southern Energy launched a scheme in association with the Royal Society for the Protection of Birds (RSPB) to offer green energy across the UK at the same price as conventional brown energy. Both parties benefited from this arrangement. Scottish and Southern became the first major utility company to offer green energy at nil premium, while the RSPB received a fee from the company for each household switching to its services.[26] A survey in 2000 found that 60% of consumers in Sweden and Germany would be prepared to pay a premium of up to 2% for green energy, while 50% of consumers in the UK would do so. That said, the highest take-up rate of green energy in the EU is in the Netherlands, with 140000 customers or a 2% market share. In the UK it is insignificant, less than 0.1% of UK households.[27]

Continental Europe has taken a leading place among the major economies of the world in actively seeking to replace coal and gas by renewable energy sources. In May 2000 the European Commission (EC) issued a directive requiring national governments to promote the use of renewables, such as solar power, wind power hydroelectric power and biomass, by setting output quotas and offering financial incentives to producers of 'green power'. The directive set the EC's aim of increasing the proportion of EU total electrical consumption generated by renewable power from 13.9% in 1997 to 22.1% by 2010. This included doubling non-hydroelectric supplies from 6% to 12% of the total. To put this into perspective, only about 1% of the world's total power capacity was produced from renewable sources by the end of 2001.

When he took office, President George W. Bush seemed to have little interest in renewable energy, as shown by his national energy policy unveiled in April 2001. However, the events of 11 September 2001 seemed to have modified that position. The administration became aware that US domestic oil and gas production was running down, leaving America increasingly vulnerable to energy supplies from the Middle East. It realised that encouraging the US to build up its supplies of renewable energy was one way of reducing this strategic risk. It therefore took a modest step in this direction with the Clear Skies Act, presented to Congress in February 2002. This proposed mandatory curbs on emissions of sulphur dioxide, nitrogen oxides and mercury by US power stations, and suggested measures to encourage emissions trading. However, the act ignored existing congressional proposals to put limits on carbon dioxide emissions.[28]

It is worth adding that even if the US federal government has been slow to move on climate change, many individual states have decided to move ahead in their own right. During 2001 New Jersey announced incentives to persuade local energy consumers to reduce carbon dioxide output, while in May 2001 Massachusetts went further by issuing mandatory reductions in carbon dioxide produced by the state's power utilities. New York, New Hampshire, North Carolina, Illinois and Florida were other states considering carbon dioxide reduction programmes.[29]

WIND POWER

Wind power has emerged as the main source of renewable power in Europe. In 1999 the International Energy Agency (IEA), an arm of the OECD, reported that installed global wind power capacity had reached the 'historic milestone' of 10000 megawatts. European countries were the leaders in this area, notably Germany, Denmark and Spain. Germany was the world leader with an installed base of 6100 megawatts of wind power, including 1600 megawatts installed in 1999 alone. While wind power subsidies have cost the German government around €2 billion a year, the emerging industry is also believed to have created some 35000 new jobs. Spain came second with an installed base of 2500 megawatts, although the Spanish government's encouragement of wind power meant that it was the fastest-growing wind power market in the world, while Denmark was third in Europe with about 2100 megawatts of wind capacity.

Given Europe's lead in this area – in 2000 it accounted for 70% of the global installed base of wind power – it is hardly surprising that Danish and German companies dominate global wind turbine manufacture. The investment bank Dresdner Kleinwort has forecast that global investment in wind power could total $27 billion in the five years to 2005. It expects global wind power generating capacity to grow from 10000 megawatts in 1999 to 60000 megawatts in 2005, and reach 400000 megawatts by 2020, equal to 200 conventional power stations.[30] France appears to be set for very rapid growth. Although only 55 megawatts of installed wind power capacity existed in France by the end of 2001, the government has recently passed similar fiscal incentives to those existing in Germany.

The UK economy is not known for its technological leadership, and it lags well behind the rest of Europe in renewable energy output.

In 1999 this stood at the relatively low level of 2.6% of the UK total, mostly deriving from old hydroelectric systems. However, in August 2001 tougher renewable energy targets for UK power suppliers were announced: all licensed electricity suppliers would be obliged to provide 3% of their sales from renewable sources by March 2003, rising to 10.4% by 2011. Suppliers would receive green certificates verifying how much renewable power they had bought, while companies falling below target would have to pay a penalty of 3 pence per kilowatt-hour. Since electricity produced by natural gas costs about 2 pence/k Wh, whereas renewable energy costs vary from about 3 pence/k Wh to 5 pence/k Wh, the idea was to make renewable energy cost-effective. The power industry lobbied hard to have electricity generated by incinerating waste classified as 'renewable', but this was rejected by the energy minister.[31]

In March 2001 Prime Minister Tony Blair announced that the government would spend £100 million to promote renewable energy in the UK. It is generally accepted that offshore wind power appears to be the most likely source, as research shows the UK's climate to be the best for offshore wind power in Europe. The potential of offshore wind power has been calculated at 30 000 megawatts, three times the UK's current power consumption. (Actual UK offshore wind power capacity in 2001 was one station off the Northumberland coast, producing 4 megawatts a year.) In April 2001 the Crown Estate, which owns the rights over the UK seabed, announced 18 leases had been granted to construct 18 wind farms off the British coast, estimated to provide about 1500 megawatts by 2004, or some 5% of the UK's total energy requirements.[32] The government's commitment to wind power was demonstrated by an announcement in November 2001 of the planned construction of a 400 mile cable linking the main offshore sites to the national grid.

Onshore wind power is a more attractive proposition in the US, a result of relatively low population density and cheap land prices. About 12 000 small inland wind power systems were built there in the 1980s, aided by federal tax credits, so that total US wind power capacity at the end of 2000 was about 2500 megawatts, the same as in Spain. However, while they were price competitive when built, a collapse in the natural gas price made wind power uncompetitive in the 1990s, and few wind farms were therefore built during that decade. However, advances in technology have halved the cost of onshore new wind power to 2 cents per kilowatt-hour, significantly below natural gas when its price rose sharply in 2000–2001. Renewable energy was made more attractive in 2001 to US consumers by the federal power tax credit (PTC) ,which gave a credit of 1.7 cents/k Wh. As a result, 2001 saw rapid construction of US wind farms for the first time for over ten years. A good example was the 470-windmill Stateline project on the border between Washington and Oregon, built by FPL Energy and due to produce 300 megawatts on completion.[33]

SOLAR POWER

The other main source of renewable electricity is likely to be solar power, i.e. electricity generated from photovoltaic cells that convert sunlight into electricity. Note that power generation depends on sunlight, not heat, i.e. the panels still generate electricity in daylight when it is dark and overcast. They have the advantage over wind power that they are quiet, and less visible blots on the landscape. Total sales of solar power products, mostly roof panels, were around £1 billion in 2000. Over half of these were in Europe, with the US following some way behind. Admittedly, President Clinton announced a Million Solar Roofs initiative in 1997 with the stated aim of 1 million US buildings having solar energy roofs by 2010. However, it provided no obligations or cash incentives to do so, although many individual states have encouraged local energy users to comply.

It seems to me that the solar industry is fast approaching the point where it moves from prototype to large-scale production. Rather like the personal computer or the video recorder, once this happens the unit costs should fall sharply and public acceptance will then rise rapidly. The oil giant Shell seems to think along the same lines, as it became the market leader in solar power in January 2002 by acquiring the photovoltaic cell businesses of two German companies, Siemens and Eon. Shell reported that the new company had sales of $200 million a year, growing at 25%, and a global market share of 15%.[34] Other major players in solar cell production include the

Japanese electronic companies Kyocera and Sharp, the independent US company Astropower, and BP. In 1999 energy expert Jeremy Leggett set up his own company, Solar Century, to promote solar power in the belief that in five to ten years UK solar power would be comparable in cost to power from fossil fuels but it would sell at a higher price. He explained:

> I expect three drivers to move the solar industry forward: large scale production to reduce cost, carbon taxes to raise fossil fuel prices, and electrical deregulation. In California and certain parts of Europe consumers can elect to buy 'green electricity', which currently sells for a premium price. This is not possible now in the UK, but it will be in the future.[35]

FUEL CELLS

The internal combustion engine must be one of the least attractive of the power technologies developed during the twentieth century. It is inefficient and produces a number of dangerous or unpleasant emissions such as carbon dioxide, sulphur dioxide, particulates and nitrogen oxides. In 2001 the IEA estimated that transport accounted for about 26% of all humanly produced carbon dioxide, and that this proportion was rising.[36] Since petroleum-based engines account for 96% of all energy used in transportation in the major economies, the need to find a renewable replacement for the internal combustion engine seems obvious. Although various technologies such as electric cars powered by batteries have been tried, fuel cells seem the most likely alternative to internal combustion engines.

Fuel cells create electricity by mixing hydrogen and oxygen, so the only waste product is water. The technology has been known for many years, but there has been great difficulty in turning it into commercial products. Fuel cells are about four time more efficient than the internal combustion engine with its 10% efficiency; their ease of use and quick filling periods makes them much more attractive than battery power for vehicles. Batteries also have the disadvantage of requiring disposal of used batteries full of toxic chemicals. However, hydrogen is a difficult gas to treat and store, and a variety of complex technological issues remain to be solved before fuel cells become commonplace in cars and as small generators. At the moment there are a number of rival technologies in development to manufacture the fuel cells themselves, while there is also uncertainty about the fuel source.

There is considerable dispute about whether the automotive industry should move directly to a 'carbon free' economy using electrolysis to produce hydrogen from water, or whether it should involve a transition stage based on fuel cells using reformulated petrol. This would not be a zero-emission technology, although it would be an improvement on the petrol engine. Another technical problem is the question of whether the industry should standardise on compressed or liquid hydrogen. Liquefying hydrogen uses up so much power that it absorbs about 30% of the power generated, although it gives a greater range to the car. Another stumbling block has been the lack of an existing infrastructure to get the hydrogen into motorists' cars.

That said, the long-term outlook for fuels cells looks bright, as fuel cell technology seems to be the only realistic zero-emission source to power vehicles. In the US the states of California and Massachusetts mandated that 10% of vehicles sold must have zero emissions by 2004. The Californian state government intends to have 70 fuel-cell-operated buses operational by 2003, as does the British city of Cambridge. Daimler-Benz has announced plans to have similar buses on the streets of Europe by 2004. Buses are the logical way to introduce fuel cells. Being short-distance carriers based in central depots, they do not need a massive chain of hydrogen 'gas stations' to be developed. The George W. Bush administration was generally sceptical about environmental concerns, but in February 2002 it put its support behind fuel cell development in what it called the Freedom CAR partnership to help establish industry standards. US energy secretary Spencer Abraham proclaimed the need to develop alternative energy sources in order to reduce American dependence on imported oil.[36]

While sales are small at present, it is generally believed that the take-off period for fuel cells will be around 2005–9. Thus global sales are estimated to reach $2 billion in 2005, $10 billion in 2007 and $20 billion in 2009. By 2015 they could approach $100 billion, with fuel cells having become the dominant power source for automotive transport. Most of the world's large automotive manufacturers have done intensive work on producing fuel cell vehicles. Ford and Daimler-Benz, are using fuel cells manufactured by the Canadian company Ballard Power, whose Mark 900 fuel stack is rated at 1310 watts per litre of hydrogen. Other large car companies developing their own fuel cell technology include Toyota and General Motors.

Fuel cells can also be used to produce on-site electric power, although the technology involved is quite distinct from that used in mobile systems. For example, the US company H-Power signed a contract to provide 12 000 local fuel cell systems to rural cooperatives throughout the US, even though the fuel cell capital cost of $2000 per kilowatt was twice that of conventional small dynamos.[37] Indeed, some experts believe that the technology used in stationary fuel cells, used to power houses and small offices, is the closest to mass production, with commercial sales expected as early as 2003−4.

THE RIO RESOLUTION 1992

Any discussion of the relationship between SRI and sustainable development must note the profound global policy statement made by the UK, US, Canadian and Australian social investment forums at the time of the 1992 Earth Summit in Rio. As the tenth anniversary of that summit approached, many bodies examined the relationship between finance and sustainable development, particularly in view of the Rio+10 summit held in Johannesburg in September 2002. Yet the 1992 Rio Resolution set a high benchmark by which later policy statements can be judged. The Rio Resolution was also a landmark event in its own right, as the first really significant occasion when socially responsible investment really became a force working on a global scale. The resolution was drafted by Tessa Tennant and Mark Campanale in the UK, Peter Kinder in the US, Marc de Sousa Shields in Canada, and Robert Rosen in Australia. (We should also note the inclusion of a chapter on sustainable finance in *Changing Course*, the business submission from the Business Council on Sustainable Development to the Rio Summit.) The resolution is shown in Box 7.1.

Box 7.1 The Rio Resolution 1992

- Whereas the United Nations Conference on Environment and Development convenes in Rio de Janeiro on June 3;
- Whereas the conference – the Earth Summit – presents an opportunity for individual and institutional investors to contribute to the environment and development debate;
- Whereas the signatories of this resolution are representatives of the social investment community; and
- Whereas the social investment community wishes to draw to the attention of investors worldwide the link between investment policy and sustainable development;

Therefore let it be resolved that:

- We call on individuals to question whether the investment policies of their mortgage, loans, insurance, savings and/or pension plans support the objectives of sustainable development.
- We call on companies and non-governmental organisations to ensure that their policies enable investments to be managed for environmental and social benefit.
- We call on financial institutions to begin the process of integrating environmental and social considerations into the investment analysis process and to have particular regard for investments in emerging capital markets.
- We call on governments to introduce incentives for private capital to invest in community enterprises that support low-cost housing, small business start-ups, education, sustainable agriculture and other projects which enhance the common good.

EMISSIONS TRADING

From the viewpoint of financial markets, emissions trading provides the possibility of major new market opportunities. The UK oil companies Shell and BP have had intracompany emissions trading schemes for some time. The stage has been set for the market to really take off by the ratification of the Kyoto Protocol in Berlin in July 2001. One research group has forecast that the emissions trading market could be worth $9 billion in its first full year, even excluding the US.[38] More speculative estimates value trading in carbon dioxide permits as potentially being worth $13 000 billion by 2050. An expert at the Chicago Board of Trade stated, 'I think what we are seeing is a convergence of capital and environmental markets.'[39]

In 2000 the World Bank set up a $150 million Prototype Carbon Fund, which enabled companies in industrial countries to get carbon credits if they invested in emissions-lowering projects in developing countries. This was a prototype venture designed to help establish the legal contracts and verification procedures involved.[40] The Sydney Futures Exchange in Australia created a joint venture with the State Forests of New South Wales to launch the world's first exchange-traded carbon sequestration credits. Buyers could offset carbon emissions with credits generated by planting trees to absorb carbon dioxide.[41]

In November 2000 the inaugural meeting took place of the Emissions Market Development Group, convened by Arthur Andersen, Crédit Lyonnais, and Natsource, with representatives of 35 large energy companies present. The group intended to establish an international carbon 'bank' which would act as a central clearing house to exchange the varying credits generated by different corporate and national trading schemes. The *Financial Times* commented:

> A group of bankers, brokers, executives and consultants are eyeing up a market that is potentially worth billions of dollars a year. They are champions of the emerging emission trading market, which would allow countries, and by extension companies, that can meet their emissions reduction targets at relatively low cost to sell emission rights − in the form of carbon permits − to countries and companies that face higher costs in meeting their targets.[42]

INVESTMENT VEHICLES

It seems fairly obvious therefore that renewable energy offers significant business opportunities. It is no great surprise that specialist investment vehicles should arise to tap the potential financial returns from this market. The first to do so was Merrill Lynch Investment Management (MLIM), which launched the Merrill Lynch New Energy Fund in October 2000. This was followed by Impax Capital, which raised £50 million for a renewable energy fund launch in the spring of 2002. Merrill Lynch's announced aim was to raise £35 million, but such was the public's enthusiasm that £200 million was subscribed. The bank identified a number of factors driving long-term growth in the sector: environmental pressure deriving from the Kyoto Protocol and green consumerism; the deregulation of energy markets which opened the way for new entrants; technological advances, particularly the falling costs of new technologies such as microturbines; and finally reliability. High-technology industries require constant supply, hence the need for back-up suppliers outside the main electricity grid. Merrill Lynch had no track record of SRI expertise, with the fund being run by its natural resources team with the explicit aim of maximising financial returns. As fund manager Robin Batchelor explained:

> The investment case is about growth – the idea is to invest for a real return. But investors can have a good conscience about it at the same time.... Investors' perception of the energy industry – growth in line with GDP growth, cyclical performance, i.e. boring doesn't apply here.[43]

Some critics were sceptical about the launch of the Merrill Lynch New Energy Fund, seeing it as narrowly focused growth stock investing within a highly restricted investment universe. Concern was also expressed that this was a very immature sector, so at the time of launch there simply weren't enough attractive quoted companies operating in the sector in which to invest. According to the magazine *Environmental Finance*:

> Some analysts are concerned about the effect that the MLIM fund and future large-scale investment flows could have in this still-developing sector. There is some danger of a bubble developing, they say, as too much capital chases too few companies.[44]

ENVIRONMENTAL MANAGEMENT AND ACCOUNTING

More and more investment funds are being managed in socially responsible ways. One of the side effects of this process is a growing demand for information and analytical tools that can be used to assess corporate environmental performance. Being able to assess accurately which companies are making a genuine effort to reduce their environmental footprint may prove a profitable strategy for investors. The problem is how to differentiate genuine improvement from public relations spin or greenwash. Part of the answer lies in corporate use of a recognised environmental management system. Two of these have come into general use over the last ten years: EMAS and ISO 14001. EMAS (Eco-Management and Audit Scheme) is a voluntary environmental management system, devised by the European Community. It came into force in July 1993 for all industrial companies operating in the EU. Its objective is to promote continuous environmental performance improvement by committing companies to evaluate and improve their environmental performance. A key requirement of EMAS is that companies seeking its accreditation must issue public environmental statements that have been independently verified.

ISO 14001 is produced by the International Organisation for Standardisation (ISO), a body that prepares global industrial standards in a variety of areas. (Since October 1997 ISO 14001 has superseded the earlier British standard BS 7750.) Unlike EMAS, ISO 14001 sets no requirement for external verification. However, the point is clear; any corporate management that claims environmental excellence should be able to demonstrate this with reference to EMAS or ISO 14001. Business in the Environment has carried out regular surveys that assess the environmental performance of the UK's largest companies. Progress in this regard has not been good. The results for 2000 showed that 20% of the top FTSE 100 companies, and 33% of those in the FTSE All-Share index, did not even measure their global warming emissions, while only 37% of the total had set targets to reduce emissions. However, 86% of the companies surveyed had policies in place to measure energy use and raise energy efficiency.[45]

A detailed survey of environmental reporting in the UK is produced every two years by Pensions and Investment Research Consultants (PIRC). The PIRC 2000 survey covered 674 companies that were included in the FTSE All-Share index. It revealed that environmental reporting was significantly worse among smaller companies, and concluded that the main drivers for compliance were strict regulation, high environmental impact and a large consumer base. In general, UK corporate environmental reporting had improved a little since the previous survey in 1998, though often from a low base. However, only a few large companies took the trouble to produce separate environmental reports. PIRC commented:

> Disclosure on environmental issues should not be seen as the preserve of a few large companies in the public spotlight. Shareholders need to know how all companies are addressing environmental issues if they are to be confident that managements are acting responsibly and effectively. There is a danger of a reporting gap opening between a relatively small number of progressive companies which are exploring reporting initiatives in an innovative way and the rest which are, at best, paying lip-service to the environment while providing little in the way of hard data to demonstrate improvements in their performance.[46]

International environmental disclosure presents a mixed picture. A 1999 study of the largest US companies prepared by KPMG disclosed the disappointing fact that a declining number were producing detailed environmental reports. In 1996 some 44% of large American companies had produced such reports, but by 1999 this number had fallen to 30%. However, the situation outside the US looked better, as 24% of international large companies were producing environmental reports in 1999, an increase from the figure of 17% seen in 1996. In part this is driven by regulatory requirements, as from 2000 environmental reporting has been mandatory for large quoted companies in the Netherlands, Norway, Denmark and Sweden.[47]

THE GLOBAL REPORTING INITIATIVE

Ultimately both companies and SRI investors will need a global standard for social and environmental analysis. This is the aim of the sophisticated sustainability reporting system currently being developed by the Global Reporting Initiative (GRI). The GRI was convened in the autumn of 1997 by CERES in partnership with UNEP. Draft guidelines were hammered out from February 1998 to March 1999, when the first version was published (known in accountancy jargon as the first exposure draft). The GRI initially concentrated on environmental reporting, before adding social indicators in 1998. The GRI's objective is simple: to develop environmental and social reporting tools that reach the same level of sophistication as conventional financial reporting.

After pilot testing involving an extended trial by 21 companies, revised guidelines were published in June 2000.[48] The GRI has tried to design a common framework for reporting on the linked aspects of sustainability – economic, environmental and social. Although the 2000 version of the guidelines treated the three elements as separate reporting items, the ultimate aim of the GRI is to move towards a reporting framework that links economic, environmental and social elements in an integrated reporting structure. Although in the long term the Sustainability Reporting Guidelines are intended to be applicable to all types of organisation, the GRI's initial development work has focused on reporting by business organisations. The key GRI concepts are shown below:[49]

1. *Economic.* This includes wages and benefits, labour productivity, job creation, expenditures on outsourcing, expenditure on research and development, and investments in training and other forms of human capital. The economic element includes, but is not limited to, financial information.
2. *Environmental.* This includes impacts of processes, products, and services on air, water, land, biodiversity, and human health.
3. *Social.* This includes workplace health and safety, employee retention, labour rights, human rights, and wages and working conditions at outsourced operations.

One last thought on environmental reporting. Some commentators give the impression that 'eco-efficiency' equals 'sustainability' equals 'financial return'. This is simplistic. Good environmental management is a useful measure of a company's progress in running its existing business in a more eco-efficient way. It tells us nothing about the strategic risk it may face of being closed down because its businesses are inherently unsustainable. Nor does this capture the 'event risk' that the company might be crippled by some kind of environmental liability. However, there is growing evidence that eco-efficiency may be a useful indication of good management.

REFERENCES

1. *Our Common Future*, World Commission on Environment and Development, Oxford University Press, 1987.
2. *Ibid.*
3. Amory Lovins, Lady Eve Balfour Lecture, London, 7 March 2001.
4. The CERES website, 8 August 2001.
5. 'Winter Drenching May be Proof of Greenhouse Effect', *Daily Telegraph*, 17 March 2000.
6. 'Breaking Down the Barriers on Climate Change', *Financial Times*, 3 August 1999.
7. 'Climate Change Poachers Turn Gamekeepers', *Financial Times*, 12 February 2002.
8. *Climate Change: A Risk Management Challenge for Institutional Investors*, Mark Mansley and Andrew Dlugolecki, 2001. Available from: Universities Superannuation Scheme, 11th Floor, 1 Angel Court, London EC2R 7EQ.
9. The Third Assessment Report of the IPPC, from IPPC website.
10. Quoted in Mansley and Dlugolecki, *op. cit.*
11. US National Academy of Sciences website.
12. 'Economists Back Bush on Kyoto Pact', *Wall Street Journal*, 8 August 2001.
13. Jonathan Porritt, *Sunday Telegraph*, 4 June 1994.
14. 'Bush's Big Backers Now Seek a Return on Their Investment, *Wall Street Journal*, 7 March 2001.
15. *Climate Change: A Risk Management Challenge for Institutional Investors*, Mark Mansley and Andrew Dlugolecki, USS 2001.
16. J. Leggett, *The Carbon War*, Penguin, 1999.
17. International Energy Agency, quoted in 'Environmental Conference Prods US to Cut Emissions', *Wall Street Journal*, 12 November 1998.
18. *World Energy Outlook 2001*.
19. Quoted in 'Winners and Losers Wait for Fog to Clear Around Kyoto', *Financial Times*, 25 July 2001.
20. Munich Re, quoted in 'Climate Change to Bring More Disasters', *Financial Times*, 13 March 2001.
21. 'Industry Marred by Worst Year of Natural Disasters', *Financial Times*, May 2000.
22. 'Climate Change May Spark Future Wars', *Financial Times*, 8 February 2001.
23. 'Future Wars "Could Be over Water" ', *Daily Telegraph*, 2 January 1999.
24. 'Climate Change Set to Affect Health', *Financial Times*, 11 February 2001.
25. 'Asia Propelled "To Brink of Environmental Catastrophe" ', *Financial Times*, 19 June 2001.
26. 'Scottish and Southern Teams up with RSPB', *Financial Times*, 20 November 1999.
27. 'Do Consumers Care about Green Energy Options?', *Wall Street Journal*, 7 September 2000.

28. 'Bush Would Link Emission Cutbacks to US Economy', *Wall Street Journal*, 15 February 2002.
29. 'States Are Stepping in to Reduce Levels of CO_2 Emissions', *Wall Street Journal*, 11 September 2001.
30. 'Wind Power Systems Set to Triple Globally', *Financial Times*, 23 January 2001.
31. 'Renewable Generation Targets May Get Tougher, Says DTI', *Financial Times*, 4 August 2001.
32. 'Britain Follows the Winds of Change', *Wall Street Journal*, 12 April 2001.
33. 'The Answer, My Friend, Is Blowin' in the Wind', *Wall Street Journal*, 29 January 2001.
34. 'Royal Dutch/Shell Will Take Control of Solar Venture', *Wall Street Journal*, 24 January 2002.
35. Jeremy Leggett, in conversation with the author 1999. Published as 'Towards a Sustainable Future', *Professional Investor*, Dec 1999/Jan 2000.
36. 'Cars that Guzzle a fresh Gas' *Financial Times*, 12 January 2002.
37. 'Seeking Solutions', *Financial Times*, 5 November 2001.
38. 'Renewable Energy Renaissance', *Financial Times*, 30 January 2001.
39. 'A Bull Market in Hot Air', *Financial Times*, 4 November 1999.
40. 'World Bank Ties New Fund to Emissions', *Financial Times*, 18 January 2001.
41. 'A Bull Market in Hot Air', *Financial Times*, 4 November 1999.
42. 'Accord at the Hague Would Boost Market in Emissions Trading', *Financial Times*, 23 November 2000.
43. 'Merrill Lynch Sees Green', *Environmental Finance*, October 2000.
44. 'Merrill Lynch Sees Green', *Environmental Finance*, October 2000.
45. 'Companies Respond Poorly to Global Warming', *Financial Times*, 2 February 2001.
46. Pensions and Investment Consultants (PIRC) website, March 2000.
47. 'Fewer US Companies File Environmental Reports', *Financial Times*, 3 September 1999.
48. 'GRI Moves up a Gear', *Environmental Finance*, April 2000.
49. Copyright the Global Reporting Initiative. Reproduced with permission.

8

Human Rights

THE NEED FOR SRI PERFORMANCE METRICS

Critics of socially responsible investment often accuse it of being based upon 'soft' or 'mushy' metrics. By this they imply that SRI issues are subjective, vaguely defined, and impossible to measure accurately. Such so-called soft performance indicators are contrasted with the 'hard', i.e. detailed and accurate, data shown in company financial statements. Well, after the sudden collapse of the energy giant Enron in January 2002, financial statements seem a lot less hard and objective than they once did. The previous two chapters of this book discussed a number of concrete environmental issues and showed how they can be measured accurately. The aim of this chapter is to do the same in the field of human rights.

Institutional investors are increasingly assessing corporate performance on the environment and on human rights. This is happening whether they have an SRI mandate or not, as complicity in human rights abuses and environmental damage can have serious implications for the reputation of the company concerned, and hence its share price. One of key themes of this book is that SRI operates as an integrated mechanism to reduce financial risk. The 1999 Turnbull Report on corporate risk control recognised this fact when it ruled that companies must take account not only of financial risks, but also 'health, safety and environment, reputation and business probity issues'.[1] The Turnbull recommendations were incorporated in the combined code of the London Stock Exchange, meaning that UK publicly listed companies were legally obliged to comply and disclose their risk control systems in future annual reports.

THE UN DECLARATION OF HUMAN RIGHTS

Human rights is one of the oldest component elements of SRI. Unrest over civil rights in the US was the initial spark that started modern socially responsible investment in the first place. The growth of SRI was fuelled by widespread concern about companies operating under the apartheid regime in South Africa. At this point it is important to clarify what is meant by human rights. The basic document asserting the value of human rights is the UN Universal Declaration of Human Rights (UDHR) proclaimed by the UN General Assembly on 10 December 1948. The declaration consists of thirty detailed clauses. It prohibits racial or sexual discrimination, and forbids all forms of slavery. It prohibits arbitrary arrest, and demands a fair trial for everybody, while asserting freedom of speech and freedom of association which includes being able to join a trade union. It also prescribes democracy based on regular and free elections as the basis of legitimate government. People may disagree with the above, but it is hard to dismiss the clauses of the Declaration as soft or mushy.

The idea of basic human rights is sometimes attacked as an attempt by Western liberals to impose their own individualistic values (i.e. those of the US) on the rest of the world. Is concern over human rights really nothing more than US cultural imperialism? This seemed a question of purely academic interest when I wrote the first draft of this chapter. However, after the events of 11 September 2001 it has become an issue of vital importance. In 2000 Amnesty International produced a book that aimed to guide business on human rights questions. This advocated a positive approach to human rights, and addressed the above question in forthright terms:

> Cultural relativists who criticise the idea of human rights as being the product of Western imperialism or individualism ignore the wide-ranging consultation across cultures and creeds that led to the drawing up of the UDHR.... Inhuman and degrading treatment of human beings is alien to all cultures, even if it is used by some governments to serve their own political ends.... The fact remains that the UHDR represents a set of fundamental and universal rights over which there is a broad

consensus transcending political and religious interpretation, as well as cultural identity. Not only are these applicable across a multitude of creeds and cultures, but they also offer the most widely accepted framework for promoting and protecting human rights.[2]

At the World Economic Forum in Davos on 31 January 1999, UN secretary-general Kofi Annan urged global businesses to adopt the Global Compact, nine principles covering corporate behaviour relating to human rights, labour and environment:[3]

1. Support and respect the protection of international human rights within their sphere of influence.
2. Make sure their own corporations are not complicit in human rights abuses.
3. Freedom of association and the effective recognition of the right to collective bargaining.
4. The elimination of all forms of forced and compulsory labour.
5. The effective abolition of child labour.
6. The elimination of discrimination in respect of employment and occupation.
7. Support a precautionary approach to environmental challenges.
8. Undertake initiatives to promote greater environmental responsibility.
9. Encourage the development and diffusion of environmentally friendly technologies.

The adoption by the EU of a Charter of Fundamental Human Rights in 2001 added further pressure for companies to recognise their responsibilities in this area, before expensive legal action forced them to do so. We should also remember that human rights consistently come top of any survey of the issues that matter most to ordinary people interested in socially responsible investment. In 2000 Scottish Life carried out its own research to establish the key ethical concerns of the public prior to launching a retail SRI fund. Scottish Life's Chris Hegarty reported back:

> Any fund wanting to be responsive to the concerns of its investors will want to incorporate a policy on human rights.... We did extensive research before we set up our fund to identify

those areas of greatest concern. Human rights were usually up towards the top.[4]

OPPRESSIVE REGIMES

Originally the 'human rights' category of SRI consisted of identifying companies operating in what were called 'oppressive regimes'. As shown in Chapter 5, major SRI funds such as Calvert in the US and Friends Provident in the UK still have 'oppressive regimes' as one of their major exclusion screens. Socially responsible investors do not normally have a direct stake in local companies operating under oppressive regimes, such as apartheid South Africa, or Burma (Myanmar) at present. The questions they have to answer involve multinational companies located in such countries. For example, South Africa prior to 1994 meant US companies such as Ford or Citicorp, or British companies like Barclays Bank or Shell. SRI investors pressed such companies to leave South Africa, and if shareholder activism failed, avoidance was the next obvious step, with shareholdings sold.

It can be extremely difficult to assess the right course of action regarding companies operating in countries with dictatorships or military juntas. People sometimes argue that large multinational companies should not leave such countries. They claim that their presence 'engages' with the authorities, and can therefore ameliorate political repression. It is often argued that giant companies like Shell or Ford should not leave a country, as their departure would adversely affect the economy, making poor people even worse off. In the author's opinion these arguments have some merit and cannot be dismissed casually. Each individual case of 'oppressive regimes' has to be evaluated on its own merits.

It seems to me that democracy is the key. Where this is lacking, recommendations made by an opposition movement that could credibly claim to win power if free elections were held, seem the best guide. They can advise whether Western companies should exit or not. This was a role played by the ANC in South Africa prior to 1993, as does the NLD in Burma at present. In both cases these opposition movements have advised overseas investors to pull out as a means to force political change, while recognising that in the short term such departures will hurt their own people. Sometimes the advice is different. Shell was the subject of widespread criticism for operating in Nigeria, particularly after General Abacha staged a coup d'état and imposed military rule. However, there was no national consensus coming from Nigeria for Shell to leave, which is not to ignore the difficult situation of the Ogoni people in the Delta.

The term 'oppressive regimes' is normally used to describe countries where the government or government-backed forces are believed to have engaged in systematic human rights abuses. For example, EIRIS has traditionally provided research information on such countries using raw data provided by UK's Amnesty International (the US-based organisation Human Rights Watch provides similar information). On receiving this information, the extensive EIRIS database of company groups is used to see which UK companies have operations in such countries. KLD and CEP provide similar information on US companies (Chapter 12). Such research merely highlights the existence of such operations; it gives no indications of their size or importance. Countries who typically appear on three or four of these lists are shown below; they include Afghanistan, Burma, China, India, Iran, Iraq, Syria and Turkey. This is calculated on the basis:

1. Extrajudicial executions or disappearances
2. Countries where torture has occurred
3. Countries where there are prisoners of conscience
4. Countries where official violence against citizens is common

I want to add a fifth criterion that I believe to be missing from the above list – democracy. Article 21 of the Universal Declaration on Human Rights defines democracy as an essential human right. Most of the countries listed above are dictatorships, and it is hardly surprising there is a close correlation between dictatorships and abuse of human rights. While there are some democratic countries where significant human rights abuses take place, they are few in number. They tend to be countries where central government is relatively weak, such as India, or where there is an effective civil war taking place, as in Colombia. In neither country is deliberate killing and torture of civilians an objective of government policy, even if regrettably it does takes place. The view that democracy is the key human right is shared by the legendary fund manager George Soros. In 1994 he instructed his funds to sell all holdings of Peregrine Investments, a company which owned a portfolio of Burmese investments. Soros had no ethical considerations in mind; he simply acted on the belief that investing in dictatorships was an unnecessary business risk.

I think that oppressive regimes can be ranked on a graduated scale, starting with the military juntas that have often seized power in Latin America, Africa or Asia. The basis of such regimes is military force, with limited or no democratic process and restrictions on the press. However, traditional military dictatorships are relatively benign compared to totalitarian regimes who rely on ubiquitous secret police and sudden 'disappearances' to terrify any potential opposition. The political scientist Hannah Arendt invented the word 'totalitarian' in the 1940s to describe the political systems established by Hitler and Stalin. One key point about totalitarian regimes is that in such countries there are no independent agencies – everything is controlled by the government.

Anybody who had business relations with Germany in the 1930s was therefore effectively dealing with Adolf Hitler. In his book *IBM and the Holocaust*, Edwin Black accuses IBM, which sold punchcard calculating machines to Nazi Germany in the 1930s, of making a significant contribution to the Holocaust.[5] Of course IBM could not have known that its machines would be later used to locate and round up Jews and send them to death camps. However, it was obvious from Hitler's accession to power in January 1933 that he headed a brutal and anti-Semitic regime. Since the collapse of Communism, the most infamous totalitarian regimes still in existence are generally recognised as being Iraq, North Korea and the Ne Win/SLORC regime in Burma. Before 11 September 2001 the political system of these countries may have been thought of as being of purely domestic concern. However, many of them, together with the late and unlamented Taliban regime in Afghanistan, are believed to be the main supporters of international terrorism. Sanctions, warfare and economic chaos mean there is minimal Western corporate involvement in Iraq, North Korea or Afghanistan. However, since the early 1990s there has been growing business interest in Burma, and in the Sudan, particularly in their oil and gas reserves.

BURMA

Burma has been ruled by a military dictatorship since power was seized by General Ne Win in 1961. Ne Win established what he called 'the Burmese road to socialism', but what was in fact a totalitarian state similar to the former Soviet Union. In 1988 widespread protests against the regime resulted in power passing to another group of generals, who called themselves the State Law and Order Committee (SLORC). SLORC also decreed that the name of the country should be changed to Myanmar, a name change not recognised by the opposition. In 1990 SLORC decided to allow elections to go ahead. The National League for Democracy (NLD) led by Aung San Suu Kyi won a landslide victory with 81% of the vote. However, SLORC refused to recognise the election result, turning instead to a policy of repression. Aung San Suu Kyi was placed under house arrest, and many NLD officials received seven-year prison terms for political offences, some of them dying in prison. Human rights groups such as Amnesty International and Human Rights Watch assembled a wealth of evidence of human rights abuses in Burma, including forced labour in chain gangs, mass rape, and 'ethnic cleansing' including summary execution of the ethnic Karen and Mons peoples. Allegations of massive human rights abuses in Burma were substantiated by the US State Department in 1997, which announced an embargo on any new US investment in Burma. The trade magazine *Infrastructure Finance* reported:

> Ethicists say that even among countries charged with human rights violations, Myanmar is unique. The abuse of human rights is so much a part of the system that it takes very creative approaches to do business ethically in Myanmar.[6]

In response to political repression, Aung San Suu Kyi repeatedly and publicly asked overseas investors to boycott Burma until there was political change. She has advised foreign tourists to stay away, and pleaded for Western trade sanctions. The 1990s saw Western companies pour into Asia in order to benefit from the Asian economic miracle believed to exist at that time. However, the opposite was true for Burma, as companies pulled out. Levi Strauss did so in 1992, stating that it was 'impossible to do business there without directly supporting the military government and its pervasive violation of human rights'.[7] US companies that exited Burma fairly quickly over the next few years included Apple Computers, Kodak, Motorola and Disney; the Dutch brewing company Heineken also left. US companies were influenced to quit Burma by a combination of intense pressure from shareholder resolutions advising them to leave, as well as local boycotts of the kind that had been aimed against South Africa. In 1996 US government influence stopped the Asian Development Bank from extending credit to Burma because of human rights violations, and the following year President Clinton signed a decree under the D'Amato Act which imposes legal sanctions on companies doing business in countries with poor human rights records. The decree banned all new investment by US companies in Burma, although it did not affect existing projects. One magazine wrote in 1997:

> It is simply not possible to do business in Burma without directly or indirectly supporting the ruthless military junta. Doing business with the Generals, against the express wish of the democratically elected representatives of Burma, is an inherently political act.[8]

In recent years the International Labour Organisation (ILO) has repeatedly criticised Burma for its use of forced labour, i.e. unpaid labour coerced by threats of violence. In 1998 the ILO described a 'culture of fear' in Burma where men, women and children were coerced into forced labour. There have been allegations that such coercion included threats at gunpoint, regular beatings and rape. In November 2000 the ILO invoked, for the first time in its history, a clause allowing it to appeal directly to the United Nations on an issue. This asked the UN to impose general sanctions on Burma to help end forced labour. In September 2001 an ILO team visited the country to see if there had been any improvement in the situation regarding forced labour. This was a high-level team, which included former ministers from Australia, the Philippines, Sri Lanka and Poland. It was believed to be a 'last chance' investigation before the imposition of sanctions.[9]

However, while the majority of Western companies pulled out of Burma, the oil industry was attracted to the country in the early

1990s by the discovery of significant oil reserves in the Andaman Sea, off the Burmese West Coast. The first major project to be developed was the offshore Yadana gas field, operated by the French oil company Total, and estimated to have reserves of 5 trillion cubic feet worth some $1.2 billion. The gas from Yadana was presold on a thirty-year contract to the Petroleum Authority of Thailand. Yetagun, a second gas field was later developed by the US oil company Texaco, although in 1997 Texaco decided to pull out of Burma on human rights grounds after intense pressure from SRI groups. It sold its 42.9% stake in the Yetagun project to Premier Oil of the UK. Total moved into Burma despite opposition from the NLD:

> The presence of big name oil companies lends much needed legitimacy to an illegal and greedy regime. In 1996 Aung San Suu Kyi said of the French company Total Oil, that they 'had become the strongest supporter of the Burmese military system'.[10]

In a press interview in February 1997 Total's chairman, Thierry Desmarest, explained the company's rationale for building up its operations in oppressive regimes such as Iraq, Iran, Libya and Burma, countries of major human rights concern. He stated that Total had not deliberately targeted countries such as Iraq, Iran, Libya and Burma for oil exploration, but that:

> It's just that the Lord put the reserves in places that are a bit hot on political grounds. We're a bit more relaxed about such countries than some of our competitors.... We're certainly more comfortable than some other European oil companies. Only some Asian companies feel as free to invest as we do.[11]

The economic viability of Total's Yadana project depended upon the construction of a 464 mile pipeline to Bangkok. This pipeline crossed 39 miles of Burmese territory, the Tenesserim peninsular, through an adverse terrain of raw jungle and mountain ranges where malaria is rife. The US State Department and human rights groups have repeatedly reported claims that this pipeline was built with forced labour, and that many of these labourers were children. Native peoples such as the Karen and Mons tribes also accused the Burmese military of forcibly expelling them from traditional tribal lands. Total claimed, almost certainly correctly, that the actual work of assembling the pipeline itself was done by French engineers without any use of forced labour. However, it is generally accepted that the pipeline was laid on a route carved out through the jungle and across mountain ranges by coerced workers. Press reports described 5000 military guards on the site, and allegations that Total's engineers were regularly accompanied by armed military escorts. Total's coordinator for Burma, Herve Chagneux, explained:

> I could not guarantee that the military is not using forced labour. All we can really guarantee is what we ourselves are doing, the contracts we make, the people we employ. What is being done near-by we do not know.[12]

As the 1990s progressed, external sanctions against Burma increased. In November 1996 the European Commission established a trade mission to investigate allegations of forced labour in Burma. The EC mission was refused entry to Burma on the grounds that forced labour did not exist in Burma, hence there was nothing to investigate. The EC subsequently revoked Burma's special trade privileges with the EU. In October 2001 the European Parliament inaugurated hearings on possible complicity of two European oil companies, Total SA and Premier Oil, in human rights abuses in Burma. The NGO Earth Rights International presented hundreds of witness statements to the hearings confirming that forced labour was continuing on a massive scale in Burma. Earth Rights accused the Burmese military of committing widespread human rights abuses, noting that the Burmese military was employed by these two companies to guard oil pipelines. A Premier Oil executive stated that the company could not be held responsible for the behaviour of soldiers it employed to protect its staff and gas pipeline. He added, 'There are no international sanctions that do not allow our operations to go-ahead there'.[13]

Total SA became the most high-profile Western company operating in Burma because of its lead role as operator and constructor of the Yadana gas pipeline. Although there was growing investor unhappiness about Total's involvement in Burma, French company law effectively precluded critical shareholder resolutions being filed. This left public disinvestment as the only mechanism for socially responsible investors to express dissatisfaction with the company's active move into Burma. The only organisation in fact to do this was the Central Finance Board of the Methodist Church. (The Pensions Board of the United Methodist Church in the US publicly stated its support for this action.) In May 1997 the following press release was issued:

> The Central Finance Board of the Methodist Church has recently sold its shareholding in the French oil company, Total SA, owing to concerns about its operations in Burma (Myanmar).... The Methodist Church is concerned that Total appears to be increasing its involvement in Burma despite the advocacy of trade sanctions against the country by both the European Commission and the US Government. We are particularly concerned by allegations of the use of forced labour to clear the route of the gas pipeline which will take natural gas from Total's Yadana gas field to Thailand. We have come to the conclusion that it would not be appropriate for us to continue to hold an investment in Total.[14]

Total may have obtained cheap oil by exploring in countries boycotted by other oil companies on ethical grounds. However this also made it vulnerable to potential penalties under the D'Amato Act. In April 1997 Total announced that it had sold its 70% stake in Total Petroleum North America to Ultramar Shamrock for $811 million. By withdrawing from the US, the company made itself relatively immune to US sanctions. However, the late 1990s saw a variety of takeovers and mergers in the US that created a super league of giant oil companies: Exxon Mobil, BP Amoco and Chevron Texaco. Total did not participate in this process, to the detriment of the company and its shareholders. In the author's opinion, Total's shareholders may have lost more from their company's self-imposed exclusion from the US than they have gained from cheap Burmese natural gas.

SUDAN

For many years Sudan has suffered from a civil war between the Islamic north and the Christian/animist south of the country. Violence intensified when the national government, based in the north, was taken over by Islamic fundamentalists in the mid 1990s. Reaction to the new regime led to armed rebellion in the south by the Sudan People's Liberation Army, campaigning for democracy and greater autonomy. There have been alarming reports that Islamic government forces have committed widespread human rights abuses against the Christian/animist civilian population of the south. These include ethnic cleansing, widespread rape, mass murder (including crucifixion), slave labour and bombing of civilians. In 1997 the US Treasury Department imposed sanctions on Sudan, identifying the Sudanese government as a human rights violator and a prime supporter of terrorists such as Osama bin Laden's Al Qaeda network. Rather like Burma, Sudan would have been of little interest to the outside world except for one thing – its possession of oil. The government was based in Khartoum, in the Arabic north of the country, whereas the oil lay in Bentiu Region in the south, historically populated by tribal peoples.

In 1999 the two main oilfields of the Greater Nile project, Heglig and Unity, commenced large-scale production with the construction of a 1000 mile pipeline to the Red Sea. It was estimated that royalties worth about 40% of the total revenue from the oilfield development would go to the Sudanese government. These royalties were estimated at $300 million a year, roughly equivalent to the total military spending of the Sudanese government. In 2000 reports came in accusing the Sudanese armed forces of using the infrastructure built to support the Greater Nile fields for military operations. In particular, it was alleged that the main oilfield airfield had been used for bombing missions attacking civilians. Local churches and aid agencies accused government forces of ethnic cleansing, including genocide of the Nuer tribe who had traditionally lived in Bentiu Region.[15]

The main financial backer of the project was the China National Petroleum Company (CNPC) which invested over $1 billion in Sudan, where it had a 40% stake. However, CNPC already held $15 billion of dollar debt, which made it expensive and difficult for it to take on additional hard currency debt. In October 1999 CNPC tried to solve the problem by an initial public offering (IPO) in the US of its upstream arm CNOOC. Although originally expected to be worth more than $2.5 billion, the CNOOC IPO was abandoned when lack of interest meant the price would have been less than $1 billion. CNPC blamed the Asian financial crisis for withdrawing the IPO, but in fact the CNOOC issue was boycotted by many US public sector pension funds in view of CNOOC's operations in Sudan. The proposed IPO was bitterly attacked by religious groups led by the Interfaith Center on Corporate Responsibility and US trade unions. They pointed out that the aim of the IPO was to fund CNOOC's share of the development costs of the Greater Nile consortium, hence indirectly it funded the Sudanese army's alleged human rights abuses in the region.

CNPC's response to this setback was to form a new subsidiary company in November 1999 called Petro China, 63 business units comprising most of CNPC's domestic energy operations. In the author's opinion Petro China looked like a vehicle created to raise equity capital for CNPC in the hope that its domestic focus would avoid the criticisms which had affected the abortive CNOOC IPO. In March 2000 it was announced that Petro China would be selling 10% of its capital in an IPO jointly in Hong Kong and on Wall Street. The initial valuation of the IPO, led by Goldman Sachs, was $10 billion, but this was quickly revised down to $7 billion. A number of the largest US pension funds such as Calpers, the New York City Retirement Scheme, and TIAA-CREF announced that they would boycott the issue on human rights grounds. The AFL-CIO (the US equivalent of the TUC) organised a campaign for investment institutions to shun the Petro China IPO. John Sweeney, AFL-CIO president, held a teleconference in March 2000 with 42 major investment institutions advising them of the ethical issues and linked financial risks of the Greater Nile project, noting that many public sector funds were entrusted with the pension savings of union members. Bill Patterson, an AFL-CIO spokesman, announced:

> We haven't found a single fund yet that wants to get near this deal. We don't intend to override the fiduciary responsibilities of the fund trustees and investment managers. We just want to share our concerns about this prospective investment of worker capital.[16]

The Petro China IPO eventually closed on 29 March 2000. The underwriters were forced to reduce the price so that the IPO was worth only $3.4 billion, one-third of the earlier total. It seems as if the issue had come to collapsing, on the lines of CNOOC. It then emerged that an unlikely saviour had rescued it – BP had bought 20% of the total IPO. BP's acquisition of a stake in Petro China led to considerable controversy. Disquiet over this action prompted the Ecumenical Council for Corporate Responsibility (ECCR) to file a shareholder resolution in January 2001 for the BP AGM due in April 2001. This resolution requested BP directors to develop a set of policy commitments consistent with the company's current ethical policy, to apply them to strategic investments, and to make them available to shareholders. It also requested that they should be applied to future investments, that BPA should engage with the boards of companies where it had strategic investments such as Petro China, and that it should make regular reports available to shareholders on the progress made in pursuing this policy. The BP board felt unable to accept this resolution, which it rejected along with three other social resolutions. This in turn led to further controversy at BP, this time over corporate governance. It is hard not to believe that BP's acquisition of the stake in Petro China in 2000, coupled with the board's hard-line tactics over social resolutions for the 2001 AGM, damaged part of the reputation for good social responsibility at BP carefully built up by CEO John Browne over the previous decade.

BP was not the only oil company to face reputational damage arising from Sudan. The operator of the Greater Nile consortium was the Canadian oil company Talisman Oil, which held a 25% stake. In Canada the Taskforce on Corporate Responsibility (TCCR) headed up a social responsibility campaign against Talisman's Sudan involvement. The Canadian government ordered an inquiry into the oilfield developments in Sudan, finding that oil revenues had played a significant part in funding the Khartoum government's military operations in the south, military activity that was believed to have cost 2 million lives. At the end of October 2001 there were reports in the Canadian press that Talisman management had been so worn down by the shareholder campaign against it that it had decided to sell its stake in the Greater Nile consortium (page 313).[17] Talisman may have felt able to ignore its local churches, but in November 2000 it faced a rather more powerful opponent, the US Congress. The House of Representative passed the Sudan Peace Act, which would have forced companies such as Talisman and Petro China to delist from the New York Stock Exchange, cutting them off from the world's largest capital markets. This was the first time that US legislators had used the threat of sanctions on access to US capital markets to press for better human rights abroad.[18] President George W. Bush declined to sign the measure, so it did not become law.[19]

In 2002 Talisman also faced significant potential legal damages when it was sued in a New York district court under the Alien Tort Claims Act, which allows organisations to be sued in American courts for human rights violations committed outside the US. Citizens of southern Sudan sued Talisman and the government of Sudan alleging the destruction of villages and the forced displacement of some 200000 people who lived in the vicinity of the Heglig oilfield. In March 2002 the court saw a copy of a document apparently produced by the Sudanese government which appeared to show Talisman had worked closely with the Sudanese security forces in arranging this 'ethnic cleansing', although the authenticity of this document has been questioned.[20]

It is hardly accidental that mining or oil companies seem to be the companies most often associated with oppressive regimes. The world's developed countries have to a large extent exhausted their own resources of oil and base metals. Energy and mining companies are therefore forced to look for significant unexploited oil reserves or ore bodies in developing countries, where oppressive regimes tend to be concentrated. In the last days of the Clinton administration, the US State Department drew up a code of behaviour on human rights for energy and mining companies. The guidelines committed signatory companies to examine closely any allegations of human rights abuses committed by their own staff, and to press governments where they operated to investigate alleged abuses committed by security forces linked to those governments. BP, Shell and Chevron were among early signatories of the code, although Exxon Mobil, the world's largest oil company was not a signatory to the agreement. Secretary of State Madeline Albright stated:

> The best companies realise that they must pay attention...to universal standards of human rights, and that in addressing these needs and standards, there is no necessary conflict between profit and principle.[21]

CHINA

The oppressive regimes described above are of relatively low importance in the context of the global economy. China by contrast is an emerging economic giant, and is therefore courted by Western politicians and Western companies. However, politically it remains under the control of the Communist dictatorship established by Mao Tse Tung in 1947. Human rights agencies have accused the Chinese government of systematic human rights abuses including torture and summary execution in its *lao-gai* prison camps; illegal detention of political prisoners; and the illegal military occupation of Tibet. For example, human rights activist Li Changjun was arrested in May 2001 for printing information on the persecution of the Falun Gong movement. He died in custody in August 2001, witnesses claiming that he had been tortured to death.[22] In May 2000 the UN Committee Against Torture condemned China for condoning practices that contributed to torture by its police.[23]

Criticism of oppressive regimes often seems to overlook China, despite the brutal destruction by tanks of its pro-democracy movement at Tiananmen Square in June 1989. There is also a paradox here: How can what is claimed to be one of the world's fastest-growing capitalist systems operate within a Communist system of rigid political control? One of China's most famous dissidents is Wei Jingsheng, exiled from the country in 1999 after 18 years in prison for daring to publicly advocate democracy for China. He has observed this paradox:

> China does not have a market economy. They don't understand contracts and the rule of law; all they know is *guanxi* (connections). The only way China will become a true market economy is with human rights laws; those are the foundation, and you'd think that companies would recognise this and be pressing for reform.[24]

In 1996 the ILO reported its belief that nearly 12% of Chinese children aged 10–14 years were in full-time employment. This was dismissed by the Chinese government, which stated that no statistics were produced on this issue as there was simply no child labour in China. The Chinese government refused to allow foreign NGOs to visit China to investigate for themselves. This policy was in stark contrast to that of the Indian government, which welcomed foreign NGOs into the country to investigate child labour despite the likelihood of adverse publicity involved.[25] China is the most important 'oppressive regime' in terms of the sheer number of Western companies operating there. Many of them are attracted by the cheap labour to be found in China, which leads on to the questions of labour conditions discussed in the next section. The early Clinton administration pushed for better human rights in China, but the president caved in after a couple of years, admitting China to most favoured nation status with the US.[26] And of course in 2001 China was accepted as a member of the World Trade Organisation. As one observer commented on the 1997 US embargo on new investment in Burma:

> The embargo has also inevitably raised questions of hypocrisy: if Burma, where the US has few economic interests, is worthy of an embargo, why not China, where the human rights record is hardly better but where US economic interests are much greater?[27]

HUMAN RIGHTS AT WORK

Oppressive regimes represented the initial human rights focus of socially responsible investors. However, over time, human rights at work have become a core issue. A main actor in this area is the International Labour Organisation (ILO), a specialised UN agency. The ILO has a unique tripartite structure including representatives of governments, as well as employers' and workers' organisations. Since its creation in 1919 the ILO has adopted a large network of international conventions on labour standards and workplace conditions. Of these, some 70 are presently up to date. ILO members ratify conventions. This triggers legal obligations, including application of a mechanism to supervise and possibilities to benefit from assistance in the implementation of these conventions. Key instruments, which are fast becoming universally ratified, include the following eight ILO conventions on fundamental human rights at work:[28]

- *Forced Labour Convention* (No. 29, adopted 1930). Requires the suppression of forced or compulsory labour in all its forms, with a few specified exceptions, such as military service. Convict labour is only permitted under tightly regulated conditions.

- *Freedom of Association and Protection of the Right to Organise Convention* (No. 87, adopted 1948). Establishes the right of all workers and employers to form and join organisations of their own choosing without prior authorisation. Guarantees the free functioning of autonomous organisations without interference by the public authorities.
- *Right to Organise and Collective Bargaining Convention* (No. 98, adopted 1949). Provides for protection against anti-union dis-crimination, for protection of workers' and employers' organisa-tions against acts of interference, and for measures to promote collective bargaining.
- *Equal Remuneration Convention* (No. 100, adopted 1951). Calls for equal pay and benefits for men and women for work of equal value.
- *Abolition of Forced Labour Convention* (No. 105, adopted 1957). Prohibits the use of any form of forced or compulsory labour.
- *Discrimination in Employment Convention* (No. 111, adopted 1958). Calls for government policies to eliminate discrimination in employment, training and working conditions, on grounds of race, colour, sex, religion, political opinion, national extraction or social origin. Advocates the promotion of equality of opportunity and treatment.
- *Minimum Age Convention* (No. 138, adopted 1973). Calls for the abolition of child labour and the fixing of the minimum age for employment or work not lower than the completion of compulsory education.
- *Worst Forms of Child Labour* (No. 182, adopted 1999). Calls for the prohibition and immediate action for the elimination of certain forms of child labour such as forced labour, debt bondage, child trafficking, prostitution, or work that is likely to harm the child's health, safety and morals.

In addition, pursuant to the Declaration of Fundamental Principles and Rights at Work adopted in 1998, all ILO member states, even if they have not ratified the conventions in question, have an obliga-tion, arising from the very fact of membership of the organisation, to respect, to promote and to realise in good faith the principles concerning the fundamental rights which are the subject of those conventions, namely:

- Freedom of association and the effective recognition of the right to collective bargaining
- The elimination of all forms of forced of compulsory labour
- The effective abolition of child labour
- The elimination of discrimination

Prior to 1990 the Iron Curtain meant that about 40% of the world's resources were off limits to global companies; following the collapse of Communism that was no longer the case. Labour-intensive consumer goods industries such as textiles and sportswear rushed to switch manufacturing from Europe and the US to developing countries where wages were a fraction of their US equivalent. They also had the advantage that additional costs of social security, healthcare and environmental protection were practically non-existent. One of the consequences of globalisation was the development of export processing zones in developing countries, regions where governments relaxed already weak labour and environmental protection laws to attract foreign business. These zones are often described as maquiladoras, as they first grew up on the Mexican side of the border with the US.

In 2000 the ILO report *Labour Practices in the Footwear, Textiles and Clothing Industries*[29] described a massive job shift in the textiles and clothing industries to Asia, which accounted for 72% of all employment in these industries by 1998. The growth in employment was most noticeable in China, followed by other Asian low-wage economies such as Pakistan, Vietnam and Bangladesh, where average wages are $0.45 per hour compared with $10 per hour in Europe and $6 per hour in the US. The ILO report noted the industry's complex supply chain, i.e. a Western company might complete the final assembly of a garment, but many subcontractors would be involved in producing the constituent parts. It also found widespread use of child and female labour at low rates of pay:

Whatever the share of female employment in the industries, one thing seems universal: women's wages in the apparel, footwear and textile industries are lower than those of men.... The primary concerns include the abundance of low skill dollar a day jobs, and the absence of social infrastructure such as sanitary facilities and dormitories [for the overwhelmingly female] work force.[30]

Defenders of the status quo often argue that such exploitation of women and children is regrettable, but assert that it is a necessary part of industrialisation that will ultimately take developing countries out of poverty. The argument goes that this was true for Manchester in the 1840s, true of New York's Hell Kitchen in the 1900s, and true of Bangkok now. They often quote conditions in Bangladesh in 1993 as an example why well-meaning Western labour campaigners should not intervene in the labour market of developing countries. It is claimed that the threat of a boycott by US clothing retailers of apparel manufacturers using child labour resulted in 50000 children being thrown on the street, to end up either begging or in prostitution. However, the garment industry did not leave Bangladesh, so child labour earning $1 a day was replaced by adult labour earning over $4 a day, enough to provide a meagre living for parent and child. In other words, the conventional interpretation of this threatened boycott is utterly wrong – it actually resulted in a net benefit to the poor of Bangladesh.

For a few years such low labour costs helped generate buoyant profits for textile suppliers in developed countries. However, by the mid 1990s NGOs and US church investors led by ICCR raised awkward questions about how these profits were made. This was very much a development that started in the US and was later copied elsewhere. US companies were accused of paying extremely low wages in overseas 'sweatshops', wages that were a minuscule fraction of the retail price. A good example was a report by the National Labor Committee published in 2001; it found that workers in El Salvador earned $0.29 for sewing National Baseball Association jerseys which cost US consumers $140 each.[31] Consumer products companies suddenly found themselves the unwelcome victims of customer boycotts, negative media articles, and shareholder resolutions demanding improvement. SRI labour shareholder resolutions not only requested compliance with the ILO conventions on page 194, but also asked for payment of a living wage, normally determined in relation to basic nutritional requirements and local food costs. A large study was produced by ICCR on this in March 2001 in association with maquiladora groups.[32]

Some of the most high-profile victims of this unwelcome scrutiny were US sportswear manufacturers such as Nike and Reebok, and fashion retailers such as Gap. These companies were extremely vulnerable to consumer boycotts and adverse press criticism, as their products sold at a premium price owing to their strong brand image. In other words, reputation was a key element of their product offering. In the early 1990s Gap was one of the leading high-flyers in US retailing with rapid sales and profits growth. However, GAPs' same-store sales growth slowed towards the end of the decade, its reputation hit by consumer boycotts, The *Wall Street Journal* commented that 'the Gap brand bears the brunt of the problems'.[33] Likewise, in March 1998 Nike announced a sharp downturn in financial results. According to the *Washington Post*, the company attributed much of its problems to 'resistance by consumers because of persistent allegations that the company mistreats its factory workers'.[34] Consultants Price Waterhouse stated:

> The management of reputation integrity is one of the greatest corporate challenges of the new millennium. As forces of globalisation continue to gain momentum, society increasingly demands that large multinational corporations improve their performance in the areas of human rights, the environment, worker health, and other governance issues. Failure to address these demands has proved damaging to a company's most important asset — its reputation.[35]

US shareholder activism is based on filing of social shareholder resolutions. A survey by IRRC for the year 2001 found that 44 resolutions on labour standards were filed with US corporations in 2001, a huge increase from the 27 submitted in 2000.[36] Three distinct SRI groups were involved in this activity: church groups led by ICCR, trade union funds, and public sector pension funds. In 2001 the New York City pension scheme was one of the most active participants, filing 14 labour standard resolutions based on the SA 8000 standard (see below). Church groups were somewhat sceptical of SA 8000, preferring independent monitoring and a commitment by the board of the targeted company to improve operational standards. It is fairly common practice in the US for social resolutions to be withdrawn if the company is prepared to discuss how it might address the issues raised with the proposer. This was the case in 2001 for the electrical conglomerate Emerson Electric, which agreed to work with the Sinsinawa Dominicans on labour issues, and they withdrew their resolution.

One of the longest-running battles over labour standards was fought between the US churches coordinated by ICCR and the retail giant Wal-Mart. Wal-Mart has been regularly criticised by labour groups on account of its policy of not allowing trade unions and its heavy reliance on overseas suppliers. In 1993 SRI shareholder activism persuaded the company to adopt a set of standards for its suppliers, but as time has elapsed scepticism has grown about the effectiveness of the scheme. The labour rights resolution tabled at Wal-Mart for 2001 included the following:

> Wal-Mart's monitoring programme is heavily dependent upon auditors who do not have the trust of workers and who miss serious labour rights violations.... Wal-Mart [should] ensure it does not purchase from suppliers who manufacture items using forced labour, convict labour, or child labour, or who fail to comply with fundamental workplace rights protecting their employees' wages, benefits, working conditions, freedom of association, collective bargaining and other rights.[37]

Unwelcome publicity over overseas labour standards has forced many companies to move beyond the production of corporate codes of conduct to examining how best to measure their effective implementation. Initially many of them relied, quite naturally, on the five giant accounting/consulting firms who advised them in other areas to measure compliance with global labour standards. However, in practice this policy does not seem to have been a conspicuous success. Although the accountancy firms have decades of expertise in financial management, monitoring human rights is a relatively new area for them. In some cases local workers felt that they were on the side of management rather than acting as an impartial adjudicator. Critics also argue that an accounting firm with strong financial links to a company faces strong conflicts of interest as an independent investigator of human rights abuses. Clearly it is impossible for any individual firm to simultaneously look for labour abuses and act as a 'reputation manager' with a mandate to cover them up.

However, while using accountancy firms for social auditing work faces a number of difficulties, the same can also be said of other potential social auditors. Individual company codes of conduct may lack real teeth and be impossible to compare across companies. Local NGOs such as trades unions and charities have strong local expertise and contacts, but it would be practically impossible for investors to compare labour data on one company produced by multiple NGOs using a variety of methods and approaches. There are some NGOs such as Amnesty International or Human Rights Watch that do possess an international reach, but their resources are much less than the accounting companies, and many of their supporters might feel uncomfortable to see them working too closely with multinational companies.

I personally see no reason why the large accounting firms should not work with their existing corporate clients as part of the internal management control systems, as long as they are not also required to act as an independent social auditor. In 2001 the UK saw the sudden collapse of large companies like Independent Insurance and Railtrack. This resulted in calls for regulation to prevent accounting firms from doing consulting work for companies while simultaneously acting as their financial auditor. The sudden bankruptcy in December 2001 of the American energy giant Enron led to similar calls in the US. The work could also be done by independent certification companies such as the Swiss company Surveillance (SGS). Neil Kearney of the International Textile, Garment, and Leather Worker's Federation made a telling point about labour issues and quality control when interviewed by the BBC television programme *Panorama* over Nike and Gap:

Major companies like the Gap, Nike, all those other retailers, they have almost total control over supplier companies. They're greatly concerned with quality, their quality controllers are there. They insist on high standards as far as quality is concerned. There's absolutely no reason why they cannot insist on the same standards for working conditions and why they cannot monitor them on a daily basis.[38]

HUMAN RIGHTS: VERIFICATION AND ANALYSIS

Socially responsible investors need accurate, verifiable and consistent data if they are to compare the record of various companies on labour issues. Pride of place for devising the first international standards for social issue analysis and performance measurement goes to the international church groups ECCR (UK), ICCR (US) and TCCR(Canada), who devised *Principles for Global Corporate Responsibility: Bench Marks for Measuring Business Performance* in 1995 (revised 1998). *Bench Marks* is an impressive document. It describes itself as an independent document not meant for corporate endorsement, but rather as an evaluative tool 'through which concerned actors may evaluate companies, their codes of conduct and their implementation'. It is based on three factors: 'principles' is a statement of business philosophy; 'criteria' are particular company policies and practices; and 'bench marks' are specific reference points for measurement to assess a company's performance. *Bench Marks* covers the following issues:[39]

- The wider community
  - Ecosystems
  - National communities
  - Local communities
  - Indigenous communities
- The corporate business community
  - The employed—conditions
  - The employed—persons
  - Women in the workforce
  - Minority groups
  - Persons with disabilities
  - Child labour
  - Forced labour
  Suppliers
  Financial integrity
  Ethical integrity

The shareholders
Joint ventures, partnerships, subsidiaries
Customers and consumers

At the moment there are a variety of competing social auditing standards. The GRI is working on adding improved social data reporting to its environmental standards, while the Institute of Social and Ethical Accountability produced its own standard, AA1000, in 2000. However, the most widely used social analysis framework is SA 8000, developed by the Council of Economic Priorities (CEP) in the mid 1990s. CEP research found that the use of internal corporate codes of practice was expensive and inefficient; codes varied widely across countries and to ensure internal consistency, factory owners had to be the subject of multiple social audits. There was also great inconsistency among the codes, making it practically impossible for SRI investors to use them to evaluate potential shareholdings. Alice Tepper Marlin, head of CEP observed:

> Major corporations already understand that a company's social accountability is a competitive asset. But companies find it extremely difficult to deliver on and verify corporate responsibility when dealing with hundreds, or even thousands, of vendors, contractors and suppliers in their home countries and abroad.... The real solution, I believe, is to adapt the same model that corporations use to ensure quality control on the part of vendors and suppliers. This solution consists of credible, verifiable and certifiable standards that can be audited by expert third parties, the best known being ISO 9000. Social Accountability 8000 (SA 8000) applies these same techniques to the assurance of social accountability, building on the same basic management system.[40]

CEP set up a subsidiary, Social Accountability International (SAI), to produce such a standard using similar ideas to those lying behind ISO 9000 on quality control. SA 8000 is based on the six basic conventions of the ILO described above, as well as the UN Universal Declaration of Human Rights and the UN Convention on the Rights of the Child. SAI requires a detailed training programme on the use of the standard before auditors are accredited to use it. Although SA

8000 is a universal standard, it is very much locally based, i.e. at the level of the local factory. Auditors are required to talk to local groups such as NGOs and trade unions, and there is a detailed complaints procedure for workers and trade unions to bring forward issues of non-compliance. The standard also requires substantial transparency, in other words, public reporting. SA 8000's stated aim is to develop, maintain and enforce policies and procedures that enable a company to manage those issues which it can control or influence, *and* to demonstrate to interested parties that its policies, procedures and practices are in conformity with the requirements of this standard. By 2001 eight large companies including Avon Products and Toys 'R' Us had signed up to the standard, while it was in use by a number of global certification companies and SRI research groups. In the author's opinion, SA 8000 is a well-thought-out and structured standard that can be usefully adopted by both the corporate sector and SRI investors; an abridged version is given in Box 8.1.[41]

Box 8.1 Social Accountability 8000

Child labour

The company shall not engage in or support the use of child labour. It shall establish policies and procedures for remediation of children found to be working which fit the definition of child labour. Such children will be allowed access to education. Children or young workers may not be exposed to situations in or outside of the workplace that are hazardous, unsafe or unhealthy.

Forced labour

The company shall not engage in or support the use of forced labour, nor shall personnel be required to lodge 'deposits' or identity papers upon commencing employment with the company.

Health and safety

The company shall provide a safe and healthy working environment and shall minimise as far as is reasonably practicable, the causes of hazards inherent in the working environment. A senior management representative shall be responsible for the health and safety of all personnel, and accountable for the implementation of the Health and Safety elements of this standard. All personnel must receive regular and recorded health and safety training; systems must be in place to detect, avoid or respond to potential threats to the health and safety of all personnel.

The company shall provide, for use by all personnel, clean bathrooms, access to potable water, and if appropriate, sanitary facilities for food storage. If dormitories are provided for personnel, they must be clean, safe and meet the basic human needs.

Trade unions

The company shall respect the right of all personnel to form and join trade unions of their choice and to collective bargaining. Trade union representatives must not be subject to discrimination and they must have access to their members in the workplace.

Discrimination

The company shall not engage in or support discrimination in hiring, compensation, access to training, promotion, termination or retirement based on race, caste, national origin, religion, disability, gender, sexual orientation, union membership or political affiliation. Personnel shall have the right to observe tenets or practices. Sexually coercive, threatening, abusive or exploitative behaviour must not be allowed.

Disciplinary practices

The company shall not engage in or support the use of corporal punishment, mental or physical coercion, and verbal abuse.

Working hours

The company shall comply with applicable laws and industry standards on working hours; and personnel shall not, on a regular basis, be required to work in excess of 48 hours per week and shall be provided with at least one day off for every seven-day period. Overtime work must not exceed 12 hours per employee per week, and must be remunerated at a premium rate.

Compensation

The company shall ensure that wages paid for a standard working week shall meet at least legal or industry minimum standards and shall always be sufficient to meet basic needs of personnel. Deductions from wages must not be made for disciplinary purposes, and wages and benefits are to be detailed clearly and regularly for workers. False apprenticeship schemes must not be undertaken in an effort to avoid fulfilling obligations to personnel under applicable laws pertaining to labour and social security legislation and regulations.

Chapter 7 described the use of kitemarks, eco-labels or logos designed to reassure consumers that their products have been made from genuinely organic food or from properly managed forests. In 1997 a similar UK initiative was launched over labour standards. Called the Ethical Trading Initiative (ETI), it was backed by trade unions and leading aid agencies such as Amnesty International, Cafod, Christian Aid, Oxfam and the World Development Movement. The UK government in the form of the Department for International Development was also an initial sponsor. Corporate supporters of ETI included some of the most famous names in UK retailing: Boots, the Co-operative Wholesale Society, J. Sainsbury, Tesco and Marks & Spencer.

The ETI's Base Code reflects the most relevant international standards with respect to labour practices to be used as the basis of its work. ETI member companies are expected to adopt this Base Code, or to adopt their own code so long as it incorporates the Base Code. ETI member companies commit themselves to requiring that suppliers meet agreed standards within a reasonable time frame, and that performance in this regard will be measured in a transparent fashion. It describes itself thus:

The ETI aims to help make substantial improvements to the lives of poor working people around the world. As consumers of the goods they produce we all have a stake in this unique and innovative initiative. The ETI aims to develop and encourage the use of a widely endorsed set of standards, embodied in codes of conduct, and monitoring and auditing methods which will enable companies to work together with other organisations outside the corporate sector to improve labour conditions around the world.[42]

In February 2001 Calpers, one of the world's largest pension funds with $151 billion under management, sent a shock wave round the world of emerging-market investment when it announced that it would be withdrawing its funds from Indonesia, Malaysia, the Philippines and Thailand. This action was taken because they did not meet its new investment guidelines on labour standards and democracy, including a free press. Calpers stated:

This is the first [action] of its kind ever done by a public pension plan that looks beyond traditional economic factors and considers basic democratic principles.[43]

Commentators suggested that others funds would follow Calpers' example.[44] This chapter began by addressing whether human rights were subjective, soft and too vague to take into account by investors. Clearly Calpers, one of the world's largest institutional investors, does not think so. Nor does George Soros, one of the most successful investors of the century.

REFERENCES

1. Accountancy Business Group, September 1999.
2. *Human Rights: Is It Any of Your Business?* Amnesty International and The Prince of Wales Business Forum, April 2000.
3. UN website.
4. Chris Hegarty, quoted in *The Ethical Investor* (EIRIS bulletin), June 2000.
5. Edwin Black, *IBM and the Holocaust*, Crown 2001.
6. *Infrastructure Finance*, March 1996.
7. Levi Strauss, quoted in *Infrastructure Finance*, March 1996.

8. *Burma News* bulletin, June 1997.
9. 'ILO to Probe Forced Labour in Burma', *Financial Times*, 18 September 2001.
10. *Burma News* Bulletin, June 1997.
11. 'Maverick Total', *Financial Times*, 12 February 1997.
12. Quoted in *Infrastructure Finance*, March 1996.
13. 'British Oil Firms Accused of Burma Abuses', *The Guardian*, 12 October 2001.
14. Methodist Church, press release, 20 May 1997.
15. 'Britain Backs Ugly War for Oil', *The Observer*, 16 April 2000.
16. 'Organised Labor Weighs in on IPO', *Wall Street Journal*, 14 March, 2000.
17. 'Talisman May Sell Sudan Assets', *National Post*, 27 October 2001.
18. 'US Legislators Want Markets to Sway Sudan', *Financial Times*, 3 November 2000.
19. 'US Urged to Use Markets to Curb Repression', *Financial Times*, 1 May 2001.
20. 'Canadian Oil Group Asked Sudanese Army to "Remove" Villagers, Document Alleges', *Financial Times*, 22 March 2002.
21. 'Rights Groups Join Companies to State Principles', *Wall Street Journal*, 22 December 2000.
22. 'Torquemada Would Have Admired China's Inquisitors', *Wall Street Journal*, 7 August 2001.
23. 'UN Committee Faults China on Torture', *Wall Street Journal*, 10 May 2000.
24. 'Dogmatic Pursuer of Democracy on China', *Financial Times*, 16 July 2001.
25. *Independent on Sunday*, 3 September 2000.
26. 'Clinton Eats Humble Pie in Asia', *Financial Times*, 28 May 1994.
27. *Prospect Magazine*, June 1997.
28. For more information on these conventions and on the ILO, contact the Department of International Labour Standards and Human Rights, 4, Route des Morillons, CH-1211 Geneva 22; telephone +41 22 799 7155; fax +41 22 799 6771; send an e-mail to normes@ilo.org or consult the ILO website at www.ilo.org.
29. Quoted in *Global Labor Standards*, Investor Responsibility Research Centre, 2001.
30. Quoted in *Global Labor Standards*, Investor Responsibility Research Centre, 2001.
31. 'Baseball Faces Sweatshop Probe', *Financial Times*, 11 May 2001.
32. ICCR website.
33. 'Gap Keeps Struggling amid Myriad Turnaround Plans', *Wall Street Journal*, 6 March 2001.
34. Quoted in 'Visions of Social Accountability: SA8000', Alice Tepper Marlin, *Visions of Ethical Business*, FT Publishing, 1998.
35. Price Waterhouse Coopers, 1999, *Earning Your Reputation: What Makes Others Respect Your Company*.
36. Quoted in *Human Rights: Is it Any of Your Business?* Amnesty International and The Prince of Wales Business Forum, April 2000.
37. Quoted in *Global Labor Standards*, Investor Responsibility Research Centre, 2001.
38. BBC Television, *Panorama*, 15 October 2000, 'Gap, Nike – No Sweat'.
39. *Principles for Global Corporate Responsibility: Benchmarks for Measuring Business Performance*, the Interfaith Centre on Corporate Responsibility (ICCR), the Ecumenical Council for Corporate Responsibility (ECCR), the Taskforce on the Churches and Corporate Responsibility (TCCR). Round Two Text, revised and released 1998.
40. Alice Tepper Marlin, 'Visions of Social Accountability: SA8000', *Visions of Ethical Business*, FT Publishing, 1998.

41. Social Accountability 8000, copyright Social Accountability International. Abridged by the author.
42. Ethical Trading Initiative website.
43. 'US Pension Fund Will Sell Holdings in Four Asian Markets', *Wall Street Journal*, 22 February 2002.
44. 'Calpers' Asian Retreat is a Victory for Ethics', *Financial Times*, 22 February 2002.

9

Corporate Social Responsibility

GROWING EXPECTATIONS

Chapter 1 described growing public concern in many countries about the way economic and even political power seem to be slipping away from democratically elected officials to unelected and unaccountable giant corporations. It was suggested that the 'anti-globalisation' riots seen in Gothenburg, Seattle, etc., were just the lunatic fringe of this general public anxiety. In such a world, institutional investors are one of the few bodies able to positively assert corporate social responsibility, and this ties in naturally with the changing nature of SRI as it evolves away from negative exclusion to active engagement and shareholder activism.

Chapter 3 ended by suggesting that corporate social responsibility (CSR) could become a critical and dominant issue for the new Millennium as a result of public fears over globalisation, and the increasing intrusion of the corporate sector into everyday life. That was initially written in late 2000, when the idea that politicians were worried about anti-globalisation concerns seemed far-fetched. I couldn't help noticing a headline in the *Financial Times* at the end of September 2001 which reported calls for a new 'ethical' association of the G8, the world's eight richest economies. The Belgian prime minister, Guy Verhofstadt, made a public plea for what he described as 'ethical globalisation', whereby the G8 would work together to establish minimum standards on working conditions and corporate governance.

At the same time, Belgium used its EU presidency to host a major conference in Brussels in November 2001, entitled 'Corporate Social Responsibility on the European Social Policy Agenda'. Topics covered by the conference included 'integrating social concerns into the corporate development strategy' and 'promoting socially responsible investment.'[1] The European Commission (EC) supported this with the publication of a Green Paper on corporate social responsibility in July 2001.[2] The EC noted the convergence of environmental and social concerns as it prepared for the Johannesburg world summit on sustainable development (Rio+10) scheduled for September 2002:

> The original Rio Summit was very much focused on the environment, but since then the social aspect has come to the fore, and it's essential that it is discussed in relation to business activity at the summit, which will be an ideal stage to raise the profile of CSR.[3]

Fears are often expressed that corporate social responsibility is just another form of 'spin', 'greenwash' or corporate public relations. After all, most companies have some kind of mission statement describing themselves as good corporate citizens or something equivalent. In this book the term 'corporate social responsibility' means simply that companies are increasingly being judged not just by the products and profits they make, but also by *how* these profits are made. Economists sometimes attack the whole idea of corporate social responsibility as being fundamentally misconceived. Using the erroneous assumption that CSR is equivalent to corporate philanthropy, they argue that the job of the corporate sector is to maximise its profits, not to give shareholders' money away. The conclusion of that argument is true, unfortunately its premise is false. CSR simply means that companies should carry out their core function of making profits by the provision of goods and services but by doing so in a socially responsible way. This also means that companies who ignore these social responsibilities are unlikely to get away with a green fig leaf by indulging in a small amount of corporate philanthropy.

In other words, companies have a responsibility to the communities and physical environment in which they operate. The need for CSR to be based on action rather than words is accepted by many large companies. According to Mark Wade, manager of the social accountability team at Shell International:

> It is not enough for companies to behave responsibly. They must be seen and believed to be doing so. This means companies finding out what it is people want to know about them, how they will be judged, and what they need to do to be believed. Our intention is to develop consistent ways of monitoring, measuring and reporting performance in a manner aligned to the expectations of society and our own business principles.[4]

From the perspective of socially responsible investors, particularly institutional investors, CSR has three core elements. I became convinced of this after discussions with a number of UK local authority pension funds in September 2000.[5]

- Responsibility to shareholders, or what we may call corporate governance
- Responsibility to humanity in the form of human rights
- Responsibility to the biosphere in terms of good environmental practice

The heart of corporate social responsibility is corporate governance, although CSR obviously has a broader dimension than that. I decided to call this chapter 'corporate social responsibility' rather than 'corporate governance' to emphasise these wider perspectives. I wanted to contrast this with the tendency of corporate governance to become bogged down in narrow box-ticking.

Corporate governance is doubly important, however. Not only is it a crucial issue in its own right, but without the corporate accountability it provides, the whole engagement approach of SRI breaks down, leaving empty discussions, or greenwash. Effective corporate governance is therefore an essential part of socially responsible investing; without it shareholder activism cannot exist.

THE HISTORY OF CORPORATE GOVERNANCE

Concern over corporate governance is as old as economics. Adam Smith identified what has since become known as the agency problem in his pioneering book of 1776, *The Wealth of Nations*:

The directors of such companies, however, being the managers rather of other people's money than of their own, it cannot be well expected that they should watch over it with the same anxious vigilance with which the partners in a private partnership frequently watch over their own.[6]

However, when Smith wrote those words, this was a question of only theoretical importance. The modern limited company which separates owners from managers was made illegal in the Bubble Act of 1720, passed in response to the frenzied speculation that had occurred in the shares of the South Sea Company. Until the late nineteenth century, business was run on a small scale, and usually by an owner or manager. Large-scale enterprises needing the additional financial flexibility provided by limited liability status did not really emerge until the 1870s, essentially to finance the expansion of railways in the UK and the US. Suspicion of the protected status and infinite life of the limited company was also prevalent in the US. Many US states prohibited business incorporation until relatively late in the nineteenth century. Justice Louis Brandeis of the US Supreme Court described their fears in a 1932 judgement:

Incorporation for business was commonly denied after it had been freely granted for religious, educational and charitable purposes. It was denied because of fear.... There was a sense of some insidious menace inherent in large aggregations of capital; particularly when held by corporations. So at first the corporate privilege was granted sparingly; and only when the grant seemed necessary in order to procure for the community some specific benefit otherwise unobtainable.[7]

Corporate governance was largely ignored during the nineteenth century, but revived as a topic of serious discussion in the 1920s and 1930s following a series of mergers that concentrated power in many industries in a few giant corporations. For example, consolidation in the chemical industry led to most British chemical companies becoming united as Imperial Chemical Industries (ICI). A similar process of almagamation in the US car industry resulted in a new corporate giant called General Motors. The first real critique of corporate governance, *The Modern Corporation and Private Property*, was written in 1933 by Adolf Berle, an economic adviser to President Roosevelt's New Deal. It states (original italics; bold italics added):

> By tradition the corporations 'belongs' to its shareholders, or, in a wider sense, to its security holders, and theirs is the only interest to be recognised as the object of corporate activity.... By the application of this doctrine, the group in control of a corporation would be placed in a position of trusteeship in which it would be called on to operate or arrange for the operation of the corporation for the *sole* benefit of the security owners despite the fact that that the latter have ceased to have power over or to accept responsibility for the *active* property in which they have an interest. *Were this course followed, the bulk of American industry might soon be operated by trustees for the sole benefit of inactive and irresponsible security owners.*[8]

CORPORATE GOVERNANCE IN THE UK

Corporate governance became an issue of general public and political concern in the UK following the report of the Cadbury Committee in December 1992. This defined corporate governance as:

> The system by which companies are directed and controlled. Boards of directors are responsible for the governance of their companies, while the shareholders' role in governance is to appoint the directors and auditors and to satisfy themselves that a proper governance structure is in place. The responsibilities of the board include setting the company's strategic aims, providing the leadership to put them into place, supervising the management of the business, and reporting to shareholders on their stewardship.[9]

The Cadbury definition is important because it illustrates the normal limits of UK thinking on corporate governance, that it is a highly technical and legalistic subject. Hence the term is normally used to describe such matters as the expected duties of a board of directors; its composition, including the number and independence of non-executive directors; the role of the chairman; reporting and control systems within the company; and the operation of audit and control functions. The Cadbury Committee was convened in May 1991 at the request of the London Stock Exchange and the accounting profession. The underlying reason was concern over the recent collapse of some large publicly quoted companies whose chief executive had dominated the board, such as Robert Maxwell at Maxwell Communications. The need to prevent a repetition of such corporate failure by controlling powerful chief executives became the central part of UK corporate governance, as Cadbury's recommendations showed. With the wisdom of hindsight, and in particular in the light of the recent collapse of Independent Insurance in the UK and Enron in the US, the committee's emphasis on auditor independence and effective control systems seems prophetic. Here are the key recommendations of the Cadbury Committee:[10]

1. That there should be a separation of authority at the head of a company to prevent a chief executive having supreme power. This would normally be achieved by separating the posts of chief executive and chairman.
2. That at least three independent non-executive directors should be appointed to each company board of directors.
3. That the majority of non-executive directors should be independent of the company.
4. That directors' service terms should not exceed three years.
5. That directors should report on the effectiveness of the company's internal control systems.
6. That fees paid to auditors for non-audit work should be fully disclosed.
7. That all companies should establish audit and remuneration committees consisting mainly of non-executive directors.
8. That institutional shareholders should recognise the responsibilities of share ownership:
   (a) by regular contact with companies at senior executive level
   (b) by regarding the voting rights of company shares they hold as an asset
   (c) by disclosing their policies on the use of their voting rights

In the early 1990s the narrow conception of the role of corporate governance within the UK as shown by Cadbury broadened to include wider issues, especially excessive executive pay. Indeed, the focus of the 1995 Greenbury Report on corporate governance was mostly on executive pay.[11] One of the most high-profile examples was British Gas, whose executives received what appeared to be large pay rises in 1995 at a time when the company's profitability looked under pressure, and a redundancy programme was being implemented. This caused intense negative publicity for the company; for example, a pig was named Cedric, after the company's chief executive and kept outside its 1995 AGM. Eleven pension funds tabled a shareholder resolution calling on the company to change its methods of determining executive pay towards best practice. This resolution won over 18% of the vote, an astonishing percentage for a resolution opposed by the company. Although it was not passed, there soon followed significant changes in the British Gas senior management and remuneration policy.

The subject of executive pay can be extremely complex, particularly when it concerns the minutiae of long-term incentive schemes for executives. However, in the author's opinion, the key point about executive pay is fairly straightforward — it should align the interests of executives and shareholders. If it does not align them, perhaps through the gift of share options, there is a risk that management may be encouraged to undertake a high-risk corporate strategy which if it works will make them personally rich. If the high-risk strategy fails, the company will suffer and could conceivably go bankrupt; the shareholders would lose everything, but all the executives would forfeit is the potential gain from their options. Large-scale corporate failures, such as Independent Insurance in the UK and Enron in the US, may go down in history as case studies of the effect of such asymmetric incentive schemes. Speaking personally, I have always believed that the best way to properly incentivise management is to pay them a large part of their basic salary in shares in the company, but not in the form of share options.

The most recent review of UK corporate governance was carried out by the Hampel Committee in 1998, which put together the main principles of the previous committees into a combined code.[12] Perhaps the most notable feature of the Hampel Report was its warning that corporate governance in the UK had degenerated into a 'box-ticking' exercise. It worried that the large UK investment institutions were going through the motions of scrutinising companies to see whether they complied with Cadbury recommendations but that nothing was really changing. Hampel also wanted companies to produce a new statement for publication in their annual report and accounts indicating how key corporate governance principles had been applied in their company. Here are the Hampel recommendations:[13]

1. That the majority of a company's non-executive directors (NEDs) should be independent, and the board should identify these.
2. That at least one-third of the board should consist of non-executive directors.
3. That all directors should be submitted for re-election every three years.
4. That the roles of chairman and chief executive should be separate.
5. That remuneration committees should consist only of non-executive directors.
6. That details of individual executive remuneration should be disclosed, and that a general statement on executive remuneration should be made to shareholders.
7. That institutional investors (i.e. fund management companies) had a responsibility to their clients to make use of their votes, and that they should make available information on their shareholder voting records.

However, despite the public uproar over executive pay that led to the Greenbury Committee report, significant improvements in the system were not apparent. A survey of executive pay of the top FTSE 100 companies was carried out by the Co-operative Insurance Services (CIS) in 2001. It found that the majority of them were not following the best practice suggestions of the Hampel Committee's combined code.[14] Indeed, the survey reported that 60% of the companies monitored had not adopted the Hampel recommendation of directors' pay being set by a remuneration committee comprising only non-executive directors. CIS chief investment officer Chris Hirst warned that excessive executive pay awards could result in damage to a company's reputation, as well as diverting the profits of the business from the shareholders who ultimately owned it. He noted:

We are surprised and disappointed at how many of the largest UK companies are not following corporate best practice. Independent scrutiny of company management and directors' pay is a very important issue of concern to us.... It is essential that those committees are properly structured so that investors can place confidence in them.... Until companies have the proper checks and balances at the heart of their management, there is the danger that shareholders... could see money due to them diverted to unjustified rewards.[15]

Under the leadership of Alastair Ross Goobey, Hermes Pension Management, the investment manager of the BT pension scheme, took a pioneering and high-profile position campaigning for better corporate governance. The philosophy behind its actions was the belief that this shareholder activism added to shareholder returns:

We see corporate governance not as a moral crusade, but as part of our fiduciary duty to our clients in identifying the business risks, financial and non-financial, to enhance our investment process accordingly.... Hermes believes that an active shareholder involvement can help release the higher intrinsic value of the company.... [Hermes' shareholder activism] grew out of our involvement in corporate governance issues, which if you are not careful could turn into a box-ticking exercise. The question is, what do you do when you come across governance that you don't like? You need some way of... facilitating change.[16]

In 1997 Hermes published a detailed corporate governance code for the companies in which it invested on behalf of its clients. It stated its policy of giving general support to companies in which it invested against hostile takeovers, but warned that such support was conditional; for example, it was unlikely to support companies hiding behind low or no voting rights. Hermes also suggested that the obvious way to align the interests of executives and shareholders would be to ensure that executives built significant personal holdings in their company's shares. Michelle Edkins, director of corporate governance at Hermes, noted the apparent conflicts of interest in the current executive remuneration system:

A director who sits on several boards is not likely to clamp down on pay at one company. That would risk lowering the value of all executives- not a very popular proposition if that includes oneself.[17]

Here are the details of the Hermes corporate governance code:[18]

- Overly large boards are not effective.
- A majority of the non-executive directors should be independent.
- At least one non-executive director should be appointed every three years.
- Non-executives should serve for a maximum of ten years.
- Non-executives should receive part of their fee in the form of shares.
- No chief executive should become chairman in the same company without a break.
- There should be separate chairmen and chief executives.
- Executives' rolling contracts should last for a maximum of one year.
- Directors should normally retire at age 70.
- Split share structures would not normally be supported.
- Voting figures should be publicised after the AGM.
- In normal circumstances the standard pre-emptive rights to new shares of existing investors should not be ignored by any share issue over 5%.

Institutional voting is the other main issue that has come to dominate the debate over corporate governance in the UK. All the committees described above expressed concern that institutional investors were behaving as 'absent owners', with voting levels running below 25%. UK shareholder voting has been monitored for many years by corporate governance specialists Pensions and Investment Research Consultants (PIRC). PIRC analysis showed that average turnout in proxy votes at UK AGMs slowly rose from 35% in 1993 to 46% in 1998, but then seemed to stagnate below 50%. PIRC's 2001 review examined 739 FTSE All-Share companies which had meetings and received results of proxy votes from 381. Five of the companies in the FTSE 100 index – the UK's largest companies – saw less than

25% of their total potential proxy votes cast at AGMs. Overall voting levels were static at 48%.[19]

Part of the problem has been the sheer mechanical difficulty faced by a major investment management house to coordinate the voting of all the hundreds, or maybe even thousands, of investment clients under its control. Nevertheless, there is still a widespread belief that the main problem is a lack of interest by large investment institutions. The Myners Report on institutional investment which appeared in summer 2001 appears to have accepted this, as it recommended that the UK should follow the US example and make the use of voting rights part of the fiduciary duty. Towards the end of 2001 there were signs that this recommendation would be given a statutory basis.[20]

As the focus of corporate governance has moved away from narrow issues of internal corporate control to cover the wider subjects of executive pay and shareholder rights, it has naturally moved towards the SRI philosophy that investment institutions have an explicit duty to engage with companies. I think it is also fair to state that the UK framework of safeguarding shareholder rights is among the best in the world. Ever since the 1960s, the National Association of Pension Funds (NAPF) and the Association of British Insurers (ABI) have fought a largely successful battle to ensure that all shareholders are treated equally using the principle of 'one share, one vote'. Very few large UK companies now have the kind of split capital structure with restricted voting rights that is common in Europe, for example, or the kind of staggered boards, tracking stocks or legal poison pills devices (anti-takeover schemes) that are regrettably fairly prevalent in the US. The City Takeover Panel also provides strong legal protection to UK minority shareholders, and tightly regulates changes in corporate control.

CORPORATE GOVERNANCE IN THE US

According to Robert Reich former US Secretary of Labor:

> Pension funds are becoming perhaps the most vigilant and influential custodians of long-term corporate strategy... as any

chief executive officer will tell you, nothing so concentrates the mind so much as an inquiry from a major institutional investor about his or her company's practices.[21]

The debate over corporate governance in the US has taken a very different shape from that in the UK. Despite the encouraging noises from Robert Reich, it has been driven mainly by individual battles over shareholder rights, rather than by government-inspired committees. As such corporate governance is generally regarded as an integral part of the US tradition of shareholder activism. Since the late 1980s this point was forcefully made in the US by the largest single institutional investor, the state pension fund of California. Normally known as Calpers, it was one of the pioneers of shareholder activism as a means of to increase returns. Dale Hanson, chief executive of Calpers, put it this way in 1993:

> Our entire investment philosophy is based on the premise that we are long-term investors. Our average holding period is between eight and ten years.... Calpers has no motives other than to improve corporate performance so that investment value is increased.... We seek a return to corporations being accountable to their shareholders. If accountability exists, we are confident that corporate performance will follow.[22]

An analysis of Calpers' shareholder activism was carried out by the consulting firm Wilshire Associates in 1993, which found that it paid strong financial dividends. From 1987 to 1992 Calpers targeted 42 US companies for shareholder action. This group had significantly underperformed the US benchmark, the S&P 500 index, in the previous five years. Wilshire found that after Calpers commenced shareholder activism, these companies produced an outperformance of the S&P 500 by 41% over the subsequent five years. The study also found that shareholder activism had the most financial benefit when it focused on corporate strategy in a dialogue with management. An academic analysis of the benefits of Calpers' shareholder activism was later published in the *Journal of Finance* in 1996. Here is an extract (emphasis added):

> It is shown that over the last five years of the sample period (1989–93), 72% of targets either adopted proposed governance

structure resolutions or made changes sufficient to warrant a settlement. There is a significant positive stock price reaction for successful targeting events and a negative reaction for unsuccessful events.... Overall, the evidence indicates that *shareholder activism is largely successful in changing governance structure and, when successful, results in a statistically significant increase in shareholder wealth.*[23]

One important difference between the UK and the US lies in the number and financial strength of charitable foundations, often church based, in America. Such institutions have a much stronger natural interest in CSR than pension funds. US pension schemes are governed by the 1974 Employee Retirement Income Security Act (ERISA), and regulated under that act by the Department of Labor. In 1988 the department stated that the voting rights attached to company shares were an asset, and therefore that US pension funds had to treat them as they would any other asset under the heading of fiduciary duty. In practice this means that they should be used in the best interests of beneficiaries, independent advice should be taken on their use, and that records should be kept of voting activity to demonstrate that such assets were being utilised. In 1995 the department extended this ruling to overseas holdings, i.e. since that date US pension funds have a statutory obligation to use their shareholder votes in the UK, Europe and elsewhere. As the Calpers evidence showed, good corporate governance pays for itself. According to Michael Claes, managing director of Burston-Marsteller in New York:

Studies show that 40% to 45% of a company's stock price is a reflection of shareholder confidence in the CEO, his strategy and management team.[24]

A landmark date in US shareholder activism occurred in April 1989, when Bob Monks informed the board of Honeywell Inc. that proposals to limit shareholder powers were unacceptable. Honeywell, a large US computer and defence company, had a recent dull profits record reflected in a stagnant share price. Monks formed a shareholder action group, including Calpers, to oppose the board's proposals, and a fierce proxy battle began. In May 1989 it was announced that the board's proposals had been defeated, and in July 1989 Honeywell announced a major restructuring. Over a three-month period the value of Honeywell shares rose 22% to $89. The 1989 Honeywell proxy battle was of historic importance, as it was the first time that institutional shareholders joined forces with private investors to support a proxy initiative to defeat a corporation's antitakeover proposals. In 1989 Bob Monks formed his own company, Lens Inc., to force change on a number of poorly performing companies. Probably its most famous campaign was a two-year battle in 1990–92 with the retail giant Sears Roebuck. Monks stood for election as an independent director of Sears. He was not elected, but the company was eventually forced into a major restructuring plan which involved selling off its financial operations to concentrate on retailing, while over the period the share price almost doubled from $24.75 to $44.75.

The name Bob Monks crops up frequently in this chapter, as an almost legendary figure in the field of corporate governance, someone who has campaigned for improved corporate accountability for over twenty-five years. His firm Lens Inc. pioneered the concept of taking stakes in underperforming companies and using shareholder activism to press for change, and over its life Lens has consistently achieved returns in excess of the S&P 500 average. In 1998 Hermes Lens Asset Management Company was founded in the UK in partnership with the BT pension scheme to promote the same investment principles in the UK. Monks has been able to combine shareholder activism with writing about it cogently and passionately Together with Nell Minow he wrote *Corporate Governance*[25], an exhaustive 550-page tome on the details of corporate governance, one of the best books ever written on the subject. Bob Monks' more recent work explores the crucial importance of corporate governance in the realm of politics and social policy. His 1998 book, *The Emperor's Nightingale*, provided a broad definition of the subject reflecting these concerns:

> Healthy corporate governance... is the relationship among various participants in determining the direction and performance of corporations consistent with the public good.[26]

In summer 2001 Monks came to the UK to publicise his new book, *The New Global Investors*.[27] I interviewed him about the book, and asked him whether his practical shareholder activism work had helped develop his thinking on corporate governance:

Absolutely yes, I would never have got there without it. Look, the real smoking gun that tells you that something is seriously wrong is the question of executive pay. In the 1990s the average American chief executive saw his pay rise sixfold, far more than the growth in profits. The ratio of the average CEO salary to that of the average factory worker is approaching 500 times, something that is obscene.

Such greed is siphoning off a lot of the benefits to society of increased productivity into a relatively few hands. It is also leading to growing 'anti-capitalist' resentment that threatens our existing free-market system — we certainly don't want this to result in a return to heavy government regulation of the economy. In a free society, institutions rest upon the popular belief in their legitimacy. I'm worried that discontent with business is growing among ordinary people — the agitators who demonstrated in Seattle, Davos, Gothenburg may have been just the tip of the iceberg.[28]

As Monks intimated, the question of executive pay has also been a major corporate governance issue is the US. One of the leading experts on executive remuneration in the US is the former compensation consultant Graef Crystal. In 1991 he wrote a book simply entitled *In Search of Excess: the Overcompensation of American Executives*. The book's dust jacket simply proclaimed: 'In the last 20 years the pay of American workers has gone nowhere, while American CEOs have increased their own pay more than 400%. This is how they've done it'.[29] About the same time as British Gas hit the headlines in the UK over excessive management rewards, Disney did the same in the US. In 1995 there was widespread discontent over a severance package given to the company's president, Michael Ovitz. A number of US SRI funds, led by Progressive Asset Management (PAM) and church investors such as the General Board of Pensions of the United Methodist Church, filed a shareholder resolution in September 1996 demanding that the company institute a system where executive rewards were based on clear performance goals. PAM chairman Tom van Dyke described the payment as perverse:

Mickey's pocket has been picked, while the shareholders and employees who give their life to work at Disney stand by and watch. That payoff is way above the market average, even by Hollywood standards.[30]

As this book was going to press, in spring 2002, corporate governance was coming under political scrutiny in the US as never before. The collapses of Enron and Global Crossing resulted in two of the largest bankruptcies in US history. Enron also caused widespread distress among equity shareholders, as a company with an equity market capitalisation of over $70 billion became worthless in just over a year. Enron's collapse was also a calamity to many of its employees, who not only lost their jobs, but saw the value of their 401k pension plans invested in Enron stock disappear. Inquiries into Enron's collapse indicated that it resulted from major failures of corporate governance. Certain senior Enron executives appeared to have made significant profits from secret deals made with the company. The board of directors appeared to have failed to control such behaviour, just as it rubber-stamped the production of accounts that failed to disclose material factors such as significant off-balance sheet debt. The Enron board also seemed to ignore reports from middle ranking executives exposing dubious practices. In February 2002 US Treasury Secretary Paul O'Neil announced planned changes in the law making it easier to punish corporate executives guilty of misleading shareholders:

> One of the things we're talking about is to move the standard for CEOs...from recklessness to negligence, which is an important change.[31]

Indeed, the Enron debacle focused attention on US accounting practices, and highlighted the relationship between companies and the accounting firms who as auditors were meant to confirm the accuracy of financial statements. Burton Malkiel, Professor of Economics at Princeton is a long-time observer of financial markets. He argued:

> In my view, the root systemic problem is a series of conflicts of interest that have spread through the financial system....Unfortunately, often the incentives facing accounting

firms, security analysts, and even in some circumstances boards of directors militate against their functioning as effective guardians of shareholders' interests....Too often, board members of US corporations have personal, business, or consulting relationships with the corporations on whose boards they sit. For some 'professional directors', large fees and other perks militate against performing their proper function as a sometime thorn in management's side. The watchdogs often behave like lapdogs.[32]

Worries over accounting policies caused the shares of the American security conglomerate Tyco to more than halve in the first two months of 2002. Reports that the Securities and Exchange Commission (SEC) was investigating the accounting practices of the computer services company Computer Associates had a similar impact on its share price. For many years corporate governance experts had worried over potential conflicts of interest when accounting firms acted as both consultants and auditors to the same firm, but these conflicts burst out into the open after Enron. The auditors to Enron were Arthur Andersen, one of the top five firms who dominate the global accounting market. The fallout from Enron's collapse left Andersen facing legal challenges including a criminal charge from the US Department of Justice. The damage to its reputation also led to a number of its major clients such as Merck replacing it with alternative auditors.

The leading socially responsible investors in America responded to the challenge. On 4 February the board of ICCR met in New York to discuss its response. Two issues dominated the agenda. First, what would be an inappropriate relationship between the level of audit fees and other consulting fees that would lead ICCR to decide to vote against the appointment of an accounting firm? Second, what were the best metrics to decide whether the audit committee was sufficiently independent of the company concerned?[33] In March 2002 Domini Social Investments (DSI) issued new proxy voting guidelines that had been revised in the light of Enron. The new guidelines stated that DSI would vote against the appointment of auditors who were not clearly independent, while it would also vote against companies whose boards did not have a majority of non-executive directors.

DSI tightened up its rules on executive remuneration, tying executive stock options to the overall performance of the company, not just the changes in its share price. Amy Domini argued:

> The Enron-Andersen scandal clearly demonstrates that conflicts can arise when accounting firms provide collateral services to the companies they audit. We know these conflicts of interest can be disastrous for shareholders, employees and the public. Henceforth, we will vote our proxies against all proposals to appoint auditors who are not sufficiently independent. We will also support shareholder resolutions requesting that these functions be performed by separate firms.[34]

Partly as a result of Enron, Patricia Hewitt, the UK Trade and Industry Secretary, ordered inquiries to be made into the role and duties of non-executive directors, and the role of accountancy firms in offering both auditing and consulting services.[35] About the same time, the SEC announced that it might seize the profits of company executives who made profits by selling company stock while earnings were inflated. It noted that Enron executives had sold $1 billion in company shares before the share price collapsed on news that charges would reduce earnings by $585 million, and revelations of off-balance-sheet debt.[36] The SEC also announced that it would assess the performance of the audit committee of any company whose financial reporting was investigated by the SEC. SEC director of enforcement Stephen Cutler explained:

> An audit committee, or audit committee member cannot insulate herself or himself from liability by burying his or her head in the sand. It just won't work that way. In every financial reporting matter we investigate, we will look at the audit committee.[37]

CORPORATE GOVERNANCE IN ASIA AND EUROPE

Interest in corporate governance outside the Anglo-Saxon world is a relatively new phenomenon. In the Far East outside of Japan many companies were only established after the war, with the founding shareholder or his family normally retaining management control. In such circumstances the idea that there could be divergent interests between shareholders and executives would be regarded as nonsensical. The Japanese *keiretsu* system, where corporate groups such as Mitsubishi or Sumitomo have widespread cross-shareholdings in each other, has similar effects, as does the related South Korean *chaebol* system.

When the Asian economic crisis erupted in 1998–99, many economists stated that the reason the Asian economic miracle proved to have feet of clay was its reliance upon crony capitalism. At best this meant a cosy partnership between the government and corporate executives, at worst it described the widespread corruption seen under the Suharto regime in Indonesia. The International Finance Corporation, the private sector arm of the World Bank, responded to such concerns in the spring of 2001 by adding corporate governance clauses to its loan agreements.[38] ASrIA (Association for Sustainable & Responsible Investment in Asia), the new SRI umbrella group for Asia, has announced the improvement of corporate governance to be one of its core aims. When the regional economic crisis hit, it was noticeable that countries such as Hong Kong which possessed relatively good corporate governance systems did much better than countries such as Indonesia with a poor record in this regard.

However, even Hong Kong got low marks from Standard and Poor's in a report produced in December 2001 assessing its relation to global corporate governance standards. S&P noted that while the Hong Kong legal system supported good corporate governance, this was obviated by the system of family control, few independent directors, and low levels of disclosure. The normal pattern of a dominant controlling shareholder meant that takeover bids were more or less unknown in the territory. The Hong Kong stock exchange announced plans at the same time to compel quoted companies to produce quarterly reports and establish audit committees.[39]

Against this background the key issues covered under the heading of corporate governance are really better described as treatment of external shareholders. These include the production of accurate and informative report and accounts, so that shareholders are properly informed about the company's affairs; equal treatment of core and external shareholders, and equal voting rights for all shareholders.

Research by CLSA Emerging Markets, based in Kuala Lumpur and carried out in the spring of 2001, found that companies operating in the emerging markets with the best corporate governance records delivered superior financial returns. CLSA studied 495 companies in 13 countries, ranking them into quartiles on their corporate governance rating. This found that the top hundred companies in the survey had an average dollar return of 127% over the three years to the end of 2000, but that those in the top quartile of the corporate governance survey returned 267% over the period. According to report author Amar Gill:

> In many markets, companies with good corporate governance have outperformed their indices in recent years and moved to valuation premia. But can that outperformance continue? Yes it can — if these companies are also value creators in their respective markets and sectors. And our research shows that companies with [good] governance are also those with high ROE and the largest value creators on an EVA analysis.[40]

Similar considerations apply to continental Europe, where until 1990s debt-based finance was the norm and equity shareholders were often second best. In countries such as Sweden and Switzerland it was common for a dual-capital system to be in existence, where A or registered shares had multiple voting rights, while the majority of shareholders were only able to buy B or bearer shares (or *Genussschein*) with limited or no voting rights. In most of the rest of the Continent, a core shareholding group (*noyau dur*) normally exercised effective control led by a dominant bank or family shareholding. The system was probably most prevalent in Italy, where a small group of industrialists and merchant banks were suspected of making changes in corporate control through private deals in smoke-filled rooms (*buono salotto*). Corporate reporting was also opaque, with a high level of provisioning distorting the real level of profits.

If Enron was the US corporate governance bombshell, ABB was its European equivalent. The Swedish-Swiss heavy engineering company ABB was one of the worst-performing large-capitalisation shares in Europe over the period 2000–2002, when its share price fell from SFr 54.5 to SFr 11. There was therefore a public outcry in

February 2002 when it was revealed that two retired ABB executives had received retirement compensation of SFr 233 million without satisfactory approval procedures of ABB's board being met.[41] ABB's recently appointed chairman, Juergen Dormann, stated that the company was pressing for the return of some of these payments. Shortly afterwards the EC commissioner Frits Bolkenstein announced plans for a pan-European code on takeovers and corporate governance. He specifically mentioned ABB when introducing the proposals, stating that excessive executive pay was a bad thing for the EU.[42] The European 'Rhineland' model of capitalism has always had a communitarian basis, valuing 'social cohesion' above the aggressive individualism of the Anglo-Saxon version. Hence the ABB pay-offs probably generated much greater disquiet than would have been the case in the US. In the words of the European Commission's Green Paper on CSR:

> An increasing number of European companies recognise their social responsibility more and more clearly, and consider it as part of their identity.... These developments reflect the growing expectations that European citizens and stakeholders have of the evolving role of companies in the new and changing society of today... in the long-term, economic growth, social cohesion, and environmental protection go hand in hand.[43]

In general the late 1990s saw a distinct improvement in corporate governance throughout Europe, in reflecting political pressure across the Continent. For example, the German government commissioned a much more stringent code which required disclosure of executive pay. While this code was voluntary, German justice minister Dauebler-Gmelin announced planned legislation for the summer of 2002 that would compel German quoted companies to declare annually whether they complied with it or not.[44] Market forces also worked for improvement, as large companies discovered the need to raise finance in London or New York, pushing them towards Anglo-Saxon levels of disclosure and treatment of shareholders. The Finnish mobile phone giant Nokia provides a good example of this process, as the company abolished its preferential voting rights in 1999, instituting 'one share, one vote' on normal Anglo-Saxon lines. It also created a global board with a number of external directors from outside Finland. Lauri Kivinen, a Nokia spokesman said:

> We've been working on our corporate governance structure for many years. As we have gained global shareholders, we have made adjustments. Currently 55% of Nokia shares are now held in the US.[45]

In summer 2001 Deutsche Bank's asset management subsidiary, DWS, carried out a survey of corporate governance across Europe. DWS analysed the top fifty European companies according to five main principles: corporate governance practice; disclosure; shareholder rights; takeover defences, and the structure of boards and their functioning. Thomas Richter, a DWS spokesman, explained:

> We hope as a big institutional investor to increase the awareness that corporate governance is important to us. We are attending general meetings, and we want to identify which companies we should be going to in order to make improvements.[46]

THE LINK BETWEEN CORPORATE GOVERNANCE AND SRI

Until recently many people, particularly in the UK, would have disagreed with the idea that corporate governance was in any way linked to socially responsible investment. One of the first people to link them was the author. In *The Ethical Investor*, written in 1993–94, I suggested that corporate governance was an integral part of corporate social responsibility, with CSR in turn being an essential ingredient of SRI:

> In December 1992 the Report of the Cadbury Committee sent a shock-wave through the boardrooms of the UK, with its explicit criticisms of the way some companies were being run. It advocated a code of good practice to improve corporate governance, stressing the need for non-executive directors to ensure this, including business ethics. Non-executive directors should bring an independent judgement to bear on issues of strategy, performance, and resources – including key appointments – and

standards of conduct. Corporate governance does not just extend to improving corporate strategy, or even increasing a company's awareness of potential liabilities for example in the environmental field.[47]

I remember many people disagreeing with me over this, although a senior business ethicist praised the book's 'far-sightedness' in this regard to me. At that time corporate governance was generally regarded as a highly technical part of company law, while negative avoidance was the basis of 'ethical investment' in the UK. This dichotomy was less true in the US, where church investors meant that shareholder activism was always on the agenda. Not everyone agrees with the author that corporate governance is really just one aspect of SRI. David Cranston, the director general of the National Association of Pension Funds sees it differently:

> SRI has been getting an increasingly high profile, encouraged by both political motives and increasing public interest. While SRI issues are clearly important, it is equally important to remember that SRI is but a subset of good corporate governance.[48]

There is no doubt that, from a practical standpoint, SRI and corporate governance are converging. Corporate governance research providers such as PIRC and NAPF in the UK, and IRRC in the US, have invested significant resources in expanding their SRI research capability. Bob Monks certainly sees a growing overlap between corporate governance and SRI. I asked him about this shift towards ethics in his work:

> It's true that this is a relatively new area for me in the context of my writing. It fact it was Peter Drucker who convinced me just a couple of years ago that corporate governance was essentially just one aspect of investment. However, questions of business ethics have always concerned me.[49]

PIRC has always considered SRI to be a core part of its work. It believes that looking beyond the purely short-term financial interests of investors is in the interests of society and in the interests of its mainly pension fund clients. The reasoning behind this was set out in 1993:[50]

1. With immense financial power comes responsibility. Not only do pension funds have duties to their members, they also have wider responsibilities which stem from their role in the economy.
2. Pension funds' investment strategies, voting policies as shareholders and relations with companies can have a profound impact upon wider society, and on the investment returns they receive. Local authority pension funds are in a leading position of influence. Their wide range of responsibilities for the environment, economic development and social welfare put them in a unique position in the investment community.
3. Pension funds are long-term investors. Over the long term there is a great deal of mutual interest between shareholders, corporations, employees, the wider community and the environment. Wealth creation, sustainable development, equality of opportunity and corporate accountability are some of the goals which are shared in common. Socially responsible investors use their position of influence as owners to initiate positive change in corporations to the mutual benefit of a company's stakeholders.

PIRC was probably ahead of its time in pointing out that the long-term time frame of pension funds mean that they have to take social and environmental factors into account. In Chapter 1 I argued that the growth of SRI represented a paradigm shift, or revolutionary new way of looking at the world, in the field of investment. A theoretical justification for these assertions was provided by an important book published in 2001, *The Rise of Fiduciary Capitalism* by James P. Hawley and Andrew T. Williams.[51] It argues that the sheer size of many institutional funds means they cannot easily liquidate or accumulate significant holdings. They are more or less forced to index the bulk of their portfolios. In the 1950s Harry Markowitz had the brilliant idea that the risk of individual holdings was not important, what was important was the overall risk of the portfolio containing them. This paradigm shift totally revolutionised thinking in the investment industry. It is arguable that *The Rise of Fiduciary Capitalism* makes a similar paradigm shift by describing large institutional investors as 'universal owners'. The point is that universal owners are unable to follow the dictates of modern financial theory and diversify their portfolios away from the index — they are stuck with it. As a result, their risk factor is no longer the risk factor of individual companies, but that of the long-term performance of the overall stock market, which is driven by the performance of the economy.

It is therefore in the fiduciary interests of such 'universal owners' to promote social responsibility and obviate environmental damage. For most investors there is what economists call a free-rider problem. It is in everybody's interests to reduce public costs such as pollution, and all investors would benefit from these improvements. However, the costs of such initiatives would be borne solely by the individual fund which promoted them. In other words, action to reduce pollution, or to promote human rights by an individual fund, could be against the dictates of fiduciary duty, as the financial costs would be higher than the financial returns. The paradigm shift derives from the fact that for universal owners this is no longer true.

Individual companies may find it profitable to offload the costs of pollution onto the public; they are what economists call externalities. But universal owners suffer the full costs of cleaning up environmental damage through deteriorating infrastructures, higher taxes, lower employee productivity, etc. At the same time, unlike individual investors, they get the benefit of positive externalities such as highly trained staff. Even if trained employees subsequently leave the firm where the expenses of training have occurred, these employees find new employment with a new firm that is simply a different shareholding of the universal owner. The promotion of corporate social responsibility is therefore in the direct financial interests of universal owners, who benefit from a country having a well-trained labour force, effective transport and communications infrastructure, low environmental remediation costs, etc. In the authors' own words:

> A universal owner is a large institutional investor that holds in its portfolio a broad cross section of the economy, holds its shares for the long-term, and on the whole does not trade except to maintain its index. As such its cumulative long-term return is determined not merely by the performance of each individual firm it owns, but by the performance of the economy as a whole.... This means that when universal owners evaluate the behaviour of the firms they own one significant dimension

should be how each firm's activities affect the economy as a whole.... Universal owners are uniquely positioned to develop and pursue a potentially virtuous efficiency cycle of minimising negative externalities and encouraging positive ones by the firms in their portfolios.... They need to begin a process of extending the definition of prudential fiduciary duty to include attention to the universal aspects of their portfolios.[52]

The above arguments may seem rather theoretical. However, they were in essence repeated recently by John Bogle, one of the most respected investors in the US, and someone with no vested interest in corporate governance. Bogle made his name as the founder of the Vanguard Group, a mutual fund company that pioneered low-cost indexed funds as the best way for ordinary citizens to build a modest investment portfolio. Currently the Vanguard Group is one of the largest mutual fund groups in America, with assets under management of over $300 billion. In a speech to the New York Society of Security Analysts in February 2002, Bogle argued that the Enron collapse had triggered what I have called 'a paradigm shift' in the expectations placed on asset managers:

> Mutual funds are the 800 pound gorillas that can make all these changes, but we aren't doing anything. It's been too long that this industry has stood back on issues such as corporate material disclosure, auditor independence, earnings quality, and executive compensation.... There are simple things that investors can do to improve corporate governance, such as voting down overly aggressive executive compensation plans, and challenging companies to release financial statements geared towards reflecting the true health of the business.[53]

Bob Monks had already come to similar conclusions in his book *The New Global Investors*[54]. This argued that the world's largest pension funds, which he calls Global Investors, should recognise that they alone have the effective power to make global business work in a responsible way. The book called for a broader interpretation of the traditional concept of 'fiduciary duty' governing the running of such funds to include issues of social responsibility. It also suggested that such funds could appoint their own independent representatives to boards to ensure that companies are indeed run on behalf of all shareholders. The book advocated five basic principles of corporate governance, based on those agreed by the OECD in June 1999. The OECD Principles of Corporate Governance are an excellent summary of the key issues in corporate governance, and well worth reading in their own right.[55] Monk's five points are as follows:[56]

1. *The corporate governance framework should protect shareholders' rights,* i.e. they should receive timely and accurate information about a company where they are investors, and they should also have the right to participate in major decisions.
2. *The corporate governance framework should ensure the equitable treatment of all shareholders, including minorities and foreign shareholders*; in particular, members of the board and executives should disclose any material interests in transactions.
3. *The corporate governance framework should recognise the rights of stakeholders in corporate governance,* i.e. there should be cooperation between corporations and stakeholders on issues like jobs, the local communities, suppliers and the environment.
4. *The corporate governance framework should ensure that timely and accurate disclosure is made on all material matters regarding the corporation.* This includes ownership and governance as well as financial disclosure, and information material should be audited.
5. *The corporate governance framework should ensure the strategic guidance of the company, the effective monitoring of management by the board, and the board's accountability to the company and the shareholders.* This clause really reflects older corporate governance principles that the board should act as an independent 'watchdog' over senior management, and carefully protect the interests of shareholders.[56]

Bob Monks is surely right to suggest that a combination of his suggested measures would move us a long way to solving the problem of growing unease about corporate legitimacy. To sum up, these include a broader interpretation of pension fund fiduciary responsibility, a more developed interpretation of corporate governance, and accurate and informative reporting on social and environmental issues. I questioned Monks over the suggestion that large institutional investors should appoint their own representative to company boards, on the grounds this could lead to major conflicts of interest between the duty owed to the company and the duty owed to shareholders:

> People have often made this objection to me – it's just nonsense! What about the conflicts of interest between the investment banks, hired by the company, when they give estimates of 'fair value' for transactions involving the management, or compensation consultants, also hired by the company, on setting executive pay.[57]

A European viewpoint on the broadening interpretation of corporate governance was given in spring 2001 by Reto Ringger, chief executive of Sustainable Asset Management (SAM). A pioneer in the field of sustainability investment, SAM advises well-known institutional and private investors, fund managers as well as several major and private banks in Europe:

> In the 21st century, it will no longer be possible to measure corporate governance solely in terms of financial success and consumer satisfaction. Instead, the successful firm will have to pay more attention to, and balance the demands of, all stakeholders, i.e. society at large and the environment. The success of a company will in future hinge on its ability to link technical and financial innovation with added value for society. Companies will have to act more transparently and be open about their decision-making process, as well as the likely consequences of these decisions for society and the environment. The increasing abundance of non-governmental organisations (NGOs) and focus groups will only add to this pressure. At the same time, growing demand for ecologically, socially and ethically sound products and services is likely to force companies to target their activities, as well as products and services, accordingly. This is undoubtedly part of the new reality of corporate governance that companies must address and from which consumers, society and the environment are benefiting.[58]

In the author's opinion the consideration of social and environmental issues, including corporate governance, in the evaluation of potential equity investments helps SRI investors to identify progressive company executives. A fund manager who analyses such considerations before buying shares in a particular company has a competitive advantage compared to others who do not. However, SRI can also function as a feedback mechanism alerting senior management to potential problems lying ahead, thus illustrating the linkages between SRI and CSR. Tim Smith, the long-time head of ICCR, always argued that others can learn from the churches' concerns, including senior corporate management:

> Church activists serve as an early warning system. If the churches are concerned about a social issue, then it is possible that the matter could be an important factor for the corporation. The fact that the churches hold stock adds to their clout − by proposing shareholder resolutions, the church representatives have the power to make public specific concerns.[59]

In the author's opinion, companies have to decide whether they are taking corporate social responsibility seriously or not. I would also suggest that in the sceptical 2000s, greenwash is unlikely to get you very far. It seems to me that the current status of CSR is rather like that of quality management in the 1980s. At that time, Western companies thought it was a matter of sampling at the end of the production process. It was only when they lost significant market share to Japanese companies who practised total quality management − the integration of quality management right from the design stage at the beginning of the production process through manufacture and assembly − that they began to regain lost market share. I suggest that the following metrics represent the minimum that will probably be acceptable to socially responsible investors and will also serve as a useful guide to a company genuinely wishing to improve its performance in this field:

1. Senior management should take responsibility for the environment or human rights, preferably at board level.
2. A detailed code of conduct should be prepared.
3. The company must commit itself to a continuing programme of education of middle-ranking executives to get the message across.

4. There should be a robust internal system to monitor CSR performance indicators.
5. Independent external social auditors should be consulted.
6. There should be a policy commitment to engage in dialogue with local NGOs when problems arise.

There seems little doubt that the pressures for better corporate citizenship will continue to grow. In 1998 I expressed my reasoning on this in a public lecture:

> Our corporate model needs updating from its Victorian format. Companies should not take the huge privilege of limited liability for granted, and mechanisms need to be put into place to ensure they use this privilege within the framework of social responsibility. Socially responsible investment would seem one obvious feedback mechanism.... [This could be] a wide-ranging justification of SRI for secular organisations, and indeed for society in general. The argument in brief is as follows: society gives companies the privilege of limited liability; such a privilege should have social responsibility associated with it, hence investors in such companies should analyse and promote corporate social responsibility.[60]

REFERENCES

1. 'Corporate Social Responsibility on the European Social Policy Agenda', Conference Programme, July 2001.
2. Green Paper, *Promoting a European Framework for Corporate Social Responsibility*, Commission of the European Communities, Brussels, 18 July 2001.
3. 'EC Plans to Promote CSR Agenda at Rio+10', *Ethical Performance*, July 2001.
4. 'Social Responsibility: An Essential Aspect of Sustainability' *International Herald Tribune*, 22 September 1999.
5. Local Authority Pension Fund Conference, St Andrews, Scotland, September 2000.
6. Adam Smith, *The Wealth of Nations*, Book V *The Expenses of the Sovereign*, page 229 of the 1977 Everyman edition, original edition 1776. I have substituted the word 'partnership' for Smith's obsolete term 'copartnery'.
7. Judgement in *Liggett v. Lee*, US Supreme Court 288/ 517 1932. Quoted in *The Emperor's Nightingale* by Bob Monks, Capstone, 1998.
8. Adolf Berle and Gardiner Means, *The Modern Corporation and Private Property*, Macmillan, 1933.

9. Cadbury Committee, *Report of the Committee on the Financial Aspects of Corporate Governance*, December 1992.
10. Summary produced by the author.
11. Sir Richard Greenbury, *Directors' Remuneration: Report of a Study Group*, Gee Publishing, 1995.
12. Sir Ronnie Hampel, *Report of the Committee on Corporate Governance*, Gee Publishing, 1998.
13. Summary produced by the author.
14. 'FTSE Groups "Failing on Directors' Pay" ', *Financial Times* 2 May 2001.
15. *ibid.*
16. 'A Flexible Approach', *Professional Investor*, October 2001.
17. Michelle Edkins, quoted in *The Sunday Telegraph*, 20 November 2001.
18. Copyright Hermes Pensions Management Ltd. Reproduced by permission.
19. PIRC Proxy Voting Survey 2001, PIRC website.
20. 'Apathy', *Financial Times,* 6 October 2001.
21. Robert Reich, quoted in 'Pension Funds Take on Watchdog Role', *Sunday Telegraph*, 10 July 1994.
22. Dale Hanson, 'Putting Investors back in Power', *Professional Investor*, April 1993.
23. Michael Smith, 'Shareholder Activism by Institutional Investors: Evidence from Calpers', *Journal of Finance*, March 1996.
24. Quoted on Social Investment Forum website, July 2001.
25. Bob Monks and Nell Minow, *Corporate Governance*, Blackwell, 1995.
26. Bob Monks, *The Emperor's Nightingale: Restoring the Integrity of the Corporation*, Capstone, 1998.
27. Bob Monks, *The New Global Investors*, Capstone, 2001.
28. Russell Sparkes, 'The New Global Investors: An Interview with Bob Monks', *Professional Investor*, November 2001.
29. Graef Crystal, *In Search of Excess: the Overcompensation of American Executives*, W.W. Norton, 1991.
30. 'No Laughing Matter at Disney', *Daily Telegraph*, 4 December 1996.
31. 'US Looks at Making It Easier to Punish CEOs', *Wall Street Journal*, 25 February 2002.
32. Burton Malkiel, 'The Lessons of Enron', *Wall Street Journal*, 17 January 2002.
33. Pat Wolf, 'Developments in Shareholder Resolutions', speech, London, February 2002.
34. 'Socially Responsible Firm Publishes 7th Annual Proxy Voting Guidelines Tightening Auditor Independence Requirements in Wake of Enron Collapse', Bloomberg newswire, 21 March 2002.
35. 'Hewitt Orders Probe into Accountants' Role', *Financial Times*, 25 February 2002.
36. 'SEC May Seize Gains when Executives Inflate Earnings', Bloomberg newswire, 22 February 2002.
37. 'SEC Says Corporate Audit Panels under Scrutiny in Agency Probes, Bloomberg newswire, 23 February 2002.
38. 'IFC Governance Plan for Loans', *Financial Times,* 21 February 2001.
39. 'Call for HK Companies to Boost Standards', *Financial Times,* 20 December 2001.
40. 'Saints and Sinners: Who's Got Religion', CLSA Press Release, 16 April 2001.
41. 'ABB Demands Ex CEOs Return Some Pay After 2001 Loss', Bloomberg newswire, 13 February 2002.
42. 'EC Commissioner Joins Attack on Barnevik Payout', *Financial Times*, 25 February 2002.

43. Green Paper, *Promoting a European Framework for Corporate Social Responsibility*, Commission of the European Communities, Brussels, 18 July 2001.
44. 'German Group Hints at Code on Executive Pay', *Financial Times*, 26 February 2002.
45. 'Investor-Friendly Firms Sought, *Wall Street Journal*, 26 July 2001.
46. *ibid.*
47. Russell Sparkes, *The Ethical Investor*, Harper Collins, 1995.
48. David Cranston, *NAPF News*, May 2001.
49. Russell Sparkes, 'The New Global Investors: An Interview with Bob Monks', *Professional Investor*, November 2001.
50. 'PIRC Services for Local Authority Pension Funds', *Socially Responsible Investment*, PIRC, 1993.
51. James P. Hawley and Andrew T. Williams, *The Rise of Fiduciary Capitalism: How Institutional Investors Can Make Corporate America More Democratic*, University of Pennsylvania Press, 2001.
52. *ibid.*
53. 'Fund Pioneer Proposes Group to Focus on Shareholder Issues', *Wall Street Journal*, 15 February 2002.
54. Bob Monks, *The New Global Investors*, Capstone, 2001.
55. OECD Directorate for Financial, Fiscal and Enterprise Affairs, *OECD Principles of Corporate Governance*, circulated 19 April 1999.
56. Bob Monks, *The New Global Investors*, Capstone, 2001.
57. Russell Sparkes, 'The New Global Investors: An Interview with Bob Monks', *Professional Investor*, November 2001.
58. 'Sustainability and Socially Responsible Investments', *Sustainable Business Investor: Europe*, Spring 2001.
59. Tim Smith, quoted in Simpson, *The Greening of Global Investment*, Economist Publications, 1991.
60. Russell Sparkes, 'Through a Glass Darkly: Some Thoughts on the Ethics of Investment', the Beckley Lecture 1998; published in the *Epworth Review*, July 1998.

10

Investment Returns

WHY INVESTMENT RETURNS ARE CRUCIAL

When carried out for institutional investors, socially responsible investing has four core components: the environment, human rights, corporate social responsibility, and investment returns. Few are likely to argue with the first three of these, but some may argue with the fourth. However, SRI will never become a credible investment strategy for pension funds and charitable foundations unless they feel comfortable that it meets the legal requirement of fiduciary duty, i.e. to get a good financial return on the funds invested.

SRI is a subject that has moved on greatly in recent years, and the research that has been carried out into the financial effect of imposing social and environmental considerations reflects this. Earlier performance studies took the approach of relatively simple index restriction, essentially seeing what would happen to financial returns if sectors like alcohol, tobacco or defence were excluded from a broad stock market index like the FTSE All-Share, or the S&P 500. However, while stock market indices are useful indicators, they can only tell you so much about the real performance of actual funds. As the 1990s progressed, analysts therefore increasingly turned their attention away from using selective stock market indices and started examining the actual performance of real-life SRI funds. One of the first people to do so was the author, in an article published in March 1994.[1]

Many studies have shown what appears to be a demonstrable link between good environmental performance and high corporate profitability. Probably the best known is the Russo and Fouts paper 'A resource-based perspective on corporate environmental performance and profitability', published in the *US Academy of Management Journal* in 1997.[2] The question of the relationship between good environmental and social practice and high corporate profitability is an interesting one, but it will not be discussed further here. The standard academic paradigm for analysing the stock market is the efficient market theory (EMT), which states that equity markets accurately discount a strong corporate performance track record by means of high valuation. In other words, in efficient stock markets, and there is little doubt that the UK and the US *are* efficient markets, a company's historic track record and the market's current view of its prospects are reflected in its share price. So even if there is a real link between environmental performance and profit margins, identifying this is unlikely to work on its own as an investment strategy. However, and this is where it gets interesting, if improving environmental performance is closely correlated with improving financial performance, then such a system could well work if it succeeded in identifying improving financial metrics before this became apparent on other measures.

Advocates of socially responsible investing sometimes suggest that SRI must be a successful investment strategy because it avoids 'bad' companies with poor growth prospects such as tobacco or alcohol. Likewise there is sometimes an assumption that because the environment is a long-term growth area, it can provide an easy road to riches in the stock market. Both of these claims are naive. In an efficient market, all companies offer the same risk/return trade-offs. If socially responsible investment portfolios consistently outperformed, this would disprove the orthodox view that markets are efficient. On the other hand, opponents of SRI sometimes argue that restricting potential investment opportunities must lower returns. This is equally naive. If SRI screening consistently produced below-average returns, the excluded 'sin stocks' would necessarily outperform. Put simply, it is extremely difficult to consistently outperform the stock market, and no mechanistic approach is likely to do so. I am *not* suggesting that expert practitioners working in specialised SRI research teams cannot produce above-average financial returns. The long-term track record of the Domini Social Index in the US, and the Central Finance Board of the Methodist Church in the UK, shows that they can. What I am suggesting is that there is no simple, mechanistic way for conventional fund managers to extrapolate such data into sustained stock market outperformance; expertise in SRI risk management and fund construction is also required.

THE DIFFICULTIES OF BACK-TESTING

Because socially responsible investment is relatively young, there is relatively little hard evidence around that can be used to analyse the effects of SRI on financial returns. Many studies have therefore used back-testing techniques. Back-testing simply means going back through existing data to calculate what would have happened in the past if a certain methodology had been used to construct an index or create an actual securities portfolio. However, over twenty-five years' experience of financial markets have convinced me to be wary of claims based on back-tested data. Over the years I have observed numerous investment strategies based on what looked like compelling back-tested data, but which then failed when tested in practice. For example, small-company investing in the 1980s, emerging markets in the early 1990s, and last but certainly not least, technology investing in 1998–2000. The following technical questions should be taken into account when considering the predictive power of any back-tested result:

- *Survival bias.* Most modern stock market indices are based on market capitalisation, which means that they try to include all companies above a certain size. Successful companies grow rapidly and therefore join the benchmark index, whereas failing companies decline in market capitalisation and are therefore ejected from it. This means that if the current members of an index are used to back-test its historical performance, the index will outperform itself. This nonsensical result arises from survival bias, i.e. companies which do badly are dropped from the index.
- *Liquidity and transactions costs.* It is obvious that administration and fund management services cost money, which put them at a performance disadvantage to a theoretical index. It is less obviously true that funds also incur dealing costs when they invest cash into equities or other securities. Actively managed funds

with high turnover levels are most highly penalised by transaction costs, but it this also true of passive index funds that have to invest new money flows. This issue is of particular concern to SRI funds as many of them have a bias to smaller companies, whose liquidity may be poor, and their dealing costs much higher.

- *Causality uncertainty*. Stock market returns are driven by a complex system of interrelationships, including profitability (return on capital), earnings growth, a risk premium and interest rates. This dynamic system of multicausality relationships makes it extremely difficult to identify genuine links between individual factors. Any back-tested result merely confirms a correlation; further performance attribution analysis is required to demonstrate the actual causality relationship. For instance, from late 1998 to autumn 2000 many environmental funds produced significantly above-average investment returns. This led to comments being made in some quarters that the environment was a major growth industry which would result in sustained high returns for investors. In fact, however, the outperformance was actually due to an upward valuation of environmental growth stocks as a side effect of the internet boom of the late 1990s. Many of the environmental funds that had earlier produced high financial returns did badly after autumn 2000 when the internet stock market bubble finally burst.

ANALYSIS USING RESTRICTED INDICES

Much early SRI performance analysis was based on back-testing analysis, exploring the impact of sector exclusion on a benchmark index such as the All-Share in the UK or the S&P 500 in the US. This approach essentially involved analysing what would have happened to financial returns when sectors like alcohol, tobacco or defence were excluded from a general index. Barra International were one of the first groups to analyse the UK equity market using a restricted index methodology in January 1989. Barra created eight 'ethical sub-indices' that avoided companies with exposure to areas of the market such as tobacco, nuclear power or nuclear weapons, or had significant exposure to South Africa. These eight restricted indices were then back-tested against the FTSE All-Share index for the five years to the end of October 1988. The difference in performance between these sub-indices and the All-Share itself was insignificant over the period, even though the 'free' indices were much less well diversified. Tracking errors were relatively low, while portfolio risk as measured by annualised volatility (beta) was relatively low, close to one. However, Barra observed that there was a strong 'small-company effect', which added 0.81% per year to the returns of the South Africa – free index over the period.[3]

Boston-based US Trust carried out similar research on the US equity market at around the same time. Five restricted indices were created based on the S&P 500 with exclusions in the following areas: South Africa, defence, the environment, employment, and harmful products. These restricted indices were then back-tested for an eleven-year period to the end of 1989. Over this period there was an insignificant difference between the screened indices and the S&P, with the average annual return of the screened portfolios 0.1% above the market benchmark.[4]

Back in 1972 Milton Moskowitz argued that socially responsible investing might produce superior financial returns.[5] Since 1996 the US Social Investment Forum has awarded the prestigious Moskowitz prize, named in his honour, for the best article on the subject of the financial impact of socially responsible investing. The first winner of the award was John Guerard's paper entitled 'Is there a cost to being socially responsible in investing?' published in the *Journal of Investing* in 1997.[6] Guerard took the broad investment universe used by Vantage Global Investors of 1300 US equities, and screened it by various SRI criteria provided by KLD. There were three screens, which eliminated 350 companies as potential investments: military; product, i.e. the classic SRI exclusions of alcohol, tobacco and gambling; and environmental. Using back-testing analysis from January 1987 to December 1994, Guerard found that the unscreened universe would have produced a total return of 177% over the period, compared to 174% for the socially screened holdings. His conclusion was:

There is no statistically significant difference in the respective return series, and more important, there is no economically meaningful difference in the return differential. The variability of the two return series is almost equal during the 1987–1994 period. One can test for statistically significant differences in the two return series using the F-test which examines the differences in series means [returns] relative to the standard deviations of the series. When one applies the F-test, one finds that the series are not statistically different from one another.[7]

Guerard returned to this subject a year later in a paper called 'Additional evidence on the cost of being socially responsible', finding no need to alter his original conclusion that there were no significant differences between returns from conventional and socially screened investment universes. Guerard did make the intriguing suggestion that the good returns from SRI funds might not reflect the desirability or otherwise of corporate products, but actually be a valid indicator of good management:

> Social screens may also be associated with better management and the generation of higher returns. Initial evidence points to the product strength variable as possibly representing 'better management', although more research and many more post-sample periods would be necessary to address the better management hypothesis.[8]

The year 1998 also saw the publication of another important piece of US SRI research by Phoebus Dhrymes, called 'Socially responsible investment: is it profitable?'. This study used cross-sectional regression analysis on a universe of 464 US equities for the period 1991–96, examining the impact of imposing 17 social screen or SRI evaluation factors provided by KLD upon financial returns. Dhrymes came to similar conclusions as Guerard, i.e. that there was no perceptible difference between the investment returns from a socially screened investment universe and that of the overall US stock market.[9]

A detailed study of UK SRI performance was produced by the research service EIRIS in 1999, called *Does Ethical Investment Pay?*[10] This examined five 'ethical indices' which stripped out a certain sector or group of activities from the benchmark. The constituent companies were those identified at May 1998, with the results back-tested to December 1990 as the inception date. The five indices

Table 10.1   *SRI performance and tracking error 1991–99*

	Relative to All-Share*	Tracking Error*	Beta	R^2
1. Charities avoidance	0.1%	3.3%	0.89	94%
2. Environmental damage	1.6%	3.2%	0.98	94%
3. Positive	0.5%	2.5%	0.96	97%
4. Ethical balanced	0.3%	4.0%	0.97	92%
5. Environmental management	−0.6%	3.9%	0.86	92%

*These percentages are annualised.

Source: Ros Haverman and Peter Webster, 'Does Ethical Investment Pay?', EIRIS, September 1999.

consisted of one based on traditional SRI exclusions, i.e. avoiding alcohol, tobacco, gambling, armaments and pornography. This was followed by an environmental avoidance index that excluded 507 companies involved in areas such as fossil fuel production and nuclear power, and a positive SRI index based on factors like community involvement, disclosure, equal opportunities and environmental initiatives. There was also a balanced index that combined the core elements of the three earlier indices, while the last of the five was based on companies who had made demonstrable progress on environmental management. The results are shown in Table 10.1.

With the exception of the environmental damage avoidance index, the EIRIS study shows little difference in performance returns compared to the All-Share, while the beta and regression coefficients also show surprisingly little variance. The author's main criticism of this study is that, like much other research into SRI performance data, it did not try to delve more deeply into performance attribution. The starting point of the research, January 1991, coincided with the start of the Gulf War, when the price of oil surged as a result. Shares in energy companies then underperformed for most of the 1990s as oil prices languished. The weak oil price may lie behind the good results of EIRIS's environmental damage avoidance index. However, the overall conclusion of the study was consistent with earlier research, i.e. that on their own SRI exclusions seem to have little impact on investment performance.

SRI UNIT TRUSTS IN PRACTICE

However, even if SRI indices produce a market average return, this does not necessarily mean that SRI retail funds will do so in real life. Mutual funds and unit trusts could have larger deviations in practice from the benchmark index than restricted indices would suggest, while there might be additional costs of running socially responsible investment portfolios that would depress returns. Any serious attempt to evaluate the impact of SRI on investment returns must therefore examine the actual performance of SRI mutual funds in practice. One of the first attempts to do so was by the author in an article called 'The Rewards of Virtue', published in March 1994 in *Professional Investor*.[11]

This study argued that the best way to observe SRI effects in unit trusts would be to compare them against others with the same stated objectives such as UK equity growth, noting the conventional wisdom that most unit trusts underperform the FTSE All-Share. The article noted the difficulties of measuring the investment performance of SRI unit trusts in view of the sector's rapid growth, which limited the number of available funds with a statistically significant track record. However, nine trusts were found that met the author's minimum requirement of possessing a three-year investment track record. In accordance with standard investment procedure, the funds' performance was ranked in quartiles, i.e. the top 25% of the sample was called the first quartile, etc. The analysis showed three of the funds were in the first quartile (out of nine) over three years, and three in the second quartile. This seemed a clear demonstration that over this time period socially responsible unit trusts had indeed yielded UK investors superior returns.

At this time the UK SRI investment universe was dominated by one fund, the Friends Provident Stewardship Trust unit trust, whose market capitalisation of £89.6 million represented 59.9% of the total UK growth SRI unit trust universe at the beginning of the period. I therefore decided that it was important to analyse the data on a weighted basis, rather than using a simple average. This seemed a better reflection of the returns received by the underlying investors, reflecting the varying sizes of the different funds. For example, if the

Friends Provident Stewardship fund had done badly, a simple average could have shown above-average returns from these SRI units, when in fact 60% of all funds invested in the sector would have underperformed. In fact, however, the Stewardship fund performed well, and this was reflected in an average weighted capital return from the nine trusts of 66.2%, which compared with a 62.4% return in the average UK growth trust over the period.[12] One point of interest was that the smaller trusts appeared to show a distinct deterioration in relative performance as the years progressed, which was not apparent in the larger funds. Eight years later I am not unhappy with the study's conclusion (emphasis added):

> The increasing outperformance of the larger funds may reflect the explosive growth of information about environmental costs and liabilities in the last year or so, as well as the increasing variety of demands from ethical investors that their funds be managed in an ethical way. Since the press have become quick to jump on any fund that they suspect is using ethical/ environmental investment purely as a marketing tool, ethical investment is becoming more complex and difficult to do. *It is becoming an asset class in its own right, and one that requires the allocation of adequate resources to do well.*[13]

Morningstar analysed US SRI mutual fund performance in the mid 1990s. This found less encouraging news on SRI investment returns.[14] Of the 24 funds studied, only 4 were above average compared to conventional funds, while the majority showed significant underperformance relative to the S&P 500 index. However, over the ten years to December 1995 US SRI mutual funds only lagged behind conventional funds by 1% a year, which the underlying investors might well have judged an acceptable price to pay. Nevertheless, publication of these results prompted an article in *Fortune* magazine describing socially screened investing as a 'dumb idea'. The author, J. Rothschild, therefore advocated 'investing with sinners'.[15]

A number of academic studies analysing UK SRI unit trusts were carried out in the 1990s. In 1994 Luther and Matatko from the economics department of the University of Exeter examined the holdings of UK ethical funds, noting their heavy bias towards smaller capitalisation issues.[16] The first UK academic research paper to examine the actual performance of socially responsible unit trusts and their conventional peers was carried out by Mallin *et al.* in 1995.[17] This study used a matched pair analysis based on size and starting date to compare the performance of the two types. It noticed that there seemed to be a weakly positive outperformance trend from the SRI funds, particularly on a risk-adjusted basis, as their average beta was surprisingly low. However, the sample was fairly limited, and I wonder whether basing the matched pair analysis upon similar size of investment assets might not impute a bias towards similar investment returns. Luther and Matatko revisited the subject in 1997, reworking the Mallin data using cross-sectional regression analysis rather than matched pairs. Luther and co-workers found that the risk-adjusted returns (calculated using a size-adjusted Jensen measure) from UK SRI unit trusts were effectively identical to other unit trusts, although they did observe that the SRI funds were significantly skewed towards smaller companies.[18]

The 1999 EIRIS study, *Does Ethical Investment Pay?*,[19] also looked at the track record of UK SRI unit trusts, analysing 15 funds in existence at June 1998 that had, as a minimum, a five-year track record. Using five-year offer to bid prices took account of initial charges and management fees. It found that the majority of UK SRI funds actually underperformed their peer group (equity growth), while the picture in the international sector was more mixed. One of the funds in the survey, Framlington Health, did extremely well. However, this is a fund that some observers, the author included, feel should not be included in a survey of social responsible investing. Excluding that fund, and one other that was not typical, the average return of UK SRI unit trusts was 0.43% less than the median, and 0.89% less than the average (mean) in the study. It also came to a similar conclusion to that of the author five years previously, i.e. that there was a distinct correlation between the size of the SRI unit trusts and their relative performance. There was one surprising conclusion from the study – the portfolio risk as measured by annualised standard deviation was lower for the SRI funds. In the UK growth sector the volatility was 10.4, compared to 10.9 for the median, and in overseas equities it was 12.6 compared to 12.0. The report concluded:

1. *On average, ethical funds have lower total risk than funds without ethical criteria.* This is a rather remarkable conclusion that runs counter to conventional wisdom outside the ethical investment world, but may also have implications for thinking within the industry. It is often supposed by financial commentators that because ethical investment can involve avoiding at least some large companies, it must be a more risky undertaking. This would appear not to be the case at the level of a portfolio of such stocks....

2. *On average, ethical funds have lower returns, although there are a number of examples of out-performance, in some cases sustained over long periods....* To an extent the average under-performance could simply be the other side of the average reduced risk, and this possibility is explored further. It is also possible that such an effect could be attributable to higher charges – at least some of the firms offering such funds make a higher charge for their ethical funds than for those funds without ethical criteria. This question has not been explored in any more detail.[20]

WM, British performance measurement consultants, produced a study in the same year called *Is There a Cost to Ethical Investing?* Its main focus was WM's client base of UK charities, which will be analysed in the next section. However, it did have a section on retail funds which showed that UK ethical unit trusts as a whole underperformed their conventional peers (Table 10.2). It also showed that they possessed higher relative volatility, or tracking error, defined as the standard deviation of their annual returns relative to the All-Share benchmark.

I decided to end this study with an up-to-date survey of socially responsible unit trusts working in the relatively homogeneous UK equity sector, restricted to trusts with a minimum three-year track record. (Although there are now a significant number of SRI unit trusts with international exposure, their widely differing asset allocation makes it difficult to draw conclusions about SRI from their financial track record.) The analysis was calculated by the author based on performance data produced by Lipper Analytics. It is based

Table 10.2 *Performance of UK ethical unit trusts 1993–98*

	Relative returns		
	Percent above All-Share	Percent below All-Share	Average deviation
Ethical funds	13.3	87.7	−3.2
Conventional funds	21.7	78.3	−1.7

	Tracking error		
	Tracking error below 2%	Tracking error above 2%	Average
Ethical funds	6.7	98.3	5.3%
Unconstrained funds	18.3	81.7	4.4%

Source: The WM Company, 'Is There a Cost to Ethical Investing?', unpublished manuscript, October 1999. Copyright the WM Company. Reproduced by permission.

on total returns using offer to bid prices, which take account of the varying management charges paid by the funds. The SRI funds had a very wide dispersion of returns. For example, over three years the top SRI fund had a return of 38.6%, whereas the bottom fund had a negative return of −11.7%. Given the limited number of funds in the sample, and the wide dispersion of returns, I decided to calculate the median return from SRI funds, as well as the usual average (the arithmetic mean). In this case the median is probably a better representative figure, as it is less skewed by outlying data points. The results are given in Table 10.3.

In any case, both the median and the normal average are shown and compared with the sector average for UK equity unit trusts. The median figures show UK SRI unit trusts as having produced roughly comparable returns to their conventional peer group over the last one and three years. However, the five- and ten-year data is less positive. Using the arithmetic mean presents an improved picture over the five- and ten-year periods, but the trend of underperformance is still clear. On the whole, UK SRI unit trusts seem to have produced long-term investment returns slightly below those of comparable

Table 10.3   *Longer-term performance of UK SRI unit trusts: annualised returns (%) for n years to December 2001*

	1 year	3 years	5 years	10 years
SRI average	−15.1	14.5	38.8	180.7
SRI median	−15.2	7.8	27.6	165.7
UK growth average	−13.6	7.0	46.9	219.3
Number of funds in sample	15	15	10	7

Source: Compiled by the author based on data produced by Lippes Analytics.

Table 10.4   *US mutual fund data: annualised returns (%) for n years to December 2001*

	1 year	3 years	5 years	10 years
Pax World Balanced	−9.1	4.5	11.9	9.9
Lipper Balanced Average	−4.4	2.1	7.6	9.4
Calvert Social Equity	−4.1	9.6	11.8	9.5
Lipper Mid Cap Growth	−21.1	4.8	7.6	n/a

Source: Based on data from Pax and Calvert websites.

unit trusts. However, relative performance was strong in the late 1980s and early 1990s, mainly due to a small-company effect, before turning down in line with that effect for much of the 1990s.

The US evidence also indicates that on average socially responsible mutual funds have produced somewhat lower returns than their peer group. The Domini Social Index Fund is discussed in the next section under institutional investment. However, two points need to be highlighted. First, a number of US SRI mutual funds have produced very good returns (Table 10.4). Second, the good performance seems to be concentrated in the larger funds, confirming the point about the correlation between SRI specialisation and good returns made earlier in the UK. I will illustrate the point using data from the $1.1 billion Pax World Fund, a balanced SRI fund that holds a mixture of stocks, cash and bonds, and the $355 million Calvert Social Equity Investment Fund equity units. I have used maximum-load data, i.e. performance data after taking account of the highest level of charges. The Pax World Fund's five-year track record ranked it 17th out of 293 mutual funds – a top-decile result.

INSTITUTIONAL SRI INVESTMENT

Pension funds and charitable endowments in the UK and the US are under the legal requirement of fiduciary duty. This means they must try to get the best financial return on the assets entrusted to them. The majority of US socially responsible institutional investors therefore concentrate their SRI efforts in terms of shareholder activism, normally in the form of filing social shareholder proxy resolutions. They carry out little or no SRI avoidance apart from excluding tobacco shares. Filing social proxies is in its infancy in the UK, but it is certainly true that most UK pension funds feel more comfortable with a policy of engagement rather than avoidance. In either case, such an approach eliminates the financial risk of SRI exclusion policies.

However, on both sides of the Atlantic there are institutional investors with SRI exclusion policies. A significant body of performance data exists on SRI retail funds, which probably explains why academic research on socially responsible investment has concentrated on this subsector of SRI. There is much less evidence available in the public domain with which to judge the track record of institutional investment for pension funds or charity clients using SRI screens. In this section I intend to look at the performance record of such funds, and examine the policies they have undertaken to moderate the risk and maximise returns.

One of the earliest sources of evidence on the financial performance of institutional SRI funds was provided in 1984 by the United States Trust Company (US Trust), one of the larger asset management companies in America that had several socially responsible accounts. The US Trust data showed that for the four years to the end of 1984 its 'socially sensitive' portfolios had produced annualised returns of 19.7%, slightly ahead of the 19.4% return from its unscreened funds. Both were well ahead of 17.1% produced by the S&P 500. Details of the screens were not revealed, although I suspect at that time South Africa would have been a major factor.[21] Robert Schwartz was one of the US pioneers of institutional SRI, his experience convincing him that socially responsible exclusions need not result in any performance cost:

> Performance in the management of assets is a function of the accuracy of judgements about the overall market, the future course of interest rates, and the ability to sort out industries with negative or positive potential in order to select investments that appreciate over time. In this fundamental approach, and with the availability of companies in every industry, I believe performance will not be hindered by restrictions on selected categories of investment.[22]

One of the earliest surveys of the impact of SRI constraints on institutional fund performance was carried out in 1991 by the WM Company.[23] WM took 126 charity funds with assets under management of £3.7 billion and examined their investment performance for the five years to the end of 1989. Forty-four of these charity portfolios were restricted by SRI constraints from investing in companies active in South Africa, tobacco, alcohol or gambling. These charity portfolios suffered no performance penalty resulting from their SRI constraints. WM also carried out the key step of performance attribution, concluding:

> Ethical constraints in their own right seem to have little impact on the performance of the constrained funds other than through the small company/large company effect. The performance of actual funds indicates that other factors, such as stock selection, can more than offset these constraints. At an extreme level of constraint, where a significant number of companies are excluded, a very large fund may find difficulties with liquidity, but in practice this is unlikely to arise. In general the message seems to be that constraints do not damage your wealth.[24]

The WM company revisited the subject in 1997, re-examining the investment performance of WM's charity fund clients for the period 1992–95. This study found that charity funds with SRI constraints, i.e. avoiding investment in tobacco, alcohol and gambling, produced annualised UK equity returns of 15.5% over the period. This was identical to the returns from unconstrained funds over the period.[25]

WM followed this up by producing a major study of SRI and their charity fund investment universe in 1999, called *Is There a Cost to Ethical Investing?*[26] The paper was produced with the intention of answering some of the fears that had been publicly expressed at that time about the possible negative impact of the UK government's proposed new SRI pension regulations on financial returns. By the end of 1998 WM's ethical universe comprised 42 funds with a total value of £1.4 billion. This seemed a representative sample compared to the unconstrained universe of 185 funds valued at £7.2 billion. WM noted, however, that the survey was skewed by the presence of one very large ethically constrained fund worth £800 million, and which had an excellent track record of financial returns. The column 'small ethical' in Table 10.5 therefore excludes the returns of this particular fund.

WM found that performance from the other 41 ethically constrained charity funds, i.e. the small-ethical universe, showed little difference in financial returns to unconstrained funds over the period. WM also examined risk/return characteristics, computing volatility on the basis of the standard deviation of monthly relative

Table 10.5 *SRI charity fund annualised returns (%) 1992–98*

	Total ethical	Small ethical	Unconstrained
1992	21.6	20.8	21.5
1993	27.2	26.7	27.4
1994	−5.4	−5.9	−5.7
1995	21.6	23.8	22.0
1996	17.6	18.4	17.1
1997	27.5	25.2	25.4
1998	14.4	11.7	11.5
1996–98	19.7	18.3	17.8
1994–98	14.6	14.0	13.5
1992–98	17.3	16.7	16.5

Source: The WM Company, 'Is There a Cost to Ethical Investing?', unpublished manuscript, October 1999. Copyright the WM Company. Reproduced by permission.

Table 10.6   *SRI and charity fund tracking error 1992–1998*

	Tracking error below 2%	Tracking error above 2%	Average
Ethical funds	44.8%	55.2%	2.5%
Unconstrained funds	61.9%	38.1%	2.1%

Source: The WM Company, 'Is There a Cost to Ethical Investing?', unpublished manuscript, October 1999. Copyright the WM Company. Reproduced by permission.

returns. In other words, each piece of monthly data was based on the return from the varying funds less that of the FTSE All-Share. I prefer to describe this as tracking error rather than volatility and show the results in Table 10.6.

Table 10.6 reveals a distinct difference between the proportions of SRI and unconstrained funds that had a tracking error below 2%. However, the absolute differences were not large: 2.5% in one case and 2.1% in the other. *Is There a Cost to Ethical Investing?* came to this conclusion:

> The evidence suggests that at the aggregate level, the exclusion of certain sectors does not appear to have a systematic impact on charity returns.... The returns of the ethically constrained charity funds sit easily within the normal range of returns produced by the unconstrained charity universe. Therefore it can be argued that the imposition of the sector exclusions (to the extent imposed by charity funds) does not inhibit the achievement of returns well within the range of those available when full investment discretion is given.[27]

Note that there are two index funds that track the Domini 400 Social Index (DSI). These are the Domini Social Index Equity Fund (DSIEF), for retail clients, and the Domini Social Institutional Equity Fund, for institutional investors. The DSI's impressive track record of producing above-average financial returns is shown in Table 10.7. This is true in absolute terms (19% a year for ten years isn't bad), and in relative terms compared to the S&P 500 index. This relative outperformance was particularly good, bearing in mind that the majority

Table 10.7   *DSI annualised total returns for 1991–2001*

Years to January	DSI	S&P 500
1 year	−5.4%	−0.8%
3 years	13.7%	13.2%
5 years	20.0%	18.4%
10 years	18.9%	17.4%

Source: Copyright 2002 by KLD Research & Analytics, Inc. Reproduced by permission. The Domini 400 Social SM Index is a service mark of KLD Research & Analytics Inc.

of active funds underperform the S&P 500 even though they have no SRI exclusions. The DSI was specifically designed to form the basis of an attractive investment vehicle for retail and institutional investors attracted to the idea of SRI. It is striking, in fact, how closely the DSI returns have tracked those of the S&P 500 but with a distinct upward bias. As the originators wrote in 1994:

> The DSI returns have closely paralleled the S&P's − something we didn't anticipate in 1988.[28]

This tight link between the two indices results from the close attention its founders Kinder, Lydenberg, and Domini (KLD) paid to minimising risk when devising the DSI index. Analysis of the new index in 1991 showed that the market capitalisation of the average DSI holding was a little less than the S&P, while the new index scored slightly higher in terms of earnings growth and return on equity. As might be expected, these characteristics were reflected in a slightly higher P/E (price/earnings multiple) and beta (relative volatility compared to the market index).[29] I thought that KLD's passionate concern to minimise the portfolio risk of social exclusion was forcibly expressed in comments it made in 1991 about a Prudential SRI index that showed a poor performance record:

> Prudential acknowledges that its 'benchmark portfolios have more risk than typical screened portfolios', essentially because

Prudential does not replace companies screened out to reduce any risk element introduced by screening.... Increased risk is only a problem if the investor is not compensated for accepting that risk. As we have seen, socially responsible investment can reasonably expect a competitive risk-reward ratio. Further, Prudential did nothing to improve the diversification of its portfolios after applying its screens, despite the fact that academic studies have shown a poorly diversified portfolio will be less efficient than a well-diversified portfolio.[30]

Any restriction of an investment universe reduces diversification and therefore causes higher risk. The key question for any active investment management strategy is whether the excess risk is compensated by higher returns. Initial analysis of the DSI performance for the period from January 1986 to October 1991 showed superior risk-adjusted returns, although part of the data was back-tested material prepared by State Street Asset Management (Table 10.8). The risk-adjusted return was calculated using the Treynor ratio

$$T = R - \mathrm{RFR}/\beta$$

where R is the return on the portfolio, RFR is the risk-free rate (normally Treasury bills) and β is the relative volatility compared to the

Table 10.8   *DSI risk-adjusted returns 1986–91*

	DSI 400	S&P 500
Monthly returns*	1.19%	1.12%
Standard deviation	5.48%	5.12%
Beta	1.07	1.00
Treynor ratio	0.56	0.53

*Geometric mean.
Lloyd Kurtz, Steve Lydenberg and Peter Kinder, 'The Domini Social Index: A New Benchmark for Social Investors', Chapter 25 of *The Social Investment Almanac*, Henry Holt, 1992. Copyright 2002 by KLD Research & Analytics, Inc. Reproduced by permission. The Domini 400 Social Index is a service mark of KLD Research & Analytics Inc.

S&P 500. In my opinion KLD deserves praise for downplaying this result, as they share my scepticism over back-tested data. The only reason for presenting the data here because there is very little information available on the risk-adjusted returns of SRI funds. However as Steve Lydenberg wrote to me:

> KLD published these figures up until about 1993 or 1994, because we had only a short track record. Backtests are notoriously unreliable and questionable. Risk adjusted returns on a backtest aren't worth much. (Unpublished letter)

When the DSI was launched it showed significant sector deviance from the S&P 500 index. The major differences consisted of underweight positions in oils, electric utilities, pharmaceuticals, tobacco and defence, whereas it was heavily overweight in sectors like retailing, insurance, services and leisure. When I perused the DSIEF fund equity holdings in the late 1990s, I noticed that many of the largest holdings were large-capitalisation technology stocks such as Microsoft, Cisco Systems, Intel and AOL Time Warner. This raised a question mark in my mind whether the DSI's good performance record could be explained by non-SRI factors. In my opinion this is a crucial question given the widespread use of the DSI's track record as a financial justification of SRI. I wondered whether SRI detailed performance attribution analysis had been carried out to answer this question.

Large-capitalisation growth stocks did very well in the second half of the 1990s. It is legitimate to ask whether the above-average returns produced by the DSI really resulted from its investment in companies with superior corporate social responsibility characteristics, or whether it was based on a combination of a large-capitalisation growth effect and beneficial sector exclusions. For example, the DSI was significantly underweight from inception in major oils and defence stocks, industry sectors that did badly in the 1990s as the price of oil fell and defence spending was cut after the collapse of communism. The S&P 500 index rose 335% during the 1990s, whereas the S&P Energy Index rose only 136%. The Nasdaq large-cap index actually rose 946%, i.e. its value increased more than ten times. I put this point to Peter Kinder when I met with him in London in 1998. Here is what he said:

We got specialist performance analysts Barra to look at the factors driving the performance of the DSI index in 1992. They discovered that the bulk of the outperformance arises not from the factor biases inherent in the introduction of social screens, but from the specific asset returns itself. There is a specific return premium to the index over the time period which is presumably related to the social screens KLD has developed. In other words, it was not due to specific sector exclusions such as avoiding arms or tobacco, but rather a general feature of the portfolio as a whole.[31]

In fact, several academic studies have scrutinised the DSI's financial performance data to address the question of factor inputs. The Barra study referred to by Peter Kinder was published in the *Journal of Investing* in 1993. Its authors, Christopher Luck and Nancy Pilotte, found that the DSI outperformed the S&P 500 by 2.33% over the period April 1990 to September 1992.[32] The Barra Performance Analysis package found that factor analysis (i.e. sector exclusion and large capitalisation bias) accounted for 0.34% of the excess return, so that individual stock selection was the major factor that comprised 1.99% of the index outperformance. In 1996 Lloyd Kurtz, one of the original analytical team that worked with Peter Kinder on the construction of the DSI, published a paper with Dan di Bartolomeo analysing the DSI's performance from May 1990 to September 1993. They found 0.19% of monthly outperformance, but claimed that the excess returns were consistent with factor exposures.[33] However, the most exhaustive survey of DSI performance was carried out by Luck in 1998, who analysed DSI returns for the period April 1990 to May 1998, again using the Barra Performance Analysis package to identify factor effects. The analysis again found that the majority of the outperformance, amounting to 0.77% a year, could not be attributed to sector exclusion; it was due to individual stock selection. Luck also discovered that the stock-specific effects were cumulative, i.e. that they seemed to be increasing over time.[34]

The DSI is the standard example used in the US to show that SRI can be a financially attractive investment policy. Its only UK equivalent in this respect is the Central Finance Board of the Methodist Church (CFB), whose track record is also used to justify SRI for institutional investors.[35] Chapter 1 noted that the civil servants drafting the 2000 SRI pension fund regulations had a problem: they could not find a UK investment institution with a proven track record of investment outperformance while using SRI constraints. Eventually they did manage to find one such organization, the CFB. At March 2001 the CFB managed over £900 million of investment assets for Methodist churches, charities and pension funds. According to CFB Investment Manager Bill Seddon (original emphasis):

As an ethical specialist we see financial and ethical performance as indivisible. This *integrated approach to investment ethics* is perhaps the most distinctive thing about the CFB – our fund managers are constantly looking for good investment opportunities. This is done by trawling through financial news, or on-line databases, or by talking to stockbrokers. However, such information is simultaneously assessed from an ethical point of view. All fund managers are expected to carry out their own fundamental research for both SRI and financial purposes.... Investment in companies wholly or mainly involved in the arms trade, gambling, tobacco and alcohol has always been avoided. However, such negative exclusion is only a part of the CFB ethical approach, which also involves engaging in constructive dialogue with company managements to influence their behaviour....We prefer companies with business practices which take into account the interests not only of shareholders but all others involved. These include employees, suppliers, customers and the community at large. The result seems to be above-average long-term returns for shareholders.[36]

Table 10.9 is based on data independently produced by actuarial consultants Combined Actuarial Performance Services (CAPS). CAPS measures the performance results of thousands of UK pension funds, ranking them in relation to the median fund in the survey. In other words, the top 10% would be described as the top decile, the top 25% as the top quartile, etc. Notice that the CFB UK and Overseas Equities portfolios achieved a first-quartile result over both five and ten years despite operating within SRI constraints. They were also ahead of their respective benchmarks, the FTSE All-Share index and the FT World Index, over ten years.

Table 10.9 *Central Finance Board of the Methodist Church: investment returns (%) 1991–2001*

	5 years to March 2001	10 years to March 2001
UK equities and convertibles		
CFB UK Equities	12.7	14.0
CAPS Median Fund	11.0	12.8
CAPS First Quartile	12.1	13.7
FTSE All-Share index	11.1	12.6
Overseas equities		
CFB Overseas Equities	9.1	12.3
CAPS Median Fund	7.3	11.0
CAPS First Quartile	8.8	12.1
FT World index (ex UK)	9.7	11.5

Source: Central Finance Board of the Methodist Church, annual report, 2001.

The first stated objective in the CFB mission statement refers not to ethics or theology, but sets out the aim of 'seeking above average returns for investors'. Its success in achieving this aim raises the question of how it has done so. Many asset managers seem to aim for top performance by taking an aggressive risk stance that may work very well or go horribly wrong. The CFB investment philosophy is quite the opposite, it is risk-averse. In baseball or cricketing terms, it aims to grind out the singles rather than going for the home run or hitting the ball for six. The CFB's investment objective is to try to be slightly ahead of the averages in most years, confident this will result in excellent long-term results. This was described by Bill Seddon in the following way:

Our portfolios tend to be widely diversified to reduce their risk profile. Consequently, we do not expect returns to be very different from the market averages in any one year. However, over the long term, our performance stands comparison with the best in the industry. The decile ranking shows this more clearly and also highlights the regular outperformance rather than the volatility which some may have expected. Although returns were in the

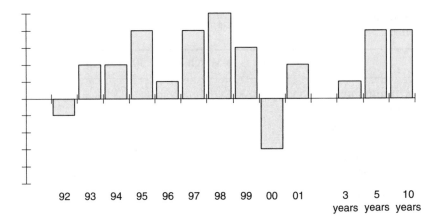

Figure 10.1 *CFB UK equities decile rankings 1991–2001*
Source: *The Central Finance Board of the Methodist Church, annual report 2001.*

top quartile in only three out of the ten years, consistent modest outperformance has led to top quartile results over five and ten years.[37]

Figure 10.1 illustrates Bill Seddon's point about the CFB's success being based on cumulative, gentle outperformance. A bar above the middle line shows that the CFB outperformed the median fund in a particular year, while a bar below it, as in 2000, shows that it underperformed the median. Over the ten-year period to March 2001, the CFB UK equity portfolios were ahead of the median fund in eight years, and below it in only two. Much of the time the outperformance was not huge, but the cumulative effect of producing consistent above-average returns was to place the CFB UK equity performance in the top decile of all UK equity funds over ten years.

The CFB gives several factors to explain why it can generate good investment returns despite the effects of SRI constraints. Heading the list would be its prime objective of generating good investment returns, something that is essential for an institutional asset management organisation like the CFB. Also important is the fact that the CFB specialises in SRI, it does nothing else. Lastly, the CFB approach to SRI is based on tight control of risk. For example, exposure to the small-, medium- and large-capitalisation sectors of the market

Table 10.10   *CFB UK equity risk/return analysis 1990–2000*

	Annualised return (geometric mean)	Volatility	Sharpe ratio*
Five years			
CFB	20.2%	32.5%	0.458
Index	18.9%	32.4%	0.417
Ten years			
CFB	16.7%	34.1%	0.297
Index	15.2%	33.7%	0.257

*The Sharpe ratio measures the portfolio's return per unit of risk. It is calculated by taking the cumulative return on a risk-free investment (short-term money market rates) and deducting it from the portfolio's cumulative return; the result is then divided by the portfolio's own standard deviation. Hence the higher the Sharpe ratio, the better the portfolio's overall risk-adjusted performance.
Source: Central Finance Board of the Methodist Church, unpublished analysis.

is closely monitored, as is relative risk compared to very large companies such as BP and Vodafone that each make up over 5% of the FTSE All-Share. The effects of this policy can be seen from the risk analysis in Table 10.10 for the five and ten years to March 2000, when the CFB UK Equity Fund produced above-average investment returns with a negligible increase in risk.

The CFB's procedures for managing the portfolio risk of SRI exclusions are particularly interesting, as very little has been written about this subject. The basis of its approach is to compensate for areas excluded on SRI grounds by having increased portfolio weightings in sectors with similar economic characteristics. In other words, SRI constraints are integrated into portfolio construction. An amended version of the FTSE All-Share index is created which adjusts sector weightings for all companies excluded on ethical grounds. The effect of SRI exclusion can then be measured in terms of SRI-adjusted economic groupings. For example, alcohol and tobacco shares have relatively low economic sensitivity, a useful asset at times of fear of a global economic slowdown. Although the CFB avoids investment in alcohol and tobacco shares, the financial risk of excluding them can be offset by overweighting other sectors within the same economic grouping which have similar characteristics, in this example food manufacturing and food retailing shares. As well as managing the portfolio risk of complete sector exclusion, the CFB also uses a 'best in class' approach within sectors. For example, it might avoid investment in some oil companies on social and environmental grounds, but compensate for this by increased investment in other oil companies with better records in these areas.

New York – based Christian Brothers Investment Services (CBIS) provide roughly similar services to US Catholic charitable foundations as the CFB does in the UK. It has found that its SRI exclusions have not resulted in below-par investment returns despite the highly competitive nature of the US asset management market. Frank Coleman, the CBIS vice president for socially responsible investing, addressed this point in a speech to the United Nations in May 2001:

> CBIS has been able to achieve competitive performance appropriate to industry benchmarks. In a study completed a year ago, we found no 'SRI effect' on performance over the long-term.[38]

THE NEED FOR DEEPER ANALYSIS

Socially responsible investment will never take off for mainstream investment institutions unless an answer can be found to the key question of whether SRI has a systemic bias to increase or reduce financial returns. The evidence from the DSI and CFB provides some comfort that the answer is yes. However, a conclusive answer requires a deeper level of analysis on the financial impact of SRI than is generally available.

In the author's opinion the greatest weaknesses of the majority of studies on SRI investment returns has been their reliance on general statistical number crunching. Financial performance is driven by a number of factors, and this makes it very difficult to separate a genuine causal relationship from an apparent correlation. The only way to do this is by performance attribution analysis of each individual fund. This involves analysing the component factors of each fund, such as its weighting in the oil sector compared with the S&P 500, as well as style bias, e.g. relative exposure to small-capitalisation or large-capitalisation stocks, bias to value or growth stocks, etc. Such sector/style variance analysis can then be used to calculate factor returns. Barra did this for the DSI, with the analysis finding that the bulk of the fund's excess returns could be attributed to a general SRI stock-picking effect, rather than deriving from sector exclusion.

INVESTING IN SMALLER COMPANIES

It is generally accepted that the many SRI unit trusts and mutual funds are heavily overweight in smaller companies. These tend to be purer plays, whereas larger companies are often of a conglomerate nature that makes them fall foul of SRI exclusion criteria. The US stock market also benefits from a dynamic venture capital industry which encourages the growth of small companies that combine innovative technologies and enlightened social practices. (This factor is less prevalent in the UK, Europe and Japan.) Such innovative small companies are natural investments for US SRI portfolios. According to Bob Zevin of US Trust:

> A lot of small, innovative companies are at the heart of socially responsible investment. You usually find better educated, younger management running the custom-tailored high-service areas. Most of these companies have good equal opportunity practices, good maternity policies, good promotions, high pay, no pollution.[39]

In the 1980s quite a significant amount of academic research was produced stating that, over the long term, small companies tend to do much better than larger ones. For example, Burton Malkiel's classic book *A Random Walk Down Wall Street*[40] found that over the sixty years to 1988 the value of shares in smaller companies grew by 12.3% a year on average, compared to an annualised rise of 10.0% in the S&P 500 index. Similar, if less extensive, data was available for the UK. However, just as smaller-company investing became generally accepted, the outperformance went into reverse. UK smaller companies shares did very badly in 1989–92, with the relative underperformance continuing in the 1990s. This same trend also occurred in the US. For the five years to the end of 2000 the S&P 100 index of the hundred largest US companies by market capitalisation rose 134%, whereas the Russell 3000 index of small-capitalisation equities was up only 53%, less than half as much.

A major bias to smaller companies seems more true of UK SRI unit trusts than it does of US-based SRI mutual funds, which tend to be more mid-cap based. However, while both smaller companies and SRI unit trusts did well in the UK in the late 1980s, the correlation was not precise. In 1994 I noted that it seemed wrong to attribute the good returns produced at that time by SRI unit trusts simply to smaller-company effects.[41] However, there is another aspect to this phenomenon that I have rarely seen mentioned. It is simply that investment portfolios with a high smaller-company bias will have a significant tracking error relative to standard benchmarks such as the FTSE All-Share or the S&P 500. Since most institutional investors and their investment consultants are wary of big tracking errors, this makes the normal approach of SRI retail funds inappropriate for them.

GREEN INVESTING

One noticeable theme of investment markets that developed during the 1990s was the trend to specialist industry, sector or theme investing. This involved the creation of specialist investment products restricted to investing in certain high-technology sectors of the economy such as pharmaceuticals or the internet. The underlying logic of theme investing was twofold:

- These particular sectors of the economy possessed underlying long-term growth rates that were significantly above average.
- The complexity of doing business in such areas required detailed analysis that was best done by experienced sector specialists in order to maximise financial returns.

Now it seems fairly obvious that environmental investment possesses both of the above characteristics. Unfortunately, this does not mean it is easy to make money by investing in the sector. Stock market sectors such as biotechnology or technology have similar profiles. Nevertheless, this has not resulted in biotech or technology investment being the road to riches for many investors; in fact, the opposite has turned out to be true. The problem is that the stock markets of developed countries like the US and the UK are extremely efficient discounting mechanisms. In other words, good growth prospects are already reflected in high equity valuation levels. Excess valuation is one concern. Another is that it can be highly unclear which of competing technologies will be ultimately successful; this is currently a major concern in the area of fuel cells. There is also a concern that the public tends to become aware of such specialist investments and, crucially, is willing to invest its savings in them only when they have already demonstrated great financial returns. In other words, there is a tendency for money to pour into theme funds at the top, i.e. when the sector is excessively valued and the returns are about to go negative. This was certainly true of the public's money that poured into internet investment vehicles in 1998–2000 on both sides of the Atlantic.

Unfortunately, this 'irrational exuberance', to use Alan Greenspan's phrase, was also true in the environmental investment area. Shares of companies operating in the renewable energy field soared in 2000 on the back of the internet mania. The public then became aware of environmental growth opportunities on the back of surging share prices of the quoted companies operating in this sector. Merrill Lynch Investment Management met the public's newly awakened enthusiasm with the launch of the Merrill Lynch New Energy Fund (MLNEF) in October 2000. However, the fund's initial performance was disappointing, with its share price more than halving in its first year (down from 103.5p to 48.25p). When the New Energy Fund was launched there was concern over whether the fund would be able to invest easily given the relatively small number of quoted companies in which to do so. The magazine *Environmental Finance* warned at the time, 'There is some danger of a bubble developing, some analysts say, as too much capital chases too few companies'.[42]

I must admit that I experienced a distinct sense of déjà vu when the environment became a hot stock market area in 2000. My mind went back to the early 1990s when there was increasing awareness that environmental services were becoming big business following the success of the Green Party in winning 15% of the vote in the

UK European elections. The stock market reaction is described in my book *The Ethical Investor*.[43] One of the City's leading stockbrokers, James Capel, produced a 'green index' of 30 companies involved in environmental services. Prospects looked good, but environmental investing peaked along with the Green vote. The Capel Green Index, having risen from an initial level of 100 in January 1989 to a high of 147 in August 1989, then fell back. Over the five years from its inception it steadily underperformed the FTSE All-Share index. US investors attracted to environmental theme investing also experienced disappointment in the early 1990s. The bottom fifty of the 1993 *Wall Street Journal* list of the worst-performing mutual funds on sale in America contained a number of environmental funds. All of these produced negative returns in 1993, a year when the average US equity mutual fund was up 12.5%.[44]

What went wrong? In retrospect, 'green euphoria' pushed share prices up to levels which could not be sustained, particularly as in reality there were few quoted companies with genuine environmental exposure. The few 'pure plays' were pushed to a huge valuation premium (an average P/E of 19 compared to 11 for the UK market average) that was unsustainable. There was also little hard analysis carried out of what the growth prospects actually were. This was pointed out afterwards by environmental analyst David Owen:

> There was a somewhat undignified rush to attach 'green' labels to any stock in the hope of its gaining an environmental premium. Much of this 'research' was more concerned with image, resulting in shops, food manufacturers, and banks being dubbed 'environmental'. This clashed with what I understood to be the sector.[45]

ESTABLISHING A THEORETICAL FRAMEWORK

When establishing a scientific theory it is not enough to notice correlation; a theoretical framework explaining the relationship is also required. However, even the academic papers on SRI investment returns have shied away from trying to explain the relationship between socially responsible investing and financial performance. Most commentators have either ignored the question or answered it in simplistic terms of avoiding 'bad' companies or supporting 'good' ones, unlikely to hold water in efficient markets like the US and the UK.

In 1992 US consultant Jeffrey Teper set out a number of reasons why socially responsible investing might not be an advisable option for the charities advised by his firm. Essentially, these boiled down to the disadvantages of reduced portfolio diversification, and the higher 'specific' risk of each individual holding if large-capitalisation blue chips were replaced by smaller companies. Teper analysed returns from a sin-stock-free index, i.e. excluding alcohol, tobacco and gambling from the S&P 500 index for the ten-year period to December 1989; this produced an annual return of 18.9%, 10.8% above the return of the S&P. However, nine actual portfolios that used sin-free criteria produced a cumulative total return 1.1% a year below that of unrestricted portfolios for a six-year period to September 1990. Teper concluded:

> The evidence presented demonstrates that there has been a consistent cost to socially responsible investing. While the cost varies with the policies and vehicles chosen, conservative investors can assume roughly a 1% annualised reduction in equity returns if they adopt restrictive criteria.[46]

I disagree with the conclusions Teper drew from his study. All it surely demonstrates is that investment managers with no expertise in SRI are indeed likely to produce lower returns if they are asked to put SRI constraints in place. There seems no other explanation for the huge disparity between the excellent return produced by Teper's sin-free index over the chosen period and the disappointing returns achieved in practice by real-life funds. While reduced diversification could be a problem if nothing is done about it, it did not seem to occur to Teper that this portfolio risk could be actively managed, as the DSI and the CFB have demonstrated successfully.

My book *The Ethical Investor* contained one of the first attempts to create an explanatory model for SRI outperformance. Here are the underlying factors:[47]

- *Diversification:* any non-financial restriction on investment selection must reduce diversification, hence risk-adjusted returns.
- *Small-companies effect:* socially responsible investors are forced to avoid large conglomerates and concentrate on smaller companies which over time grow faster.
- *Anticipation effect:* exclusion of certain companies on grounds of moral or environmental repugnance anticipates later legal action and financial problems.
- *Information effect:* to do it properly, SRI needs a higher level of knowledge about the companies invested in than ordinary investment managers possess.
- *Positive selection effect:* the positive criteria used by such funds help them target well-run companies.

With hindsight, I find it interesting that I avoided suggesting that SRI generates excess returns by identifying new growth areas such as environmental investing. The anticipation effect should not work as it falls foul of the efficient markets hypothesis, although asbestos litigation suggests otherwise. Diversification is standard financial theory and the small-companies effect has already been explored in depth. Both the DSI and the CFB have generated above-average investment returns that cannot be explained simply by portfolio risk or sector exclusions. Where are these superior risk-adjusted returns coming from? I suspect the answer lies in the information effect and the positive selection effect. In other words, the 'best in class' methodology used by both funds results in them identifying superior corporate management in a way that is not available to conventional fund managers.

To my mind one of the most interesting papers on SRI performance drivers was produced by the former DSI analyst Kurtz in 1997, who noted what he called 'three apparent contradictions':[48]

- Despite apparently unavoidable diversification costs, the universe of SRI stocks as evidenced by the DSI index did not appear to have underperformed the market on either a nominal or a risk-adjusted basis.
- Some management science studies found that the factors monitored by social investors, such as environmental policies and

employee relations, could be associated with positive abnormal returns. However, the evidence was mixed, and studies using complex attribution models had failed to demonstrate the existence of a social factor in the returns of screened portfolios.

- Money managers who handled both screened and unscreened portfolios had reported that over time there was no significant difference between the performance of these two account types.

Kurtz made the perceptive comment that although the portfolio risk of most average SRI exclusion screens could be diversified away if the screens were random, in fact the screens were not random and this created uncompensated risk. He also found a persistent bias towards smaller companies and higher valuation in SRI funds. Kurtz suggested a variety of mechanisms that might generate a positive bias to SRI returns, in particular evidence of skilful management, a result of corporate success, i.e. prosperity, and SRI activism as a catalyst for change. Kurtz was dismissive of these, and highlighted the lack of hard evidence that SRI really could identify good management:

> It could also be true that the DSI (which, like most SRI products, is not optimised to any broader benchmark) suffers diversification costs, and that these have been offset by information effects. If this were the case, SRI practitioners would be faced with a dilemma — information effects would likely be arbitraged away as they became well-known, while diversification costs would be permanent in unadjusted portfolios. At present it appears that portfolio managers wishing to eliminate active exposures of social screens may do so without incurring material costs.[49]

I believe there are two factors which, for now at least, enable skilful SRI fund managers to produce above-average investment returns despite operating within social and environmental constraints. The first is the identification of good management. The Innovest approach described in Chapter 11 uses objective environmental metrics to try to identify good practice in companies operating across a range of industrial sectors. Innovest claims that their evidence indicates this approach has been successful in generating excess stock market returns. Repeated surveys show that financial analysts working in the City of London have little interest in environmental or social factors. As long as this is the case, SRI fund managers and analysts also have an information edge over their competitors. At the moment, the good long-term financial performance record of the DSI and the CFB is not well known outside the SRI community. However, if SRI methods become generally accepted on the basis that they can produce higher returns then they will be increasingly adopted, and these excess returns are likely to be arbitraged away. The growth of SRI means that it is being taken seriously by some of the most famous names in finance. In 2000–2001 both Goldman Sachs[50] and UBS Warburg[51] produced papers examining the financial effect of SRI. However, obtaining specialist SRI expertise may not be that easy to obtain. History suggests that capital moving into areas that suddenly become 'hot' can find it extremely difficult to replicate the high returns which attracted it in the first place. Examples of this include emerging markets in the early 1990s, private equity in the late 1990s, and I suspect hedge funds presently. The shortage of SRI expertise (see page 349) suggests that SRI funds may well be able to generate excess returns for the foreseeable future.

I will end this chapter with some thoughts on the matter by Mark Mansley of Claros Consulting, one of the UK's leading thinkers on SRI:

The argument about whether the current pattern of investment works is essentially about whether maximising a series of short term investment periods succeeds in maximising long term investment returns. Mathematically, for this to work, it must be the case that the return prospects in each period are 'independent' of each other. Put another way, a necessary condition for short term investment to deliver the best long term returns, is that: 'the process of investing for each short term period does not affect the ability to generate returns in any future period'. This condition may sound familiar, and indeed is essentially the same as that of sustainable development.[52]

REFERENCES

1. Russell Sparkes, 'The Rewards of Virtue', *Professional Investor*, March 1994.
2. Michael Russo and Paul Fouts, 'A Resource-Based Perspective on Corporate Environmental Performance and Profitability', *Academy of Management Journal*, Vol. 40, No.3, 1997.
3. Barra International, 'Survey of Ethical Investment 1983–1989', EIRIS, 1989.
4. L. Livak, 'Do Social Screens Harm Performance?', *Values*, June 1992.
5. Milton Moskowitz, 'Choosing Socially Responsible Stocks, *Business and Society*, Spring 1972.
6. John Guerard, 'Is There a Cost to Being Socially Responsible in Investing?', *Journal of Finance*, Summer 1997.
7. *Ibid.*
8. John Guerard, 'Additional Evidence on the Cost of Being Socially Responsible in Investing', *Journal of Investing*, Winter 1997.
9. Phoebus Dhrymes, 'Socially Responsible Investment: Is It Profitable? *The Investment Research Guide to Socially Responsible Investment*, Colloquium on Socially Responsible Investing, 1998.
10. Ros Haverman and Peter Webster, *Does Ethical Investment Pay?* EIRIS, September 1999.
11. Russell Sparkes, 'The Rewards of Virtue', *Professional Investor*, March 1994.
12. *Ibid.*
13. *Ibid.*
14. 'Principia for Mutual Funds, *Morningstar*, March 1996.
15. J. Rothschild, 'Why I Invest with Sinners', *Fortune*, May 1996.
16. Robert Luther and John Matako, 'The Performance of Ethical Unit Trusts: Choosing an Appropriate Benchmark', *British Accounting Review*, Vol. 26, 1994.
17. C.A. Mallin, B. Saadouni and R. J. Briston, 'The Financial Performance of Ethical Investment Funds', *Journal of Business Finance and Accounting*, Vol. 22, June 1995.
18. Alan Gregory, John Matatko and Robert Luther, 'Ethical Unit Trust Financial Performance: Small Company Effects and Fund Size Effects', *Journal of Business Finance and Accounting*, Vol. 24, 1997.
19. Ros Haverman and Peter Webster, *Does Ethical Investment Pay?* EIRIS, September 1999.
20. *Ibid.*
21. US Trust statistics, quoted in Domini and Kinder, *Ethical Investing*, Addison-Wesley, 1984.
22. Dr Robert Schwartz, *Socially Responsible Investment: the American Experience*, GLC, 1984.
23. The WM Company, 'The Implications of Ethical Constraints on Investment Returns', unpublished manuscript, 1991. Available from The WM Company, Crewe Toll, Edinburgh EH4 2PY1.
24. *Ibid.*
25. The WM Company, 'You Can Have Your Ethical Cake and Eat It', press release, 7 March 1997.
26. The WM Company, 'Is There a Cost to Ethical Investing?, unpublished manuscript, 1999.

27. *Ibid.*
28. Peter Kinder, Steven Lydenberg, Amy Domini, *Investing for Good*, Harper Business, 1994.
29. Lloyd Kurtz, Steve Lydenberg, and Peter Kinder, 'The Domini Social Index: A New Benchmark for Social Investors', Chapter 25 of *The Social Investment Almanac*, Henry Holt, 1992.
30. *Ibid.*
31. Russell Sparkes, notes from a conversation with Peter Kinder, London, 18 January 1998.
32. Christopher Luck and Nancy Pilotte, 'Domini Social Index Performance', *Journal of Investing*, Fall 1993.
33. Lloyd Kurtz and Dan Di Bartolomeo, 'Socially Screened Portfolios: An Attribution Analysis of Relative Returns', *Journal of Investing*, Fall 1996.
34. Christopher Luck, 'Domini Social Index Performance', *The Investment Research Guide to Socially Responsible Investment*, Colloquium on Socially Responsible Investing, 1998.
35. See for example Mark Mansley, *Socially Responsible Investment: A Guide for Pension Funds and Institutional Investors*, Monitor Press, 2000.
36. Bill Seddon, speech, 'SRI in Global Portfolio Management', London, April 2000.
37. Bill Seddon, speech: 'Socially Responsible Investing: The UK Experience', European Pension Fund Investment Forum, Stockholm, August 2000.
38. Frank Coleman, vice president of socially responsible investing at Christian Brothers Investment Services (CBIS), speech to UN Finance for Development Conference, 2 May 2001, New York.
39. Bob Zevin, quoted in Domini and Kinder, *Ethical Investing*, Addison-Wesley 1984.
40. Burton Malkiel, *A Random Walk Down Wall Street*, 4th edn, W.W.Norton, 1985.
41. Russell Sparkes, *The Ethical Investor*, Chapter 6, Harper Collins, 1995.
42. 'Merrill Lynch Sees Green', *Environmental Finance*, October 2000.
43. Russell Sparkes, *The Ethical Investor*, Chapter 6, Harper Collins, 1995.
44. *Ibid.*
45. David Owen, 'Looking for Life Beyond the Green Paint Job?', *Professional Investor*, April 1994.
46. Jeffrey Teper, 'Evaluating the Cost of Socially Responsible Investing', Chapter 28 of, *The Social Investment Almanac*, Henry Holt, 1992.
47. Russell Sparkes, *The Ethical Investor*, Chapter 6, Harper Collins, 1995.
48. Lloyd Kurtz, 'No Effect or No Net Effect? Studies on Socially Responsible Investing', *Journal of Investing*, Winter 1997.
49. *Ibid.*
50. Goldman Sachs Investment Management, 'The Risk Management Implications of Custom Guidelines', unpublished manuscript, December 2000.
51. UBS Warburg, 'Sustainability Investment: The Merits of Socially Responsible Investing', unpublished manuscript, August 2001.
52. Mark Mansley, Claros Consulting, submission to the Myners Commission, June 2001.

PART III

A Global Revolution

Parts I and II gave a structural overview of socially responsible investment on the basis of developments in its two oldest and largest markets, the US and the UK. This was designed to show the common structural factors of issues, methods and customer profiles that underpin SRI on both sides of the Atlantic. They show how SRI has moved beyond simple negative screening to a more sophisticated consideration of issues such as the environment, human rights and corporate governance, involving active dialogue with companies.

However, it is important to note the geographical breadth of socially responsible investing, something reflected in the internationalisation of SRI research provision. Socially responsible investing has become well established in both Canada and Australia, which are also important markets in terms of SRI funds under management. Their alternative approaches are therefore covered in Chapter 12. In recent years SRI has become a core aspect of UK and US mainstream investment management, a process described in Chapter 13. Chapter 14 highlights the geographical expansion of socially responsible investing, as it truly becomes a global revolution.

11

Information Services

THE NEED FOR SRI RESEARCH

Good analysis requires quality data. Anyone wishing to analyse a company's financial performance is a beneficiary of the explosion that has occurred in the provision of financial news coverage over recent years. There is much less available information on which to analyse a company's social responsibility performance. This chapter therefore highlights the crucial role of the specialist research organisations that meet the demand for social and environmental research on companies. Without such external research providers, many SRI funds would struggle to exist in their current form. This is not an easy task, as it may require uncovering things that corporate executives would prefer left unnoticed.

The vast majority of large companies in developed countries are publicly quoted, meaning that they have to produce detailed financial accounts, while they also have to abide by stock market listing requirements. Company executives may well wonder whether any further analysis of their company really needs to be carried out. However, a growing number of people feel that financial reporting does not provide a complete picture of the impact of a company's operations; they want to know where, and how, these profits are being made. In other words, close scrutiny of environmental and social performance is simply a contemporary requirement of a company's licence to operate, something increasingly recognised by more progressive company executives.

Recent years have seen a proliferation of research services analysing SRI or related issues. This chapter describes five of the leaders in the field, three of them American and two British. They include the Council on Economic Priorities (CEP) and EIRIS, the pioneers in the US and the UK respectively. The demands placed on SRI research providers reflect the changing nature of SRI itself. Over time SRI analysis has shifted from the provision of relatively simple data identifying areas of investor concern such as alcohol or defence, to a broader approach trying to assess an individual company's social responsibility profile. The increasingly global nature of SRI has also resulted in international developments in SRI research and analytical procedures, as well as the introduction of SRI stock market indices.

THE COUNCIL ON ECONOMIC PRIORITIES

The Council on Economic Priorities (CEP) is a non-profit body. It was founded in New York in 1969 in response to the Vietnam War, making it the oldest specialist SRI research organisation in the world. Its aims are described as the accurate and impartial analysis of corporate social and environmental performance. CEP's work targets ethical consumers as well as socially responsible investors. Its 1987 book *Rating America's Corporate Conscience* was a pioneering study of the social performance of 130 US companies, mostly selling consumer products. *Shopping for a Better World* has sold over a million copies. This is a pocket-sized book rating over 200 companies with over 2100 brand names in 23 product categories from cereals to home appliances. CEP also pioneered the production of in-depth studies examining corporate America from a particular viewpoint. The first was *Efficiency in Death* (1970) which identified producers of anti-personnel weapons to the Vietnam War. Other examples included *Short-changed* (1972), noting the lack of senior women or ethnic minorities in the banking industry, and *Star Wars: The Economic Fallout* (1987), reviewing weapons contractors and their exposure to that project. One of CEP's greatest achievements in recent years was the development of SA 8000 (Chapter 8).

CEP uses its research database to assess the social and environmental performance of more than 300 large- and mid-cap publicly owned US companies. Like other SRI research providers, its staff examines newspapers, magazines, government statistics and company accounts to produce detailed company profiles. Questionnaires are sent to corporate executives requesting information on areas of concern. Its main research headings are the following: environment, women's advancement, minority advancement, charitable giving, family benefits, workplace issues, disclosure. Other subjects researched are animal welfare, community outreach; gay and lesbian issues, and military involvement. Private subscribers to the CEP Company Analysis service receive research reports six times a year summarising its findings, while in-depth industry reports are also produced. In 1992 CEP launched the Institutional Investor Research Service (IIRS) to supply its information in a format appropriate to the needs of professional investors. IIRS produces monthly reports tabulating the performance of the 300 companies it follows. Companies are rated top, middle or bottom, with alert columns highlighting corporate activity such as defence exposure that is outside its 12 research categories but may well result in exclusion from many SRI portfolios.

CEP's Global Ethics Award has received widespread recognition. For example, in 2000 Bristol-Myers Squibb received this award for its work in establishing a five-year $100 million initiative designed to stem the tide of illness and death from AIDS in partnership with the nations of South Africa, Botswana, Namibia, Lesotho and Swaziland. Another winner was the Japanese company Ricoh Corporation for environmental achievement through its development of energy-efficient office equipment, including digital copiers, facsimile machines, printers and scanners. CEP also provides a consulting service to corporate America to help executives make their companies more socially responsible. CEP's head, Alice Teppler Marlin, described the growing market for social and environmental research:

> Public awareness and outrage have grown steadily and corporate reputations are now at stake, not simply − like Texaco − in a company's headquarter country, but whenever consumers watch TV, log on to the Internet, have made 'fax' a verb, and whenever thoughtful investors hold portfolios with international components. The momentum for global social change in this era of instant communication is unprecedented.[1]

THE ETHICAL INVESTMENT RESEARCH SERVICE

The Ethical Investment Research Service (EIRIS) was set up in 1983 to provide UK churches with more information on corporate involvement in South Africa and other issues. There are in fact two EIRIS organisations. EIRIS Services Ltd is a company providing commercial services to clients; its parent, the Ethical Investment Research Service, is a charity that carries out research into ethical investment. EIRIS is governed by a council and run by a board of directors. The charity was the original organisation, but it has been overshadowed by the growth of its commercial arm. In 1999, for example, the parent had income of £17 675, whereas EIRIS Services had a turnover of £910 873. The current aims of EIRIS Services are as follows:[2]

- To provide independent research into corporate behaviour needed by ethical investors.
- To help charities and other investors identify the approach appropriate to their requirements.
- To publish guides to help investors and advisers identify and choose between funds with ethical criteria.
- To enable each investor to create a portfolio that reflects their own ethical concerns.
- To offer services for all types of client, from checking a portfolio to creating and implementing an ethical investment policy.

EIRIS's core activity is the production of detailed ethical profiles of company groups. The analysis is based on published data, including company reports and accounts, but it also uses statistics produced by government regulators and non-government organisations. EIRIS prefers to use the term 'company groups' rather than the straightforward word 'company', as its aim is to identify all the activities that a quoted company may carry out, which requires analysis of its subsidiaries and affiliates. Every 18 months a copy of the data EIRIS holds on each company is sent to an executive of that company for comment and checking. A good illustration of EIRIS's methods was given by head of research Karen Eldridge in 1991 when she described a large research project carried out on water pollution:

Table 11.1 *EIRIS research categories*

Negative criteria			
Alcohol	Animal testing	Gambling	Genetic engineering
Greenhouse gases	Health and safety	Human rights	Intensive farming
Military, MOD	Military, nature of	Nuclear power	Ozone depletion
Pesticides	Pollution convictions	Pornography	Roads
Third World	Tobacco	Tropical hardwood	Water pollution
Positive criteria			
Community work	Disclosure	Equal opportunity	Environment, positive
Positive products			

Source: Abridged from *EIRIS Annual Review of 1999*, June 2000.

We spent over 400 hours analysing and entering the data. We had to approach each of the ten NRA and seven River Purification Boards (RPB) individually for information. Then we checked whether the consent holder was owned or controlled by a stock exchange group. By the end of February 1991 we had reached some 6858 conclusions about 800-odd company groups.... We create consistent factual benchmarks that help investors choose between them. Not a complete picture, but a clearly defined basis for decisions with many practical attractions.[3]

EIRIS's core research products are based on negative screening presented in a fairly straightforward way (Table 11.1). Over time the sales of such screening services to the burgeoning ethical unit trust industry have grown rapidly. Clients identify areas of concern such as alcohol or defence, and stipulate thresholds of turnover such as 5% or 10%. Companies that exceed these limits are identified, and if necessary, excluded from an approved list of possible equity holdings. EIRIS's current research capability consists of an in-house team of 12 researchers analysing 1200 company groups in the UK and 500 in Europe. Research is carried out using 200 social, economic and ethical performance indicators grouped under 28 main different research headings: EIRIS has always dominated the market for SRI services in the UK. Over 67% of all UK SRI retail funds use its services, a number exceeding 90% when measured in terms of fund values. However, in the late 1990s it recognised the need for more sophisticated products specifically designed for the institutional investor. Such investors want a system that does not just identify areas of ethical concern, but can analyse how an individual company is changing over time, or how a company compares with its peer group in the same industry. In 1999 EIRIS launched *Corporate Ethics Overview*, a publication aimed at updating such clients on a wide range of corporate social responsibility issues. In 2000 *Ethical Portfolio Manager* (EPM) was distributed to clients, a computer-based version of its traditional screening procedures, allowing the client to select an analytical framework and then work with this on an interactive basis. EIRIS director Peter Webster is only too aware of the rapid rate of change in SRI (emphasis added):

> Anyone offering services in this field who has not reviewed what they offer several times in the last twelve months could well be left behind. The new research methodology grades company groups according to their performance in three key areas: policy and commitments, management systems and reporting. *Companies are categorised as having either weak, moderate, good or exceptional records. This allows clients to identify the best-performing companies within a particular sector, and to monitor a company's progress.*[4]

KINDER, LYDENBERG AND DOMINI

Well known as the compiler of the DSI index, Kinder, Lydenberg and Domini (KLD) is also a major producer of SRI research services in its own right. It was founded in 1988 by Peter Kinder, a lawyer with a special interest in corporate social responsibility, and Amy Domini, an investment counsellor (in British parlance, a financial adviser), both based in Cambridge, Massachusetts. Steve Lydenberg brought extensive SRI analytical skills to the new company, most recently as a senior researcher for Franklin Research in nearby Boston. Work began on compiling the prototype DSI index in March 1988, although it was not officially launched until two years later. Peter Kinder later remembered:

We could see a clear need for an SRI product that met the needs of institutional investors, i.e. one that was unlikely to significantly underperform the S&P 500. However, it took a long time to develop the right product and then market it, incurring significant costs and no revenue. Essentially we only kept it going financially by judicious use of our personal credit cards.[5]

Since then Boston-based KLD has grown into a provider of social research for 150 US institutional investors employing 33 people, 22 of them SRI analysts. The company's official name has also been changed from Kinder, Lydenberg and Domini to KLD Research & Analytics Inc. to reflect its research provision function. KLD's current research services also include corporate accountability research, as well as consulting services designed to help individual clients such as charitable foundations devise their own SRI guidelines and implement them. The firm's mission statement sets out the following aims:[6]

- To remove barriers to socially responsible investing.
- To provide superior research and support services to the socially responsible investment market.
- To operate the company in a manner that meets our own standards for judging other companies.
- To analyse data and distribute information on publicly traded companies.
- To influence corporate behaviour toward a more just and sustainable world.
- To respect employees by seeking to involve them in decisions.

KLD's main research product analysing corporate social responsibility is Socrates, a large SRI database on US companies. I remember visiting the KLD offices in 1997 and being amazed at the power of the program, the first interactive database available on CD-ROM designed specifically for investment professionals. The 2001 version of Socrates contains data on over 1600 companies. It has been designed to have flexible sorting and reporting features to enable users to find the required information quickly and easily. Socrates contains KLD's profiles of over 650 US corporations, including every company in the S&P 500 index and the Domini 400 social Index. The profiles include narrative coverage based on 11 research headings, as well as social ratings evaluating each company's strengths and concerns. There is also information about current shareholder actions, including the text of proxy resolutions compiled by the Interfaith Center on Corporate Responsibility. Here are the KLD primary data points:[7]

- Alcohol
- Charitable contributions
- Defence
- Environmental concerns, including Superfund or hazardous waste sites
- Executive representation of women and ethnic minorities (diversity)
- Gambling
- Non-US operations (outsourcing)
- Nuclear power
- Shareholder actions
- Tobacco
- Union representation

In my opinion the most innovative aspect of Socrates lies in its interactive character, i.e. a multiple-query capability. This enables companies to be ranked on social ratings or statistical data, using a single criterion or multiple criteria. It is specifically designed to enable investment managers to devise their own search criteria, e.g. to identify companies with military contracts over 5% of revenues or $10 million. Companies are then ranked by a weighting system based on the values assigned to the social rating issues by the particular asset manager. The portfolio management feature also allows institutional investor to store clients' portfolios in Socrates so they can run updated reports on their holdings whenever they wished. In April 2001 Steve Lydenberg made the following prediction:

> SRI will become a 'standard service' required by institutional investors. There will also be universal corporate reporting of social issues – globalisation and ease of communication means that what used to be implicit now has to be made explicit – and the GRI is leading the way in this respect. We are also seeing the growth of a wealth of resources for SRI research, including

diverse NGO participation. This all means that it is becoming much easier to engage with companies on social responsibility issues.[8]

INNOVEST

Innovest was launched in 1997 by Matthew Kiernan, previously director of the World Business Council for Sustainable Development (WBCSD). This is a coalition of 120 international companies which seeks business-based solutions to global environmental problems. For many years the WBCSD was frustrated at the indifference shown by US financial markets to environmental issues.[9] The City of London appears no better in this respect than Wall Street. A Business in the Environment survey carried out in May 2001 showed that only 3% of UK investment analysts and only 4% of fund managers thought environmental and social factors were important.[10] In the words of WBCSD's 1996 report *Environmental Performance and Shareholder Value*:

> At the end of 1995 we asked a number of financial analysts and investment managers what they thought were the most important drivers of shareholder value. They mentioned environmental drivers only when there was evident downside risk to business results. Historically, the financial market's recognition of environmental performance has been restricted to legal liabilities and to negative risk factors.[11]

The idea of creating Innovest therefore grew out of WBCSD's Capital Markets Task Force. It was designed to demonstrate the benefits of good corporate environmental performance to asset managers in terms they would accept, i.e. that it led to above-average profits growth and share price outperformance. As Linda Descano of Salomon Smith Barney wrote in 1998:

> Since the perceptions of the capital markets are shaped primarily by information provided by companies, the challenge for the corporate community is to communicate the immediate and long-term financial implications of their progressive

environmental practices. Until the linkages are clear, 'beyond compliance', environmental performance will continue to be undervalued by the markets.[12]

Correlations between environmental and financial factors were therefore 'hard-wired' into the Innovest EcoValue 21 research model, based on regression analysis of 350 out of the 500 stocks in the S&P 500 index. The basic idea underlying the Innovest research process is to identify superior eco-efficiency, defined as 'simply the capacity to produce greater shareholder value with lower levels of environmental risk and resource inputs than one's competitors'. The philosophy is simple: these drivers determine whether a company will be able to generate sustainable competitive advantage, profitability and shareholder value. According to Matthew Kiernan:

> The gut instinct is to say this is nonsense, that if you want to buy environmental performance it will be at the expense of financial performance. In fact environmental performance ratings are a potent, pregnant, robust proxy for superior strategic management which translates into stronger earnings and greater shareholder value.[13]

Here are the six aspects of the Innovest risk model:[14]

1. *Historical contingent liabilities*: ongoing risk exposure arising from past actions. This includes Superfund liability, likely remediation expenditure and adequacy of insurance cover.
2. *Operating risk exposure*: risk exposure arising from current operations, calculated by analysis of factors like toxic emissions, product risk liabilities, hazardous waste disposal issues and waste discharges.
3. *Eco-efficiency and sustainability risk*: future risk exposure caused by potential undermining of the company's material sources of long-term profitability and competitiveness. Examples include energy intensity and efficiency, raw material dependency, product life-cycle durability, and exposure to shifts in consumer values.
4. *Financial risk capability*: ability to overcome environmental risks through balance sheet strength and adequacy of insurance cover.

5. *Managerial risk efficiency*: environmental competence, or management's ability to drive an environmentally aware business strategy. Such factors include strategic corporate capability, i.e. board-level environmental responsibility, strong environmental management systems and accounting, supply chain management, and a business culture supportive of business innovation.
6. *Strategic profit opportunities*: the company's ability to position itself to benefit from environmentally driven business opportunities. This could be via demographic or product differentiation, using superior environmental performance as a marketing-led competitive tool.

EcoValue 21 calculates the median score for each industry, using this to generate environmental credit ratings: AAA is the best, AA is the second best, then come A, BBB, BB, B and CCC (worst). Hence Eco-Value 21 is essentially a 'best in class' methodology that is trying to identify the best companies in each industry. A consequence of the Innovest methodology is that the scores have no absolute meaning, i.e. a top rating in the chemical industry might still mean greater environmental risk than a low rating in a service industry with a low environmental footprint. EcoValue 21 aims to identify the balance of environmental risk facing a company together with its capacity to manage that risk strategically and profitably into the future. It is not designed to assess the absolute level of environmental risk facing a company, but rather the combination of risk and the company's ability to manage this risk. Innovest believes it is this relationship that determines the financial consequences of environmental risk for industrial companies and their investors. Back-tested results provided strong support for Innovest's basic claim that eco-efficiency is an identifiable variable with a strong correlation with stock market returns. Innovest found that that a portfolio consisting of the top 50% of their S&P 500 universe outperformed a portfolio of the bottom half by almost 72% for the three years to December 1998:

> Back-test evidence published this year [1998]...indicates that a diversified portfolio of eco-efficient companies can be expected to outperform its less efficient competitors by anything from 240 to 290 basis points per annum [i.e. 2.4% to 2.9%]. In sectors

with particularly acute environmental risk exposure, chemicals and petroleum for example, Innovest research has revealed that the 'outperformance premium' can easily reach or exceed 500 basis points [i.e. 5%].[15]

It was a natural and easy step to use the EcoValue 21 ratings to develop 'enhanced eco-efficiency' stock market indices or create related portfolios. Companies with below-median scores in each sector are underweighted or eliminated. The positive scores, or alphas, of the companies with above-median scores are then determined, the amount invested in each company being proportional to alpha, while the overall industry weight is kept neutral. The fact that the scoring is industry-specific means it can be used to generate portfolios or indices with little market risk (tracking error) relative to benchmarks such as the S&P 500 index. It is hardly surprising that a number of investment management firms have adopted the model to launch funds based on its findings. By 2000 Innovest research was being used by some of the world's leading investment management groups such as Fidelity, Mellon Capital, Scudder Dreyfus, Schroder Investment Management and Lombard Odier as well as by investment banks such as Morgan Stanley and Bear Stearns. In 1999 Dreyfus Investment Advisors launched an Eco-Enhanced Index fund based on EcoValue 21 research, containing approximately 200 S&P constituents with industry weights similar to the S&P 500 index. Schroders explained that its decision to subscribe to Innovest environmental research was based on its expected financial benefits:

> Schroders doesn't sell any ethical funds yet and shouldn't be classified as a pure ethical investor. Our primary objective is, and will remain, to achieve optimal financial returns for our clients.[16]

I have made my scepticism of back-tested investment performance well known throughout this book. As described in Chapter 10, many environmental stocks produced high investment returns in 1998 to 2000, leading to some incautious suggestions in some quarters that such 'industries of the future' could be expected to generate such high returns. In fact, however, the outperformance was actually a side effect of the internet boom of the late 1990s, and many environmental stocks did badly in 2001–2. Chapter 10 raised the question of performance attribution. It seems pertinent to ask the question of whether the outperformance found by Innovest might have been a simple reflection of the massive large-capitalisation bull market of the late 1990s; large companies have the resources to publish and implement environmental policies that small companies do not. Only time will tell whether eco-efficiency is the strong determinant of stock market outperformance that Innovest obviously believes, or whether the actual relationship is more complex. However, a quantitative study of the Innovest data was carried out in 2001 by QED International, which found that the outperformance continued even when the factor bets were neutralised.[17]

PENSIONS AND INVESTMENT CONSULTANTS

Some people may be surprised to see Pensions and Investment Consultants (PIRC) described as an SRI research provider, as it is best known for its UK corporate governance work. PIRC's Corporate Governance Service (CGS) was launched in 1991 at a conference addressed by Sir Adrian Cadbury, and is now used by private and public sector pension funds and investment managers with combined assets of over £300 billion. In fact, however, PIRC has always seen SRI as a core part of its activities, according to PIRC managing director Alan McDougall:

> We had an imperative to make socially responsible investment financially acceptable.... It was our view that there was nothing socially responsible about losing money. If we were dealing with money, it had to be commercial. PIRC aims to enable its pension funds clients to develop prudent long term investment strategies which both meet the wider economic best interests of beneficiaries and which recognise pension funds' wider responsibilities.[18]

PIRC publicly entered the SRI market with the launch of its SRI service in January 2000, as it recognised that that the data compiled by CGS could easily be used for SRI purposes. PIRC's CGS database contains detailed reports on each of the over 800 companies that constitute the FTSE All-Share index, not just on corporate governance but also on issues of shareholder concern such as environmental policy, and the appointment of women to the board. PIRC's SRI service is based on the belief that 'wealth creation for the benefit of shareholders is achieved by companies establishing best practice standards in relations with key stakeholders. Institutional investors thus have a common interest with other stakeholders in issues of corporate responsibility and corporate performance over the long term'.[19] Its SRI reporting is based on the following issues:[20]

- *Environment*: corporate policies, quality of reporting, management systems, independent verification
- *Employment*: training programmes, consultation procedures, representative structures, participation, equal opportunities
- *Human rights*: overseas labour standards, involvement with repressive regimes, arms industry
- *Community policy*: charitable and political donations, community involvement
- *Corporate governance*: shareholder rights, best-practice compliance, board structures, remuneration, investor relations

PIRC was one of the first organisations in the UK to argue persistently and cogently that pension funds should look beyond their purely short-term financial interests in the interests of society and of a pension scheme itself:

> Pension funds are long term investors. Over the long term there is a great deal of mutual interest between shareholders, corporations, employees, the wider community and the environment.... Wealth creation, sustainable development, equality of opportunity and corporate accountability are some of the goals which are shared in common. Socially responsible investors can use their position of influence as owners to initiate positive change in corporations to the mutual benefit of a company's stakeholders.[21]

TWO GLOBAL SRI NETWORKS

The globalisation of the world economy has led to growing demands for SRI research to be provided on a worldwide basis. Two international SRI networks have therefore grown up in response to this demand. The Global Partners for Corporate Responsibility Research network was founded in 1995 as an international grouping of 11 international organisations conducting research on corporate social and environmental responsibility to effect positive change. Annual working meetings are held to discuss topics such as increasing research quality and corporate disclosure.

The second international SRI research network is the Sustainable Investment Research International Group (SIRI), a coalition of 10 research organisations devoted to the global advancement of social investing. Each SIRI member covers its national markets and provides services to its local financial community but I suspect that SIRI's ultimate objective is for the network to allow the sharing of research between partners and their clients. In other words, SIRI appears to be building the first common platform for global SRI research. By the end of 2001 SIRI consisted of 11 research organisations with a combined total of over 70 researchers, covering more than 1500 companies in the major markets worldwide. Membership at that date was as follows: AReSE, (France), Avanzi (Italy), Caring Company (Sweden), Center Info (Switzerland), Fundación Ecología y Desarrollo (Spain), KLD (US), Michael Jantzi Research Associates (Canada), PIRC (UK), Scoris GmbH (Germany), Stock at Stake (Belgium) and Triodos Research (Netherlands). SIRI's global ambitions and reach are illustrated in its mission statement:[22]

- To provide and promote high-quality social investment research products and services throughout the world
- To provide global coverage of all major financial markets
- Publication of harmonised profiles of the largest publicly traded companies throughout the world
- Promotion and the development of socially screened national and transnational financial indices
- Maintenance of the highest possible standards for social investment research and product

The rapid growth of SRI research provision has not occurred without leaving problems in its wake. In particular, I am becoming increasingly concerned that the exponential growth of SRI information services creates the risk that investors may suffer from information overload due to the sheer volume of data presented to them. Corporate executives have also already expressed concern about the growing numbers of questionnaires they receive requesting social and environmental information, not just from specialist research providers, but also from the ever-increasing number of SRI funds themselves. Business in the Environment in its 2001 survey warned about 'the dissipation of impact caused by the fragmentation of measurements'.[23] The same point was made more strongly by Tom Woollard of Environmental Resources Management, a UK consultancy:

> The proliferation of eco-rating tools is muddying the water of companies' environmental performance and confusing the analysts and investors for whom they are intended.... There should be less focus on [environmental] policies and plans, and more on the hard data of companies' environmental impact. But investors and fund managers are still unsure as to what information they should demand, and which eco-raters they can rely on.[24]

I end this section with some thoughts of Steve Lydenberg on social research. To me they seem as perceptive and valid as when they were first uttered in 1992:

> As corporate social accountability research develops – and as the market for social investing expands – the task of the researcher will become easier in some ways but more difficult in others. Some factual research will become easier as independent resources develop and sources of information expand. But as has already happened with the environment, when these issues become important to the investing public, different sources – including the companies themselves – often put forth contradictory claims. Along with methodologies for obtaining and evaluating factual data, a social researcher must develop judgement – a sensitivity to the nuances and the

relative importance of issues. Issues will change, as will the companies being evaluated. A researcher's task is to be attuned to these changes and to formulate a combination of data and evaluation in ways that can be used by money managers and investors alike.[25]

SRI MARKET INDICES

The public's growing interest in socially responsible investing has been reflected in the development of specialist SRI stock market indices. Few people give much thought to the subject of equity market indices, but they are a relatively new invention. It was in 1897 that Charles Dow and Edward Jones had the brainwave of measuring the short-term movements of the US stock market using a basket of leading shares. From the 1960s onward, the rise of institutional investment management led to requirements for a different type of stock market index. Pension funds needed a broadly based investment index that would define the optimum investment universe and accurately track its performance over time. Typical examples are the S&P 500 index in the US, the FTSE All-Share index in the UK, and the TOPIX index in Japan. In the 1990s the development of theme investing led to the creation of a third type of index, specialist sector indices that tracked areas like technology or biotechnology, e.g. the UK TechMark index, or the US Amex Biotechnology index.

A further development occurred on Wall Street in 1993 with the launch of exchange-traded funds (ETFs) based on specific indices. ETFs are essentially tradable securities with hedging potential, designed to offer small investors the benefits of passive fund management at a low cost. The first ETFs were the US Spiders (SPDRs) series, a good example of the type. Investors can buy and sell units in the S&P 500 itself or subsectors of it. In the five years to the end of 2000, the market value of ETFs quoted on the New York Stock Exchange soared from $1.1 billion to $57 billon. ETFs arrived in Europe in 2000, and by the end of 2001 there were 80 ETFs traded on the main European bourses with a combined market capitalisation of €5 billion.[26] The demand for ETFs has led to the creation of market

Table 11.2 *Types of stock market index*

Aims and objectives	Illustrative example
Track short-term market movements	Dow Jones Industrials, FTSE 100
Investment performance benchmark	S&P 500, FTSE All-Share, TOPIX
Sector specialist	Techmark, AMEX Biotechnology
Force for social change	DSI, DJSI, FTSE4Good

indices designed with the specific intention of providing the base for an ETF.

Any SRI index that aims to command general acceptance requires a combination of generally accepted social responsibility criteria and the financial characteristics of a low tracking error compared to a standard benchmark such as the S&P 500 or FTSE All-Share index. Issues of liquidity are also important, as such an SRI index must identify an investable universe that could be used by large institutional investors. The varying functions of equity market indices can be summed up as in Table 11.2. SRI indices of course add one more objective to the list − stock market indices designed to be a force for social change.

THE DOMINI SOCIAL INDEX

One of the core themes of this book has been the expression of the author's belief that the essence of SRI lies in a combination of social objectives and reasonable financial returns. Further, that this is only likely to be achieved as an integrated policy objective. The Domini 400 Social Index (DSI) seems a good example of this approach. It was inspired by KLD's objective of constructing a benchmark index for US equities with robust social and environmental criteria whose financial performance would not deviate significantly from that of the S&P 500. The Domini Social Index Equity Fund (DSIEF), an index tracker linked to the DSI index was launched at the same time. The three founders, Peter Kinder, Steve Lydenberg and Amy Domini, later reminisced:

It had become clear to us in the mid-1980s that social investors needed benchmark indices tailored to their requirements. Financial professionals needed a generally accepted definition of the universe of US equities social investors could buy. In March 1988 we set out to address those needs. The result was a benchmark equities index, the Domini Social Index.[27]

The DSI was constructed using a mixture of negative screening, social evaluation and risk management procedures (Box 11.1).[28] The greatest weight has been placed on social evaluation, i.e. excluding companies whose records are on balance negative and including companies with positive scores in these areas. The DSI's exclusion screens are zero-tolerant, i.e. a company scoring in these areas is automatically dropped from the index; note the 2% tolerance in the case of military weapons. However, the social evaluation criteria are based on an overall evaluation of each company, combining positive and negative indicators. The question of diversity tends not to be a big issue in European socially responsible investing. It describes the representation of women and ethnic minority groups on company boards or at senior executive levels. Perhaps Europe (including the UK) should take diversity issues more seriously. A survey carried out in November 2001 of the UK's largest boardrooms found that only 2% of all FTSE 100 company directors were women, with 43 out of the 100 companies having no female directors at all.[29]

Box 11.1 DSI Screening and Evaluation Criteria

Exclusion Screens

- Two percent or more of sales derived from military weapons systems
- Any revenues derived from the manufacture of alcoholic or tobacco products
- Any revenues derived from the provision of gaming products or services
- Electric utilities owning interests in nuclear power plants, or deriving electricity from nuclear power plants in which they had an interest

Social Evaluation Criteria

- The environment
- Diversity
- Employee relations
- Product safety
- Community or non-US operations

In the author's opinion one of the most distinctive aspects of the DSI 400 was the close attention its compilers paid to minimising financial risk (tracking error relative to the S&P 500). KLD started by screening the S&P 500 index constituents, eliminating those companies that failed to qualify under the exclusionary and qualitative screens. Firms with stock prices below $5 per share were eliminated, as were firms with financial problems so serious that their long-term viability was questionable. Approximately 250 companies were eliminated through this process. KLD then looked for large-capitalisation potential company holdings that were not constituents of the S&P 500 to give the industry representation that would otherwise have been lacking. Approximately 100 companies fitting these criteria were added. Finally, 50 companies were added on SRI grounds, on the basis that they possessed exceptional social characteristics, so reaching the specified 400 company membership of the index.

Turnover on the DSI has been kept low, typically 5% a year. The most frequent reason for removal from the index has been acquisition by another firm, corporate demerger, or imminent bankruptcy proceedings. Exclusion from the DSI for social reasons has been a fairly rare occurrence. However, if a company has entered a business explicitly excluded by the DSI's screens, such as military contracting or gambling, it has been dropped immediately. This low level of change in the index constituents was intended to confirm that the DSI was a passive index offering an SRI benchmark against the S&P 500. When an index member has been dropped, a replacement has been immediately added to keep the DSI at 400 holdings. Replacement holdings are identified using four main criteria: strong social responsibility characteristics, relatively large market capitalisation, industries in which the DSI is underrepresented, and existing membership of the S&P 500 index.

The DSI regularly publishes its top holdings, a good example of transparency and disclosure. At 31 December 2000 they were Cisco Systems, Wal-Mart Stores, Microsoft, American International Group, Merck, Intel, SBC Communications, Coca-Cola, Johnson & Johnson and EMC. These was a mixture of large-capitalisation corporate America with a high-technology bias. While this holding list gave no precise measure of the index's tracking error relative to the S&P 500, the presence of a relatively diversified list of highly liquid investments meant that the general portfolio risk of the DSI appeared to be fairly low. In 1999 the DSIEF also became the first mutual fund in the US to publish all the proxy votes it cast on the companies held in its portfolio. Critics have questioned the holding of Wal-Mart, the largest retailer in the world. For several years there have been fairly high-profile battles over labour standards between the company and the US churches coordinated by ICCR. There has also been criticism of Walmart's refusal to accept trade unions, and allegations that it discriminates against women. It was therefore no great surprise to see that the DSI had decided to drop Walmart from the index in May 2001, expressing concerns over workplace vendor conditions. KLD issued a statement saying that:

> KLD removed Wal-Mart from its Domini 400 Social Index primarily because the company has not done enough to ensure that its domestic and international vendors operate factories that meet adequate labor and human rights standards. Wal-Mart's vendor contracting policies and procedures have failed to meet the standards set by prominent human and labor rights activists or those attained by other prominent companies that are similarly exposed to sweatshop controversies.[30]

In my opinion the DSI appears to be a well-constructed SRI index. It has surely fulfilled its intended role of providing a useful SRI benchmark for the domestic US equity market, and also of proving to an initially sceptical Wall Street that socially responsible investing can produce good investment returns. In my analysis of the DSI, I have deliberately focused on index construction and financial risk management. However, we should not forget the pioneering achievement of the DSI/DSIEF in challenging conventional thinking about investment. One of the DSI's original objectives was 'to communicate the standards of mainstream social investors to corporations and the general public in a viable format'.[31] In June 2001 the DSI hosted a reception in New York to celebrate its tenth anniversary. Amy Domini used the opportunity to make this point:

> The Domini Social Equity Index has played a vital role in changing the investment world. It has helped set in motion a movement that is changing companies, changing financial markets, and laying the groundwork for new ways of doing business in a more sustainable and humane economic system.[32]

THE DOW JONES SUSTAINABILITY INDEX

If socially responsible investors genuinely wish to encourage corporate social responsibility (CSR), they need to persuade company executives that taking account of social and environmental factors is an integral part of long-term business success. In Chapter 9 I argued that CSR only really works if it is integrated throughout a company's operations, just like total quality management in many leading companies. The example of quality management suggests that CSR is unlikely to be done well if regarded as an afterthought of core activities. The Dow Jones Sustainability Indexes (DJSI) seem based on similar thinking, called 'corporate sustainability'. This is defined as the ability to increase long-term shareholder value through the integration of economic, environmental and social factors into business strategies, using the five key factors shown below (emphasis added, slightly abridged):

> They facilitate a financial quantification of sustainability performance by focusing on a company's pursuit of sustainability opportunities – e.g. meeting market demand for sustainable products and services – and reduction, ideally, avoidance of sustainability risks and costs. *As a result, corporatec sustainability is an investable concept. This relationship is crucial in driving interest and investments in sustainability to the mutual benefit of companies and investors.*[33]

The DJSI sustainability principles are set out overleaf:[34]

1. *Strategy*: Sustainability leaders integrate long-term economic, environmental and social aspects in their business strategies.
2. *Innovation*: Sustainability leaders invest in product and service innovations that focus on technologies and systems, which use economic, natural and social resources in an efficient, effective and economic manner.
3. *Governance*: Sustainability leaders implement the highest standards of corporate governance, including management quality and responsibility, organisational capabilities and corporate culture.
4. *Shareholders*: Sustainability leaders meet shareholders' demands for sound financial returns, long-term economic growth, long-term productivity increases, sharpened global competitiveness, superior intellectual capital and reputation.
5. *Employees and other stakeholders*: Sustainability leaders encourage long-lasting social well-being in communities where they operate, engage in an active dialogue with different stakeholders, and respond to their specific and evolving needs, thereby securing a long-term 'licence to operate' as well as superior customer and employee loyalty.

DJSI World was launched in September 1999, the result of a partnership between the American Dow Jones & Company and the Swiss group SAM. Dow Jones is one of the world's leading index providers, as well as being the publisher of the *Wall Street Journal*. It therefore provided the expertise in index construction. SAM is a Zurich-based asset manager specialising in integrating corporate sustainability. In October 2001 the two partners were joined by the leading European equity index provider STOXX Limited to launch a series of European sustainability benchmarks, the DJSI STOXX. SAM's CEO Reto Ringger described the reasoning behind the index:

> The DJSI provides a bridge between companies implementing sustainability and investors wishing to profit from their superior performance and favourable risk/return profiles. For investors, the DJSI provides rational, consistent and flexible performance tracking of the leading sustainability companies world-wide. The integrity of the sustainability assessment and the index calculation provides an investable sustainability concept. For

companies, the DJSI provides a financial quantification of their sustainability policy and strategy and their management of sustainability opportunities, risks, and costs.[35]

The DJSI World series is based on the DJGI, an investment universe comprising nearly 5000 stocks from 34 countries covering 51 industry groups and 89 subgroups. At the end of April 2002, the DJSI World consisted of around 300 companies in 62 industry subgroups with a total market capitalisation of $5.6 trillion. The basic methodology underlying the DJSI World was simple: to use sustainability criteria to select the top 10% of the companies in each industry subgroup of the DJGI, i.e. the best in class. Following the same approach, the DJSI STOXX series includes the leading 20% in terms of sustainability out of the Dow Jones STOXX 600 index. For both index series, DJSI World and DJSI STOXX, subsets are available which exclude tobacco, alcohol, gambling and/or armaments and firearms, for clients who wanted such an approach. In my opinion it seemed rather strange for the DJSI index to depart from its logical and clear 'best in class' approach and adopt negative SRI exclusions. The logic behind this was not explained.

The corporate sustainability assessment process is produced by SAM using social, environmental and economic factors: strategic opportunities 15%, management opportunities 20%, industry-specific opportunities 15%, strategic risks 15%, management risks 20%, industry-specific risks 15%. The DJSI assessment process is based on industry-specific questionnaires sent to each company, as well as an analysis of corporate policies and company reports and accounts. The sustainability ratings are reviewed once a year, each September, to ensure that the index composition accurately reflects the leading companies in each of the DJSI industry groups. In addition, the components are continuously reviewed and monitored throughout the year.

Although the DJSI is based on corporate sustainability using a 'best in class' approach, it also takes reputational factors into account via what it calls corporate sustainability monitoring (CSM). In essence this tests the extent to which index constituents live up to their stated CSR principles, looking out for such incidents as illegal commercial practices, human rights abuses, large-scale lay-offs or labour disputes, and large disasters or accidents A striking example of corporate monitoring occurred in October 2000 when SAM downgraded the rating of the large Swiss bank Credit Suisse, although it was not expelled from the index. Credit Suisse was one of the banks most heavily criticised by the Swiss Federal Banking Commission over involvement in money transfers from Nigeria on behalf of the former dictator Abacha.[36] Credit Suisse is one of the two dominant banks in Switzerland, and it cannot have been easy for the Swiss-based SAM to reduce its rating. That it did so is a tribute to its impartial treatment of index constituents. SAM Indexes commented:

> The decision was taken after an in-depth corporate monitoring procedure was declared to have shown a systematic weakness of internal compliance systems in dealing with money transfers from the former Nigerian dictator Sani Abacha's entourage.[37]

The creation of the DJSI was based on the premise that its methodology could identify companies producing above-average investment returns. Five-year data for the five years to February 2000 showed annualised returns over the five-year period of 19.3% for the DJSI compared to only 12.1% for its benchmark with a similar level of risk (beta). However, I think it is fair to criticise the DJSI for not always making clear an absolute distinction between back-tested returns of what might have been, and real results of what actually has occurred. Real-time performance data of the DJSI can only be calculated from its actual launch in September 1999. The author's calculations of the DJSI in practice are shown in Table 11.3

Table 11.3   *DJSI financial performance (%)*

	DJSI	DJGI	FT World
Year to September 2000	1.1	6.0	8.3
Year to September 2001	−27.8	−29.9	−29.0
Two years to September 2001	−26.7	−25.7	−23.1

Source: Table compiled by author using DJSI and index data.

and confirm his repeated caution about using back-tested results as a guide to future stock market returns. As can be seen, in its first full year of operation the sustainable index significantly underperformed two comparable benchmarks, although it regained some of the lost ground in the second year. That said, it should also be noted that attribution analysis showed that the disappointing relative performance over the period was not due to any negative bias in the sustainability indices, but rather to asset allocation — principally being overweight in Europe and due to the weakness of the euro. David Moran of Dow Jones commented on the poor relative performance:

> Is the market performance of sustainability stocks unsustainable? One might be tempted to leap to such a conclusion after the difficult year that stocks the world over experienced last year. The Dow Jones Sustainability Index under-performed its benchmark, the Dow Jones Global Index, by nearly 450 basis points.... It is wholly legitimate for investors to wonder if the stocks of companies committed to sustainability offer downside cushioning as well as upside potential.[38]

One of the signal successes of the DJSI has been to produce an index that has been widely taken up, particularly in continental Europe, to form the basis of retail SRI funds. By April 2001 the DJSI had been licensed to 34 leading investment management groups across Europe, as well as in Japan and Australia. These included continental leading names in finance such as Credit Suisse, HypoVereinsbank, Robecco, ING and Aegon. Total funds under management linked to the DJSI at the end of April 2002 amounted to €2.1 billion.[39] These included index-tracking mutual funds, segregated accounts and portfolio baskets. The biggest single fund was a SFr 500 million mandate won by the US asset manager State Street Global Advisors to be invested in the DJSI on behalf of the Swiss Federal Social Security Fund.[40]

In the author's opinion the DJSI seems a good example of an equity index based on 'sustainability' principles. The general methodology appears robust and well thought out, essentially a global 'best in class' approach, and therefore well suited to institutional investors wishing to combine social concerns with above-average investment returns. The index has also played a useful role in forming the basis of SRI index funds that have significantly contributed to the growth of SRI in Europe.

FTSE4GOOD

FTSE4Good is the most recent addition to the family of SRI indices, being launched in July 2001. At the same time Close Fund Management issued the FTSE4Good UK Fund, in essence an index tracker linked to the FTSE4Good UK index. FTSE recognised the need for a partner to add SRI expertise to its own skills in index construction, so the FTSE4Good index series was therefore created in association with EIRIS. The underlying concept was to construct a broadly based SRI index for a number of regional markets: UK, US, Europe and the world, with the objective of producing a benchmark to measure SRI fund performance in these regions. The following exclusions were then used to filter out unacceptable companies: tobacco producers, companies providing strategic parts or services or manufacturing nuclear weapons systems, manufacturers of whole weapons systems, and owners or operators of nuclear power stations and those mining or processing uranium.[41]

> A need has arisen for a clear definition of 'socially responsible' to be applied to companies and for a benchmark index to be developed according to this definition. FTSE is addressing this need with the creation of the FTSE4Good index series... to express a coherent view on these matters and to set a global standard for corporate responsibility.[42]

The basic philosophy underlying the index was to include only companies moving towards best practice in the areas of the environment, human rights and stakeholder relationships. FTSE explained that its entry into the field of SRI indices was driven by the convergence of the recognition by business leaders of the need for corporate social responsibility, coupled with growing acceptance by large institutional investors of the case for SRI. An independent committee of reference meets every six months to review the indices and define the guiding principles lying behind the index, 'the ground rules'. The committee's decisions are based on the general methodology and the individual company data provided by EIRIS. FTSE stated:

> The FTSE4Good Advisory Committee is a key element in achieving this goal as it provides an expert and dependable body of opinion to guide decision-making. Committee members include fund managers who understand the needs of retail and institutional investors and nominees of UNICEF and the Co-op Bank.[43]

The United Nations Childrens Fund (UNICEF) agreed to be associated with the project in return for the right to nominate three members of the advisory committee. UNICEF also gained the commitment of FTSE to pay it all the net licence income FTSE received from its clients in the first twelve months of operation, as well as a 50p charge on each trading screen showing the data. FTSE International hoped this would generate revenues estimated at $1 million for donation to UNICEF:[44]

> The initial size of the new Fund is vitally important to the success of the new initiative. In conjunction with FTSE and UNICEF, Close are raising seed money so that the Fund launches with significant initial capital on day one. The initiative will serve as a platform
>
> - to help raise the issue of socially responsible investing in way that has hitherto not been possible;
> - to encourage companies to behave in a socially responsible way;
> - to provide an important source of revenue for UNICEF.

Excluding investment in tobacco, defence and nuclear power operations rules out about 10% of the All-Share index, while aspirational objectives on environment, human rights and social issues have further restricted the approved list. FTSE4Good's first investable universe comprised 288 out of the 757 companies in the All-Share index, and 64 out of the 100 larger companies in the FTSE 100 index.[45] However, no indication was given as to what proportion of the All-Share or FTSE 100 index by value would be excluded. Some back-tested data on investment performance was provided, which showed 15% outperformance of the FTSE All-Share over the previous five years, although risk-adjusted returns do not seem to have been calculated.[46] FTSE chief executive Mark Makepeace stated:

> We expect less than half of all companies to qualify. FTSE4Good represents an aspirational framework for change. We want it to be a step towards encouraging companies to adopt socially responsible principles.[47]

The aims and objectives of the FTSE4Good index are clearly laudable. FTSE4Good seems to have made a genuine and praiseworthy attempt to construct an SRI index that would be as inclusive as possible. However, I wonder if the attempt at inclusivity may have caused the index compilers to lose sight of its natural client base. Pension funds would be attracted to FTSE4Good's three key principles of the environment, human rights and corporate social responsibility. However, it is inconceivable that any UK pension fund would benchmark itself against an index that excludes over 50% of the All-Share index. In March 2002 Commerzbank, a German banking group, published an analysis of the FTSE4Good European index which showed that the new index had a tracking error of 2.6% compared to the standard FTSE Europe index. Commerzbank warned its clients about the higher risk involved in using FTSE4Good Europe.[48]

FTSE4Good therefore seems best suited to act as a benchmark index to track the performance of SRI unit trusts, an important role that may raise the profile of retail SRI investing in the UK. However, the majority of UK SRI unit trusts may not want to be compared against it, as each SRI unit trust has its own proprietary methodology that is used as a selling point. The two market leaders in UK SRI retail funds, Henderson Investors and Friends Provident, both stated at the time of the FTSE4Good launch that they had no intention of using the new index as the benchmark for their own funds. Craig Mackenzie of Friends Provident commented:

> FTSE takes a different view to ethical investing. It's a pragmatic view, whereas we take the purist view.[49]

The initial evidence showed relatively little take-up of the index so far by investors or by independent financial advisers (IFAs). Lee Coates of Ethical Investors Group, an independent financial adviser specialising in socially responsible investment commented in October 2001:

> Only two of the 3,000 clients to whom we sent information on the Close [FTSE4Good] fund wanted to invest in it. The FTSE4Good index just isn't ethical enough for them.[50]

REFERENCES

1. Alice Tepper Marlin, 'Visions of Social Accountability', *Visions of Ethical Business*, Financial Times Management, 1998.
2. Abridged from 'EIRIS Annual Review of 1999', June 2000.
3. Karen Eldridge, quoted in *The Ethical Investor* (EIRIS bulletin), May 1992.
4. Peter Webster, quoted in *The Ethical Investor* (EIRIS bulletin), August 1999.
5. Author's notes from a conversation with Peter Kinder, London, February 1999.
6. Copyright 2002 by KLD Research & Analytics, Inc. Reproduced by permission. The Domini 400 Social Index is a service mark of KLD Research & Analytics Inc.
7. Copyright 2002 by KLD Research & Analytics, Inc. Reproduced by permission. The Domini 400 Social Index is a service mark of KLD Research & Analytics Inc.
8. Author's notes on a speech by Steve Lydenberg, Germany, April 2001.
9. Matthew Kiernan, quoted in *Tomorrow*, September/October 1998.
10. 'Green Companies Sell Themselves Short in the City', press release, Business in the Environment, 24 May 2001.
11. World Business Council for Sustainable Development, *Environmental Performance and Shareholder Value*, 1996.
12. Linda Descano, quoted in *Tomorrow*, September/October 1998.
13. Matthew Kiernan, quoted in 'Go Green, Invest, and then Prosper', *Financial Times*, 25 January 1999.
14. Copyright the Innovest Group. Reproduced by permission.
15. Copyright the Innovest Group. Reproduced by permission.
16. 'Schroders to Adopt "Green" Guidelines for Investments', *Wall Street Journal*, 15 June 2000.
17. 'Research Shows Efficiency of Eco-efficiency', *Environmental Finance*, June 2001.
18. PIRC Services for Local Authorities, *Socially Responsible Investment*, PIRC, 1993.
19. PIRC website, November 2001.
20. *Ibid.*
21. PIRC Services for Local Authorities, *Socially Responsible Investment*, PIRC, 1993.
22. SIRI presentation, July 2001.
23. 'Green Companies Sell Themselves Short in the City', press release, Business in the Environment, 24 May 2001.
24. Tom Woollard, quoted in *Environmental Finance*, March 2001.
25. Steve Lydenberg, 'Researching Social Performance', published in *The Social Investment Almanac*, Henry Holt, 1992.
26. 'Exchange-Traded Funds Gain in European Markets', *Wall Street Journal*, 5 November 2001.

27. Peter Kinder, Steven Lydenberg and Amy Domini, *Investing for Good*, Harper Business, 1994.
28. Copyright 2002 by KLD Research & Analytics, Inc. Reproduced by permission. The Domini 400 Social Index is a service mark of KLD Research & Analytics Inc.
29. 'Women Lose More Ground in Top Boardrooms', *Financial Times*, 26 November 2001.
30. KLD 'white paper' 17 May 2001.
31. Peter Kinder, Steven Lydenberg and Amy Domini, *Investing for Good*, Harper Business, 1994.
32. Amy Domini, quoted in 'Domini Social Equity Fund Celebrates 10th Anniversary', *Business Wire*, 14 June 2001.
33. Dow Jones Sustainability Group Index, document circulated in September 1999.
34. *Ibid.*
35. Dow Jones Sustainability Group Index, quarterly report, 3/99.
36. 'Berne Raps Banks over Dictator's Dubious Dollars', *Financial Times*, 5 September 2000.
37. 'Credit Suisse Downgraded over Nigeria Involvement', *Ethical Performance*, November 2000.
38. David Moran, 'Well-Managed Companies Mean Well-Managed Risk', *Sustainable Business Investor: Europe*, Spring 2001.
39. 'SRI Indexes Come of Age, *Environmental Finance*, June 2001.
40. 'DJSI World: Two Years On', *Environmental Finance*, October 2001.
41. FTSE4Good, series overview, July 2001.
42. 'Aim', FTSE4Good website, 3 March 2001.
43. 'Role of Committee', FTSE4Good website, 3 March 2001.
44. FTSE4Good website, 25 January 2001.
45. 'Ethical Indices Bar 40pc of Companies', *Daily Telegraph*, 28 February 2001.
46. 'FTSE4Good Aims for a Clear Conscience', *Financial Times*, 11 July 2001.
47. 'Adopting a Responsible Approach to Standards', *Financial Times*, 11 July 2001.
48. 'Commerzbank Report Highlights Risks of Ethical Investing', *Financial Times*, 25 March 2002.
49. 'The Green Funds Are Growing', *Sunday Telegraph*, 21 October 2001.
50. Lee Coates, quoted in 'Business and the Environment', *Financial Times*, 5 November 2001.

12

Alternative Approaches: Canada and Australia

CANADIAN BEGINNINGS

Canada has played an important part in the growth of socially responsible investment, even if this has been overshadowed by the sheer volume of activity south of the border. Church groups were the initial pioneers as elsewhere. In 1973 the Young Women's Christian Association (YWCA) published *Investment in Oppression*, a report showing how Canadian companies were supporting the apartheid regime in South Africa. This report led to the foundation of the Taskforce on the Churches and Corporate Responsibility (TCCR) in 1975. TCCR criticised the mining company Noranda over expansion plans in Pinochet's Chile, and was one of the first groups to actively campaign for Canada's giant forest products companies to adopt environmentally sustainable practices, as well as for better corporate governance standards in Canada. In the late 1980s TCCR filed shareholder resolutions criticising the tractor/motor components company Massey-Ferguson (later renamed Varity) over its involvement in South Africa, and the Canadian banks over their loan practices in that country. However, in 1987 the Canadian courts upheld a legal challenge by Massey-Ferguson that this contravened the Canada Business Corporations Act (CBCA), a ruling that effectively killed any attempts to file wide-ranging US-style social proxy resolutions in Canada for the next fourteen years.

At the same time, the Canadian government has been pushing for greater corporate social responsibility from Canadian companies. For example, in September 1997 foreign affairs minister Lloyd Attworthy announced a new voluntary initiative called The International Code of Ethics for Canadian Business. Signatories to the code committed themselves to promote human rights, protect worker health and safety, avoid child labour, protect the environment, promote social justice, and allow workers freedom of speech and freedom of association in the workplace.[1] However, this code was only voluntary. An examination of actual Canadian corporate practice published at the same time found that:

> The largest Canadian companies, like many of their US counterparts, are beginning to consider human rights issues in their international practices. This awareness is gratifying. At the same time, the report flags a number of shortcomings in codes of conduct....The majority of Canadian businesses operating or sourcing overseas do not have codes containing reference to even the most basic human rights standards. Second, most codes lack the independent monitoring viewed as essential by many code analysts. Third, companies appear to be reluctant to share their codes with the public...this recalcitrance runs counters to calls for transparency in code development, implementation, and administration.[2]

In the late 1990s the Canadian churches suffered major setbacks which caused a serious deterioration in their financial position. This has forced all the Canadian churches to significantly reduce their spending, including big cutbacks at TCCR. Despite this TCCR has managed to carry out a major campaign to raise public awareness and concern over the operations of the Canadian oil company Talisman Energy in Sudan. (The terrible human rights abuses believed to be occurring in Sudan are described in Chapter 9.) At the Talisman annual general meeting held in May 2000 in Toronto, TCCR proposed that the company should adopt the following measures for its operations in Sudan:[3]

- Adopt clear human rights standards for its operations.
- Create an independent organisation to verify compliance with those standards.

- Cease operations if the independent monitor concludes the company cannot comply with its own standards.

The TCCR proposals were backed by major investment institutions such as the Ontario Teachers' Pension Plan Board, the Ontario Municipal Employees Retirement Board, and the Caisse de Depot de Quebec. Although it was not carried, the proposal obtained the support of 27% of the company's shareholders, the highest level of support ever seen for a social resolution. The controversy was judged to have hung over the Talisman share price. Analysts quoted in the main Canadian financial newspaper, the *Toronto Globe and Mail*, estimated that the company's Sudanese involvement reduced its overall market value by up to 25%.[4] A year later there were signs that the company accepted this and was looking for an exit, as Talisman's chief executive, Jim Buckee, stated that he was prepared to sell the company's stake in the Sudan project. It seems likely that pressure from TCCR played a part in this decision. Buckee said:

> It's a good asset, and if they come up with what we see as a good price, then we will sell it... [Sudan] takes up more than 10% of my time for 10% of our assets.[5]

Canadian socially responsible investing really took off in a big way in the mid 1980s. In 1986 stockbroker Larry Trunkey founded the Canadian Network for Ethical Investing (CNEI), spending three years on whistle-stop tours across the country explaining and advocating SRI. In 1989 the think-tank Caledon Contemporaries organised the first Canadian National Conference on Social Investment, the first national gathering on the subject which attracted more than three hundred delegates.[6] This led directly in 1990 to the creation of the Social Investment Organisation (SIO), formed with a mandate to promote SRI in Canada. Founding members included Eugene Ellmen, a former business journalist; Ted Brown, a manager at the progressive Toronto Credit Union; Stuart Coles and Don Warne, two ministers of the United Church; and Carolyn Langdon, a women's rights activist.[7] Ellmen was later to become Canada's leading authority on SRI, writing four books on the subject and being appointed director of the SIO in 1999. He later reminisced:

In 1988 and 1989 I wrote the first Canadian books on ethical investing. At the same time a group of organisers – myself included – started to think about a national organisation to advance social investment. It started in 1988 with an ethical investment workshop at the alternative summit coinciding with the Group of Seven meeting in Toronto. The workshop led to the first Canadian social investment conference, which agreed on the need for a national organisation.[8]

Within four years the SIO felt confident enough to host the first ever international conference on socially responsible investment, held in Montreal in June 1994, assisted by the US Social Investment Forum and UKSIF. The conference was called, appropriately enough, Going Global, and brought together over two hundred specialists for two days of intensive discussions. Two specialist SRI research services also appeared around this time. In 1987 Earthscan Canada launched the *Corporate Ethics Monitor*, a bimonthly monitor on the social and environmental performance of 1500 Canadian companies. The *Monitor* analyses corporate practices in depth in such areas as community relations, charitable giving, progressive staff policies, labour relations and environmental records. It also provides a broad coverage of socially responsible investment in Canada. In 1992 Earthscan published a 'green consumer' guide called *Shopping for a Better Canada*, which examined the environmental performance of the companies producing the most common consumer products sold in Canada.

Michael Jantzi Research Associates (MRJA) was set up by the eponymous founder in 1988 to produce reports on the environmental and social performance (including labour issues) of over 300 publicly quoted Canadian companies. It was also one of the first SRI research organisations to put its research onto a large computer database, the Canadian Social Investment Database. This enables portfolio managers to make quick social or environmental 'snapshots' of companies or their portfolio holdings, and has become widely used by Canadian SRI funds. MRJA went on to launch the Jantzi Social Index in 1999, the first Canadian SRI index, wrote a book called *The 50 Best Ethical Stocks for Canadians*, and has worked with the

Active Shareholder Working Group to promote shareholder activism in Canada.

SRI MUTUAL FUNDS IN CANADA

The first Canadian SRI mutual fund, the Ethical Growth Fund, appeared in 1986. Industry growth was rapid. Six years later there were six socially responsible funds, with assets under management of C$200 million. By the tenth anniversary of the Ethical Growth Fund's launch there were 14 Canadian SRI mutual funds in total with investment assets of over C$1 billion and 100 000 investors. Five years later still, the number of Canadian SRI mutual funds had risen to 49, with assets under management of C$5 billion. Four groups dominate the Canadian SRI mutual fund market: Ethical Funds, Clean Environment, Investors Group and Desjardins Trust.

The Ethical Funds Group now has a range of 12 SRI funds, including balanced, bond and money market funds, as well as special situations and Pacific Rim funds. This gives it one of the broadest ranges of socially responsible funds in the world. However, the C$500 million Ethical Growth Fund remains its flagship product. The fund screens investments for industrial relations, racial equality, tobacco, armaments, nuclear energy and the environment, as well as a general 'best in class' methodology, and is noted for a record of steady investment performance. The Ethical Growth Fund is sponsored and distributed by Canada's largest credit union, VanCity (previously called Vancouver City), although the actual investment management has always been carried out by the professional asset management firm of Connor, Clark & Lunn. Corporate governance has traditionally received little attention from Canadian SRI mutual funds, but in 1997 the Ethical Funds Group commenced working with Michael Jantzi Associates on shareholder activism proposals.

The Clean Environment Group has a range of funds based on the Brundtland definition of 'sustainable development', although it rejects any description of them as 'ethical'. The C$170 million Clean Environment Equity Fund is the group's flagship. This is an 'industry of the future' fund whose policy is to find companies working towards sustainability with zero-emission products or alternative energy policies. The Clean Environment Equity Fund was therefore one of the earliest investors in renewable energy plays like the Canadian fuel-cell producer Ballard Power. The fund's investment performance was extremely impressive during the late 1990s when such investments did very well, and has suffered along with them in the new millennium.

The Summa Fund was launched in 1987 by the Investors Group, Canada's largest mutual fund company, with traditional avoidance screens based on alcohol, tobacco, gambling, armaments, environments and oppressive regimes. It has made a number of SRI divestments over the years, e.g. Northern Telecom for operating in apartheid South Africa, and Austral Communications for allegedly broadcasting pornography. By September 2001 investment assets had reached C$2.4 billion, in part resulting from a consistent record of good investment performance. The C$100 million Desjardins Environment Fund was launched in September 1990. It is part of the Desjardins group of *caisse populaires* (savings banks), and therefore sold mostly through the Desjardins network in Quebec. It may be classified as a mixture of an 'industry of the future' and 'best in class' fund. In other words, the Desjardins Environment Fund targets growth companies operating in the environmental sector, as well as the best environmental performers in the other sectors of the economy. Noranda Forest, one of the more environmentally aware forest products companies, is an example of the latter.

Many of the underlying investors in Canadian SRI mutual funds have probably done so via a registered retirement savings plan (RRSP). The RRSP is essentially a flexible tax-efficient vehicle that enables individuals to invest money in a variety of assets of their choice with the aim of building up a substantial lump sum to pay their pension. It is therefore the Canadian equivalent of the US 401k plan, and much more user friendly than UK personal pensions plans. Investment performance is a critical factor for pension fund investors, and potential RRSP investors in SRI funds may have been put off by a general perception that SRI produces poor long-term investment returns. As was shown in Chapter 10, the US and UK evidence demonstrates that this need not be the case. However, Canada's leading financial newspaper, the *Toronto Globe and Mail*, seems to focus

Table 12.1 *Largest Canadian SRI funds: return (%) for n years to September 2001*

	1 year	3 years	5 years	10 years
Clean Environment	−38.3	−3.5	1.9	n/a
Desjardins Environ	−20.0	−4.5	6.1	7.3
Ethical Growth	−21.0	−1.0	3.7	7.0
Investors Summa	−29.3	11.2	11.8	11.1
SRI average	−27.2	0.6	5.9	8.5
Weighted SRI	−28.1	7.8	9.7	9.7
Sector average	−18.9	8.8	6.5	9.2

Source: Compiled by the author using statistical data published in the SIO bulletin, December 2001.

on the negatives when it comes to SRI. In this respect it is like many of its peers overseas. For example, the newspaper ran an article in October 2001 with the headline 'Some Socially Responsible Funds Aren't as Pristine as You Might Think. And Their Returns are Lacklustre'. It went on:

> If you buy into the adage that no good deed goes unpunished, you won't be surprised that socially responsible investing, sometimes called ethical investing, has had a rough year.... Socially responsible investing may be good for the soul, but what about the bottom line?... Whatever fund you choose, don't count on beating the market. In many cases, you'll be lucky to keep within shouting distance of market benchmarks.[9]

Table 12.1, produced by the author, shows the long-term performance of the largest SRI funds for periods to September 2001. It only covers four funds; many Canadian SRI mutual funds are small and only recently established, i.e. they do not have the three-year track record that the author regards as being the minimum for a statistically valid analysis. The four funds also had investment assets at September 2001 of C$3.1 billion, i.e. they constituted over 75% of the C$4.0 billion universe of Canadian SRI mutual funds at that time. The data suggests that the *Globe and Mail* was right to say that

SRI funds had 'lacklustre' short-term returns. Using simple averages shows Canadian SRI mutual funds as having produced long-term returns for their investors which lagged slightly behind comparable funds.

However, the excellent and consistent financial returns generated by the Summa Fund should be noted. Its 'best in class' methodology has been able to generate above-average long-term investment returns for investors. Since the Summa Fund is by far the largest Canadian SRI fund, its good track record pushes up the weighted average return from SRI mutual funds. Since the weighted average gives a better reflection of the experience of the average investor, it seems fair to state that over five and ten years the average investor in Canadian SRI mutual funds has received better returns than they would have obtained by investing in the average Canadian growth mutual fund.

One last point on performance. Through much of the 1990s, Canadian socially responsible investment funds produced excellent financial returns. For example, the *Globe and Mail* published a survey in July 1997[10] which showed that all four SRI funds had above-average performance records. This begs the question of why performance deteriorated in the period 2000–2001 and whether it was a function of using SRI screens. The answer is no; it resulted from the technology investment mania that swept across all the major stock markets of the world in 1998–2000. When the bubble burst, it dragged down environmental stocks in sympathy. For example, the share price of the fuel-cell company Ballard Power fell from over C$200 in March 2000 to C$25 in September 2001. This was true even though the fundamental trading position of many environmental companies did not deteriorate over the period, unlike the majority of technology companies. Technology mania was particularly pronounced in Canada. One company, Nortel Networks, saw its share price rise so much that at its peak in September 2000, its market capitalisation accounted for over 35% of the entire value of the Canadian stock market. (Eighteen months later this had fallen to 3.1%.) Since Nortel had operations in Burma, it was boycotted by many SRI funds. Ironically, Nortel got out of Burma just as the bubble burst. Ethical Growth Fund portfolio manager Martin Gerber attributed much of its relative underperformance in 1999–2000 to the 'Nortel effect':

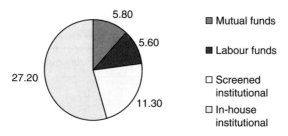

5.80

5.60

27.20

11.30

■ Mutual funds

■ Labour funds

☐ Screened institutional

☐ In-house institutional

Figure 12.1 *Canadian SRI market (C$bn) 2000*

The underperformance took place, not as technology stocks came down, but as they went up. The Nortel phenomenon was a 'once-in a lifetime' event in the Canadian market.[11]

In December 2000 the SIO carried out the first ever systematic survey of socially responsible investment in Canada, in conjunction with the MBA programme at Wilfrid Laurier University.[12] The survey was based on a questionnaire sent to 219 money management firms in Canada, and used the SIO's definition of SRI as possessing three identifiable component factors: positive or negative screening of equity portfolios, community investing, and shareholder advocacy and engagement. It discovered there was some C$50 billion of investment assets using SRI criteria in Canada, a much higher figure than had been expected, as shown in Figure 12.1. The Canadian SRI investment community was well aware of the C$5.8 billion then invested in SRI mutual funds, and the C$5.6 billion of labour-based funds. What was totally unexpected was the fact that many of Canada's leading asset managers were found to be running socially and environmentally screened portfolios for institutional clients. In sum these institutional screened portfolios amounted to C$11.3 billion, with the majority of the underlying clients falling into four categories: religious institutions, particularly religious orders; pension plans, particularly union trustee pension schemes; public sector bodies such as universities and hospitals, and charitable foundations.[13]

The survey also found there were a number of large charitable foundations and religious bodies which managed their investment assets in-house using SRI criteria. These organisations had a cumulative total of C$27.2 billion in socially responsible funds. The

Table 12.2 *SRI screens used by Canadian money managers*

Issue	Percent of funds using issue
Tobacco	83
Environment	64
Alcohol	63
Military	62
Employee relations	50
Human rights	48
Nuclear power	47
Gambling	41
Diversity	36
Aboriginal	20
Animal rights	5

Source: Canadian Social Investment Review 2000: A Comprehensive Survey of Socially Responsible Investment in Canada, Social Investment Organisation, December 2000.

data also identified the most popular SRI exclusion screens used by Canadian money managers for their institutional clients (Table 12.2). It was hardly surprising that tobacco was top of the list, but the environment, alcohol and defence, labour relations and human rights also scored strongly.

In many ways the Canadian experience closely parallels the way SRI has developed in other countries such as the UK and the US. Yet it has some unique features, particularly in the role played by trade unions, and their associated work in local development through venture capital funding. The largest trade union in Quebec, the FTQ, set up the Solidarity Fund in 1983 with the aim of providing a pension fund for its members, and also promoting economic and social development in Quebec. The FTQ Solidarity Fund invests 60% of its assets in small and medium-sized companies, normally unionised. By 1988 the fund had assets of C$100 million, and 41 000 investors. It calculates that it has saved or created 3 000 Quebec jobs since inception. Over its first five years the Solidarity Fund produced annualised returns of 6.1%, less than those produced by the average equity fund, but better than the 4.5% return from money market funds over the same period.[14] Labour funds with similar objectives have since set up in other provinces. Currently there are seven significant labour-sponsored funds in existence in Canada, whose combined assets amount to C$5.8 billion. In 1986 the Canadian Labor Congress passed a resolution that:

> The C$100bn in pension fund assets represents a powerful economic and social force. The goals of organised Canadian workers, working through the labor movement, are to achieve greater control and direction over the investment of pension funds so that, consistent with the financial integrity of the plans, pension funds are invested to further the economic and social objectives of Canadian organised workers.[15]

In November 2000 FTQ hosted a major conference in Montreal, together with the Shareholder Association for Research and Education (SHARE), to consider the use of pension fund voting power in the field of shareholder activism. FTQ decided it would encourage trade union representatives to press their pension funds to press for greater corporate responsibility.[16] Together with Ethical Funds and the firefighter union Ville La Salle, FTQ filed proposals on labour standards at two of Canada's largest retail chains, Hudson's Bay and Sears Canada. In fact, shareholder activism has become a growing movement in recent years, with 63 corporate governance and social responsibility resolutions filed with Canadian companies in 2000. As noted earlier, the 1987 Massey Ferguson judgement made it extremely difficult to file social resolutions on the US model under the Canadian Business Corporations Act (CBCA). The act empowered corporate boards to summarily reject any shareholder resolutions they judged to be outside 'normal business', e.g. on social or environmental matters, from being circulated with the standard proxy circular. However, in November 2001 the federal government issued new regulations on the CBCA that made the Canadian rules on proxy resolutions similar to those in the US. The *Globe and Mail* commented:

> Canadian institutional investors will have a lot more power in the nation's boardrooms under sweeping revisions to rules governing shareholders activity. Under amendments to the

Canadian Business Corporations Act that took place on Saturday, shareholders of publicly traded companies will now be able to challenge management without preparing a formal proxy circular. Liberalising the dissident proxy rules will make it much easier to communicate with each other and organise campaigns to force management to respond to their concerns. The new legislation effectively alters the balance of power between institutional shareholders and corporate Canada.[17]

The *Globe and Mail* article focused on the general implications of the changes to the CBCA, and actually ignored the fact that the specific clause prohibiting social and environmental shareholder resolutions had been abolished. Eugene Ellmen of the SIO highlighted the crucial aspect of this particular amendment to the CBCA:

We believe that the rules of the shareholder game have been stacked against shareholders wishing to discuss issues of social and environmental importance....We commend the government for eliminating this language from the new Act. By eliminating this clause, the government is recognising the importance of providing shareholders with the right to make proposals on issues of substantial importance to the corporation, including legitimate and prudent matters involving social and environmental issues.[18]

There has also been growing popular pressure for the Canadian authorities to follow the example of the UK and compel pension funds to disclose their policy on social responsibility issues. In October 2001 Stephan Tremblay, a member of the Bloc Quebecois tabled a private member's bill (Bill C-394) in the Canadian Federal Parliament introducing this measure. He also had discussions with finance minister Paul Martin on the subject. As a private member's bill, it was unlikely to become law, but it succeeded in putting the subject onto the political agenda. This book began by noting how SRI had moved from fringe to mainstream in the UK. The year 2002 seems likely to be the take-off point for this process in Canada. In the SIO's words:

This is the first time in its ten-year history that the SIO has systematically reached out to the investment community. Our aim is to bring the mainstream financial community into the SIO and into the socially responsible investment industry.... Large pension funds have been pressing for more say over corporations for governance reasons. These new [CBCA] rules will also serve to make social and environmental rules a more common part of the relationship.[19]

THE AUSTRALIAN APPROACH TO SRI

Generally speaking, most Australian commentators continue to use the older term 'ethical investment' rather than SRI to describe socially responsible investing. In this section I shall continue the standard practice of this book and use SRI as the basic descriptive term except when quoting directly from other people. In Chapter 2 I made a distinction between socially responsible investment or 'ethical investment', which is equity based, and socially directed investment or 'ethical banking', which is debt based. Both are 'social investment' in the sense that they combine social objectives and financial returns, but only equity investment has the power to assert corporate social responsibility through the voting power of share ownership. This distinction is particularly important in Australia, where church investors have significant investment assets run along ethical lines, but the majority of these funds are debt based. When calculating the value of Australian SRI funds I have therefore excluded loan funds, in common with my practice in the rest of this book.

Church-based investment funds in fact were the original 'ethical investors' in Australia. For many years the Catholic Development Fund has operated loan-based funds based in Perth and Melbourne. Parishioners lend money to the fund either through a passbook or on a fixed-term bond, with the money loaned to Catholic schools, hospitals, childcare, etc. By 1997 it had assets of A$88 million in Perth with a further A$250 million in Melbourne. Note that the churches in Australia are primarily organised along state lines, hence in financial matters the state bodies are much more important than national organisations. Another major church investor is the Uniting Church Investment Services (Queensland), whose funds are invested according to a 1982 resolution of the church prohibiting investments that could damage the environment or human health, lead to human rights abuse or racial or sexual discrimination.[20] Unsurprisingly, the largest of them all is based in Sydney. This is the Sydney diocese of the Anglican Church, which had investment assets of A\$300 million in 1996, mostly in property and cash deposits.[21] In 1995 the Sydney diocese decided to set up a specialist organisation to run its investment portfolios called Glebe Asset Management, recruiting a senior banking executive called David Andrews (previously with Westpac and EquitiLink) to run the new venture. Glebe's SRI policy is as follows:

> Glebe's portfolios are managed according to an ethical investment policy which includes restrictions on investments in companies primarily involved in tobacco, alcohol, gambling, and armaments.[22]

Australia has an economy whose exports are largely based on natural resources, principally mining, agriculture and forestry; forestry is mainly in Tasmania and Victoria. Hence many Australian SRI funds have added criteria such as uranium mining and woodchip production to the traditional sin stocks of alcohol, tobacco, armaments, gambling, etc. Mining raises questions over the treatment of native peoples, the spoiling of the physical environment, and also over worker rights. Trade unions have always played an important role in Australian society. In the late 1990s the unions alleged that the big mining companies were attempting to limit trade union power by shifting workers to individual contracts of employment, something that caused considerable public disquiet. These questions are well covered in a book called *Ethical Investment*, one of the first books on the subject specifically designed for the Australian market that appeared in 1997.[23]

The first public trust offering SRI to the public was launched by Australian Ethical Investments. This had been in existence since 1981 as a private company with the objective of encouraging and supporting sustainable business practices in Australia. In 1989 the directors decided that its objectives would be better achieved by conversion to a publicly owned investment trust (open-end fund). Australian Ethical Investments' investment policy is set out in detail in its Australian Ethical Charter (Box 12.1).[24]

Box 12.1 The Australian Ethical Charter

The Trusts shall seek out investments which provide for and support

(a) The development of workers' participation in the ownership and control of their work organisations and places
(b) The production of high-quality and properly presented products and services
(c) The development of locally based ventures
(d) The development of appropriate technological systems
(e) The amelioration of wasteful or polluting practices
(f) The development of sustainable land use and food production
(g) The preservation of endangered ecosystems
(h) Activities which contribute to human happiness, dignity and education
(i) The dignity and well-being of non-human animals
(j) The efficient use of human waste
(k) The alleviation of poverty in all its forms
(l) The development and preservation of appropriate human buildings and landscapes

The Trusts shall avoid any investment which is considered to unnecessarily

(a) Pollute land, air or waters
(b) Destroy or waste non-recurring resources
(c) Extract, create, produce, manufacture, or market materials, products, goods or services which have a harmful effect on humans, non-human animals or the environment
(d) Market, promote or advertise products or services in a misleading or deceitful manner
(e) Create markets by the promotion or advertising of unwanted products or services
(f) Acquire land or commodities primarily for the purpose of speculative gain
(g) Create, encourage or perpetuate militarism or engage in the manufacture of armaments

(h) Entice people into financial overcommitment
(i) Exploit people through the payment of low wages or the provision of poor working conditions
(j) Discriminate by way of race, religion or sex in employment, marketing, or advertising practices
(k) Contribute to the inhibition of human rights generally

Australian Ethical Investments is a fairly small and illiquid company, a factor which can make its shares difficult to deal in. In 1994 the group therefore decided to launch another unit trust (open-ended fund), the Australian Ethical Equities Trust, in order to offer the same objectives to a wider investing public. This has a specific equity focus with a mandate, as set out in the existing Australian Ethical Charter, to positively support socially and environmentally beneficial enterprises involved in such areas as energy conservation, recycling, wildlife protection, health promotion, and education. As always, rainforest logging, human rights abuses and animal exploitation were on the excluded list.[25] In 1989 Ethinvest Pty Ltd, the first Australian financial adviser specialising in SRI, was set up by Ross Knowles. Knowles later went on to compile *Ethical Investment*, and in the spring of 2000 he became co-president of the new Ethical Investment Association, a trade body designed to promote awareness of socially responsible investing. Ross Knowles described its objectives thus:

> We hope to bring together like-minded people to promote ethical investing to the consumer. It's about investing so you know what your money is doing and you feel good about where it's going. It's easy to identify areas like tobacco companies, uranium mining, woodchipping, but there are grey areas that the fund managers need to consider.[26]

GROWTH OF SRI UNIT TRUSTS

The Young Women's Christian Association of Australia (YWCA) launched another socially responsible investment trust in 1989, originally known as the YWCA Ethical Investment Trust. Originally this was managed by Global Funds Management with a small-company bias, before being acquired by the Tyndall Group in 1995.[27] Sales growth of the fund was not spectacular, and in 2000 the fund management contract was sold on to the Challenger International group, who were expected to put greater resources into marketing the fund and to developing its SRI research capability. A number of SRI unit trusts were established in the 1990s but not all were successful. In 1996 the EquitiLink group issued the Greenlink Trust, a unit trust based on the philosophy of sustainable development, while a few years earlier the Over Fifties Friendly Society launched the Over 50s Green Bond in association with the Australian Conservation Foundation. Neither fund reached the desired level of minimum assets, and both were eventually closed.

However, one highly successful launch was the Hunter Hall Value Growth Trust in May 1994. This was founded by Peter Hall with support from the Anglican Diocese of Sydney. The fund's stated policy is to avoid investment in companies engaged in activities considered to harm people, animals or the environment: armaments, tobacco, gambling, animal testing, factory farming and logging. I remember meeting Peter Hall in London in 1996, and being struck by his passionate belief that he could find enough attractive small-company investments in both the UK and Australia to meet the fund's SRI policy and to generate good financial returns for investors. (Hunter Hall Value's track record has proved him right.) Peter Hall has attributed his success in part to the fact that Hunter Hall is an SRI specialist, i.e. it integrates social and environmental factors into its decision-making process, rather than using SRI issues simply as the basis of exclusion screens. This integrated approach is something it shares with other successful SRI asset managers. In Hall's words:

> I don't think a larger fund manager can run a non-ethical fund alongside an ethical fund. It's a whole approach which includes issues such as corporate governance in stocks under investment.[28]

Just how big is SRI in Australia? The figure generally quoted is one produced by Ross Knowles of the Ethical Investment Association, that Australian managed SRI investments totalled about A$1 billion in 2000. This is a huge increase on earlier figures; for example, the total value of Australian SRI mutual funds amounted to no more than A$48 million in June 1996.[29] David Andrews of Glebe has questioned that figure, claiming it is too high if it is based on retail products, and too low if it includes the assets managed by church investors. He points out that Glebe itself managed A$77 million for external clients in 2000, with a further $450 million managed on behalf of the Sydney diocese. Andrews adds:

> If we combined the Sydney, Melbourne, and Brisbane dioceses, the Anglican Church would represent almost half the [SRI] market in Australia.[30]

I decided to check Knowles' figures, and so added up all publicly available information on Australian SRI unit trusts and superannuation funds. This produced a figure of total Australian SRI assets under management of A$617 million in May 2001.[31] The difficult bit was to calculate the SRI equity assets of the church investors. I evaluated this as being A$77 million for Glebe, A$150 million for its Sydney diocese parent, and around A$200 million for the Uniting Church, making a total of church-managed SRI funds of A$427 million. Adding the two figures together and eliminating double counting produces a total figure of A$1020 million. Knowles' figure therefore seemed right for 2000.

In September 2001 the Ethical Investment Association released data calculating the total size of Australian investments using SRI criteria as A$10.5 billion. However, this headline figure included assets of A$6.3 billion belonging to church investors, and A$2.62 billion relating to shareholder activism. Ethical unit trusts were calculated to be worth A$1.5 billion. Since the shareholder activism figures related to a one-off event, the AGM of the mining company Rio Tinto in May 2000, I think they should be excluded from the total. I have no doubt that shareholder activism will take off as a major component of SRI in Australia, but it has not happened yet. Adding the equity component of the church investors to ethical unit trusts produces a figure of some A$2 billion, which would be my preferred estimate of SRI in Australia. It is worth adding that an Australian SRI investment universe of A$2 billion is big enough to be significant in a global context.

Table 12.3 *Australian SRI funds: return (%) for n years to May 2001*

	1 year	3 year	5 year
Australian Ethical Equities	14.3	18.2	15.9
Challenger SRI	12.5	2.9	7.1
Australian Ethical Balanced	14.2	10.4	9.9
Hunter Hall Value Growth	13.8	23.3	28.9
Tower Super Ethical	10.7	11.7	12.0
Rothschild Conservative Ethical	9.2	7.3	8.4
SRI fund average	12.5	12.3	13.7
All-Ords Accumulation index	10.5	10.1	11.5

Source: Table compiled by the author using data copyright *Ethical Investor* magazine. Reproduced with permission.

Relatively little work has been carried out on the investment performance of Australian SRI funds. Table 12.3 has therefore been produced by the author. The data is limited as there are only six funds that meet the author's minimum criterion of possessing a three-year track record. However, the evidence indicates that the average Australian SRI fund has managed to outperform the standard equity benchmark, the ASX All-Ordinaries index, over one, three and five years.

The statistics in Table 12.3 derive significant benefit from the stellar performance of the Hunter Hall Value Growth Fund, whose compound five-year return of almost 29% a year makes it one of the best-performing equity unit trusts in Australia. It would be useful to possess deeper performance attribution analysis of this fund performance. For example, it would be interesting to know how much, if any, of its excellent performance derives from an Australian smaller-companies effect. The Australian dollar was weak compared to most major currencies throughout most of the 1990s. As Hunter Hall is an international fund, it would have benefited from the Australian dollar's weakness, giving it a competitive edge over purely domestic Australian funds. Nevertheless, the overall conclusion from this study seems to be that Australian SRI unit trusts have managed to provide their underlying investors with a combination of social and environmental exclusions and good financial returns.

In March 2001 AMP, Australia's largest insurance company, decided to enter the domestic SRI market. AMP was already a big player in the UK SRI market as the parent company of Henderson Investors/NPI Global Care, and it used its UK expertise by seconding in-house expert Mark Campanale from Hendersons to Sydney. AMP announced that it would be launching three SRI funds in the AMP Sustainable Future Funds range: a balanced growth fund, an international equity fund and an Australian equity fund. Campanale's influence could be seen in the wide-ranging criteria of the funds – a first for Australia. These were based on the environment, human rights, labour practices and corporate governance, with the investment philosophy that the fund would benefit financially from 'industries of the future' such as renewable energy.[32]

AMP is also one of Australia's largest landowners, and news that it was launching such products caused considerable furore. Environmentalists noted that its subsidiary, Stanbroke Pastoral, had actively cleared thousands of acres of Queensland and held permits to clear a further 100000 acres of virgin bush. AMP held discussions with environmental groups prior to its new fund launch, and agreed not to clear any of the 8000 acres due to be cleared by Stanbroke before an independent environmental audit of the relevant area. The company also agreed to conduct an environmental audit of all Stanbroke's property holdings.[33] Stephen Dunn of AMP accepted that owning Stanbroke did not sit easily with offering SRI funds:

> We had to get our own house in order before we launched an SRI product. We saw the growth of ethical investment overseas and, based on feedback from retail and institutional clients, wanted to build on the expertise of our UK subsidiaries Henderson and NPI.[34]

SOCIALLY RESPONSIBLE PENSIONS

One of the most distinctive features of the Australian market for financial services is that all employees are legally obliged to invest in a pension fund. However, this is based on the fundamental concept of employee choice. The May 1997 Federal Budget ruled that all employees must have a choice of at least five superannuation funds by July 1998. (Pension funds are normally called superannuation funds in Australia, often shortened to supers.) Pension fund investors in Australia have the choice between superannuation bonds (i.e. managed funds) issued by insurance companies, and master funds, rather like US 401k funds, where the investor has a choice of underlying funds within an overall tax wrapper.

The potential for ethical supers became obvious after the 1997 Budget. In 2000 Resnik Consulting and KPMG were commissioned to carry out a survey to see how many Australians would be interested in SRI pension products. The Resnik/KPMG survey, called *Money Where Your Mouth Is*, found that '69% of all Australian would consider investing their superannuation in an ethical option'.[35] In fact, ethical supers have taken off rapidly. VicSuper, the A$1.2 billion pension fund for the 135000 employees of the state of Victoria has made an 'ethical option' available for its members, as does the Commonwealth Super Scheme and UniSuper, the national university superannuation fund with A$8.5 billion of assets.[36] James Their of Australian Ethical Investments has estimated that SRI pension products could treble the size of the Australian SRI market:

> Member choice could change the whole landscape. Then those numbers are out the window, because you have individuals making their own decisions.[37]

The current market value of Australian superannuation funds is estimated to be around A$700 billion, and it is believed this figure will quadruple by 2020. The first attempt to exploit the potential market for ethical supers was Friends Provident Life in 1986. It launched a socially responsible superannuation product that excluded investment in armaments, alcohol, gambling, tobacco and the production of CFCs. However, the fund was before its time and public interest remained low; in 1997 Friends Provident Life was therefore sold to the Tower Life insurance group, which rebranded it as the Tower Life Ethical Growth Portfolio superannuation bond.[38] A successful attempt to offer ethical supers had to wait until February 2000, when Westpac Investment Management (WIM), a subsidiary of one of Australia's Big Three banks, launched the Eco Pool 'environmentally friendly' institutional SRI fund. This fund was sponsored by the HESTA public sector superannuation fund with 400 000 members, meaning that it started life with A$20 million of assets.[39] Such was the demand for the new product that within a year of its inception the Westpac Eco Pool fund had more than doubled in size to A$50 million.

The Westpac Eco Pool fund broke new ground in that it was developed in association with Monash University, one of Australia's leading universities. The fund was clearly institutional, as its investment policy was designed to create a portfolio with a low tracking error compared to the standard Australian equity market index, the ASX All-Ordinaries Index. It consists of 150 fairly large stockholdings, which are then assessed on environmental performance grounds using international standards such as ISO 14000 as well as environmental shareholder value models developed by the World Business Council for Sustainable Development. Monash University's Centre for Environmental Management then assesses each potential company investment on the following basis:[40]

- *Strategy* assesses the extent to which companies address environmental management as a strategic concern and how management responds to changing business drivers, risks and market conditions.
- *Management* assesses the extent to which good environmental management is integrated into day-to-day business management processes, systems and functions.
- *Product/operations* assesses the implementation of best-practice environmental techniques, technologies and product design.
- *Ratings*: companies are assessed by Monash University on a scale from 1 to 6, where 1 is good environmental performance, 6 is poor, and 0 means environmentally neutral.
- *Investable universe*: the Eco Pool funds may only invest in companies ranked 0, 1 or 2.
- *Assessments* are based on a variety of assessment tools, including proprietary survey, search of public records, and interview and audit.

- *Final Share Portfolio*: WIM then uses its risk analysis software to create a first-pass portfolio of around 45–75 holdings, although this may be adjusted by WIM's investment team to reflect additional market factors that may impact the portfolio.

In 2000 management consultants Allen Consulting Group were commissioned to produce a report. The result, *Socially Responsible Investment in Australia*,[41] was not so much a description of the existing Australian SRI market, as an exploration of the underlying institutional and structural factors that presented opportunities and barriers to the growth of SRI in Australia. It concluded:

> Socially responsible investment (SRI) in Australia is on the verge of a transition from being a niche activity to having a place in the mainstream investment options. This review has identified a change in attitude to investing ethically, and gradual growth in SRI is already evident. This is not surprising as it is consistent with changes in community attitudes to business more generally. Companies in Australia are increasingly expected to meet broad social and environmental responsibilities as well as their traditional financial objectives. The growth of socially responsible investment is a logical next step in the minds of some investors.[42]

Don Stammer, head of investment strategy at Deutsche Bank in Australia, estimated that the total assets of Australian SRI will be A\$35–40 billion by 2010. He backed up this opinion by leaving Deutsche to become a director of the first Australian specialist research service, Sustainable Investment Research Institute (SIRIS), which started operation in 2000.[43] *Socially Responsible Investment in Australia* estimated that the total investment assets of Australian churches, charitable foundations and educational establishments could be A\$20 billion, a potentially highly lucrative market for asset managers seeking institutional SRI clients. Glebe Asset Management is a natural candidate to manage such funds, and in December 2001 it announced a restructuring aimed at doing just that. David Andrews was appointed executive chairman with the mandate to significantly increase third-party funds under management which at that time amounted to A$95 million, compared to Sydney diocese funds of A$500 million. Andrews commented:

> The Diocese see us as an investment, and wish to develop the Glebe as an additional source of income – one which is inherently more stable than market returns. With almost A$600 million under management we are the largest manager of ethical funds in Australia, and next year we aim to double our 'commercial' funds to A$200 million.[44]

The investment group Challenger International moved into SRI by taking over the fund management contract for YWCA Ethical Investment Trust Funds in 2000. At the same time Challenger launched the Challenger Socially Responsive Investment Fund in association with the US investment management company Neuberger Berman. This fund is targeted at charitable foundations as well as superannuation funds. It is based on a 'best of class' methodology, seeking to invest in companies that meet a variety of social criteria. Allen Consulting describe such products as second generation:

> The *second generation* SRI funds aim to compete in the mainstream. They have greater portfolio diversification than *first generation* funds and are more appealing to the mainstream market as their risk-adjusted performance is more reflective of mainstream investments. They are more explicit about selection and screening, with some systematically identifying company performance indicators for environment or social sustainability.[45]

One of the consistent themes of this book is that socially responsible investing is simply the mirror image of corporate social responsibility. Both are reflections of growing societal unease about the unadulterated worship of wealth creation typical of the 1980s and 1990s. At the end of 2001 the New South Wales Chamber of Commerce published a report on SRI called *The Unseen Revolution: Ethical Investment in Australia*. This report was written by Margy Osmond, chief executive of the NSW chamber and therefore one of the leading business people in the state. She urged Australian business to recognise that SRI, and therefore the demand for CSR, was not going to go away. I am struck by how Osmond's conclusions concur with those of Allen Consulting, i.e. that SRI and CSR could no longer be dismissed as a fringe issue:

> What we do in this report is look at what's happening in Australia, round the world, and put it in context. There's an old attitude that social responsibility is not relevant or, worse, will go away. CSR may not be *de rigeur* now, but it will be in five, ten years. A company that doesn't plan for that is not planning ahead, It's no longer a fringe issue. The bottom line is still the key, but companies have to answer to the board and the wider community.... It's important that CSR is not some sort of strange graft on the company, because of the need to be seen to be doing it. It needs to be a part of overall strategy.[46]

There have been a number of legislative changes in Australia that should assist in moves to promote corporate social responsibility. The 1998 Company Law Review Act amended the requirements of Australian company law regarding the minimum requirements needed to call a company general meeting. This was changed from 5% of a company's share capital to 100 registered shareholders, making it much easier for Australian shareholders to call a general meeting to advocate social or environmental policies. It was first used for this purpose in October 1999 when shareholders of the mining company North Ltd proposed a resolution committing that company to adopt sustainable development policies. The 1998 Company Law Review Act also made it mandatory for Australian companies to include details of environmental performance in their directors' report.

Consistent with this policy, the Australian government not only followed the UK's SRI pension fund disclosure regulations, but in fact advanced beyond them. The Financial Services Reform Act (FSRA) was passed by the Australian Senate in August 2001, coming into force in March 2002. Investment products covered by its clauses include superannuation funds, managed investment funds, and investment life insurance. Financial services in Australia are regulated by the Australian Securities and Investment Commission (ASIC), which does a similar job to the SEC in the US or the Financial Services Authority in the UK. Australian pension funds have to produce periodic disclosure statements (PDS) to their members, and from March 2002 each PDS will have to disclose its fund's compliance with the SRI regulations, placing an obligation on ASIC to monitor this. There are two key clauses:[47]

(a) Any seller or issuer of investment products must disclose to investors the extent (if at all) to which labour standards or environmental, social or ethical considerations are taken into account in the selection, retention, and realisation of the investments.
(b) ASIC may develop guidelines that must be complied with where a product disclosure statement makes any claim that labour standards or environment, social, or ethical considerations are taken into account in the selection, retention or realisation of the investment.

During 2001 the Australian business community and political establishment was rocked by the sudden collapse of three large companies: HIH, Ansett and One.Tel. Joe Hockey, the minister for financial services, described Australian institutional shareholders as being 'lazy' regarding their failure to intervene earlier in the affairs of these companies. This put improved corporate governance in Australia high up the political agenda. Sandy Easterbrook of Sydney-based Corporate Governance International stated, 'It's obvious that in both of those cases the governance defects in the company had a lot to do with what happened'.[48]

Margy Osmond described Australian superannuation funds as being angered by these corporate collapses, and determined to use their voting power to improve corporate governance. 'The recent collapse of One.Tel, Ansett, and HIH has put them on red alert,' she said.[49] Signs of this process occurred quickly. In December 2001 the giant Commonwealth public sector pension fund CSS/PSS formally appointed Westpac Investment Management (WIM) as its corporate governance adviser. This meant that in future WIM would engage in dialogue with CSS/PSS top 200 Australian company holdings on areas of business risk, including corporate governance and environmental and social factors.[50]

In May 2002 Corporate Monitor, Australia's leading specialist researcher of ethical and socially responsible funds, upgraded its rating on two of Glebe's trusts. The Glebe Pan-Asian Growth Trust now has a four star rating, and the Glebe Blue-Chip Equities trust has a 3.5 star rating. Commenting on the Blue-Chip equities trust, Corporate Monitor noted that 'In 2001 performance was above benchmark and among the top performing Australian share-based ethical funds.'

REFERENCES

1. 'Global Business Ethics Code Unravelled', *The Toronto Star*, 6 September 1997.
2. Craig Forcese, *Commerce with Conscience? Human Rights and Business Codes of Conduct*, 1997, Canadian Lawyers Association for International Human Rights and the International Center for Human Rights and Democratic Development.
3. 'Church Investors Query Talisman', *The Catholic Register*, 18 February 2000.
4. *Ibid.*
5. 'Investors Eye Talisman's Sudan Stake', *The Globe and Mail*, 17 October 2001.
6. Marc de Sousa-Shields, 'Social Investment in Canada', Chapter 56 of *The Social Investment Almanac*, Henry Holt, 1992.
7. *Ibid.*
8. Eugene Ellmen, *The 1998 Canadian Ethical Money Guide*, Lorimer, 1997.
9. 'Some Socially Responsible Funds Aren't as Pristine as You Might Think. And Their Returns Are Lacklustre', *The Globe and Mail*, 26 October 2001.
10. 'Report on Mutual Funds', *The Globe and Mail*, 17 July 1997.
11. 'Manager Sees Bargains in Current Climate', *The Globe and Mail*, 8 November 2001.
12. *Canadian Social Investment Review 2000: A Comprehensive Survey of Socially Responsible Investment in Canada.* The Social Investment Organisation, December 2000.
13. *Ibid.*
14. Ted Jackson, 'SRI and the Canadian Labour Movement', EIRIS, Spring 1988.
15. Quoted in Anne Simpson, *The Greening of Global Investment*, Economist Publications, 1990.
16. *Prospectus*, a newsletter of the Shareholder Association for Research and Education, Fall/Winter 2001.
17. 'Investors Given Power to Fight Boards', *The Globe and Mail*, 26 November 2001.
18. 'New Shareholder Rules Become Law', *SIO Newsletter*, December 2001.
19. *Ibid.*
20. Ross Knowles, editor, *Ethical Investment*, Choice Books, 1997.
21. Glebe Asset Management, July 1996.
22. Glebe Strategic Objectives, August 1998.
23. Ross Knowles, editor, *Ethical Investment*, Choice Books, 1997; see especially Chapter 5 by Robert Rosen, Chapter 17 by Jeff Atkinson and Chapter 18 by Tim Cadman.
24. Copyright Australian Ethical Investment Ltd. Reproduced by permission.
25. Ross Knowles, editor, *Ethical Investment*, Choice Books, 1997.

26. Ross Knowles, quoted in *Personal Investor*, May 2000.
27. Robert Rosen, 'The History of Ethical Investment in Australia', *Review of 2000*, Ethical Investment Association.
28. Peter Hall, quoted in 'The Good Word on Investing', *Money Management*, 13 April 2000.
29. Assirt and *Money Management*, July 1996.
30. David Andrews, quoted in 'Ethical Size Really Does Matter', *Investor Weekly*, 17 July 2000.
31. Author's calculation using data from *Ethical Investor*, issue 1, and other sources.
32. 'Shareholders Want Their Money to Behave', *Sydney Morning Herald*, 21 April 2001.
33. 'AMP Funds Prompt Ethical Shake-up', *Environmental Finance*, April 2001.
34. *Ibid.*
35. Paddy Manning, 'The Year That Was, *Review of 2000*, Ethical Investment Association.
36. 'Earn 130% and Feel Good about It', *Personal Investor*, May 2000.
37. James Their, quoted in 'Ethical Size Really Does Matter', *Investor Weekly*, 17 July 2000.
38. Ross Knowles, editor, *Ethical Investment*, Choice Books, 1997.
39. 'Shareholders Want Their Money to Behave', *Sydney Morning Herald*, 21 April 2001.
40. 'Linking Screened Investments to Shareholder Value', Westpac Investment Management 2000. Copyright Westpac Financial Services. Reproduced with permission.
41. Allen Consulting Group Pty Ltd, *Socially Responsible Investment in Australia*, 2000.
42. *Ibid.*
43. 'Ethical Investments Set to Increase', *Australian Financial Review*, 14 February 2001.
44. 'Anglicans Restructure Glebe for Growth', *Ethical Investor*, 19 December 2001.
45. Allen Consulting Group Pty Ltd, *Socially Responsible Investment in Australia*, 2000.
46. Margy Osmond, quoted in *Australian Financial Review*, 14 December 2001.
47. 'Upfront and Ethical', *Australian Financial Review*, 28 August 2001.
48. Quoted in 'Flaws and Failures Behind Some Fine Facades' *Financial Times*, 8 June 2001.
49. Margy Osmond, *op. cit.*
50. 'CSS/PSS Confirms Westpac as Governance Adviser', *Ethical Investor*, 19 December 2001.

13

Into the Mainstream

Chapter 1 argued that the SRI pension fund regulations which came into force in July 2000 have fundamentally changed the nature of socially responsible investment in the UK. It was suggested that these new regulations have caused a major paradigm shift in the general perception of SRI, transforming it from a fringe pursuit carried out by a small number of retail funds into an approach accepted by the major institutional investors. This chapter investigates the extent to which these claims can be justified.

The most visible confirmation that SRI has become a realistic option for pension funds and charitable foundations has been the significant increase in investment mandates won by asset managers specialising in the field. This development has been described in detail, as it may offer some useful pointers to other markets such in Europe and Australia that have followed the UK example. I have highlighted the way Henderson/NPI took advantage of the market opportunity to build a significant institutional business based on socially responsible investing. It seems to me that it is not only of interest to students of SRI, but serves as an interesting case study in investment management.

The US is obviously the home of the world's largest financial markets. SRI has not yet received the legislative backing of the federal government in Washington, although it is being promoted by an increasing number of state legislatures. Nevertheless, the major US investment institutions have followed a similar path to the UK in recognising the value of SRI. The American experience is considered in the second half of this chapter. The rapid growth of socially responsible investment in the US, to a massive size, demonstrates beyond a shadow of a doubt that SRI has truly entered the mainstream.

The recent growth of US plan sponsors wanting to offer their clients an SRI pension option suggests this trend will continue.

THE UK: GREAT CHANGES AFTER JULY 1998

The UK SRI pension fund regulations were laid before Parliament in July 1999, and came into force in July 2000. However, they were first mooted in a speech by the then pensions minister John Denham in July 1998. Organisations potentially affected by the new regulations started to position themselves to benefit from the legislative changes as soon as the minister finished speaking. In other words, the implementation of the pension fund SRI regulations in July 2000 marked the end, rather than the beginning, of a process that began two years earlier.

Socially responsible investment in the UK was traditionally dominated by the mutually owned insurance company Friends Provident, the pioneer of SRI unit trusts in the UK with its Stewardship range of funds. Stewardship essentially pioneered the approach that has been copied by the majority of UK SRI unit trusts ever since. This is based on what I describe as a twin-track model, i.e. a strict dichotomy between ethical research and fund management. The fund managers are not deeply involved in SRI, their task being to maximise investment returns using the 'ethically approved' list given to them. There is normally a high level of SRI exclusion; for example, Stewardship's SRI constraints rule out investment in excess of 50% of the UK equity market. This business model was well suited for the retail investment market, and Stewardship's market share in socially responsible unit trusts remained above 50% during the 1990s despite the entry of many new players. However, it was not really appropriate for pension fund clients. This did not really matter until 1998, as there were no significant pension fund clients to be had outside the church and charity sectors. However, all that was about to change.

The first indication of a new positive climate for SRI occurred in September 1998, when the Nottinghamshire County Council pension scheme announced its intention to invest up to £150 million of its £1 billion pension scheme in environmentally friendly companies. The Council's Roger Latham announced that the fund had commissioned an independent, detailed report investigating the linkages between environmental excellence and long-term financial returns. Although it was not disclosed at the time, it later became known that this had been produced by Mark Mansley of Claros Consulting. Since the study found a strongly positive correlation between environmental and financial performance, the council decided this path could be justified on financial grounds alone.[1]

This development did not go unnoticed. The National Provident Institution (NPI) was another mutual insurance company that had followed Friends Provident's move into SRI unit trusts. In 1994 NPI recruited the team of Tessa Tennant, Mark Campanale and Anne Maree O'Connor from Jupiter Asset Management to form the core of its SRI effort. Tennant and Campanale were already well known for their public commitment to sustainable development (see Box 7.1), and also as pioneers of a more active 'engagement' approach for SRI unit trusts. In February 1998 it also appointed Mike Shaw from Framlington as a new institutional sales and marketing director, with the responsibility to build an institutional SRI business for the company by targeting local authority pension schemes and charity foundations potentially interested in this area. He described the market opportunity he saw:

> Councils are an obvious target for ethical funds. Our research shows that the typical ethical investor tends to be in the ABC1 social group, often working in one of the caring professions such as dentistry, medicine or teaching. Administrative staff working in the public sector are also typical ethical investors. At the same time one of the purposes of local authorities is to create a better environment for their ratepayers. So it makes sense that many councils want to adopt an investment approach that reflects this aim.[2]

The UK trade union movement put its energies behind promoting socially responsible investment. The annual conference of the Trades Union Congress (TUC) held in November 1998 urged pension fund trustee members to advocate a stronger line on SRI issues.[3] These were defined as corporate governance, executive compensation, human rights and the environment. In November 2001 the TUC issued a range of five 'stakeholder' pension plans for its members, one of them being an SRI plan run for the TUC by Standard Life.[4] Mike Shaw's point about the strong interest of local authority workers in social responsibility issues was confirmed at the Unison conference in November 1998. Unison, the trade union for workers in local government with 1.3 million members, passed a resolution at its annual conference declaring:

> A socially responsible approach to pension fund investment is required to ensure sustainable pensions in the future.[5]

NPI's intention to attack the institutional market was made clear by the launch in July 1998 of the NPI Social index, which seemed inspired by the American DSI index. In contrast to the Friends Provident twin-track model, Shaw recognised that winning institutional SRI mandates required an integrated approach. He was therefore able to make good use of a specialist SRI team under the NPI Global Care name, combining analysts, fund managers and marketing professionals. Many of these individuals became well-known names in the field, such as marketing manager Mark Campanale, who already had ten years' experience of SRI research with NPI and elsewhere. Anne-Maree O'Connor headed the research effort when Tessa Tennant moved to Asia to inaugurate the first ever Pacific-based SRI fund. Campanale in particular became associated with NPI's drive to make SRI be seen as a positive investment approach. This was achieved through emphasis on a 'best in class' approach, seeking investment in 'industries of the future'. Indeed, the NPI Global Care Fund was the first thematic SRI fund based on the concept of sustainability and the positive benefits of investing in industries that would benefit from this. In 1998 Campanale worked with the World Wide Fund for Nature (WWF) to launch an SRI fund suitable for their client base. He later explained:

> We have tried to take the screened ethical fund into new territory. We are trying to see what a sustainable future will look like and investing in businesses which are likely to be part of the future.[6]

A 1998 survey of independent financial advisers carried out by NPI found that the majority were experiencing growing sales of SRI unit

Table 13.1 *UK consumer recognition of SRI: all figures are percentages*

	1994	1995	1996	1997	1998
Heard of it	16	21	21	21	38
Never heard of it	84	79	79	79	62

Source: NOP/Friends Provident 5th Annual Ethical Investment Survey, 1998.

trusts. Sixty percent of them reported sales higher than two years previously, 38% were experiencing unchanged sales, and only 2% noted sales were down on previous years.[7] The US has shown similar developments according to a Calvert-sponsored study of mutual fund investors whose employers offered them retirement plans. The study was carried out in 2000 and found that 35% of them were offered SRI investment plans, more than double the level of 16% found in the previous survey carried out in 1996.[8] An NOP survey for Friends Provident also showed steadily growing consumer recognition of socially responsible investment (Table 13.1).

In September 1999 NPI joined forces with Henderson Global Investors, a UK investment management group itself recently acquired by AMP, the largest insurance company in Australia. Henderson brought £200 million of SRI funds to NPI's existing total of £350 million. The Henderson name was used for institutional SRI accounts, with NPI Global Care being kept on as the SRI unit trust brand name. The new Henderson SRI investment team of four fund managers and six specialist research analysts quickly began to win sizeable institutional mandates. By spring 2000 the Henderson SRI team had essentially doubled its total SRI assets to over £1 billion within a year. This was achieved primarily on the back of mandates to run a number of segregated local authority pension fund mandates.[9,10] Henderson also commissioned a survey of public sector employees on their knowledge of socially responsible investment. This showed that the proportion of public sector workers aware of and interested in SRI had risen from 16% in 1994 to 38% in 1998.[11] Equity markets were weak throughout 2000–2001, but by the end of 2001 Henderson's actively managed SRI assets had grown to £1.2 billion.

It has since remained the UK market leader in segregated SRI port-folio management.

Friends Provident reacted quickly to the competitive threat, hiring Craig Mackenzie from Bath University to beef up its internal SRI research capability. In October 1998 Friends announced the creation of a six-person 'engagement unit' whose numbers doubled by December 2001.[12] The company stuck to its traditional approach of keeping SRI research and fund management strictly separate. However, it hoped that its in-depth analysis of social and environmental problems could be used by pension funds to 'engage' with companies over such concerns. Friends Provident promoted its engagement product under the name of Responsible Engagement Overlay (REO), the idea being that REO could be used alongside an index or active fund without affecting the stockholdings.[13] In June 1999 the company won a £20 million mandate for REO from Aberdeen City Council, followed by Lothian Council in June 2000 for a £350 million REO agreement.[14] Other REO customers include the AEW trade union pension fund and the giant Dutch pension fund PGGM.

PENSION FUNDS: GROWTH IN SRI ACTIVITY

The main driver in the period 1999–2000 promoting the growth of UK SRI fund assets was the announcement by three very large pension schemes that they would be incorporating SRI principles into their statements of investment principles (SIPs). The first to do so in June 1999 was the £20 billion British Coal pension scheme, followed early in 2000 by the £33 billion BT pension scheme and the £22 billion Universities Superannuation Scheme (USS). The BT scheme manager, Hermes, has actively pursued corporate governance issues, while USS has recruited a two-person SRI team and sponsored a major report on the implications of climate change for pension funds. Thus, within a year of the SRI regulations being announced, £75 billion of pension scheme assets were actively using SRI principles. The SIP for the BT Pension Scheme is representative:

> The letters of appointment of every investment manager of the Scheme instruct the appointee, in its investment policy, to consider the following when selecting the shares in which they

invest the Scheme's assets: A company run in the long-term interests of its shareholders will need to manage effectively relationships with its employees, suppliers and customers, to behave ethically and to have regard for the environment and society as a whole.... Similarly, the letters of appointment request that the manager uses its best endeavours to exercise the ownership rights associated with shares.[15]

In summer 2000 the UK Social Investment Forum (UKSIF) commissioned a study to determine the response of UK pension funds to the new regulations.[16] Letters were sent out to the top 500 UK corporate pension funds by size and 97 local authority pension funds. In total the funds surveyed possessed investment assets of £540 billion, accounting for about 65% of all UK pension fund investments at that time. Responses were received from 171 funds, with 6.4 million members and £302 billion of funds under management. The survey's main conclusions are shown below. There was, however, a noticeable difference between company and local authority pension schemes. In general, company pension funds delegated the decision over SRI to their asset manager, whereas local authority schemes retained control of their SRI policy, normally adopting a policy of engagement. Numerically this difference was striking: 71% of local authorities mentioned the use of engagement, compared to only 23% of company pension funds. The report concluded that:

> These results are clearly significant, and have considerable implications for the fund management industry as well as the companies it invests in.[17]

Here are the main conclusions of the survey:[18]

1. Fifty-nine percent of funds were incorporating SRI principles into their investment process, either via the fund manager, directly through engagement, or both. These funds represented 78% of the assets surveyed.
2. Forty-eight percent of funds representing 69% of assets requested their fund manager to take account of the financial implications of environmental, social and ethical concerns when investing.
3. Larger pension funds were more likely to take SRI considerations into account than smaller funds.

4. Only 14% of funds clearly stated that they would not take environmental, social and ethical concerns into account, and because these funds tend to be the smaller funds, they only represented 4% of the assets surveyed.
5. Twenty-seven percent of funds delegated the decision over SRI to their fund manager.
6. Thirty-nine percent of funds mentioned the approach of 'engagement' in their statement of investment principles.

The survey showed the rapid adoption of socially responsible investment by institutional investors, confirming other evidence such as the growth of institutional SRI mandates at Henderson, of REO at Friends Provident, and the use of SRI policies by giant pension schemes such as BT and USS. Many people working in the field were therefore rather surprised to hear a lecture in September 2001 that appeared to contradict these findings. Called 'The Impact, to May 2001, of the UK Government's Summer 2001 Legislation on SRI', it was produced by Prabhu Guptara on behalf of the National Association of Pension Funds (NAPF). Guptara claimed that the new rules had had minimal impact and had not achieved their stated objectives, using the performance indicators shown below.[19] Guptara did, however, accept that the legislation had changed the general perception of SRI in the UK, i.e. it was no longer regarded as the preserve of the lunatic fringe:

> The legislation has changed the atmosphere of institutional investment in the UK. SRI is no longer something that 'funny Green people' do. It has changed the context in which everyone in the financial services industry operates.[20]

Guptara analysed the impact of the new regulations using the following five metrics: money, recruitment, time, results, and impact. He argued that although there was a common belief that the legislation had resulted in a greater flow of investment assets into SRI funds, none of his respondents could identify any instance where this had occurred in practice. He found a similar situation regarding recruitment, where again a general feeling that that there was greater level of SRI recruitment could not be substantiated. Guptara found that one or two of his respondents were spending more time on SRI as a direct result of the legislation, but that the majority had not noticed a significant difference.

Guptara's findings on results were mixed. He found that some companies had appointed SRI specialists, while others had increased personnel numbers working in this area. However, few of them had changed the structure of their investment management operations as a result. He did not that a shortage of people with SRI expertise seemed to be a limiting factor on expansion plans. Lastly, he considered impact. The opinions of his respondents on the impact of the legislation varied widely; some people thought it was significant, while others felt that nothing had really changed. Some respondents stated that it was too early to tell, although Guptara was critical of this attitude, arguing that: 'Time itself won't create any additional momentum for change'.[21]

A QUANTUM LEAP IN UK SRI ASSETS

In the author's opinion Guptara's work performed a salutary function in combating possible complacency about the inexorable growth of SRI in the UK. However, the evidence suggests that his conclusions are debatable even when evaluated using his criteria of money (the amount of SRI funds under management), recruitment and results. The big move by large pension funds who started to use SRI approaches from 1999 onwards was described earlier. Another major development, at least as important, was the move by a number of large insurance companies to apply SRI criteria across all their equity funds. Friends Provident was the first to do so in the summer of 2000, moving beyond the Stewardship unit trusts to all their equity funds with investment assets worth £15 billion. The company announced:

> This new policy is the Responsible Engagement Overlay (REO™) developed by Friends Ivory & Sime, Friends Provident's asset management arm. REO builds on Stewardship's long-standing

Table 13.2 *Growth in UK SRI Investment universe (£bn) 1997–2001*

	1997	1999	2001
Church investors	12.5	14.0	13.0
SRI unit trusts	2.2	3.1	3.5
Charities	8.0	10.0	25.0
Pension funds	0.0	25.0	80.0
Insurance companies*	0.0	0.0	103.0
Total	22.7	52.2	224.5

*Unit trust assets have been netted off from insurance totals.
Source: Produced by the author using industry data.

pioneering work to seek to use its influence as an investor to encourage companies to improve their policies on social, environmental and ethical issues. In the past we could only use Stewardship's relatively small pool of assets to push companies to change, now we can speak on behalf of Friends Provident as a whole. This gives our voice significantly more weight. We believe that Friends Provident is the largest investor in the UK to have ever applied a social responsibility policy to all of its investment.[22]

Friends Provident's example was quickly followed by three other major UK insurance companies: Co-operative Insurance Services (CIS), Henderson/NPI and CGNU. By the end of 2001 these four insurance companies had added £103 billion of UK equity assets to the SRI UK investment universe. Table 13.2 and Figure 13.1 show the explosive growth and rapidly changing nature of SRI in the UK over the four years to the end of 2001.

In December 1997, the last year before Denham mentioned the introduction of SRI legislation, total SRI assets in the UK were some £22.7 billion. Although SRI unit trusts were growing very rapidly, they accounted for less than 10% of UK SRI funds, which were dominated by church and other charity investors. By the end of 2001 the overall total of SRI funds in the UK had almost risen tenfold to £224.5 billion, as shown in Table 13.2. Churches and charities were

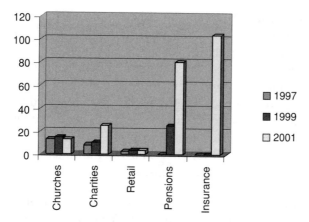

Figure 13.1 *Growth in total UK SRI investment assets (£bn)*

overtaken by pension funds and insurance companies as the major players. The continued growth in SRI from 1999 to 2001 deserves highlighting as it occurred despite a significant fall in the UK stock markets over the period. (The value of the UK equity market as measured by the FTSE All-Share index declined 22.2%).

The evidence of money therefore suggests that the SRI regulations had a major impact on investment markets in the UK. Using recruitment as a performance metric produces a similar picture. The evidence suggest steadily rising recruitment levels at all the specialist SRI asset managers; indeed there is ample evidence that a shortage of experienced people has been a limiting factor on expansion plans.[23] Deloitte & Touche carried out a survey of UK investment management companies in January 2001 to see how they were reacting to the new regulatory climate. It found that 62% of them reported high or medium levels of interest in SRI from their clients, and the majority of respondents expected the level of interest to increase. Interest in SRI was particularly strong in the larger organisations, defined as having £10–100 billion under management, but not as strong for those managing less than £10 billion.[24]

Recruitment shifted into a new gear in August 2000 when seven people, including Clare Brook and Anne Maree O'Connor, widely regarded as key members of the Henderson SRI team, were headhunted to join Morley, the investment management side of CGNU, one of the

UK's largest insurance companies. The *Financial Times* even thought this event worthy of being a distinct story with its own headline accusing Morley of 'poaching' SRI specialist expertise.[25] To the best of my knowledge, this was the first time anywhere in the world that socially responsible investment professionals were thought important enough to be 'poached'. The pattern was repeated in December 2001 when Craig Mackenzie and some of his senior colleagues from Friends Provident left en masse to join Clerical Medical, the fund management arm of HBOS. This is how Mark Miller of Morley Fund Management explained their decision:

> The reason we wanted to build our presence in SRI was the increase in demand for SRI products. You cannot do it with one or two people; you need scale. But it is a very small pool of talent to choose from.[26]

THE QUESTION OF ENGAGEMENT

The period since July 1998 has also seen increased interest in SRI from the professional bodies who advise the UK financial services sector. In May 2001 the UK Society of Investment Professionals (UKSIP) organised a discussion evening on SRI for its members. The National Association of Pension Funds (NAPF) is the main trade body for UK pension funds, whose clients manage over £650 billion of investments, including £300 billion in UK equities. For many years NAPF has offered the Voting Issues Service (VIS) to its members, providing technical advice on corporate governance and shareholder voting. In July 2000 NAPF announced that henceforth VIS would be incorporating social and environmental issues into its corporate governance reports.[27] In July 2001 NAPF went further with the publication of a substantial report, *Engaging for Success: Engagement Guidance on Socially Responsible Investment for Investors and Companies*, written in association with the Institute of Business Ethics.[28] The report stated its aim as providing guidance to investors and companies on SRI issues. For investors it provided a range of indicators that could be used to assess corporate behaviour on social and environmental issues in the light of their own policy statements. The

NAPF report was particularly helpful in my opinion in trying to measure the success of engagement (Box 13.1).[29]

Box 13.1 NAPF Measures of Engagement Success

Engagement outcomes

- How successful is the current engagement process at achieving its objectives?
- How many companies have changed policies or practices as a result of engagement?
- How substantial are these changes?
- What other signs of response in the corporate sector have resulted from engagement activity?
- How well substantiated are claims of engagement success?

Reporting on engagement

- How clear is the communication of engagement activity?
- How detailed is the fund manager's reporting of engagement activity?
- How frequent?
- How well substantiated is it?
- How good is communication to trustees?

Shortly afterwards the Association of British Insurers (ABI) produced a major report of its own, *Investing in Social Responsibility: Risks and Opportunities*.[30] The philosophy behind the ABI report seemed primarily negative; that is, it concentrated on SRI techniques as mechanisms to identify social, environmental and ethical (SEE) risks. It did not really identify SRI as a positive force to target and support industries of the future. However, to be the fair to the ABI, risk avoidance would seem to be the main concern of its client base. More positive developments occurred in January 2002, when Dresdner Kleinwort Wasserstein and HSBC, two of the UK's largest investment banks, announced plans to produced regular investment research on socially responsible investment issues. HSBC stated:

- An innovative new research service to help clients profit from the growing market for socially Responsible Investment (SRI)
- Reviews companies' current environmental and social performance and analyses the catalysts for, and barriers to, future performance
- Facilitating contact between clients, company management and environmental and social opinion formers[31]

The SRI Forum was formed at the beginning of 2001. It was an informal grouping of major institutional investors, and it consisted mainly of representatives of the UK's largest investment fund managers, organisations traditionally with little experience or interest in SRI. The Forum's stated aims were to discuss matters of common interest, including the development of a set of guidelines for corporate reporting on SEE matters, focusing mainly on governance-related disclosures of the board's approach. One objective was to displace the 'proliferation of codes and questionnaires' that companies were believed to face in the absence of a commonly accepted market standard.[32]

Guptara's final criterion was impact, which I think deserves further consideration. His point seemed to be that even if SRI had been adopted by major institutions, and there was a flurry of apparent activity, it was debatable whether anything of substance really had been achieved. He noted the widespread use of the term 'engagement', which he argued 'covers too wide a range from active pushiness to absolutely nothing'.[33] What has been highlighted here by Guptara is the UK's unique reliance on discussion with companies, 'engagement', as its core SRI mechanism. In the author's opinion, Guptara's critique of UK SRI has considerable force in this respect. SRI has traditionally been considered to involve stock selection or shareholder activism. Stock selection on social and environmental grounds may be either positive or negative, i.e. it may be about excluding tobacco or defence shares, it may be about investing in the 'best in class' in all industries, or it may be about allocating capital to 'industries of the future', industries preferable to others on environmental grounds.

Legal factors have prohibited pension funds in the US from adopting the disinvestment route, with the important exception of tobacco

shares. However, they do have vigorous shareholder activism programmes. Dialogue with corporations is one important aspect of this
process, but it is only one part. If dialogue does not lead to a satisfactory improvement in the behaviour of the corporation, other sanctions normally follow. These include public disclosure of investor
concern, which may adversely affect a company's reputation and its
share price, or filing a shareholder resolution, and using the voting
power of share ownership to press for change. Some market participants will argue along with the ABI that it is useful for investors to
be aware of social and environmental risks. So it is. But when this
is done for purely financial reasons I don't think it can be called socially responsible investment. Simon McCrae of Friends of the Earth
criticised the engagement approach in June 2001:

> We are seeing survey after survey which tells us that peo-
> ple want socially responsible pension funds — but the message
> does not appear to be getting through to trustees or pension
> fund managers. Many pension funds are not taking the mat-
> ter seriously — their behaviour is tantamount to 'greenwash'. A
> large number [of funds] are unable to give proof of how they
> were fulfilling their stated SRI objectives. Prejudices need to be
> overcome.[34]

In May 2001 I addressed this issue in a speech given to UKSIP. It
seems appropriate to end this section with the closing part of that
presentation:

> The last point I want to make is about 'engagement'. It is impor-
> tant not to unthinkingly proclaim this a great success. A critic
> might well say: 'So what! The majority of pension funds have
> delegated their SRI policy to their investment managers. The
> latter consider SRI consists of having polite discussions with
> corporate executives on social and environmental issues. Is this
> really going to make any difference to achieve greater corporate
> social responsibility? Look at all the time and effort spent on
> corporate governance over the last ten years! It seems to have
> done nothing to stop the scandal of excessive corporate pay
> awards.'

I think that the (hypothetical) critic has a point. Venture capital may provide a useful example of another investment approach that has moved from fringe to mainstream. When this shift occurred in the early 1990s, the British Venture Capital Association standardised the calculation of rates of return for the industry, as varying approaches were confusing clients. I hope that the same will happen for SRI, and that the leading SRI asset managers will come together to produce a common standard of best practice in the engagement field. If this does not happen, I fear that the Government may feel it necessary to revise the SRI pension regulations, say in 2003, adding a clause about demonstrating compliance. It could then ask the Financial Services Authority (FSA) to audit these claims as part of its normal function of inspecting City firms.[35]

THE US: A MAJOR MARKET FOR SRI

Growth in US socially responsible investing has been equally dramatic. Every two years the Social Investment Forum (SIF) produces a detailed survey, *Trends of Socially Responsible Investing in the United States*; the latest survey appeared in November 2001.[36] It found that SRI in America was 'healthy and expanding'. All the three categories of socially responsible investment – screening, shareholder advocacy and community investing – had enjoyed robust growth over the two years since the previous survey. This was all the more remarkable as it occurred despite a significant fall in the US stock market over the period. It is curious how similar were the declines in the UK and US markets; the FTSE All-Share dropped 22.2%, the S&P 500 fell 21.9%. In common with the rest of the book, I will ignore community investing when assessing the total of US socially responsible assets. This is not because I think it unimportant, far from it, but because in my view it is not socially *responsible* investment. In any case, the sums involved are small, amounting to $8 billion out of a total SRI universe of $2332 billion.

Figure 13.2 shows there has been dramatic growth in the US universe of assets managed according to SRI criteria over the last five

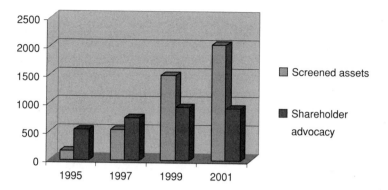

Figure 13.2 *Growth in US assets ($bn) 1995–2001*

years. In 1995 this amounted to $635 billion, before almost doubling over the next two years to $1181 billion. The total almost doubled again in the following two years to reach $2154 billion in 1999. Growth of socially responsible investment assets was relatively modest in the years 1999–2001, as the fund total grew by 8.3% to $2332 billion. However, this should be seen in the context of a falling US equity market. Adjusting for this, US SRI assets increased by over 30% in market-adjusted terms. The growth of SRI in the UK has been primarily driven by pension funds adopting an engagement approach, whereas exclusion, mostly of tobacco stocks, has been the most dynamic aspect in the US during recent years. In 2001 the total assets of professionally managed investment portfolios using SRI exclusion screens increased by 36% from their 1999 level to exceed $2 trillion for the first time. The main screens are listed in Table 13.3.

In contrast, the amount of funds relying solely on shareholder advocacy remained fairly constant: $922 billion in 1999, $906 billion in 2001. There was, however, a surge in the amount of assets that used both social screens and shareholder advocacy; this jumped from $265 billion in 1999 to reach $601 billion in 2001. Excluding double counting, the total assets of the SRI universe grew from $2.16 trillion in 1999 to $2.34 trillion in 2001 (this total includes community investment). The report concluded:

Table 13.3 *Main US exclusion screens*

Generally used *At least 50% of* *portfolios*	Common *30–49%* portfolios	Rare *Less than 30% of* *portfolios*
Tobacco	Labour relations	Executive pay
Environment	Animal testing	Abortion
Human rights	Community investing	Birth control
Employment equality	Community relations	ILO standards
Gambling		
Alcohol		
Weapons		

Source: 2000 Report on Socially Responsible Investing Trends in the United States, Social Investment Forum, SIF Industry Research Program, 28 November 2001.

Nearly one out of every eight dollars under professional management in the United States today is involved in socially responsible investing. The $2.34 trillion managed by major investing institutions, including pension funds, mutual fund families, foundations, religious organisations, and community development financial institutions, accounts for nearly 12 percent of the total $19.9 trillion in investment assets under professional management in the United States, according to the 2001 *Nelson's Directory of Investment Managers.*[37]

Socially Responsible Investing Trends in the United States also discovered continued growth in the total amount of mutual funds in the US who were incorporating social screening into the investment process. The number of screened funds jumped from 168 in 1999 to 230 funds in 2001. Overall assets of US socially responsible mutual funds were essentially unchanged: $154 billion in 1999 and $153 billion in 2001. However, that was 22% better than the US equity market as a whole. This demonstrated, once again, a distinguishing feature of socially responsible investors – they are more loyal or resilient clients. Socially screened mutual funds were able to keep investor assets much better than their unscreened counterparts in the adverse climate of a steady market decline. Lipper Analytics reported that during the first nine months of 2001 net new money flows into SRI mutual funds declined 54%. Although this was a negative number, it held up much better than the average equity mutual fund which experienced a drop of 94% in new dollars invested.

Divestment of tobacco shares by state and local governments was a major driver of growth in screened assets. In October 1997 Massachusetts became the first state in the Union to actually prohibit its pension funds from investing in tobacco shares, although Maryland and Florida had previously set out avoidance policies. It is often said in the UK that pension funds will not and cannot adopt an exclusion model. While it is certainly true that the widespread SRI avoidance approach typical of unit trust/mutual funds is unlikely to be adopted by many pension funds, the US experience shows that institutional investors can exclude whole areas of the market on social grounds. Many US foundations and pension schemes avoid investment in tobacco shares, something which has never been challenged on legal grounds even though tobacco shares led by Philip Morris were one of the best-performing sectors of the market during the market decline of 1999–2002. In October 2000 the $160 billion California Public Employees Retirement System (Calpers) decided it should sell all its holdings of tobacco shares; this was a board decision made in direct opposition to advice from its in-house investment team. Calpers' board member Philip Angelides, the California State Treasurer, successfully argued for a tobacco-free investment policy:

> This is the right financial decision. It recognises the fact that the tobacco industry faces an extraordinary and unprecedented barrage of litigation that makes its stocks a risky investment. We ought not to be risking our pensioners' money betting on the future of tobacco, when there are sound, alternative investments available.[38]

At the same time, Calpers also announced that it would be evaluating its investment portfolios on seven different human rights criteria. The new human rights policies were particularly designed to strengthen the standards used for evaluating its funds invested in emerging markets. At that time the fund had approximately $2 billion invested in stocks and bonds in foreign emerging markets such as Indonesia, Malaysia and Argentina. While Calpers had launched a programme focusing on global corporate governance beginning in 1996, it had never previously included social issues in its investment decisions. The fund justified these policies on the grounds of political risk management. In other words, it was based on the assumption that countries lacking fundamental human rights were, over the long term, likely to prove politically unstable, and therefore unlikely to generate sustainable returns for Calpers' pensioners. 'Human rights' in this context meant excluding investment in countries lacking fundamental democratic institutions including a free press, and basic labour rights including the absence of child labour and slavery. Calpers's new policy also screened out US companies with demonstrated abusive labour practices in emerging markets. Angelides stated that the fund's new human rights policies were

> a much needed step that recognises the correlation between political stability and human rights, and the long-term stability and profitability of our investments.[39]

I suspect that one of the main growth drivers behind socially responsible investment over the next ten years will be pension fund sponsors offering their beneficiaries a specific SRI option among a menu of possible choices. Much the same point was made by Barbara Krumsiek of Calvert Group, who said in April 1997, 'I see enormous potential for growth for Calvert Group, particularly in the defined contribution retirement plan area'.[40] In spring 2001 signs of this occurred as the Domini Social Equity Fund (DSIEF) won a number of defined contribution SRI pension fund mandates. These included the $17 billion Ford Company 401k plan, and the $4.7 billion State of California Savings Plus deferred compensation plan. The DSIEF's origins lie in Cambridge, Massachusetts, although it is now based in New York. I suspect the DSIEF people were therefore particularly pleased when the Commonwealth of Massachusetts announced that the fund would be offered to all 111 000 members of the state's $2.8 billion deferred compensation plan. Massachusetts State Treasurer Shannon O'Brien commented:

> We think it is very important to offer a socially responsible investment option to our plan participants. And we are very

pleased to include the Domini Social Equity Fund as a core offering within our menu of investment options.[41]

SHAREHOLDER ACTIVISM IN THE US

One of the first US institutional investors to go down the path of shareholder activism was the Episcopal Church, which filed its first shareholder resolution back in 1971. This led directly to the foundation of the Interfaith Center on Corporate Responsibility (ICCR), an association of 275 Protestant, Roman Catholic and Jewish institutional investors, including national denominations, religious communities, pension funds, endowments, hospital corporations, economic development funds and publishing companies. Under the legendary Tim Smith, who led ICCR from its inception in 1973 until his retirement in 2000, ICCR has been 'the engine room' of the corporate social responsibility movement in the US. Its work is channelled into six focus groups: energy and the environment, global corporate accountability, international health and pharmaceuticals, militarism and violence, equality, and global finance. One US fund manager said to me in 1993, 'When Tim Smith rings up corporate America, they don't just listen, they stand to attention!'.[42] Many US companies will testify that ICCR has brought issues to their attention that they otherwise would not have considered, functioning as an 'early warning system' of growing societal concern over aspects of their activities that they need to address. Chemical giant Du Pont put it thus:

> They've contributed an awful lot to Du Pont, and to our understanding of how the general public might view certain issues.[43]

Each year the institutional investors who are members of ICCR sponsor over 100 shareholder resolutions on major social and environmental issues. Since the combined value of their investment assets exceeds $110 billion, they have considerable clout when they do so. Although Tim Smith retired in 2000, ICCR's shareholder activism has continued to grow under the leadership of Patricia Wolf. The role played by ICCR and its UK and Canadian sister organisations in developing the Global Principles for Global Corporate Responsibility (Bench Marks) was described in Chapter 9. In January 2002 Pat Wolf came to London to talk about ICCR's work:

> ICCR has used the Global Principles in corporate dialogues and shareholder resolutions and had seen improvements in company codes on a range of labour rights issues and monitoring mechanisms.... [They] have been the framework for ICCR's work with Walt Disney on labour conditions in the supplier plants producing Disney products. ICCR shareholders have pressed Disney to use its influence to raise labour standards by strengthening the code of vendor conduct, by creating and improving its internal auditing system and by working with non-governmental organisations in training and independent monitoring programs. A relationship which was rocky at first has now turned into a productive collaboration to take concrete steps to improve Disney's approach to change the conditions in its supply chain.[44]

Socially Responsible Investing Trends in the United States 2001 also examined shareholder activism. Preliminary data for the 2002 shareholding season showed that 251 socially responsible shareholder resolutions had been submitted to a total of 177 companies, a significant increase from the previous year's total of 226 shareholder resolutions submitted to 160 companies. The major source of these resolutions was ICCR, whose members sponsored 144 resolutions to 99 companies. The 2002 shareholder season included a number of new resolution topics for ICCR, such as:

- Pharmaceutical companies should improve access to HIV, tuberculosis and malaria pharmaceuticals, especially in developing countries.
- Appliance manufacturers should reducing greenhouse gas emissions.
- Computer manufacturers should take back and recycle their products.
- Corporations should continue in-person annual general meetings.[45]

Many US companies are registered in the tiny state of Delaware for legal reasons. The majority of Delaware annual shareholder meetings are fairly quiet, almost routine affairs. I think a good flavour of ICCR's work is given by the following comments made at the annual shareholder meeting of financial services group MBNA in June 1999. Don Kuespert, an ICCR member, criticised the MBNA board in front of assembled shareholders for consisting solely of seven white men. He added:

> There are people in our society who are not white males. It is distressing that the company refuses to even make an effort.[46]

Apart from ICCR, American trade unions are the other major sponsor of US shareholder resolutions. The American Federation of Labor and Congress of Industrial Organisations (AFL-CIO) has become one of the major forces in this area. The AFL-CIO monitors the shareholding voting records of all the major US asset management firms, and makes these voting records available to its members who are trustees of pension funds. It is estimated that worker trustees have supervisory positions on US pension schemes who possess assets under management of $11 trillion. Indeed, I suspect that the next few years will see growing use of shareholder activism on a global basis by trade unions. They can use their influence as shareholders to push the case for better labour conditions, and also to make mainstream investors more aware of labour issue problems. This was the subject of an international conference of trade union organisations held in Washington DC on 5–6 April 2001.

The conference used the giant mining company Rio Tinto as a case study. Rio Tinto has a two-part corporate structure, being based in the UK and also in Australia. For many years the Australian Construction, Mining, Forestry and Energy Union (CFMEU) has been in dispute with the company over allegations that Rio Tinto has imposed individual work contracts on employees, obviating their rights to collective bargaining. In 2000 CFMEU decided to file a shareholder resolution at the joint AGMs of the company being held in London and Sydney to challenge it on this issue. The campaign was organised by CFMEU's Peter Colley, who said:

> After several years of disputes in various forms we felt frustrated with management as we could not get through to them, not necessarily the particulars of each dispute but our overriding aim of minimum labour rights.[47]

The CFMEU shareholder resolution was backed by a coalition of international and domestic unions representing 41 million workers across the world. These included the Australian Council of Trade Unions, the UK's Trades Union Congress (TUC), the American Federation of Labor and Congress of Industrial Organisations (AFL-CIO), and the International Chemical, Energy, Mine and General Workers' Union. The campaign filed two shareholder resolutions. The first was on corporate governance, requesting the company to appoint an independent non-executive chairman. The second asked the company to adopt ILO conventions safeguarding rights in the workplace, in particular on collective bargaining.[48] Although these resolutions were not carried, they obtained votes of 20.3% and 17.3% respectively, some of the highest levels of support ever achieved by social shareholder resolutions.

The unions claimed this as a great victory over one of the world's largest companies. They stated that, following the vote, Rio Tinto had indicated its willingness to resume discussions over collective bargaining with the trade unions in Australia. The company was also believed to be improving its corporate governance standards by adopting a policy of having a majority of non-executive directors on the board.

The Washington conference was the third ever meeting of the Committee on Workers' Capital. Fifty-five trade union representatives from around the world attended. The conference agreed that the Rio Tinto campaign had demonstrated that shareholder activism could be an effective way of pressurising company executives, particularly on disputes involving human rights in the workplace. It was decided that trade unions should work together to develop much greater expertise in this area, and allocate resources for future international campaigns. It was also agreed that unions should aim to educate their members about socially responsible investment. The ultimate objective was to raise awareness among pension fund trustees about SRI, with human rights in the workplace being one of the key issues, as this book argued in Chapter 8.

I mentioned earlier concerns over the efficacy of the engagement route in the UK, amid fears that it might lead to 'greenwash'. Similar fears have arisen in the US over the launch in late 2000 of low-cost SRI index funds by two of America's largest money management firms, TIAA-CREF and the Vanguard Group; Vanguard is a specialist in index mutual funds. The management fee charged by these funds was less than 0.3%, compared to an average fee for a US SRI mutual fund of 1.16%. using Morningstar industry data. The point at issue was that a management fee of only 0.3% was not adequate to pay for detailed SRI research, nor would it finance shareholder activism campaigns. Critics argued that all such funds could really offer was a screened index fund based on simple exclusion formulas. One commentator called this 'social investment lite'.[49] Others such as Frank Coleman of Christian Brothers Investors Services (CBIS) worried that this development risked 'diluting' the whole concept of socially responsible investment in America.:

> Over the past twenty years the SRI industry in the US has grown up. It has moved beyond just screening and now defines itself as screening plus activism plus community development. If Vanguard and TIAA-CREF only do screening, and if they draw from the established customer base, they could take the SRI industry back thirteen years.... The social activism and research required for socially responsible investment costs money. At CBIS we estimate that shareholder activism alone represents a 0.25–0.3% premium over the standard costs of managing a mutual fund.[50]

Let me end this chapter with some thoughts on the development of SRI in America from someone who has lived through it in the beginning, Steve Lydenberg. Steve and I were both at the SRI in the Rockies Conference in September 2001, and I remember talking with him as we were both stunned by the terrible events of September 11. One of the few happy memories of that conference is the Service Award given to him for lifetime achievement in socially responsible investment. He recently looked back:

> In the 1970s SRI was not even recognised. It was treated with suspicion in the 1980s, and it was only in the 1990s that it won recognition both as a market and as a legitimate investment tool. In 1992, if you had asked me, I would not have known whether SRI would be around in five years. Now, I believe it has won a permanent place. I believed it would happen, but I did not necessarily believe I would see it my lifetime.[51]

REFERENCES

1. 'Local Authority Plans Ethical Pensions', *Financial Times*, 15 September 1998.
2. Mike Shaw, quoted in 'Really Too Good to Be True', *Pensions Management*, February 1998.
3. *The Ethical Investor*, October 1998.
4. 'Union Members Offered Ethical Pension Option', *The Ethical Investor*, December 2000.
5. *The Ethical Investor*, November/December 1998.
6. Mark Campanale, quoted in *Tomorrow Magazine*, July/August 1999.
7. Author's notes on a presentation by Mark Campanale of NPI, London, March 1999.
8. Calvert Group website 2000.
9. 'New Henderson Team Wins £100m Brief', *Investment Week*, 27 September 1999.
10. Author's notes on a presentation by Mike Shaw of Henderson, London, April 2000.
11. *Ibid.*
12. 'Friends Provident Raises Its Profile with Ethics Unit', *Investment Week*, October 1998.
13. 'Friends Provident Establishes Engagement Unit', *The Guardian*, 28 October 1998.
14. 'Conscience Money', *Pensions World*, June 2000.
15. Hermes Pensions Management, press release, July 2000.
16. 'Response of UK Pension Funds to the SRI Disclosure Regulations', UKSIF, October 2000.
17. *Ibid.*
18. *Ibid.*
19. 'Profile: Prabhu Guptara', *Environmental Finance*, October 2001.
20. *Ibid.*
21. Prabhu Guptara, 'The Impact, to May 2001, of the UK Government's Summer 2001 Legislation on SRI', speech to the Sustainable and Responsible Investment Forum, London, September 2001.
22. 'Friends Provident to Apply Social Responsibility Policy across £15bn of Investment Funds', *Friends Provident Stewardship Newsletter*, Summer 2000.
23. See for instance 'City Finds Added Value in Green Credentials', *Financial Times* 31 August 2000; Mike Shaw, 'The Development of a Credible SRI Policy Requires Levels of Expertise Which Are beyond the Scope of Many Fund Managers', *Pensions Week*, 28 June 1999; Mark Mansley, 'Rise to the Challenge', *Pensions Week*, 28 June 1999.
24. 'Deloitte & Touche Report Fund Manager Interest in SRI', *UKSIF Newsletter*, June 2001.
25. 'Morley Poaches Ethical Investment Specialists', *Financial Times*, 8 August 2000.
26. 'City Finds Added Value in Green Credentials' *Financial Times*, 31 August 2000.
27. *The Ethical Investor*, March 2000.
28. *Engaging for Success: Engagement Guidance on Socially Responsible Investment for Investors and Companies*, National Association of Pension Funds, July 2001.
29. Copyright the National Association of Pension Funds. Reproduced by permission.
30. *Investing in Social Responsibility: Risks and Opportunities*, Association of British Insurers, October 2001.
31. 'Sustainability & Securities' HSBC 22 January 2002.
32. *PIRC Intelligence*, April 2001.
33. Prabhu Guptara, 'The Impact, to May 2001, of the UK Government's Summer 2001 Legislation on SRI', speech to the Sustainable and Responsible Investment Forum, London, September 2001.

34. Simon McRae, quoted in 'Friends of the Earth Slates Pension Funds', *Sunday Telegraph*, 17 June 2001.
35. Russell Sparkes, 'Socially Responsible Investment: Past, Present, and Future', speech to UK Society of Investment Professionals, May 2001.
36. *2000 Report on Socially Responsible Investing Trends in the United States*, Social Investment Forum, SIF Industry Research Program, 28 November 2001.
37. *Ibid.*
38. *UKSIF Bulletin*, January 2001.
39. *Ibid.*
40. Barbara Krumsiek, quoted in *Wall Street Journal*, 8 April 1997.
41. Quoted in Domini Social Equity, *Business News Wire*, 2 April 2001.
42. Quoted in Russell Sparkes, *The Ethical Investor*, Harper Collins, 1995.
43. Quoted in 'Social Activists Get to Work', *The News Journal* (Wilmington DE), 8 June 1999.
44. 'Developments in Shareholder Resolutions', talk by Pat Wolf, London, 13 February 2002.
45. ICCR website.
46. Quoted in 'Social Activists Get to Work'.
47. Quoted in 'Shareholder Campaign Profile: RIO vs. CFMEU', *Ethical Investor*, 26 February 2001.
48. 'Rio Tinto Unions Call for Board Changes at AGM', *Wall Street Journal*, 10 May 2000.
49. Quoted in 'SRI Meets the Mainstream', *Environmental Finance*, March 2001.
50. Frank Coleman, quoted in 'SRI Meets the Mainstream', *Environmental Finance*, March 2001.
51. Steve Lydenberg, quoted in 'The Power of Research', *Environmental Finance*, January 2002.

14

A Global Revolution

JAPAN: A NEW MARKET FOR SRI

Japan is one of the youngest markets in the world for socially responsible investment. However, it is growing rapidly. The huge size of the Japanese savings market gives Japanese SRI the potential to become a force of global importance in socially responsible investing. The love of the natural world that is embedded in traditional Japanese culture makes it easy for the Japanese to embrace the concept of sustainability. However, Japanese people also remember how they suffered from environmental pollution when Japan industrialised rapidly after the Second World War. One of the worst cases was the fishing village of Minamata, whose citizens were badly poisoned by mercury dumped into the bay in the 1950s and 1960s.

The Japanese economy stagnated throughout the 1990s after the bursting of the economic bubble of the 1980s. In the new Millennium that stagnation seemed to deepen. The Bank of Japan has cut effective interest rates to zero, but even this failed to boost the economy. Unemployment has risen to a post-war record, and the Nikkei 225 stock market index has plunged to levels last seen almost twenty years ago. Against this bleak background, SRI gives Japanese investors a rare chance of hope in the future.

The Japanese consumers' association, the Asahi Shimbun Foundation, has interested itself in socially responsible investment for many years, and is a member of the Global Partners network. Good Bankers is Japan's first specialist SRI research provider. It was launched in 1998 to introduce the idea and mechanisms of socially responsible investment to Japan. During 1998–99 Good Bankers worked with

Nikko Asset Management to launch the Nikko Eco-Fund in August 1999, the first SRI product for the Japanese market.[1] In February 2000 Good Bankers and Nikko Asset Management became the first Japanese signatories of the UNEP financial initiative, with Nikko stating its objective of achieving ISO 14001 certification.

The partners decided that the Japanese market was not suitable for negative screening, and therefore the focus of the new fund was placed on positive environmental themes. Its stated objective is to facilitate sustainable development of Japanese society by investing in environmentally friendly companies. The two partners also announced that part of the profits from the new fund will be used to create a charitable foundation, working with the World Wide Fund for Nature to support environmental protection measures in Japan. The fund's launch exceeded all expectations, as it quickly reached ¥170 billion of assets. Mizue Tsukushi of Good Bankers recalled:

> The Nikko Eco-Fund collected more than four times the projected initial sales, reflecting stronger than expected interest among Japanese individual investors in this new investment vehicle. It is now Japan's 17th largest mutual fund and one of the largest green funds in the world. Additionally, six more financial institutions have followed this new trend by launching similar mutual funds. The total assets of Japanese green funds under management have now reached ¥200 billion [$1.5 billion] in January 2000, only six months after Nikko Eco-Fund's initiation. The immediate popularity of these funds has caused a sensation in Japanese financial services industry. Over 90% of investors are individuals, including women and the younger generation who have not traditionally been major players in the stock market. This shows the great potential of socially responsible investment in Japanese society[2]

The Japanese public's strong support for green consumerism makes it fertile soil for environmental investing. According to a survey carried out in 1998 by the *Keidanren* (the Japanese employer's federation), 90% of women agreed that they were prepared to accept a lower standard of living in order to protect the environment. These findings agreed with those of a survey produced by Nippon Dentsu (Japan's largest advertising company) in 1997, which showed that 70% of people aged between 15 and 59 in the greater Tokyo area were ready to pay a price premium for environmentally friendly goods. This was a significant increase on the 55% of green consumers identified by a similar survey carried out in 1993.

Such fertile soil for SRI meant that the Nikko Eco-Fund found plenty of imitators. For example, T. Rowe Price Asset Management, one of the largest asset managers in the US, used Japan to launch its first ever SRI fund, the Global Eco Growth Fund, in July 2001. This is a large-capitalisation growth fund specialising in the environmental investment area (80% of its assets), and with specialist environmental research provided by Innovest in New York. Marketed by Daiwa Securities, the fund quickly gained assets of ¥26 billion. Peter Wiles of Innovest stated (original emphasis):

> The fund will invest in a combination of large-cap blue-chip issues with superior environmental credentials as well as small and mid-cap 'eco-pioneers' that are leading the way in solving the environmental problems of the future. T. Rowe Price screens the investment universe for the top business franchises in all the sectors around the globe. [Then] Innovest provides *positive*, not negative environmental screens on these companies, so the portfolio includes the best of the best.[3]

Currently the Japanese social responsibility market consists of 10 mutual funds with assets under management of ¥250 billion. However, they are rather unusual by Western standards. All are based on positive criteria without making any use of negative exclusion, while only two of them have moved beyond a narrow environmental focus to consider broader social responsibility issues. One of these is Nikko's second SRI fund, the Nikko Global Sustainability Fund. However, the launch of this fund was less successful than its predecessor, drawing in a relatively modest ¥13 billion of investments. Takejiro Sueyoshi of Nikko Asset Management explained why this was so:

> Japanese citizens have been quick to embrace eco-funds, but investors have been more uncertain about newly emerging SRI funds that take account of companies performance using broader social criteria. This is because there is a common

understanding about eco-funds, but not about funds that have a broader focus than just environmental performance.[4]

The rapid growth and publicity attached to the new SRI mutual funds has awakened attention of Japanese institutional investors to the possibilities of socially responsible investment. In the summer of 2000 the Rengo federation of trade unions announced that it would be investigating eco-fund type guidelines for its investment assets of ¥1 trillion invested on behalf of its 8 million members. Rengo noted that some trade union funds were already investors in the Nikko Eco-Fund. In October 2000 the Tokyo Teachers' Mutual Aid Association announced similar plans. In fact, the president of Nikko Securities, Masahi Kaneko, announced at the UNEP conference in May 2000 that he expected the total Japanese SRI market to expand to ¥1 trillion.[5] The outlook for SRI in Japan appears bright, particularly if it is taken up by Japanese public pension funds on behalf of their investment assets of ¥170 trillion.

Corporate governance is also an issue of growing public interest in Japan. Historically this has not been of great importance in view of the *keiretsu* system of corporate families such as Sumitomo, Mitsubishi and Mitsui. Many of these are old-established company groupings that go back to Japan's initial industrialisation during the Meiji period of the late nineteenth century. Members of such corporate families typically maintain an elaborate system of cross-shareholdings in each other. However, the *keiretsu* system appears to be coming under pressure as the government encourages restructuring of the Japanese economy. In July 2001 the International Corporate Governance Network held its first ever meeting in Tokyo, discussing proposed changes to the Japanese Commercial Code being considered by the Diet, the Japanese parliament. One of these proposed changes was a new legal requirement that every quoted company should have at least one external director (i.e. outside the *keiretsu)*. The Ministry of Economy, Trade and Industry (METI) has also mooted the idea that Japan should adopt the US ERISA regulation that shareholders should have a legal obligation over the use of their shareholder voting rights.

The rapid growth of SRI in Japan confirms that investing with values has global attractions. Yet its also demonstrates how the social and environmental issues taken into account are shaped by local traditions and customs. I asked Mizue Tsukushi why negative screening had not caught on in Japan, and what were the prospects for shareholder activism. Her reply was fairly defensive:

> In Japan it is considered impolite to criticise others. If you exclude companies because they fail certain screens of environmental or social performance you are obviously criticising them, so it is hard to see how negative screening could work in Japan. Shareholder activism is even more difficult. In traditional Japanese custom, only rude or uneducated people would publicly criticise other people; you just cannot do this.[6]

SRI IN THE PACIFIC

Until recently there has been little interest in SRI in Asia apart from Australia (Chapter 12). The first Asian SRI fund to be established outside Australia was the United Global Unifem Fund, launched as recently as 1999 in Singapore. This was created by a group of leading businesswomen in Singapore and run by UOB Asset Management. The fund's investment universe is limited to companies that encourage female advancement at work. The fund sponsors hoped it would reach $30 million of assets fairly quickly.[7] In the same year, the UK firm Henderson set up a sustainable fund to invest in Asia under the guidance of Tessa Tennant. Called the NPI Global Care Asia Pacific Fund, it had grown to $60 million of funds under management by the end of 2001.

Tennant stayed in the region and in 2000 it was one of the key founders and the first executive chair of the Association for Sustainable and Responsible Investment in Asia (ASrIA). In 2000 the Hong Kong–based Kingsway group announced that it was applying SRI screens to all of its $64 million assets under management.[8] The same year saw the production of a report on the prospects for SRI in Hong Kong by Christine Loh, formerly a member of the Legislative Council and now head of the Civic Exchange think-tank. Loh argued that little was likely to happen over the short term, but that within five years there was likely to be a substantial SRI presence in Hong Kong. She noted that the introduction of the Mandatory

Provident Fund (MPF) in Hong Kong in December 1999 was likely to be a highly positive factor. The MPF requires all employers to pay 5% of an employee's wages into a pension fund, resulting in inflows of HK$24 billion ($3 billion) a year into financial assets. It is widely believed that many Hong Kong employers would like to offer their employees an SRI pension option.[9] ASrIA estimated that the total of socially responsible funds under management in Asia was less than $2.5 billion at the end of 2001, but that this figure was expected to increase substantially.[10]

The relatively undeveloped financial markets of Latin America have seen little interest in SRI up to now. All credit therefore to Unibanco, Brazil's fourth largest private bank, which announced in January 2001 that it would be producing SRI reports for its clients on Brazil's largest quoted companies. These reports cover information on emissions, child labour, ISO 14001, the Amazon, employee diversity, environmental reporting and community relations. The SRI research unit is headed by an American, Chris Wells, who has lived in Brazil for many years. He is proud that:

> Unibanco has achieved two firsts. One, we are the first investment bank in the world to include an SRI assessment in the research we send to our fund manager clients. Secondly, we are producing the first SRI coverage of emerging markets. We have recently produced reports for example on companies as wide-ranging as CST (steel); Sadia (food), and Pao de Acucar (supermarkets). Our ultimate aim is total coverage of all Brazilian quoted equities. Our SRI research has caught the public's attention in Brazil; there is growing coverage of the issues in the business press, and ABN Amro has just launched a domestic SRI mutual fund for Brazilian investors.[11]

SRI IN CONTINENTAL EUROPE

References to Europe in this chapter exclude the UK. Although the European single currency seems to be leading to the formation of a single pan-European financial market, the UK stands outside it at present. That is one reason why I have treated the UK separately from Continental Europe. The two areas are also quite distinct in terms of their positioning in the development of socially responsible investment. The UK has always been one of the leaders in SRI, and is second only to the US in terms of socially responsible assets under management. Although some Nordic countries were early pioneers of SRI mutual funds, these have operated on a small scale. SRI in Europe has therefore been relatively small and low profile, at least until recently.

Since the 1950s most continental European countries have experienced low inflation, which has limited investor interest in equities as an inflation hedge. Investment in mutual funds/unit trusts has therefore been slow to develop, and has remained relatively small compared to Anglo-Saxon levels. With the important exception of the Netherlands, funded pension schemes have not developed in Europe, with future pensioners relying on 'pay as you go' state guarantees. Unit trusts and pension funds have been the main drivers behind the growth of socially responsible investment in Anglo-Saxon countries, and in Europe they have been lacking until recently. However, things have changed dramatically in recent years. The cult of the equity seems to have caught on, while governments across Europe are rushing to introduce funded pension schemes in view of the demographic time bomb they would otherwise face.

Until recently there was little information available on socially responsible investment across Europe. In the summer of 2000 the Italian sustainable development research agency Avanzi made one of the first systematic calculations of how big the European market for SRI might actually be. Their report, *Green and Ethical Funds in Europe 1999*, was produced for the Global Partners network with the help of local SRI researchers for their respective markets: EIRIS (UK), Caring Company (Sweden), Ethibel (Belgium), Centre Info (Switzerland), Imug (Germany), L'Observatoire Ethique (France). This came out with a widely quoted headline figure of €11 billion in pan-European SRI investment assets.[12] However, this figure needs to be treated with caution for three reasons: it includes the UK, it is rather out of date, and it excludes institutional investment, counting only mutual funds.

To be fair to the Global Partners report, it does highlight these features, but the headline figure has been repeated elsewhere without any mention of such caveats. To be included in the survey, funds

had to be explicitly marketed as being socially responsible investment, and to use clearly identified ethical, social and environmental
screens for portfolio selection. The report was commissioned by the
Global Partners network on the basis that there was little detailed
or reliable information available on green and SRI investment in
Europe. It aimed to find answers to questions such as the size of the
investment universe of green and ethical funds in Europe, how many
SRI funds there were, and what were the main criteria being used.[13]
Thus the research specifically excluded institutional funds such as
charitable foundations, or pension funds. *Green and Ethical Funds
in Europe 1999* concluded that total SRI assets under management
in Europe had reached €11 billion at the end of 1999, invested in
188 mutual funds.

However, over one-third of the 188 funds covered were based in
the UK, which was also by far the largest market, with €4.6 billion of
assets. The author believes that SRI in the UK should be considered
on a stand-alone basis as regards developments in socially responsible investing. Once the UK funds are removed from the survey, the
headline total of European SRI assets is reduced significantly from
€11 billion to €6.4 billion. The geographical breakdown is shown
in Figure 14.1

The relative dominance of Italy may seem surprising. However, it
reflected two funds (over €1 billion each) that were open to both
institutional and private investors. Perhaps the most important conclusion reached by the Avanzi report was that although retail SRI
investing had been slow to take off in Europe in the past, the late
1990s had experienced 'exponential growth'. This is undoubtedly
true. For example, the number of Belgian socially responsible mutual

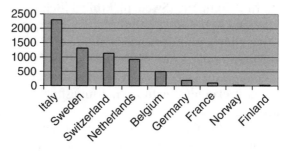

Figure 14.1 *European SRI assets in 1999 €m*

funds more than doubled over the course of 2000 from 10 to 24, while their total investment assets increased from €500 million to €1000 million.[14] The German market experienced a similar development The number of German SRI funds increased from 10 to 18 in 1998–2000 with their assets under management rising from DM 600 million to reach DM 3 billion (€1.5 billion).[15]

SCANDINAVIAN PIONEERS

The Scandinavian financial markets were the real pioneers of socially responsible investment in Europe, probably a reflection of the strong social and environmental awareness felt throughout the region. Once again church investors were the pioneers. As early as 1965 church groups founded the Ansvar SRI fund in Sweden. In 1980 Robur Investment Management launched the Svenska Kyrkans VP Fond on behalf of the Church of Sweden. This fund avoided investments in companies dealing with South Africa or armaments. Currently the Swedish Church has some Skr 5 billion (€570 million) invested in financial securities. In 2000 the Church Synod issued an order that assets of the Church of Sweden must be invested 'in an ethical and accessible way in keeping with the fundamental values of the Church'.[16] The Church of Sweden set up a Council for Ethical Investment to discuss ethical questions in the management of capital. According to Lars Friedner of the Kyrkokansliet:

> The Church Investment Fund Board has decided that the central Church funds should not be invested in tobacco or weapons manufacturers. Instructions to this effect have been sent to the banks who invest the Board's money. Some of the local church trusts have added alcohol and pornography to the excluded list, although the sums involved are still small. The Church of Sweden recently set up a new initiative to make a mathematical model to assess the ethical scores and business risk of company investments. The Church of Sweden hopes that all these measures will take forward in a meaningful way the discussion on ethical investment. It looks like our discussions have a lot further to go, but this is perhaps an area where the journey is more important than the destination.[17]

A number of environmental funds appeared at the end of the 1980s. These included two Danish funds launched in 1987: Danske Invest Miljo and DK Miljo Invest. In 1989 the Gront Norge (Green Norway) fund was issued by environmental specialist asset manager MiljoInvest, later acquired by Sweden's Skandia, while in 1991 the environmental growth fund SE Banken Miljofond was launched by Enskilda Asset Management, a subsidiary of Skandinaviska Enskilda Banken, one of the largest banks in Sweden. In 1999 the medium-sized Danish bancassurance group Almene Brand launched the Almene Brand Invest 6 Environmental Technology Fund together with the UK environmental finance boutique Impax Capital. This is a pure-play fund specialising in environmental technology investment, which is currently worth around €30 million. The fund's performance was excellent in 2000, as it was the best-performing Danish mutual fund in that year, although it suffered along with the sector after that.

The two market leaders in the Swedish SRI retail market are Banco Funds and Robur, the latter a subsidiary of the Forenings Sparbanken savings bank, which runs environmental mutual funds worth SKr 1 billion (€110 million).[18] The Banco Funds group was a pioneer of SRI in Sweden, launching the Swedish Environmental Fund in September 1994. This invests in the top 300 companies quoted on the Stockholm Stock Exchange that passed its rigorous environmental screening tests. The Banco Ethical Global Fund is noted for its strong use of human rights evaluation in which it uses data supplied by the UK merchant bank Dresdner Kleinwort Benson. Sweden also possesses one of the oldest SRI providers in Europe in the Stockholm-based Caring Company. This has produced social and environmental research on Scandinavian companies since its foundation in 1992.

Currently there are around 40 Swedish SRI mutual funds in existence with total assets under management of SKr 15 billion (€1.7 billion), which gives them a market share of 1% of total Swedish mutual fund assets. There are three distinct types of fund in Sweden: general SRI funds with some social screens and possessing a positive commitment to sustainable development; environmental technology funds; and charitable funds, often linked to churches which rebate part of the management fee to a specific charity. The charitable funds deserve further comment. The system works by the underlying investors being charged a higher fee, but with this being passed on to a charity client of their choice.

In June 2001 the development agency Diakonia decided to coordinate the efforts of a group of six Swedish churches and NGOs such as the Save the Children Fund and the World Wide Fund for Nature to explore the potential of this market together. A specialist company called Humanix was created that launched a series of socially responsible index funds whose financial value is calculated daily by the financial news service Bloomberg. Administrative support and financial expertise is provided by Den Danske Bank, the largest bank in Denmark. These indices include the Humanix 50, which consists of the 50 largest companies on the Swedish stock market that pass its ethical screens, as well as other European, US and global indices. Humanix worked together with the churches and NGOs to develop its SRI criteria, i.e. the churches provided standard exclusions such as companies deriving over 3% of sales from alcohol, tobacco and armaments, while the other NGOs offered their specialist advice on the environment and human rights.[19]

A new Swedish law that came into effect in December 2000 has obliged the giant SKr 400 billion (€43 billion) AP pension funds to take ethical and environmental considerations into account. However, they remain obliged to get the best financial return on their investments. The law obliges Swedish savers to invest in private pension schemes, but they have a choice in where the money goes, rather like the US 401k rules. They may choose among a range of AP funds or to invest in private schemes. If no choice is made, AP fund number 7 becomes the default option. The AP funds do not screen out traditional sin stocks such as alcohol, tobacco and gambling, although they do exclude companies discriminating against women or involved in landmines. The AP funds currently exclude some 30 stocks quoted on the Swedish stock market. It has been calculated that such avoidance would have had a minimal effect on investment performance over the previous two years.

KPA is the Swedish local authority workers pension fund that has investment assets of SKr 1.5 billion (€170 million). In 2001 it became a subsidiary of the Folksam insurance group. In recent years KPA has received growing number of requests from its municipal customers for their funds to be run using SRI constraints. It therefore decided to carry out a high-profile advertising campaign to promote its services using photographs of women 'angels' stating how their investments were frustrating the devil, e.g. 'I put the Devil in his place'. Carina Lundberg of KPA described the logic thus:

> The fact that the three people in the advertising are female is due to the fact that 80% of KPA's target group, local and municipal workers, are also female.... The advertising campaign also has a general purpose, which is boosting the recognition factor for KPA's name and brand name. This is important because SKr 50 billion in new monies will be invested in the securities market next year, followed by a further SKr 15 billion every year after.[20]

Although Norway is a relatively small economy, it has played a significant role in the development of socially responsible investment. This is particularly true of Storebrand, the largest insurance company in Norway. The Norwegian government has invested some of the country's oil revenues in the giant NKr 400 billion (€50 billion) Petroleum Fund. In 2000 it decided on a three-year trial of socially responsible investment, particularly human rights, using NKr 1 billion (140 million) of the fund's assets. In 1996 Storebrand established the Storebrand Global Principle Fund, one of the first publicly available SRI funds to explicitly incorporate human rights criteria into its investment decision-making processes. These criteria were developed with the help of organisations like Amnesty International and Human Rights Watch as well as the University of Oslo, and are based on generally accepted UN declarations and the major ILO conventions, described earlier. Storebrand explained the decision to focus on human rights issues (as opposed to conventional ethical and social criteria (e.g. good employers, employment for disabled persons, executive compensation) as follows:[21]

1. Ethical and social criteria are built upon how basic human rights are assured.
2. An increasing share of corporate activity occurs in developing regions of the world, and human rights issues are a concern in many of these areas.
3. At the same time, society's concerns about human rights issues, such as the use of child labour, has increased.

4. There is a positive relationship between human rights performance and financial performance.

Storebrand has achieved particular recognition outside Scandinavia for its positive and thoughtful statements on the environment. The company is a member of the United Nations Environment Programme (UNEP) and the World Business Council for Sustainable Development. In 1994 the company announced a ten-year action plan to integrate environmental considerations into its products, pricing and management systems. For example, the company encouraged customers to have damaged car bumpers repaired rather than replacing them, saving an estimated NKr 25 million (€3.4 million) a year and reducing waste and landfill volumes. Its marine insurance operation started to refuse to cover ships that did not meet its environmental criteria.[22] Storebrand's vice-president, Carlos Joly, describes the company's philosophy in the following way:

> I believe that the fiduciary responsibility we have in relation to our life insurance savers extends beyond the purely financial aspects of return on investment to include some of the social and environmental conditions in which they and their beneficiaries will live. What we invest in the long term, how we manage the assets we are entrusted with, should take into consideration avoiding harm to our clients through environmental deterioration. What good does it do us to cash in on investments 20 years from now if the world goes to hell partly as a result of what we invest in?[23]

Storebrand has also developed 'charitable' funds on the Swedish model, i.e. in 1999 it set up the Norwegian Red Cross Fund.[24] At the same time it has become one of the leading global managers of institutional SRI funds around the world, with SRI client assets of over £3 billion for IBM, Swiss Re, World Wide Fund for Nature and Statoil. In August 2001 Storebrand announced a partnership with the Australian asset manager Tower Asset Management to offer a global SRI fund to the Australian market. Carlos Joly stated:

> We're not in the business of imposing values on our clients or defining what is or isn't a socially responsible line of business. This is reflected in our pragmatic 'best of sector' approach to

the global market. Our resulting portfolio represents the highest standards of financial prudence and environmental and social responsibility.[25]

OTHER EUROPEAN MARKETS

The pioneering efforts of Dutch SRI funds should also be recognised. One distinctive aspect of financial markets in the Netherlands has been the important role played by the 'ethical savings bank's SNS Reaal Groep and Triodos. SNS's ASN Aandelenfonds subsidiary launched the first SRI fund quoted on the Amsterdam Stock Exchange in 1993, the ASN Groenprojectenfonds. The fund's investment performance has been good, with annualised returns of 31% for the five years to December 2000, with its net assets reaching €50 million.[26] In 1996 SNS started to offer SRI consultancy services and in 1998 two further sustainable development funds were launched, so that SNS's total SRI assets amounted to €697 million by the end of 2000.[27] In July 2001 ASN sponsored a new environmental technology fund called ASN Milieufonds in partnership with Impax Capital of the UK. Michel Negenman of ASN stated:

> As one of Europe's leading ethical banks, ASN is pleased to launch a new fund in the rapidly growing environmental technology sector. We look forward to working closely with the team at Impax, and believe that Dutch investors can benefit significantly from the partnership.[28]

Triodos operates social savings accounts in the Netherlands and the UK, and is well-known for its targeted savings accounts. It began to produce corporate social and environmental research in 1996 for its Meerwaarde Fund, and in 1998 it produced its own sustainable development stock market index based on 34 companies quoted on the Dutch stock market.[29] Triodos has become recognised for its Dutch SRI research services as well as its banking and fund management operations. Triodos Research started out in 1996 to provide SRI data for its own clients, but the research coverage was later expanded and is now supplied to external institutional investors in the Netherlands.

The Netherlands' largest banks and insurance companies such as ABN AMRO and Aegon have discovered the potential of SRI. ABN's Groen Fond has become the largest single SRI fund in the Dutch market, with assets under management of €300 million at the end of 2001. In 1999 the University of Amsterdam created its own SRI index for the Dutch stock market in response to requests from the Wereld Natuur Fonds, the Dutch arm of the World Wide Fund for Nature, with € 80 million of assets. Aegon Asset Management runs the €50 million AEAM Sustainable World Fund for institutional investors based on the DGSI index. Aegon commented:

> Demand from the Dutch institutional market at this moment is mainly from non-commercial organisations, like charities and environmental organisations and the labour unions. In addition we see interest from commercial entities with a sustainable investment charter.[30]

There is little public information available about the Swiss market for socially responsible investment. However, in July 2001 UBS reported that the total value of its in-house SRI assets (including individual portfolios of private and institutional investors) broke through the SFr 1 billion (€680 million) barrier for the first time.[31] Zurich-based Sustainable Asset Management's role in creating the Dow Jones Sustainability Group indices was described in Chapter 11. Reto Ringger, the head of SAM, also played a key role in the foundation of the Sustainable Performance Group (SPG) in August 1997.[32] This is a Swiss-based global growth fund that aims to generate above-average investment returns by investing in companies demonstrating superior sustainability performance. SPG's investment assets at the end of 2001 were SFr 450 million (€307 million). Also worth noting is Geneva based Ethos fund. This was set up in 1997 as an SRI investment vehicle for local authority pension funds and charitable foundations. Investment assets were over SFr 1bn at the end of 2001.

Socially responsible investing has been relatively slow to take off in the southern half of Europe. However, by the end of 2001 there were some 20 SRI funds in Italy, although only two were of any size. In 2001 a specialist SRI fund management company called Etica SGR, a joint venture of the ethical bank Banca Etica and Milan savings bank Banca Populare di Milano, was set up to launch a broad range of SRI funds for the Italian market.[33] Avanzi was created in 1997 to provide independent research to organisations engaged in designing and implementing sustainable development strategies. The production of SRI research is only one aspect of Avanzi's work, which also covers consulting and advice to organisations wishing to develop in sustainable ways. Social and environmental research on Spanish companies has been available since 1997 from Fundación Ecología y Desarrollo (FED), a long-established Spanish NGO that promotes business sustainability. FED developed an environmental research capability in order to set up the first Spanish environment fund in 1999. Its coverage was subsequently expanded to include social issues, and it publishes the first newsletter in Spanish dealing with corporate social responsibility issues.

The most dynamic market for socially responsible investment in southern Europe has undoubtedly been France, a fact reflected in the rapid growth of research providers meeting the demand for SRI information. AReSE was created in July 1997 as the first specialist French environmental and social rating agency. Its objective is to provide institutional investors with specific social analysis and research tools. AReSE currently dominates the market, as 15 French SRI funds use its sector-based social and environmental ratings. L'Observatoire Ethique is a French NGO specialising in corporate social responsibility issues which has also produced SRI research since 1998. The French consulting firm Terra Nova Conseil produces a regular report, *SRI in Progress*, which describes developments in the field of socially responsible investment and sustainability in France and overseas. In May 2000 ORSE, a network to study and promote corporate social responsibility was set up in France, announcing plans to encourage French business to develop and improve performance on corporate governance and sustainable development.

In May 2001 a comprehensive survey of SRI mutual funds in France was published by the newly established Social Investment Forum (Le Forum pour l'Investissement Responsable, or FIR). This found evidence of explosive growth. Nineteen new funds were launched in 2000 alone, and the amount invested in French SRI mutual funds more than doubled from €325 million in 1998 to €777 million.

The survey noted three types of SRI fund in France: funds carrying out the value systems of their investors, often churches; funds with specific objectives such as creating employment; and sustainable development funds investing in businesses respecting financial, environmental and social criteria.[34] Virtually all the growth in French SRI during 1998–99 occurred in the last category, normally using AReSE research. In Chapter 12 I noted the distinctive character of some SRI products in French-speaking Canada, in particular the labour-backed venture capital funds. Two of the big French savings banks, the Caisse des Dépôts and the Caisse d'Epargne, tried out a similar idea in 1994 via the launch of the Insertion-Emplois fund. By 2000 total assets had risen to over €50 million, making it one of the larger SRI mutual funds in France. Its prospectus states:

> 10% of your savings will be invested in businesses that create employment for the excluded [i.e. the unemployed]....This is an investment fund whose objective is to combine financial performance and the growth of employment.[35]

The growing interest in socially responsible investment across Europe has been reflected in the profusion of specialist research services that have grown up to meet the demand for social and environmental data. The relatively recent development of organisations such as AReSE and Avanzi is proof of that. I can remember having lunch in 1994 with Herwig Peeters over his plans to set up one of the first European SRI research agencies in Belgium. His company, Ethibel, is now one of the largest SRI research agencies and consultants in Europe, employing 12 people. However, the honour of being the oldest provider of SRI research on the continent of Europe probably belongs to the Friburg-based Centre Info (Switzerland), which was founded in 1990. It provides corporate research, country sustainability research and consulting services to clients interested in corporate social responsibility. Its clients include institutional investors, pension funds and financial institutions, and it was the first institution in Switzerland to provide corporate governance services such as proxy voting recommendations.

The German market has also seen dramatic developments in SRI research provision, as there are now four German SRI research providers. Hanover-based Imug (Institute for Market, Environment and Society) was founded in 1992 as an environmental research consultant, but it soon ventured out into the production of green shopping guides. It also carries out social and environmental analysis of German companies. Also based in Hanover, Scoris was founded in September 2000 as a joint venture of several members of SIRI. Its corporate sustainability research covers the main German stock-indices as well as pioneer companies. Other German SRI researchers include Oekom, based in Munich, and Suedwind, operating in Siegen. The churches in Germany have significant financial resources, and church investors are significant users of social and environmental research.

SOCIALLY RESPONSIBLE PENSIONS

There is growing interest at the highest levels of European politics in socially responsible investment. In November 2000 the European Commission hosted a Brussels conference on corporate social responsibility. The European Social Investment Forum (Eurosif), designed to promote and advise on socially responsible investment across Europe, was launched during this conference. Financial support for the new venture came from the European Commission. Administrative support and advice was provided by the UK Social Investment Forum (UKSIF). Emma Howard Boyd, vice-chair of UKSIF, became the first chair of Eurosif.[36] I remember being struck in 2000–2001 by the strong interest shown by members of the European Parliament about introducing SRI across the European Union. A journalist reported my thoughts at that time, followed by those of Richard Howitt MEP:

> (a) There is a 'paradigm shift' taking place in Europe, and it is inevitable that other governments will follow the UK line. It's only a matter of time before they apply similar regulations in other countries, and I suspect that the European Union will come out with some incentives on SRI along the lines of the UK regulation.[37]
> (b) It's certainly being talked about in Brussels, and I think that will be transferred into a European Directive within

the next five years. Things are at a very early stage, but I do believe that there will be a Directive and there's a big political interest in this issue.[38]

There has also been growing political interest in promoting socially responsible investment in Europe at the national level. In May 2001 the Belgian minister of social affairs stated that he would be introducing legislation requiring pension funds to disclose their approach to SRI in their annual reports. In January 2001 the German Green party, part of the governing coalition, inserted the following SRI disclosure clause into the new German Riester pension legislation:

The provider shall give written information whether and how he considers ethical, social and environmental matters when using the contributions that have been paid in.[39]

In France the National Assembly adopted an article to encourage socially responsible investment in a draft law to generalise employee savings plans, but this was initially removed by the Senate, the upper house of the French parliament. At this point the Social Investment Forum (FIR) wrote an open letter to the French parliament, 'A Plea for Socially Responsible Employee Savings'[40] the regulation was then passed:

The regulation specifies that when appropriate the investment management company must take social, environmental, and ethical considerations into account in the purchase or sale of securities, as well as the exercise of the voting rights attached to them. The fund's annual report shall describe the application of these considerations within the terms defined by the Commission des operations de bourse (French stock market regulator).[41]

With the important exception of the Netherlands, funded pension schemes on the Anglo-Saxon model do not exist in Europe. The deteriorating demographic profile of all European countries means that the existing 'pay as you go' pension and social security system are not sustainable over the longer term. In recent years European governments have faced up to this potential crisis. In Germany the labour minister, Walter Riester, presented plans to the Bundestag in November 2000 to reduce the state's guaranteed pension from its current level of 70% of net wages to 64% by 2030. However, in

compensation the state will offer tax incentives to encourage workers to build up their own funded pension schemes on similar lines
to American 401k plans. Workers will be able to invest up to 1% of
gross wages in such schemes free of tax from 2002, rising to 4% of
gross wages by 2008. It has been estimated that the German Riester
pensions law could generate annual contributions of €10 billion into
pension schemes.

Intense opposition from the trade unions has prevented the French
government from moving away from the state-guaranteed pension
system and introducing funded pension plans. Pension reform is a
major political subject in France, unlike the UK. However, *epargne
salariale* 'employee savings plan' schemes were introduced in 1999
that to Anglo-Saxon eyes bore a distinct resemblance to pension
schemes. Other European countries are also working on the introduction of funded pension schemes. For example, in December 2001
the Italian government announced plans to amend the existing social security system so that monthly payments could be paid into
a funded pension scheme. It was estimated that this could lead to
€10 billion a year of contributions flowing into Italian private pension schemes. In January 2002 the Spanish government passed various tax incentives to try to increase pension savings.

The growth of funded pension schemes across continental Europe
implies investment flows of immense magnitude. The European
Commission has estimated that overall reforms of corporate pensions could increase their total assets by €1.2 trillion.[42] The consultants Pricewaterhouse Coopers forecast that sales of European
private savings and long-term savings products are set to rise by
€300 billion a year over the next five years.[43] Pension consultants
William Mercer calculated that the total value of European pension
assets grew from €2.1 trillion in 1996 to €3.9 trillion at the end
of 2001, and Mercer estimated that the figure would probably double again over the next five to ten years.[44] Whereas pension funds
in the UK and the US are essentially a mature and in some senses
a declining market, the rapid growth of funded pension schemes in
continental Europe makes them one of the most attractive areas for
asset managers throughout the world.

To put this into context, pension fund assets in the UK in 1999
amounted to 106% of GDP, compared to 7% in Germany and 5% in

France. The move from pensions guaranteed by the state to independently funded pension schemes has major implications for savings markets. These are likely to be defined contribution pension schemes similar to US 401k. Such pension schemes tend to have certain characteristics, such as a higher equity content, and they offer future beneficiaries a much greater choice of savings vehicles. Hence there seems a strong case that banks and insurance companies wishing to maximise their sales of pension products would be advised to offer their clients a credible 'socially responsible pension' alternative among a menu of other pension choices.

Such trends have also prompted existing pension schemes to adopt socially responsible investing. The Dutch public sector pension scheme ABP Investments is one of the largest pension funds in the world, with investment assets of €150 billion. In November 2001 it announced that it had commissioned Innovest to provide the research to enable it to move its portfolios towards environmental and social sustainability, including setting up two small €100 million portfolios to invest along SRI lines both domestically and overseas. Its smaller counterpart PGGM has also announced that it will be experimenting with SRI on a small part of its €50 billion portfolio using criteria provided by the UK's Friends Ivory & Sime.

THE SRI UNIVERSE IN EUROPE

I will end the discussion of SRI in Europe by returning to the question raised earlier, the size of socially responsible investment assets in continental Europe. My calculations indicate that the assets under management of European SRI mutual funds grew from €6.5 billion at the end of 1999 to €10.3 billion at the end of 2001. As this book went to press, I received an updated survey from Avanzi on this topic.[45] This time it was produced for SIRI rather than Global Partners. The new report stated that European SRI funds amounted to €15.1 billion in June 2001. However, the UK accounted for €5.9 billion of that. Excluding the UK, the continental European figure was €9.2 billion. Given the strong rallies that occurred in equity markets in the fourth quarter of 2001, my calculation and that of Avanzi seem consistent with each other.

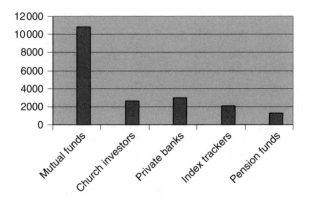

Figure 14.2 *SRI in Europe (€m) 2001*

However, the figure of €10.3 billion refers only to SRI mutual funds. I have therefore gathered together all the information I can find on European pension funds, charitable funds, private banking and index trackers all practising socially responsible investment. On this basis I have estimated that institutional SRI assets in continental Europe amounted to €9.5 billion at the end of 2001. In fact, this is almost certainly a major underestimate, as it is well known there are large amounts of private banking assets and church funds run on an SRI basis, but their amount is undocumented. A guess, and it is only a guess, would be that total European institutional funds invested in a socially responsible way amount to €20–€30 billion. In any case, adding the author's estimate of €9.5 billion to the €10.3 billion of SRI mutual funds produces a European SRI investment universe of €19.8 billion at the beginning of 2002. This is shown in Figure 14.2. All the evidence suggests this total is growing very rapidly.

THE GLOBAL REVOLUTION BEGINS

One of my ambitions in writing this book has been to produce the first systematic, rigorous and consistent coverage of SRI as a global phenomenon. This includes producing a detailed calculation of the

Table 14.1 *Socially responsible investment assets 2001*

	$bn	£bn	€bn
United States	2332.0	1603.2	2621.7
United Kingdom	326.6	224.5	370.0
Canada	31.4	21.6	35.0
Europe	17.6	12.2	19.8
Japan	1.9	1.3	2.2
Australia	1.1	0.7	1.2
Total	2710.6	1863.5	3049.9

total socially responsible investment universe. In September 2001 Cerulli Associates, a Boston-based financial services consultancy, published figures giving their estimate of the world of socially responsible investing. Cerulli came up with a figure of $1.42 trillion, dominated by US SRI investments amounting to $1.35 billion. Other significant SRI markets according to the report were Europe (including the UK) valued at $38 billion, Canada $33 billion, and Asia $2.5 billion. Cerulli stated that institutional SRI funds amounted to $1.4 trillion, while socially responsible mutual fund assets were a relatively insignificant $33 billion.[46]

However, Cerulli's figures seem hard to reconcile with the statistics produced by the Social Investment Forum in the US, nor do they agree with my own calculations for the UK. In fact, my calculations indicate that the Cerulli figures seriously underestimate the global SRI investment universe. They are shown in Table 14.1 using dollars, pounds and euros.

Total investment assets managed using socially responsible methods therefore amounted to $2.7 trillion at the end of 2001. This was practically double the Cerulli figure given earlier. Of course the US SRI market dominated the table, accounting for 86% of global SRI funds under management.

It is my intention to update this table in a few years. I will end the book by making two forecasts of what I expect to find:

- The total will have grown significantly.
- Despite rapid growth in the US, faster growth elsewhere will cause the American proportion to decline.
- Frank Coleman of CBIS recently put it thus:
  'I think we are seeing a growing number of people interested in integrating their faith, beliefs, morals, and values across all aspects of their lives, including investing . . . for some reason, women seem to be more interested in exploring SRI options than men.'[47]

The global revolution has begun.

REFERENCES

1. Mizue Tsukushi of the Good Bankers Co. Ltd, 'Japanese Perspective and Present Position of SRI', speech to Triple Bottom Line Investing Conference, Rotterdam November 2000.
2. *Ibid.*
3. 'Innovest Named as Environmental Research Provider for New Global Eco Fund', Innovest press release, New York, 11 July 2001.
4. Takejiro Sueyoshi, quoted in 'SRI with Asian Characteristics', *Environmental Finance*, September 2001.
5. Quoted in Mizue Tsukushi of the Good Bankers Co Ltd, 'Japanese Perspective and Present Position of SRI', speech to Triple Bottom Line InvestingConference, Rotterdam, November 2000.
6. Author's notes from a conversation with Mizue Tsukushi, Rotterdam, 3 November 2000.
7. 'Singapore Will Offer Ethical Mutual Fund', *Wall Street Journal*, 19 November 1999.
8. 'Think Globally, Analyse Locally', *Environmental Finance*, January 2002.
9. 'SRI with Asian Characteristics', *Environmental Finance*, September 2001.
10. ASrIA website, January 2002.
11. Author's notes of presentation by Christopher Wells, 'SRI in the Rockies', September 2001.
12. *Green and Ethical Funds in Europe 1999*, Global Partners for Social Responsibility Research, 2000.
13. *Ibid.*
14. Dirk Van Braeckel, Ethibel, author's notes of a speech in Rotterdam, 3 November 2000.
15. Kirein Franck, 'Der Markt für ethisches Investment in Deutschland', Bad Boll, Germany, 4 April 2001, author's translation.
16. Lars Freidner, 'The Investment Policy of the Church of Sweden', Bad Boll, Germany, 4 April 2001, author's translation from the German.
17. *Ibid.*

18. Anna Nilsson, 'SRI in Sweden', author's notes of a speech in Rotterdam, November 2000.
19. 'Swedish Humanix Launches Ethical Indices on Bloomberg', Bloomberg newswire, 17 October 2001.
20. Carina Lundberg, KPA, 'The Growth of SRI in Scandinavia', author's notes of a speech in London, April.
21. Jan-Olaf Willums, Storebrand ASA, *Sustainable Business Investor Europe*, Spring 2001.
22. Carlos Joly, 'Insurance Strategies for Greenhouse Risk-Abatement', in *Climate Change and the Financial Sector: The Emerging Threat and the Solar Solution*, Jeremy Leggett (editor), Gerling Akademie Verlag, 1996.
23. *Ibid.*
24. Storebrand website.
25. 'New Socially Responsible Alliance', *Australian Financial Review*, 31 August 2001.
26. 'Impax Advises New Dutch Fund', Impax Capital press release, 30 July 2001.
27. Kajetan Hetzer, 'On the Construction of a "Sustainable" Investment Universe, Ethical Investment Conference, Bad Boll, Germany, 4 April 2001, author's notes.
28. Quoted in 'Impax Advises New Dutch Fund', Impax Capital press release, 30 July 2001.
29. Bas Ruter, Triodos Bank, author's notes of a speech in Rotterdam, November 1999.
30. Monique van Gils of Aegon Asset Management, quoted in *Environmental Finance*, June 2001.
31. Newsletter No. II 2001- UBS, *Eco Performance Newsletter*.
32. 'The DJSI: A Story of Financial Innovation', *Environmental Finance*, December 2001/January 2002.
33. Davide Dal Maso, 'Italian Market Set For Growth', *Environmental Finance*, November 2001.
34. Author's translation of 'Le Forum pour l'Investissement Responsable Fait le Point de l'ISR en France.' *Terra Nova*, Spring 2001.
35. Author's translation of 'Une Placement Performant Pour L'Emploi', April 1994.
36. 'Europe Move on Socially Responsible Investment', *Financial Times*, 27 November 2001.
37. Russell Sparkes, quoted in *Ethical Performance*, December 2000.
38. Richard Howitt MEP, quoted in *Ethical Performance*, December 2000.
39. Walter Kahlenborn, 'German Disclosure Rules Promise SRI Boost', *Environmental Finance*, April 2001.
40. Author's translation of 'Plaidoyer en Faveur d'une Epargne Salariale Socialement Responsable', *Les Echos*, 26 September 2000.
41. Law 19 February for Employee Savings Plans. Translated from the French by the author Article 21.
42. 'Europe Takes on Pension Reform', *Wall Street Journal*, 30 October 2000.
43. 'Defusing the Demographic Timebomb'. *Financial Times*, 10 November 2000.
44. 'Companies' Funding of Pension Plans Grows in Europe', *Wall Street Journal*, 14 May 2001.
45. *Green, Social and Ethical Funds in Europe 2001*, SIRI Group, January 2002.
46. *The Cerulli Edge: Global Edition*, quoted in *Ethical Investor*, September 2001.
47. Frank Coleman, quoted in *Environmental Finance*, February 2001.

Index